Culture and Crisis Communication

Culture and Crisis Communication

Transboundary Cases from Nonwestern Perspectives

Edited by

Amiso M. George

Kwamena Kwansah-Aidoo

IEEE PCS Professional Engineering Communication Series

IEEE PRESS

WILEY

Published by John Wiley & Sons, Inc., Hoboken, New Jersey.
Published simultaneously in Canada.

For general information on our other products and services or for technical support, please contact our Customer Care Department within the United States at (800) 762-2974, outside the United States at (317) 572-3993 or fax (317) 572-4002.

Wiley also publishes its books in a variety of electronic formats. Some content that appears in print may not be available in electronic formats. For more information about Wiley products, visit our web site at www.wiley.com.

Library of Congress Cataloging-in-Publication Data is available.

ISBN: 978-1-119-00975-7

Printed in the United States of America.

To our students of global and crisis communication, who, spanning many cultures and boundaries, yearn for an understanding of, and emphasis on, culture in crises. And to communication practitioners everywhere who constantly contend with crisis and conflict situations that challenge their abilities and professional deontology. We hope that the cases and tips provided in this book will bring some welcome reprieve!

Amiso M. George & Kwamena Kwansah-Aidoo

Contents

A Note from the Series Editor

The IEEE Professional Communication Society (PCS), with Wiley-IEEE Press, continues its book series titled *Professional Engineering Communication* with a volume collected guided and shaped by Amiso M. George and Kwamena Kwansah-Aidoo titled *Culture and Crisis Communication: Transboundary Cases from Nonwestern Perspectives*. In the field of risk communication, there are few sustained, focused collections about practices from a nonwestern perspective. This book aims to fill that gap and show everyone how communication is, foremost, always contextualized and never inert.

With the knowledgeable and steady vision provided by the book's editors, who also contributed to writing chapters, this tome will help anyone unpack assumptions and presumptions about appropriate actions to take while (sometimes literally) in the eye of the storm. From intense human tragedy to the follies of the rich, these chapters examine how companies, organizations, news outlets, health organizations, technical experts, politicians, and local communities communicate in crisis situations.

As with other books in this series, we aim to do more than theorize. Thus, each chapter provides lessons learned, discussion questions for interactive training, and some expert opinions. Use these resources to enrich your own thinking about the complexity of international and intra-national communication when an emergency is at hand.

When this book series began, we were looking for a collection that could address these issues, and here it is. The series has a mandate to explore areas of communication practices and application as applied to the engineering, technical, and scientific professions. Including the realms of business, governmental agencies, academia, and other areas, this series has and will continue to develop perspectives about the state of communication issues and potential solutions when at all possible.

While theory has its place (in this book and this series), we always look to be a source where recommendations for action and activity can be found. All of the books in the fast-growing PEC series keep a steady eye on the applicable while acknowledging the contributions that analysis, research, and theory can provide to these efforts. You will see Brewer's active synthesis between on-site realities and research coming together. There is a strong commitment from the Professional Communication

Society of IEEE and Wiley to produce a set of information and resources that can be carried directly into engineering firms, technology organizations, and academia alike.

For the series, we work with this philosophy: at the core of engineering, science, and technical work is problem solving and discovery. These tasks require, at all levels, talented and agile communication practices. We need to effectively gather, vet, analyze, synthesize, control, and produce communication pieces in order for any meaningful work to get done. This book, like others in the series before it, contributes deeply to that vision.

Traci Nathans-Kelly, Ph.D.

Author Biographies

Dila Beisembayeva (M.A., Unitec, New Zealand) is a lecturer at the Department of Computing in the Unitec Institute of Technology, New Zealand. Originally from Kazakhstan, Beisembayeva's interests include social media, national identity, and censorship in authoritarian states such as China, Russia, and Kazakhstan. Her international communication master's thesis explored the impact of online political activism on political process in Kazakhstan. She has presented papers at conferences in Ireland, Japan, and Canada. Email: dbeisembayeva@unitec.ac.nz

Ronald Carr (M.F.A., University of California, Los Angeles) is an associate professor and director of the Communication Studies Department, with specialization in broadcasting and documentary filmmaking, at Temple University, Japan. He is also executive producer of *Global Lives, Asia*, and of *Urban Villages*, a recent Temple University-funded project that brings awareness and solutions to serious issues plaguing Asian urban communities. Professor Carr has produced stories on disaster relief in Manila, Philippines, and the struggles facing informal settlers, and on nuclear energy crisis following the 2011 Tohoku earthquake. His projects have taken him to far-flung places such as Beirut, Sapporo, Damascus, and Varnasse. He resides in Tokyo with his family. Email: carr@tuj.temple.edu

Christabel Reena David (BComms (Hons), Nanyang Technological University, Singapore) is a senior consultant at DeVries Global. To date, she has worked on several accounts, including Head & Shoulders, SK-II Local and Global, Prestige Fine Fragrances, Samsonite, and CÉ LA VI Singapore. She has experience in both regional and local work such as media relations, traditional and social media communication strategy, event execution, and regional toolkit creation. David graduated from Nanyang Technological University's Wee Kim Wee School of Communication and Information in 2014, specializing in public relations. She worked on creating awareness among youths for social enterprises for her final year project and on a paper on social media crisis communication in Singapore. Email: christabel.rdavid@gmail.com

Uttaran Dutta (Ph.D., Purdue University) is an assistant professor in the Hugh Downs School of Human Communication, Arizona State University, USA. His research interest includes intercultural communication, communication for social change, indigenous and folk culture, and visual communication. He has published in several peer-reviewed journals including *Qualitative Health Research*, *Journal of International Communication*, and *Communication Design Quarterly*. Email: uttaran.dutta@Asu.edu

Amiso M. George (Ph.D., Ohio University; Accredited in Public Relations by the Public Relations Society of America [PRSA]; Fellow, PRSA) is an associate professor of strategic communication at Texas Christian University (TCU), Fort Worth, Texas. She is former chair of the Strategic Communication Department and former director of the graduate program at TCU, where she coaches the award-winning PRSSA Bateman team. George also directed the Public Relations program at the Reynolds School of Journalism, University of Nevada, Reno, where she developed and taught the first course in crisis communication. She was a visiting professor of strategic communication at Swinburne University of Technology, Melbourne, Australia, in 2012. Before entering academia, George worked as a journalist and freelance broadcaster in radio and television at Nigerian Television Authority, Voice of America international radio network (Africa Service), and WOUB Radio in Athens, Ohio. She also served as a consultant for C-SPAN-Television, Washington, D.C. In addition to journal articles and book chapters on crisis communication, she is the co-editor of *Crisis Communication: An International Perspective on Hits and Misses* (Routledge/Taylor & Francis, 2012) and *Race, Gender and Other Minorities: Readings for Professional Communicators* (Cognella, 2012). She consults in risks and crisis communication. Email: a.george2@tcu.edu; Twitter: @tampriye

Yi-Hui Christine Huang (Ph.D., University of Maryland) is a professor at the School of Journalism and Communication in the Chinese University of Hong Kong. Previously, she taught at School of Communication in National Chengchi University in Taiwan and as a visiting professor in the Negotiation Program at Harvard University Law School. Her research interests include cross-cultural communication and relationship management, crisis communication, conflict and negotiation, public relations management, and communication studies in China. She has received distinguished public relations research awards from the National Communication Association, USA; National Science Council, R.O.C.; and Research Chair Professorship Award by the National Chengchi University in Taiwan. A recipient of numerous top paper awards and teaching awards at various international conferences, including the International Communication Association, Dr. Huang has also served on the editorial boards of major international SSCI journals in communication and public relations, including *Journal of Public Relations Research*, *Asian Journal of Communication*, and *International Journal of Strategic Communication*. She is associate editor-in-chief and editorial board member of major Chinese TSSCI scholarly publications, including *Chinese Journal of Communication Research*. She has also served as the vice president and the secretary-general of the Chinese Communication Society as well as a board member and consultant for the Foundation of Public Relations of the Republic of China. Email: yhuang100@gmail.com

Jangyul Robert Kim (Ph.D., University of Florida; Accredited in Public Relations by the Public Relations Society of America [PRSA]; Fellow, PRSA) is the director general of Customer Risk Prevention Bureau at the Ministry of Food and Drug Safety of South Korea. A former associate professor in the Department of Journalism and Media Communication at Colorado State University, USA, he is the first Korean awarded the professional designation of Accredited in Public Relations (APR) by the Public Relations Society of America. He is also the first Korean to be inducted into the prestigious Public Relations College of Fellows. He was a visiting professor at Ewha Womans University in Seoul, South Korea, in 2013–2014. Prior to joining academia, he was the founder of KorCom Porter Novelli, a full-service public relations firm based in Seoul, and has consulted numerous domestic and multinational firms, governments, and non-profit organizations. Kim's research interest includes issues and crisis communications, public diplomacy, corporate social responsibility, international public relations, and strategic and marketing communications. His manuscripts are published in top peer review journals including *Journal of Public Relations Research*, *Public Relations Review*, *Asian Journal of Communications*, *Asia Pacific Public Relations Journal*, and *Journal of Public Relations (Korean)*. Email: jangyul.kim@colostate.edu

Elena Kolesova (Ph.D., University of Auckland) is a senior lecturer and programme leader for postgraduate programmes at the Department of Communication Studies in the Unitec Institute of Technology, New Zealand. She developed and teaches courses in Asian studies and in international and intercultural communication. Her research interests include the re-emergence of nationalism in Japan and Russia, media and multiculturalism in New Zealand, and East Asian popular culture in a local context. In 2011, she organized a "Cool New Asia" international symposium followed by the ePublication *Cool New Asia: Asian Popular Culture in Local Context*. In 2014, she co-organized an Ethnic Media Forum. Elena is also involved in research on international/transnational education and international students, and has published in the area of the history of Japanese education, international students and also a comparative analysis of history textbooks in Japan and Russia. She is the reviews editor for *New Zealand Journal of Asian Studies*. Email: ekolesova@unitec.ac.nz

Kwamena Kwansah-Aidoo (Ph.D., Queensland University of Technology, Australia) is an associate professor of marketing/public relations at Swinburne University of Technology, Melbourne, Australia. In the early 2000s, he established Monash University, Gippsland's Public Relations Program before moving to Swinburne in 2007, as head of Academic Group of Communication, Marketing and Tourism, and Associate Dean, International from 2011 to 2013. He has been a consultant for Ghana Social Marketing Foundation, visiting professor of marketing communication at the Ghana Institute of Management and Public Administration, visiting scholar at Texas Christian University, and consultant for AusTraining in cross-cultural communication/issues in Africa. He is experienced in leading course and curriculum development in public relations, advertising, and communication studies. Dr. Kwansah-Aidoo has authored two books on media communication and crisis communication. He has also published several refereed journal articles and book chapters on public relations, communication and media, with emerging streams on Ghanaian film and also the African diaspora in Australia. Email: kkwansah@swin.edu.au

Joanne Chen Lyu (Ph.D., The Chinese University of Hong Kong) is an assistant professor at the School of Communication in Hang Seng Management College, Hong Kong. Prior to joining academia, she served in the Public Relations Department of a transnational media corporation for years. In her doctoral study, she won Top Student Paper in the public relations division of the annual conference of International Communication Association (2012). Lyu's research interest includes public relations, crisis communication and management, relationship/guanxi studies, and Chinese communication. She has published in *Public Relations Review*, *Communication & Society*, and many English and Chinese scholarly books. Email: joannelyu@hsmc.edu.hk

Heba Metwali (M.A., American University of Cairo) is a researcher, English translator, and media specialist at the Egyptian State Information Service since 1997. Metwali has previously worked as an expert and media coordinator at the Population and Migration Department, League of Arab States. She obtained a B.A. in English literature from Ain Shams University, a Diploma in Journalism from Cairo University, M.A. in Journalism and Mass Communication from the American University in Cairo, and a postgraduate studies in anthropology and visual anthropology from the African Institute, Cairo University. She is a Ph.D. candidate in the Faculty of Mass Communication at Cairo University. Metwali's research interests include media and journalism, image of women, children, countries, and peoples in the media, the role of media in shaping perceptions, and effects of media on developmental issues. Email: bobba@aucegypt.edu

Juan-Carlos Molleda (Ph.D., University of South Carolina) is a professor and the Edwin L. Artzt Dean of the School of Journalism and Communication, University of Oregon. He was the former chair of the Department of Public Relations and director of the Online Master's in Public Relations and Communication Management at the University of Florida's (UF) College of Journalism and Communications. He is also an affiliated faculty of the UF Center for Latin American Studies. Molleda is academic trustee of the Institute for Public Relations, member of the board of directors of the LAGRANT Foundation, Latin American liaison of the Public Relations Society of America's Certification in Education for Public Relations, and co-director of the Latin American Communication Monitor, a multinational study organized by the European Public Relations Education and Research Association. Dr. Molleda introduced to the international academic community the concept and theory of cross-national conflict shifting (*Journalism Studies*, *Public Relations Review*), the Latin American School of Public Relations (*Journalism Studies*), as well as the social roles of public relations in Brazil (*Journal of Public Relations Research*) and Colombia (PRSA Educators Academy and *Anagramas*, a peer-reviewed publication from Universidad de Medellín, Colombia). Dr. Molleda has a national and international record of conference papers, lectures, and publications in Europe, the Americas, and Asia. Email: jcmolle@hotmail.com

Augustine Pang (Ph.D., University of Missouri) is an associate professor and program director of Master of Mass Communication at Wee Kim Wee School of Communication and Information, Nanyang Technological University, Singapore. He specializes in crisis management and communication, image management and repair, media management, and corporate communication management. His chapters have appeared in leading communication books like the *Handbook of Crisis Communication* (Wiley-Blackwell, 2010), *SAGE Handbook of Public Relations* (2010), *Handbook of Communication and Corporate Social Responsibility* (Wiley-Blackwell, 2011), and *Handbook of Research on Crisis Leadership in Organizations* (Edward Elgar, 2013). He has also published in many top journals, including *Journal of Public Relations Research*, *Journal of Contingencies and Crisis Management*, *International Journal of Strategic Communication*, *Australian Journalism Review*, and *Asia Pacific Media Educator*, amongst others. Dr. Pang has won top research awards at leading international conferences such as the International Communication Association, Corporate Communications International, the Association of Educators in Journalism and Mass Communication (AEJMC), and the International Public Relations Research. He won a highly commended paper published in *Corporate Communication: An International Journal* for 2014. A member of the Arthur W. Page Society (US), he was appointed Honorary Fellow by Hong Kong Polytechnic University in 2015 in recognition of his expertise in the field. Email: Augustine.Pang@ntu.edu.sg

Cornelius B. Pratt (Ph.D., University of Minnesota at Twin Cities; Accredited in Public Relations by the Public Relations Society of America [PRSA]) is a professor in the Globalization and Development Communication Program and in the Department of Strategic Communication at Temple University, Philadelphia. He also teaches at Temple University Japan. Pratt is an honorary visiting professor of mass communication at Bingham University, New Karu, Nasarawa State, Nigeria. Widely published in top communication and public relations journals, he is the co-editor of *Crisis Communication: An International Perspective on Hits and Misses* (Routledge/ Taylor & Francis, 2012). Additionally, he serves on the editorial-review boards of six journals, including the *South East Asian Journal of Management*, *Public Relations Review*, and the *Journal of Public Relations Research*. His research interests include international communication, ethics, public relations and communication for national and regional development, particularly in emerging economies. Email: cbpratt@temple.edu

Ibrahim Saleh (Ph.D., Cairo University) is an associate professor of political journalism and mass communication at Future University in Egypt, chair of Political Mass Media Department, and director of Future Public Opinion Polling Centre (FPOPC). Saleh is Fulbright scholar, a senior media expert on the Middle East and North Africa (MENA), and an indexed scholar in the Media Sustainability Index (MSI). Saleh is the chair of Journalism Research and Education (JRE) section at the International Association of Media and Communication Research (IAMCR). Saleh is the linchpin editor of the *Journal of Transnational 'Worlds of Power': Proliferation of Journalism and Professional Standards*, book series on *Visual Politics of War*, and *Global Media Journal*, African edition. He is the author of the following books: *Unveiling the Truth about Middle Eastern Media—Privatization in Egypt: Hope or Dope?* (2003), *Prior to the Eruption of the Grapes of Wrath in the Middle East* (2006), and *Visual Politics of War* (2015). Email: Ibrahim.Saleh@uct.ac.za and jre09is@gmail.com

Soumitro Sen (Ph.D., Purdue University) is an assistant professor of public relations in the Department of Journalism and Mass Communication at California State University, Long Beach. Prior to joining the academe, he was a public relations practitioner, performing media relations for Purdue University. He also is a former print journalist. His research interests include new media and public relations, coverage of news in the neoliberal press, and health communication. His research has appeared in peer-reviewed journals such as *Journal of Creative Communications* and *Health Communication*. Email: soumitrosen@gmail.com

Regina Coeli da Silveira e Silva (Ph.D., Ohio University) is a professor in the Department of Social Communication at Universidade Salgado de Oliveira in Rio de Janeiro, Brazil. She is the coordinator of the Núcleo de Estudos em Comunicação e Pesquisa – NECP (Nucleus of Communication Research Studies). Dr. Silva has taught at the University of North Carolina in Chapel Hill, University of Connecticut in Storrs, and Ohio University. She has conducted seminars in Brazil and Argentina. Among her extensive publications on communication and new technologies is one focused on R&D quality in Brazilian universities and research centers. Professor Silva is the recipient of Cátedra Interamericana de Pesquisa 2000 (Interamerican Research Chair 2000) from College of the Americas—COLAM/UN, for her research on women's rights. She is the chief editor of her university interdisciplinary research journal, *Cadernos de Estudos e Pesquisas*. A member of the International Communication Association (ICA) and the Brazilian Studies Association (BRASA), Dr. Silva is also the current president of the International Association for Journals and Conferences—IAJC—Latin America Chapter. In 2011, she was elected a voting member of Niterói City Council for Women's Rights. In 2016, Rio de Janeiro State Government awarded her the title of *Citizen Woman* as a tribute for her contribution to women's human rights. Email: silvaregina4@yahoo.com.br

Gabriel C. Stephen (M.A., Maryville University of St. Louis) is a public relations doctoral student and instructor at the University of Florida. In addition, Stephen is an account supervisor for a strategic communications agency in Gainesville, Florida. He obtained a Master of Arts in Strategic Communication and Leadership from Maryville University and a double bachelor's degree in Advertising and Public Relations from Southeast Missouri State University. Stephen worked as marketing assistant at Maryville University and a media relations specialist at Saint Bernard & Associates of St. Louis. Email: gcstephen@ufl.edu

Selin Türkel (Ph.D., Ege University, Turkey) is a lecturer in the Faculty of Communication, Public Relations and Advertising Department at Izmir University of Economics since 2005. She received a B.A. degree in Public Relations and Advertising (Istanbul Bilgi University, 2004) and an M.A. degree in Business Administration (Izmir University of Economics, 2007). Her research interests are corporate communication, corporate social responsibility, and marketing communication research. Dr. Türkel is a co-author of the SSCI journal article, "A Strategic Approach to CSR Communication: Examining the Impact of Brand Familiarity on Consumer Responses" (*Corporate Social Responsibility and Environmental Management*, doi:10.1002/csr.1373) and the international book chapter "Corporate Social Responsibility (CSR) Communication: A Turkish Industry Example." Dr. Türkel has also attended many international conferences to present her studies. Email: selinturkel@gmail.com

Ebru Uzunoğlu (Ph.D., Ege University, Turkey) is an associate professor and the head of the Public Relations and Advertising Department at Izmir University of Economics (IUE). Currently, she is acting dean of the Communication Faculty at IUE. She teaches courses on marketing communications, campaign design in integrated marketing communications (IMC), IMC projects, principles of public relations, and brand management. Her research interests include integrated marketing communications, brand communications, and social media implementations. She is a co-editor of the book *Integrated Communications in the Post-Modern Era* (Palgrave MacMillan, 2014). She has published in many journals, including *Journal of Marketing Communications*, *Public Relations Review*, *Corporate Social Responsibility*

and Environmental Management, International Journal of Information Management, International Journal of Human Sciences, and the *Global Media Journal*. She worked in several national and international companies as a public relations and advertising specialist, marketing communication specialist, and product manager for 12 years. She is a member of the Izmir Public Relations Association and was a board member for three terms. Email: ebru.uzunoglu@ieu.edu.tr

Reidinar Juliane Wardoyo (MMassComm, Nanyang Technological University, Singapore) is a communications coordinator at the World Resources Institute, Indonesia. She was a research associate at the Wee Kim Wee School of Communication and Information, Nanyang Technological University (NTU), Singapore. Her research interests include communication for development (e.g., maternal health, the use of information and communication technology for education and the use of digital interventions in health communication) and strategic communication. Prior to joining the master's degree program at NTU, she worked as a consultant for Edelman Indonesia, specializing in corporate and public affairs practice, with issues revolving around crisis management, government engagement, and corporate communication. She holds a bachelor's in humanities from the University of Indonesia and a master's degree in mass communication from NTU. Email: reidinar001@e.ntu.edu.sg

Kyung-Hyan Yoo (Ph.D., Texas A&M University) is an associate professor and graduate director of Communication Department at William Paterson University of New Jersey, USA. Prior to pursuing her academic career, she worked as a public relations specialist at KorCom Porter Novelli, a full-service public relations firm based in Seoul, Korea. Her research interests focus on online communication, online trust, electronic word-of-mouth, persuasive technology, online information search, and decision-making. She has worked on research projects on online travel reviews and social media use by travelers funded by TripAdvisor, Travel Industry Association of America, and several local destination marketing organizations. Yoo has authored journal articles and book chapters on social media marketing, consumer-generated media, and online trust. Her manuscripts have been published in top peer review journals including *Public Relations Review*, *Computers in Human Behavior*, and *Journal of Information Technology & Tourism*. Email: yook2@wpunj.edu

Foreword

The global nature of crises foregrounds the importance of communication scholarship that takes culture seriously and theorizes pathways, processes, mechanisms, and message characteristics that are deeply rooted in cultural contexts. Within the crisis communication literature, there is a dearth of scholarly work that addresses culture seriously, especially from the frameworks of multiple global cultures. Often missing from the overarching concepts of crises are cultural worldviews, contextual understandings, and engagement with the anchoring values that drive the theorizing of crises. To take culture seriously and to create conceptual maps for theorizing crisis communication from cultural worldviews calls for communication scholarship that roots itself in the diversity of worldviews, approaching the theorizing of culture from within these worldviews. The refreshing part of this collection, *Culture and Crisis Communication*, lies in its treatment of culture as an anchor for the development of communication theories of crises. In doing so, the book adopts a polymorphic approach to the theorizing of crisis communication, depicting the multitude of ways in which meanings are assigned to crises, crises are constructed, and processes of communication are constituted around crises. In the chapters that follow, the reader is offered a conceptual map for journeying through a plethora of understandings of crises and communication, thus offering different pathways for addressing the questions of theory, methodology, and practice.

One of the key contributions of the book is its theorizing of crisis communication from nonwestern contexts, thus opening up the possibilities of theorizing from cultural vantage points that reside outside of the western mainstream of communication theorizing. In doing so, the cases presented in the book bring forth analyses of communication strategies in crises contexts in often under-represented and globally salient contexts such as the Nigerian response to the Ebola virus, the crisis response in the context of the conflict between the workers, the KazMunaiGaz oil company, and local government authorities that took place between May and June 2011 in Kazakhstan, the response of European countries to Syrian refugees amidst the broader Syrian civil war, the crisis negotiations of the US-based transnational corporation Chiquita Brands International® in Colombia and Guatemala, crisis management in the context of the Niterói landslide in Brazil, the response of the Chinese political and media institutions in the context of the melamine-tainted milk powder crisis in

China, the response of the Indian government to the terrorist attacks in Mumbai in November 2008, the layers of Indonesian government response to the forest fires that led to the transboundary haze crisis of 2013, and the Singapore government's crisis response strategy in the context of the large-scale penetration of social media. This impressive array of case studies from diverse nonwestern contexts depict the interplay of cultural context and communication in crisis response. The very nature of what is communication and how to conceptualize the role of communication in the realm of crises is polymorphic, thus rendering as evident the various culturally constituted taken-for-granted assumptions that go into how we come to understand "what is communication?" and "what is the role of communication in crises?" Moreover, the contextual location of the authors of the chapters in relationship to the Western mainstream of communication scholarship offers unique vantage points for theorizing crisis communication practices.

Crises are socially constructed. They are constituted in relationships and in relationship to the structures within which we come to experience them. The ways in which we respond to these crises thus are rendered meaningful through our values, identities, and relationships. Whereas a large number of examples covered in the book result from human actions, others originate naturally from the environments within which we live, although contemporary writings on the Anthropocene depict the ways in which these crises too often result from aggregating human action over an extended period of time. Even as we consider the immediate responses that are constituted as solutions to the crises, the chapters in the book also point toward long-term and big picture questions we ought to be asking in theorizing crises and in conceptualizing responses to crises. Particularly salient are notions of global dialogues, conversations, and collaborations across cultural boundaries in the articulation of solutions that require collective efforts, especially in the realm of problems that are global in nature. How then can organizations and institutions, situated within particular and local meaning communities, come to create common communicative entry points for mutual collaboration and problem solving? What are the challenges to collaboration and how can these challenges be meaningfully addressed?

Another key contribution of the book is in the treatment of the multiple layers and levels of cultures in the conceptualization of communication. The notions of transboundary and within-boundary crisis communication attend to the criss-crossings and cross-boundary movements in the negotiation of stakeholder groups and contexts. The concept of boundary raises important theoretical questions about the constitution of cultural boundaries, the textures of boundaries, and the intersections and demarcations of boundaries. How then is communication negotiated as crises cross boundaries, engaging with stakeholders that are globally dispersed and globally connected? The chapters depict the constitutive role of communication in the maintenance and reproduction of relationships in crisis situations. They also pay careful attention to the nuances of the very definition of crisis and the ways in which communities come to be formed around a crisis. That crises are situated within broader social, political, and economic contexts, weaved into intricate local–national–global relationships is a thematic lesson that emerges across the chapters. In the array of examples depicted in the chapters, we are drawn into the complexities that constitute crises and the challenges of cultural understanding. That the risks, vulnerabilities, and responses to crises are constituted through the lens of culture is an invaluable lesson that emerges across the chapters. As you read through these chapters, consider the ways in which our practices of communication are shaped by the institutions, structures, and cultures within which we reside. What values do we take for granted when we come to define crises and map out specific solutions? What other values are backgrounded or erased? The tentative conceptual maps offered in these pages are excellent seeds for crisis communication that is attentive to the cultural diversities and differences within which crises are constituted.

Mohan J. Dutta
Provost's Chair Professor
Department of Communications and New Media
National University of Singapore

Preface

The frequency, intensity, and transboundary reach of crises have increased steadily for more than three decades. More corporations, countries, and continents experience crises of a significant magnitude than could have been imagined by earlier generations. Current crises defy regional, national, and cultural boundaries as they impact the lives of diverse publics in unforeseeable ways. Simply put, the growing complexity, severity, and interconnectivity of crises defy long-standing expectations for effective crisis communication.

Current scholars who hope to generate best practices for mitigating and managing these events must do so from a transboundary perspective. Crises may begin locally, but they rarely end there. Instead, diseases spread internationally in days. Natural disasters impact food security for multiple nations. An unfortunate incident in one country can impact an organization's reputation world-wide. Economic and political crises in one nation result in mass dislocations of populations to others. These are only a few examples of how crises expand and compound in their impact.

The evolving nature of crises has demanded innovative outlooks in theory-building and crisis communication consulting. The fact that much of the original research on crisis communication was done from a western perspective and bias has created a gap in understanding how various crises evolve and how publics respond in other parts of world. In short, our current body of work on crisis communication fails to fully account for the impact of culture on crisis and crisis communication.

Kwamena Kwansah-Aidoo and Amiso M. George and the authors of their edited text take a bold step forward in bridging this gap in their edited text, *Culture and Crisis Communication: Transboundary Cases from Nonwestern Perspectives*. Their book captures the distinct characteristics of crises initiated in nonwestern contexts. The cases selected by the authors are diverse, compelling, and thought provoking. Combined, the cases reveal the pattern through which crises begin locally and extend to international levels, impacting seemingly unrelated audiences with devastating consequences.

Most importantly, the authors adopt and adapt theories with a cultural focus to crisis communication contexts. This theory-building effort provides a much-needed expansion of the crisis communication literature. The case studies are designed to both expand our understanding of transboundary crises and to provide explicit strategies for managing them. Thus, the book contributes to crisis planning on multiple fronts.

The authors and editors have succeeded in finding the consistency that weaves through diverse crisis types in a variety of nonwestern cultures. Crises stemming from political revolution, national sports teams, pandemics, xenophobia, food fraud, terrorism, natural disasters, nuclear disasters, worker unrest, inept crisis planning, reputational threat, homeless refugees, violations of cultural expectations, and cross-national conflict are analyzed through a consistent lens emphasizing cultural nuances.

The authors also recognize that, although crises are expanding in both their reach and consequences, we are also living in a time of unprecedented access to information and communication. Publics once considered remote now have immediate access to vital information. Audiences that once had little understanding of one another are now intertwined in commerce. The sprawling networks created by new media can exacerbate crises, particularly those involving reputation, but they can also introduce new ways of collecting and distributing information that aids in crisis mitigation. The authors of *Culture and Crisis Communication: Transboundary Cases from Nonwestern Perspectives* recognize this paradox and offer new insight into how the shifting landscape of communication technology is influenced by cultural differences.

Crises will always bring danger and disruption. And, unfortunately, the scope and scale of crisis will continue to expand. This book, however, offers a degree of optimism. The authors recognize the crucial role of culture in managing crises. The understanding and advice offered in this text advances our capacity for more effectively managing these transboundary crises. In doing so, these authors make a valuable contribution to the crisis communication literature.

Timothy L. Sellnow and Matthew W. Seeger
Authors of *Theorizing Crisis Communication and Narratives of Crisis: Telling Stories of Ruin and Renewal*

Acknowledgments

This book is a reflection of two things: the state of interconnectedness of the world in the latter years of the second decade of the 21st Century, and the collaborative nature of academic work. Given the nature of the subject of this book, it stands to reason that the final product could not have been achieved without the cooperation of many, and we want to express our gratitude to them. First, we would like to thank all the authors who responded to our call for contributions to this volume. Without their input, this book would never have seen the light of day and we deeply appreciate the time and effort they put into their chapters.

Next, we would like to thank Dr. Traci Nathans-Kelly, the Series Editor, for her professionalism, support, and guidance throughout the preparation of this manuscript. Our sincere thanks also goes to the publisher, John Wiley & Sons, for sticking with us throughout the entire process, in spite of some changes and delays. Many other people, whose names we cannot mention for lack of space, provided moral and other forms of support for which we are also eternally grateful.

Finally, we wish to extend our immense appreciation to our families, for their patience and understanding.

Amiso M. George & Kwamena Kwansah-Aidoo

Introduction

Setting the Scene

Communication, Culture and Crisis in a Transboundary Context

Kwamena Kwansah-Aidoo and Amiso M. George

Chapter Preview

As international crises increasingly dominate the news headlines, it is imperative to examine how crises are communicated and perceived from a viewpoint that is often ignored in most crisis literature—the nonwestern perspective. This book, Culture and Crisis Communication: Transboundary Cases from Nonwestern Perspectives, attempts to fill that gap by examining the role that culture plays in crisis communication in nonwestern settings. Considering the emergence of new spheres of power in the form of the BRIC countries (Brazil, Russia, India, and China) and other emerging economic powers that are not western countries, this book is timely.

Also, the responses to major crises that have rocked different parts of the world in the last few years—including the disappearance of Malaysia Airline (MH370), the Boko Haram kidnapping of nearly 300 school girls in Nigeria, the mass migration of refugees from the ongoing Syrian war and others, by both western and nonwestern societies—illustrate the importance of examining crisis communication

Culture and Crisis Communication: Transboundary Cases from Nonwestern Perspectives, First Edition.
Edited by Amiso M. George and Kwamena Kwansah-Aidoo.
© 2017 by The Institute of Electrical and Electronics Engineers, Inc. Published 2017 by John Wiley & Sons, Inc.

from standpoints that are nonwestern. The responses also reinforce the assertion that crises are becoming more transboundary than in the past.

After reading this chapter, you will be able to

- *Understand what crisis is, as well as the definition of crisis that we have adopted in this book*
- *Define more deeply what culture is, and the definition of culture that we have adopted in this book*
- *Review our definition of transboundary, as applied in this book*
- *Comprehend the argument for understanding the role of culture in crisis communication*
- *Assess the importance of looking at cases from a transboundary perspective*
- *See an overview of all the chapters and how the rest of the volume is organized*

Introduction: An Ever-Intertwining World

In a world where there is increasing interdependence of countries, and one in which globalization and technological advancements have made it possible for almost any-one to witness, report on, and/or experience what is happening elsewhere irrespective of location and time, local issues can instantly become internationalized and interna-tional issues can become localized in the same way. An issue or crisis that might seem to be a problem for one country or local setting can become a matter of global con-cern and spawn serious consequences for many who at first glance may have thought themselves far removed from the particular issue or crisis. This situation is exempli-fied by events that have happened in different parts of the world over the past decade, and how various countries have responded. In some cases, countries have responded in a certain way, only to be forced later to deal with unforeseen consequences, usu-ally borne out of the deeply entrenched differences that are a function of different worldviews or cultural positioning.

The wave of Syrian and other refugees moving to Europe in 2015 was initially welcomed by most countries—Germany alone took in 800,000 in 2015; Sweden accepted 160,000; and Austria, Hungary, and Denmark also took in tens of thou-sands. While the numbers keep fluctuating based on the numbers that apply for asylum or turned back at original entry countries, the welcome carpet is being withdrawn as news reports indicate a clash of cultures. At a 2015 traditional New Year's Eve event in Cologne for instance, police reported that about 80 German women were sexually assaulted and robbed by men who were allegedly of Arab or North African extraction [1]. Other reports of assault at the city's central train station were also recorded. Swedish media reported an unprecedented onslaught of pickpockets and vagrants described as North Africans at Stockholm's central train station. While the government response has been to suspend acceptance of additional refugees (Germany), propose a repatriation (Sweden), seize assets to pay for their upkeep (Denmark), and build fences (Hungary), local groups have taken it upon themselves to demonstrate their displeasure with the influx of refugees whose culture they consider as fundamentally different from theirs and has the potential of creating serious social and political problems in future. An example occurred in Sweden's Stockholm central train station where members of a large masked gang distributed flyers calling for the expulsion of foreigners and physically attacked "foreign" looking persons. They reportedly justified the attacks as revenge for a 15-year-old Somali refugee who fatally stabbed a Swedish refugee worker [2].

Media pundits argue that these reports illustrate a glimpse of Europe's future if the refugees are not assimilated into European culture. Even Angela Merkel, the Chancellor of Germany as of this writing, has stepped backed from her open door policy. In a reversal of previous statements, she contends that refugees will be expected to return to their countries after the war; but, not all Germans are that patient. The outcome of a March 2016 regional election in Germany shows the anti-immigrant Alternative für Deutschland (AfD) Party gaining influence [3]. At the core of all of these statements, activities, and confusion is culture. So, what is culture?

Culture, Crisis, and Transboundariness

Many definitions of culture abound, but a few will suffice here. *Culture* is the traditional shared behavior of any society, race, or people at a particular time. It includes values, customs, beliefs, and attitudes; it is communicated through generations via language, objects, ritual, institutions, and art. It is also transmitted through learned and shared assumptions, beliefs, attitudes, values, knowledge, norms, clothing, language, and more [4]. As Hofstede [5] aptly puts it, culture is the "collective programming of the mind which distinguishes the members of one human group from another." Schein [6] compares culture to an iceberg, arguing that culture exists in layers, with the first invisible layer found just beneath the surface. This first layer is that of values or that which we believe is important and the deepest layer—that of fundamental belief—is the one most difficult to observe, measure, or change.

The refugee crisis in Europe highlights the intersection of culture and crisis on many levels. While research on impact of culture on communications features much of Geert Hofstede's seminal work on theory of cultural dimensions, studies on the impact of culture on crisis is gaining grounds [7]. The Toyota recalls, Volkswagen scandal, BP Deepwater Horizon, Nigeria's Shell Oil crisis, Malaysia Airline crisis, and many others illustrate not just the influence of culture on crisis communication in global environments, but also the transboundary nature of crisis. We use the term *transboundary* here to imply the crossing of inter- and intranational boundaries where there are significant geopolitical, cultural, religious, ideological, and socioeconomic differences which are significant enough and easily discernible with set systems based on both formal and informal patterns of observation. In other words, we acknowledge that boundaries can exist both within and outside geopolitical entities or countries.

Threats such as "Terrorist attacks, water shortages, critical infrastructure failures, unexpected flows of illegal immigrants, progressive climate change, and new pandemics" would overwhelm countries and turn into crises that would challenge even the best organized government.

Boin and Rhinard [8] describe *transboundary threat* as that "characterized by the potential to cross geographical and functional boundaries." They argue that "these characteristics outstrip the capacity of nation-states and national bureaucracies that were designed to deal with more classic threats." They further contend that threats such as "Terrorist attacks, water shortages, critical infrastructure failures, unexpected flows of illegal immigrants, progressive climate change, and new pandemics" [8] would overwhelm countries and turn into crises that would challenge even the best organized government. Using the European Union (EU) as an example, Boin and Rhinard not only identified the challenges of transboundary crisis management, but also opportunities therein. Their proposal to deal with such crises is for nations to collaborate and cooperate across their political, ideological, and geographic boundaries to respond to the crisis.

This book takes the Boin and Rhinard [8] concept a step further by examining transboundary crisis communication cases from a nonwestern perspective. Much of the international crises emanate from nonwestern countries, yet, there is a dearth of research on the topic.

Second, given the nature of current transboundary crises as mentioned by Boin and Rhinard and illustrated by recent humanitarian crises such as the refugee crisis in Europe, health scares such as the Ebola virus and Zika, corporate crisis such as Volkswagen and others, there is an urgency for case studies of transboundary crisis communication in nonwestern cultures. Whether one wishes to conduct business or research in a nonwestern culture, an understanding of the culture would enable the organization or individual to effectively navigate crises situations in that country.

Crisis, Communication, and Culture

The literature on crisis management and crisis communication suggests that there are many different definitions of what constitutes crisis but for our purposes here, we describe a crisis as a major occurrence that can potentially have a negative effect on the individual, organization, or industry experiencing it, as well as its publics, products, goods, services, and reputation [9]. By its very nature, a crisis unsettles and interrupts normal functioning and creates a sense of unease among some groups, at the very least [10]. Thus for many communicators, crisis and conflict situations are some of the hardest tests of ability and professional deontology [11] that they will ever face. This is because communication sits at the core in the hierarchy of "crisis issues" [12]. That means that (a) communication or the lack of it can cause crises, and (b) when crisis threatens or occurs, communication is central to averting, containing/resolving it, and/or leading the way to restoration.

For many communicators, crisis, and conflict situations are some of the hardest tests of ability and professional deontology that they will ever face.

The link between communication and crisis then, is not only obvious, but absolutely important in thinking about crisis and crisis planning. Within this mix is also culture, which can be seen in simple terms as "that complex whole which includes knowledge, belief, art, morals, law customs and many other capabilities and habits acquired by the members of society" [13]. On the basis of that definition, one can argue that what constitutes crisis would necessarily be influenced by culture or cultural predilections, and so would communication about crisis since communication is an inevitable part of culture.

Indeed, available empirical evidence suggests that culture significantly affects the way people communicate [11, 14], and on that basis, various writers/scholars have suggested communication strategies to adopt or follow during conflict/crisis situations. While there are keen differences in these suggested strategies, what is common to all of them is the observation that during the elaboration process, knowing what the recipient/public/audience wants, what its social, professional, cultural, and psychological characteristics are and what its needs are, is germane to successful communication in that situation.

The implication here is that without in-depth knowledge and understanding of the cultural setting where a crisis situation has occurred, the crisis communication strategy stands the risk of not achieving its intended purpose [11]. While culture does not always readily provide us with an explanation of the main reasons why crisis erupt and how they evolve, including cultural dimensions in crisis management thinking is a very positive step. An approach that takes cultures into consideration has great potential for achieving long-term and sustainable outcomes in crisis communication plans [11].

From a transboundary perspective then, culture is even more significant in the sense that it is responsible for the differences in the collective programming of the mind, which ultimately results in significant differences in ways of perceiving, knowing, and being.

From a transboundary perspective then, culture is even more significant in the sense that it is responsible for the differences in the collective programming of the mind [5], which ultimately results in significant differences in ways of perceiving, knowing, and being. This implies, for example, that "[w]hat is appropriate in one sociocultural/national setting can be seen as wholly offensive in another, and what is rational in one sociocultural/national setting is wholly irrational in another." How, then, do communicators achieve success with such varying and varied environments?

Paying Attention to Cultural Specificities

It has been suggested that because of cultural differences in the publics' preferences in terms of direct or interpersonal communication during crisis situations, and also the cultural differences relating to the adequate "translation" of communication strategies, Western-style communication strategies are inadequate for dealing with global and transboundary issues of concern [11]. In view of this, getting to know what different cultural and multicultural groups expect and how they analyze, evaluate, and articulate their views during a crisis will ensure that the activities of different publics are considered when planning the crisis communication process; a process which must in itself be considered to be veritably dynamic.

Thus crisis communication practitioners must necessarily acknowledge that having an adequate understanding of basic features related to international cultures and subcultures is of utmost importance if one wants to communicate effectively in an environment that is becoming increasingly global. They must not only recognize, but also acknowledge the existence of cultural diversity and differences and how these influence not just behavior, but communicative behavior especially in times of crisis—situations where there is a threat to a community's core and life sustaining values [15]. The communicator must also develop and exhibit intercultural sensitivity toward such differences within and across nations [16] and across boundaries. This must be seen as an important attribute in the arsenal of the successful communicator.

Crisis communication practitioners must not only recognize but also acknowledge the existence of cultural diversity and differences and how these influence behavior—especially communicative behavior—in times of crisis.

Culture matters when two parties (the sender and the recipient(s) of the message) are communicating, but it becomes even more significant in a crisis situation because of heightened stakes, due to the potential for a disruption of "the normal flow of things," and the human trait that desires to protect its own; what is known – one's known way of life that is seen as normal, which is being threatened. This situation, as exemplified by many of the cases presented and discussed in this volume, implies that to be able to effectively handle issues and crisis situations, crisis managers and communicators need to be increasingly more versatile in their understanding of contexts that are often times beyond their immediate spheres of operation and direct influence.

Organization of This Volume

In our call for contributions, we asked authors to write about cases that had significant transboundary implications and which were clearly influenced by cultural specificities. We asked them to consider the following questions:

- How do cultures, in this case, these specific nonwestern cultures, respond to crises?
- What happens when the crisis occurs outside the country, but leads to consequences within the country and also outside the country?
- What are the factors that influence the crisis response by the affected countries?
- What are the lessons that scholars and practitioners can learn about the important role of culture in crisis communication in nonwestern cultures?

The result is a collection of cases that together provide a strong justification for considering crises in a transboundary sense, and also the role that culture plays in the understanding and resolution of crises in nonwestern contexts. The chapters (representing countries where the crises occurred) are drawn from the broad geo-political regions of Africa, Asia/Euro-Asia, the Middle East and Latin America. While not every single chapter has a transboundary angle to it, collectively they go beyond a mere presentation of cases to provide unique perspectives into the various influences – cultural and otherwise, tensions and dilemmas – that affect crisis and crisis communication in the specific settings. Each chapter examines how the specific culture impacts communication and response to crisis, using a case study or two as illustration. The aim is to show how different nonwestern cultures perceive crisis, how they manage all aspects of crisis within and across national, political, and ideological boundaries, and lessons that organizations and others that wish to operate or are operating in those cultures could use in preparing for and managing crisis. This chapter has tried to frame this volume within the adopted conceptual boundaries of culture, crisis, transboundariness, and crisis communication. The remainder of *Chapter 1* is devoted to an overview of the rest of this volume, described in the subsequent paragraphs.

Setting the tone is *Chapter 2,* which examines the political and cultural crisis of violence in Egypt, a situation where protesters express their grievances through violence, which is, in turn, met with state brutality. The chapter looks at several incidents surrounding the volatile situation in Egypt between 2011 and 2015 and identifies some of the key sociopolitical and cultural issues such as human rights violations, police brutality, and politicization of religion, as well as the breaking of the social contract, that has led to a fragmented social fabric. The consequences, according to the authors, are dire for the practice of democracy, and have resulted in battles that are being waged in inquisition courts. In this confusing and fluid state of affairs, many of the issues relating to an "authentic" Egyptian identity are being questioned, particularly the view that a critical mass of Egyptian civil society can participate in producing a political consensus in which civil and political freedoms may be legitimately sacrificed in the name of national unity and security.

Chapter 3 provides an example of a national crisis with truly transboundary implications: a crisis for one country (Ghana), that unfolded in a different country (Brazil). We see stakeholders across different nations, including a worldwide governing body. Using the Ghana Black Stars' threatened boycott of their last group match against Portugal at the 2014 Fédération Internationale de Football Association (FIFA) World Cup as an example, this chapter shows how the Ghanaian cultural traits of high power distance, respect for elders, and a general *laissez faire* attitude toward what constitutes crisis influenced the way both the handlers of the national team and government officials responded to this crisis that unfolded in the full view of an enthusiastic footballing world. The Ghanaian government's rather unconventional approach to resolving the issue in order to avoid what was shaping up to be a crisis of immense proportions, while averting the immediate crisis of an actual boycott, created major embarrassment for Ghana on the international scene. The chapter shows the difficulty in framing the issues and subsequently the narrative/s that are spawned when a crisis is unfolding in full glare of the international media; the story also exemplifies the shared human trait of failing to learn from earlier crises.

Using the case of the detection of an Ebola-infected person as a starting point, *Chapter 4* interrogates how the Nigerian government dealt with the threat and managed to beat the Ebola virus disease (EVD) with few deaths in only 3 months when other West African countries struggled to contain the deadly virus with devastating and fatal results. The Nigerian government's swift and decisive action in implementing effective strategies and tactics that involved the use of existing health infrastructure and personnel, effective communication, mobilization of technology to trace, track, quarantine, and treat Ebola-infected patients and contacts saved the situation. A concerned but patient public complied with new government directives; religious, traditional, opinion leaders and local and international health organizations cooperated and collaborated with the government in an unprecedented manner to bring what would have been a nightmare, to a quick end. This chapter showcases how quick thinking, planning, and adequate mobilization of people and resources can yield the desired results.

Chapter 5 uses the April 2015 violent xenophobic attacks in South Africa as a basis to raise and discuss some important questions around xenophobia in that country. Observing that the legacy of apartheid has made it easy for South Africans to be suspicious of, and often antagonistic to, people who are different, some key questions are raised: Do these xenophobic attacks represent a deep-seated suspicion of other people and/or an in-bred intolerance of others? Are there multiple causes that simmer under the surface and—from time to time—explode violently? Do the South African media report on foreigners in ways that perpetuate stereotypes and invariably encourage xenophobia? The authors point out that, on the basis of the country's violent history and also previous incidents, this was one crisis that should have been foreseen. Yet when it happened, the ruling African National Congress (ANC) government seemed to be caught by surprise and its initial reaction was a denial that the attacks were xenophobic, a response which only added fuel to an already incendiary situation. The chapter examines the government's response to the April 2015 attacks in its entirety, while trying to interrogate the culture of xenophobia in South Africa and the validity of claims against foreigners. It concludes by noting that the case reveals the complex nature of South African society and the dynamics of the relationship between South Africans as hosts, and foreigners who live in their midst, particularly those foreigners from north of the River Limpopo.

In *Chapter 6*, the melamine-tainted milk powder crisis in China—one of the most serious transregional crises of the twenty-first century in Greater China—provides the basis for illustrating the role traditional Chinese culture and various institutions, especially political and media systems, play in dealing with crisis situations. Through a comparative analysis of the form and content of crisis communication strategies (CCSs) used to mitigate public anger over the contaminated milk powder, this chapter presents a holistic approach to examining crisis communication practice and its effects in the Chinese context. The chapter also contributes to theory advancement by using a Chinese perspective to enhance the cultural and contextual sensitivity needed for crisis communication practitioners and policy makers in various regions in China.

The subject of *Chapter 7* is the terrorist attacks in Mumbai in November 2008, which provides the basis for interrogating the response of the Indian government, including how crisis communication was carried out in that crucial period. The transboundary nature of the crisis lies in the supposed control or coordination points of the attacks (Pakistan) and the vast number of foreigners who were among the casualties. The terrorists targeted the specific locations to fulfill a three-pronged political agenda, which was anti-India, anti-Israel and anti-Jewish, and also anti-US and anti-NATO. The attacks unfolded live on mainstream television over 3 days, and many ordinary citizens used smartphones and social media to post a constant stream of information to websites, leading to the claim that for the first key hours of the attacks, Flickr® rather than the New York Times® or BBC World® had more detailed and relevant information [17]. The Indian approach to crisis response in general, which is typified by tolerance tempered with caution and the generally easy-going and relaxed pace of life, resulted in a situation where the police forces were in a state of confusion during the first hours of the attack, with no one knowing what was going on or what to make of the pieces of information that were filtering in.

Chapter 8 deals with the way Indonesia responded to the forest fires that led to the transboundary haze crisis of 2013. It discusses the different responses provided at the different levels of government—the national and the local. While the local government approached the whole crisis lackadaisically, the national government's responses varied according to the respective institutions; while some Indonesian ministry officials adopted a denial and evasion response strategy, others took a more progressive approach that sought to assuage their neighbors' concerns. The authors point out that some of the responses were influenced by the Indonesian cultural characteristics of high power distance, weak concern regarding uncertainty avoidance, high in-group collectivism, and low institutional collectivism, as described by the Hofstede and GLOBE studies.

In *Chapter 9*, the authors use Japan's worst nuclear disaster to showcase how the culture and communication practices of Tokyo Electric Power Company® (TEPCO), which operates the world's largest nuclear power plant, influenced its response to the nuclear disaster such that its transboundary effects continue to reverberate across the globe, more than 5 years later. The chapter examines TEPCO's failure to demonstrate consistently high standards in its crisis management and its failure to be transparent with stakeholders, particularly the everyday public protocol, while holding to the cultural expectations of employee loyalty and of harmony with stakeholders. The chapter proposes a communication plan, which has the potential to restore the company's public image and to reduce the growing public disaffection with it over its perceived *mis*handling of a major nuclear crisis.

Chapter 10, on Kazakhstan, analyzes the deadly conflict between the oil workers, the KazMunaiGaz oil company, and local government authorities that took place between May and June, 2011, using the national ideology of Eurasianism as a framework for understanding the role that culture played in the response to that conflict. While official reports of the crisis gave very low numbers of civilian casualties (17 dead), social media reports painted a very different picture, reporting that, at least 100 people died as a result of the clash with local police. Social media reporting of the conflict forced the Kazakhstani government to abandon its initial denial of the existence of conflict/crisis in the region and to work toward ending it.

An event that stunned the whole world, and continues to baffle industry expects – the disappearance of a Malaysia Airlines Boeing 777 (Flight MH370) on a routine flight from Kuala Lumpur to Beijing, China – is the focus of *Chapter 11*. Precisely 327 days (on Thursday 29 January 2015) after the flight literally vanished without a trace, Malaysia officially declared that the disappearance of the aircraft was an accident and added that it presumed all the flight's passengers and crew were dead. On January 17, 2017, it was announced that the search for Flight MH370 had been suspended, making the incident a major mystery in aviation history, and creating an unresolved crisis for the Malaysian government. The chapter discusses how the Malaysian government responded to the vanishing of Flight MH370 and how communication was carried out with the relatives of people who were on board the flight and their governments, as this was an international flight. The influence of culture on the initial responses and general communication around the crisis, and the role played by social media as the crisis unfolded, are also discussed. Through the lenses of communication, culture and social media, the chapter examines the various aspects of the Malaysian response within the context of transboundary crisis. This case reveals the complex nature of transboundary crisis and the dynamics of the relationship between communication, crisis and culture in an era of widespread social media use that knows no geographic and/or communicative boundaries.

The crisis preparedness, particularly social media crisis preparedness of Singaporean organizations is the subject matter of *Chapter 12*. The authors argue that despite Singapore's success as a hub of commerce, knowledge, and research and development in a fiercely competitive global environment, and a national culture characterized by diligence, continuous learning, improvement, growth, and always needing to be ahead of the curve, its lack of crisis preparedness, particularly social media crisis preparedness constitutes an Achilles heel. This is particularly so given the heavy social media use among organizations in that country. Using two instances of a breakdown in Singapore's mass rapid transit (SMRT) operator as a case point, the authors conclude that organizations have a lackadaisical approach toward social media use and are totally unprepared for social media crisis. Despite practitioners' claim of understanding the importance of crisis preparedness, few have actually put in place practical and rigorous mechanisms to help manage potential and actual crises. The authors conclude that the lack of preparedness for a crisis engendered and/or given fillip by social media is a function of the corporate culture of Singapore's top organizations; a culture that is characteristically cautious and prudent, seeking to maintain the status quo and has a preference for utilizing "safe" traditional media in order to exert control over communication.

In *Chapter 13*, the Korean Air® "ramp return" crisis provides insights into how Korean culture affects public relations practice and crisis communication within that context. Though Korean Air had a strong public relations department with seasoned crisis communication experts, its crisis management system did not work as effectively as one would expect. This was because, as the authors argue, in South Korea's Chaebol system where the owner of an organization exercises absolute power, any recommendations or plan of action suggested by the internal public relations department is futile unless the owner agrees to it. The chapter shows how, in this instance, Korean Chaebol culture combined with Confucianism to negatively impact Korean Air's crisis management and its response to a crisis which could be seen as largely owner generated.

Focusing on the ongoing war in Syria and the subsequent refugee crisis that it has spawned, *Chapter 14* discusses what has been described as the worst humanitarian disaster since World War II. Noting that the civil war has claimed over 200,000 lives and forced about 12 million Syrians to flee their homes into other parts of Syria as well as to some major European and Middle Eastern countries, the chapter looks at the part that culture has played in both the war and the ensuing refugee crisis, including the resettlement process. The authors ask important questions such as these: What is the rest of the world doing in response to the humanitarian disaster unfolding right before their eyes? What are key Western and Middle Eastern countries doing to help resolve the refugee situation? How are the media covering the crisis and how does this coverage affect refugees in their efforts to settle in their host countries? Providing answers to these questions help bring to the fore the complex and problematic nature of the civil war in Syria and the refugee crisis that it has inevitably created. In the end, the chapter concludes that the Syrian refugee crisis is not just a Gulf Arab issue but one for the Gulf, as well as Western countries, to work on together. The authors also note that the crisis represents a battle for hearts and minds, and suggest that giving the refugees hope through good refugee policies backed by effective communication can help win that battle.

In *Chapter 15,* the authors use the Borusan crisis of 2011 in Turkey as a basis for discussing the complex relations between business, culture, politics, and religious sensitivities. Borusan withdrew sponsorship for a woman race car driver giving the official reason as budget cuts, but it was alleged that the real reason was because the woman wore a headscarf in a television interview which did not sit well with the company's policy of political and religious neutrality. In this case, the controversial issue regarding the true meaning of a headscarf, in terms of whether it represents religious devotion or political Islam, became an issue and showed how sociopolitical, cultural, and religious differences and inclinations can interact to turn what at first glance might seem to be a simple business decision, into a full-blown crisis, aided by social media. The Borusan crisis is regarded as the first major crisis occurring along the sociocultural fault line that Turkish corporations witnessed, and one that the business world was not prepared for and was unable to deal with in a satisfactory manner. The chapter concludes that the case shows that sociocultural factors have major influences on business success, while highlighting recently amplified sensitivities of the Turkish society.

Chapter 16 examines the Niterói landslide, which occurred in Rio de Janeiro, Brazil, and how cultural practices accentuated the disaster and also influenced the way in which authorities responded to it. In that situation, two factors came together to turn a natural disaster into a serious tragedy that could have been avoided. The disaster was compounded by a sequence of careless activities strongly influenced by cultural attitudes and state and municipal government (in)action and lack of preparation for effective crisis management. The landslide was partly a result of a terrible series of management misconduct and organizational misdeed. The handling of the Niterói disaster highlights how culture and politics negatively influenced Brazil's response to the crisis and provides important lessons in how effective risk analysis and crisis communication may save lives; and the need to prioritize lives over houses or votes.

Two countries in Latin America – Colombia and Guatemala – are the subject of the discussion in *Chapter 17.* The case, which is also a prime example of a transboundary crisis, involves the United States-based transnational corporation Chiquita Brands International®, which has been involved in crises originating in Colombia and Guatemala, each of which rapidly spread to the United States with different consequences in each respective nation. The chapter describes these crises, how they shifted from the corporation's host countries (Colombia and Guatemala) to Chiquita's home country (the United States), and the specific controlled public relations and communication strategies and tactics that Chiquita adopted to face those challenging situations. The authors point out that it is essential to understand these crises in the context of global public relations because in a globalizing world, transnational corporations (TNCs) need to understand how cross-national conflict shifts happen. They suggest that corporations need to have the ability to develop a "glocal" strategy that responds to the needs and concerns of different publics in the home and host countries and propose a practical framework for addressing transnational crises, using cross-national conflict shifting theory (CNCS) as a basis.

The final chapter (*18*) offers a fitting conclusion to the volume by providing practical tips on how to plan for crisis communication across cultural and transboundary contexts. As the summary of the chapters in this section has shown, and as history has consistently taught us, most organizations and institutions will experience a day of crisis in their lifetime. Given that certainty (almost), the authors suggest that it makes sense to put in place plans for that day of eventuality. This is particularly important in an era where a local crisis can quickly cross boundaries – physical, ideological or virtual, and become an international crisis, and crisis seemingly happening far off from a nation's shores can quickly become a matter of concern for local authorities away from the maiden point of crisis. Thus, planning for the day of crisis, the authors point out, is imperative. The chapters in this volume indicate that there is usually a common theme running through most crises; that is, failure to plan in advance. To deal with that, the last chapter attempts to tie it all together with tips on preparing for that day of inevitability. In crisis situations, things can be chaotic and not as orderly as the crisis handlers would have it, and usually implementing any plan at all, is difficult. Nonetheless, planning is essential and the concluding chapter seeks to provide some guidelines on how to plan for communication on that crisis day, noting that, when a crisis hits, what is said in the early moments can go a long way to not just define how the crisis is perceived but also how the organization recovers from the crisis. The thrust of the chapter is that, despite the focus on culture and transboundary concerns, certain commonalities can be found among crises across all settings, and that, allows for the provision of broad guidelines in planning and preparation.

Conclusion: The Value of Transboundary Crisis Case Studies from Nonwestern Societies

This book, *Culture and Crisis Communication: Transboundary Cases from Nonwestern Perspectives,* aims to fill the gap in an area of crisis communication that is now getting some attention from scholars. Globalization has ushered in new spheres of power in the form of the BRIC countries (Brazil, Russia, India, and China) and other emerging economic powers [18, 19]. These countries, with their attendant cultural views, are reshaping business communication. Sriramesh's pioneering fieldwork on Indian organizations in 1988 set the stage for linking cultural "environment" to the practice of public relations. Today, while some organizations recognize the important role of culture in their communication to communities in host countries, others are still debating whether adapting their communication to fit cultural mores of a host country is necessary. This debate is heightened when an organization faces a crisis situation. The responses to the burning of the Quran by the US military in Afghanistan, Arla and the Danish cartoon crisis in the Middle East, among others, provide excellent examples. We believe that as more countries and regions assert their influence, organizations and public relations professionals must consider culture in their design of public relations programs and response to crisis situations in nonwestern countries. We believe that culturally significant issues such as religion and the political chasm that exists between developed and developing countries would be highlighted within the project.

Within the emerging literature, there is support for the contribution of this book from those who stress the role of culture in crisis management [20], those who criticize crisis communication scholarship for its "managerial bias" and the tendency to marginalize the perspective of the public [21], and also those who point to the heavy domination of American/Western viewpoints [22, 23]. Since the focus of this book is on case studies from nonwestern contexts, it provides a different perspective to the literature, by addressing some of the aforementioned criticisms while filling a lacuna in the literature.

As individuals and organizations are integral parts of any society, crisis communication cannot be considered in a vacuum; it needs to adopt a holistic approach by considering the broader cultural context in order to better deal with the concerns of stakeholders. For international managers, communicators, and researchers, it is essential to understand the culture of the country or region in which they are operating. Understanding the effect of the differences in context provides a knowledge base and cultural intelligence that can oftentimes be the difference between success and failure.

We believe that this book will appeal not only to students of culture and communication, but also to organizations with business interests in those parts of the world that have been discussed here. It will broaden the scope of research in crisis communication from cultural and nonwestern perspectives. The epistemological value of culture cannot be understated in any attempt to understand how individuals, groups, organizations, and nations around the world recognize and respond to crisis. Ultimately, it is our position that an ontological understanding of crisis and the role culture and communication play in crisis response is an absolute necessity, hence this book.

References

1. "Germany shocked by Cologne New Year gang assault on women" (2016, January 5) [Online]. Available: http://www.bbc.com/news/world-europe-35231046, March 13, 2016 (last date accessed).

2. "Sweden masked gang 'targeted migrants' in Stockholm" (2016, January 30) [Online]. Available: http://www.bbc.com/news/world-europe-35451080, March 13, 2016 (last date accessed).

3. "Angela Merkel's CDU suffers German state election setbacks" (2016, March 13, 2016) [Online]. Available: http://www.bbc.com/news/world-europe-35796831, March 14, 2016 (last date accessed).

4. "What is culture: Definition and meaning," Business Dictionary. [Online]. Available: http://www.businessdictionary.com/definition, March 14, 2016 (last date accessed).

5. G. Hofstede, *Culture's Consequences: International Differences in Work-related Values* (Abridged ed.). London: Sage Publications, 1980.

6. E. H. Schein, *Organizational Culture and Leadership.* Jossey-Bass, 1985.

7. J. Falkheimer and M. Heide, "Crisis communication in a new world: Reaching multicultural publics through old and new media," *Nordicom Review*, vol. 30, pp. 55–66, 2009.

8. A. Boin and M. Rhinard, "Managing transboundary crises: What role for the European Union?" *International Studies Review*, vol. 10, no. 1, pp. 1–26, 2008.

9. K. Fearn-Banks, *Crisis Communications: A Casebook Approach*, 2nd ed. New Jersey: Lawrence Erlbaum Associates, 2002.

10. C. Galloway and K. Kwansah-Aidoo, "Getting to grips with issues management and crises communication," in *Public Relations Issues and Crisis Management*, C. Galloway and K. Kwansah-Aidoo, Eds. Melbourne: Thomson/Social Science Press, 2012, pp. 1–12.

11. E. Minty. (2015, April 29). *"Culture and crisis communication"* [Online]. Available: https://www.linkedin.com/pulse/culture-crisis-communication-ella-minty-chart-pr-mcipr-miod-mspe, May 15, 2017 (last date accessed).

12. International Risk Governance Council. (2012) [Online]. Available: http://www.irgc.org/wp-content/uploads/2015/04/An_introduction_to_the_IRGC_Risk_Governance_Framework_final_v2012.pdf, March 4, 2016 (last date accessed).

13. E. B. Tylor, *Primitive Culture: Researches Into the Development of Mythology, Philosophy, Religion, Art and Custom.* London: Bradbury, Evans and Co. Printers, 2010.

14. G. Hofstede, *Cultures and Organizations: Software of the Mind.* New York: McGraw-Hill, 1991.

15. A. Enander, O. Lajksjo, and E. L. Tedfeldt, "A tear in the social fabric: Communities dealing with socially generated crises," *Journal of Contingencies and Crisis Management*, vol. 18, no. 1, pp. 39–48, 2010.

16. R. Sriussadaporn, "Managing international business communication problems at work: A pilot study in foreign companies in Thailand," *Cross Cultural Management: An International Journal*, vol. 13, pp. 330–344, 2006.

17. Kaplan, C. (2009). "The biopolitics of technoculture in the Mumbai attacks," *Theory, Culture and Society*, vol. 26, nos. 7–8, p. 305.

18. K. Sriramesh, "Globalization and public relations: Opportunities for growth and reformulation," in *The Handbook of Public Relations*, 2nd ed. R. L. Heath, Ed. Thousand Oaks, CA: Sage, 2010, pp. 691–707.

19. K. Sriramesh and D. Vercic, *Culture and Public Relations.* New York and London: Routledge, 2012.

20. K. Campiranon and N. Scott, "Factors influencing crisis management in tourism destinations," *in Crisis Management in Tourism*. E. Laws, B. Prideaux, and K. S. Chon, Eds. London: CAB International, 2007, pp. 142–156.

21. D. Waymer and R. L. Heath, "Emergent agents: The forgotten publics in crisis communication and issues management research," *Journal of Applied Communication Research*, vol. 35, pp. 88–108, 2007.

22. M. Ayish, "Communication research in the Arab World: A new perspective," *The Public*, vol. 5, no. 1, pp. 33–57, 1998.

23. D. R. G. Padgett, S.S. Cheng, and V. Parekh, "The quest for transparency and accountability: Communicating responsibly to stakeholders in crises," *Asian Social Science* (April, 2013) [Online]. Available at: http://dx.doi.org/10.5539/ass.v9n9p31, March 8, 2016 (last date accessed).

Africa

Egypt

2

Dealing with Political and Cultural Crisis in a Troubled Middle East Region

Ibrahim Saleh and Heba Metwali

Chapter Preview

After several years (since 2011) of ongoing political and cultural crisis in Egypt and the region, failing to make progress in attaining freedom, and obvious delinquency in taking any steps towards democratization, there is an alarming phenomenon of a fragmented social fabric in Egypt. In addition, there is a form of escaped violence – a situation where protesters express their grievances through violence, which is, in turn, met with state brutality – instigated by an acute national political identity crisis and an alienated culture of enclaved ghettoes. The chapter delves into several incidents surrounding the current volatile situation in Egypt while identifying some of the relevant issues such as human rights violations, police brutality, and the politicization of religion, as well as breaking of social contracts. All of these aspects have influenced the potential practice of democracy and put the culture in reverse, leading to a situation where people are fighting battles in inquisition courts. In this

Culture and Crisis Communication: Transboundary Cases from Nonwestern Perspectives, First Edition.
Edited by Amiso M. George and Kwamena Kwansah-Aidoo.
© 2017 by The Institute of Electrical and Electronics Engineers, Inc. Published 2017 by John Wiley & Sons, Inc.

confusing and fluid state of affairs, many of the issues relating to an "authentic" Egyptian identity are being questioned, particularly the view that a critical mass of Egyptian civil society can participate in producing a political consensus in which civil and political freedom may be legitimately sacrificed in the name of national unity and security. This is in spite of the cost of trying to reach the main goals of the 2011 revolution: gaining bread, social justice, and dignity.

After reading this chapter, you will be able to

- *Offer multiple explanations of interventions because no single reason suffices*
- *Move beyond the euphoria of political changes in Egypt into a contextual analysis*
- *Provide clarity to the underlying and short-term socioeconomic reasons for military intervention*
- *Describe the group-think structure of Egyptian society and the changing social contract*
- *Explain the growing sense of polarization and radicalism as a cultural reservoir*
- *Analyze the goals, objectives, strategies, and tactics of military, political Islam, and secularists in dealing with public discontent*
- *Clarify the role of technology and social media in the political fluidity in Egypt*
- *Understand the role of culture in coping with the performance of political actors during the crisis*

Introduction: Overview of Egypt

Egypt, one of the oldest civilizations in the world, lies in Northeast Africa and is bordered by Israel, the Gaza Strip, Libya, and Sudan. It has a population of over 90 million [1] with the vast majority living within 40,000 square kilometers along the banks of the River Nile, less than 4% of the total land area.

Life in Egypt is based around the River Nile, whose annual flood is central to the country's prosperity. Over 85% of the population is Sunni Muslims with the remaining population being predominantly Coptic Christians. Arabic is the official language of Egypt, although English is widely spoken and understood.

Roughly 45% of Egyptians live on less than US$2 a day and inflation reached as high as 12.97% in 2014. Tourism revenue is the primary source of foreign currency along with Suez Canal tolls and remittances from Egyptians working abroad. "Unemployment remains high at 13.4%. Among unemployed Egyptians, 71% are between 15 and 29 years old" [2].

This chapter examines the political, economic, and cultural crisis in Egypt, which has led to protesters expressing their grievance through violence that is met with state brutality. The fragile political scene might have also been aggravated by the role played by families of local tribes who submit themselves to the dictates of the ruling regime in exchange for influence [3].

The majority of Egyptians are desperate to attain political rights and social justice.

The majority of Egyptians are desperate to attain political rights and social justice [4]. Yet, what they get is increasing impoverishment which is worsened by the "liberalization" policies implemented by Mubarak's regime in a Russian-style "oligarchization." Egypt's old middle class is unable to help because it is both corrupt and unrepresented—a situation which helped to create a societal void that was quickly filled with political Islam that only exacerbated the crisis and opened all doors for bloody clashes and disruptions [5].

Confusion about how to react to political Islam led to the rise of grassroot movements of young people and disenfranchised workers, and ordinary Egyptians rose up and got rid of Hosni Mubarak's autocratic regime [6]. Yet, there continues to be anger and disappointment over the continuous exploitation by police forces [7], conflicts of interest, and fragmented public opinion. The spread of Islamic fascism also created concern among Egypt's neighbors.

Situation Analysis: 2011: A Year of Hope and Despair

These events created divisions inside Egypt and the rest of the Middle East and North Africa (MENA) region. Undemocratic Arab states such as Saudi Arabia, Jordan, and the United Arab Emirates (UAE) watched on with discomfort as various factions, including secular camps, fought over the role that Islam should play in politics and society [8].

In January 2011, large-scale anti-Mubarak regime demonstrations developed leading to the resignation of President Hosni Mubarak and the collapse of his 30-year regime. On June 30, 2012, an alternate candidate of the Freedom and Justice Party, Mohamed Morsi, was elected Egypt's fifth president and the first nonmilitary leader. Less than 3 months later, on August 12, Morsi nullified a declaration by the military and put all executive and legislative powers in his hands, excluding the military establishment. Following those actions, revolutionary activists declared in the socialist party newspaper that "Egypt is like a house where the curtains have been changed but everything else is the same" [9].

The two key slogans of the Egyptian upheaval are (a) *'aish, horreya / adala igtema'eya* (bread, freedom, social justice) and (b) *'ash-sha'b yurid / isqaat an-nizaam'* (the people want the downfall of the regime).

The two key slogans of the Egyptian upheaval are (a) *'aish, horreya / adala igtema'eya* (bread, freedom, social justice) and (b) *'ash-sha'b yurid / isqaat an-nizaam'* (the people want the downfall of the regime). Regardless of the political gains and outcomes, both slogans reflected an undeniable shift in the increasing level of political awareness among Egyptians since the January 25 Revolution. Hence, 2011 was the year that offered hope and dreams, but also disappointments that led to cultural and identity crisis for millions of Egyptians. The country's cultural identity has been shaken by inquisition-type religious courts that decide what is religiously acceptable. For example, blasphemy cases between 2011 and 2012 exceeded the cumulative cases during Mubarak's whole 30-year reign. Yet, Egypt's secular society, though conservative, prefers to keep religion in the private sphere [10].

In less than a year, Morsi was impeached and an interim President Adly Mansour was sworn in on July 4, 2013. On June 8, 2014, presidential elections were held, and Abdel Fattah El-Sisi was elected with almost 97% of the votes, and he was sworn into office as president [11]. However, the violent culture and polarization that marked Egypt since 2011 provided a veritable context for chaos, riots, and vandalism. Consequently, Egypt erupted with crowds that attempted to storm government buildings, setting fire to public and private properties, blocking roads and railroads, and surrounding government buildings. Authorities responded with force, triggering more confrontations and fatalities among protesters [12].

The Egyptian cultural violence entailed much more than just regimes' removal, elections, and democratization; it was an ideological confrontation fueled by the will to, and the search for a way to redefine identity and establish a culture of acceptance of the other. The protest culture endured continuous swings between revolution and counter-revolution movements that occurred simultaneously and led to bloody, unsettling, and confusing scenarios. Violence and bloody conflict became the tools utilized by contenders and these destabilized Egypt's sociopolitical and economic structure and order.

The Egyptian cultural violence entailed much more than just regimes' removal, elections, and democratization; it was an ideological confrontation fueled by the will to, and the search for a way to redefine identity and establish a culture of acceptance of the other.

Egypt became a dysfunctional culture, a space for naming and shaming, that was strategically manipulated by the Muslim Brotherhood (MB), who sold its narrative to the global audiences that the army's intervention on July 3 was a coup.

The narrative was picked up and disseminated widely by such international media as *Al-Jazeera*, *CNN*, and *BBC*.

In contrast, many Egyptians rejected this discourse by criticizing foreign media channels and emphasized that mass protests erupted to defy the religious fascism that was imposed by Morsi and the MB in Egypt. Thomas Friedman captured the sentiments of many Egyptians when he wrote: "Egypt's first revolution was to get rid of the dead hand, the second revolution was to get rid of the dead heads and the third revolution was to escape from the dead end" [13]. In explaining this point, Friedman noted that the dead hand referred to President Mubarak whose hand was "so dead that way too many young Egyptians felt they were living in a rigged system, where they had no chance of realizing their full potential, under a leader with no vision" [13]. The *dead heads* referred to the military generals who replaced Mubarak and had no idea of how to govern, and the *dead end* was a reference to Morsi who was "more interested in consolidating the Brotherhood's grip on government rather than governing himself, and he drove Egypt into a dead end" [13]. Friedman summed up the overarching concerns of the majority of Egyptians concisely thus:

> Add it all up and there is a message from the Egyptian majority: No more dead hands; we want a government that aspires to make Egypt the vanguard of the Arab world again. No more dead heads; we want a government that is run by competent people who can restore order and jobs. And no more dead ends; we want a government that will be inclusive and respect the fact that two-thirds of Egyptians are not Islamists and, though many are pious Muslims, they don't want to live in anything close to a theocracy. [13]

In spite of these concerns, the violence continued, mostly perpetuated by the state. Moataz Salah, El Wafd Party media advisor and the president of the group "Popular Initiative to Recover Egypt's Looted Funds," noted the resurgence of state-sponsored violence. He cited the break-ins into his apartment with threats to prevent him from continuing his efforts to recover Egypt's looted money [14]. However, Ramy Jan, founder of Christians Against the Coup/Christian Anti-Coup, explained that he followed an uninvolved and disengaged pattern to avoid the repercussions of the revival of the police state in Egypt [15].

Such political fluidity resulted in a very disturbing clash of power in Egypt's cultural crisis that is stained with blood and gore everywhere, where peaceful demonstrations are silenced with gunshots, helicopters, and bulldozers. The intercultural and inter-religious polarization led to targeting, looting, and burning of churches and Christian institutions, thereby dashing hopes of a harmonious existence between the majority Muslim population and its tiny Christian minority [16].

The military and remnants (feloul) of Mubarak's old regime have alienated the society and worsened the situation, eliminating opportunities for any healing in Egyptian society [17]. Average citizens have become victimized by all political actors, although each of these groups had separate agendas and conflicts of interests that fueled antagonism and caused more violence at the societal level [18]. Ordinary

Egyptians believe that law enforcement is not designed to protect them; rather, they revived the dreaded "midnight visitors phenomenon" whereby security forces break into homes of the suspected rebels, arrest those persons, in some cases, never to be seen again.

Research on Crisis in Egypt

There is continuous failure to connect ideas and concepts developed around any scholarly work about MENA. Reasons might be the result of the strong western influences and also low indigenous theoretical features [19]. Besides, "managerial bias" and the lack of context and understanding of the region [20] are two main hurdles in this understanding. However, such absence of local knowledge only serves to escalate some of the external crises and internal conflicts in the region [21].

Research on crisis in Egypt runs the gamut—from studies that opine that political figures like Gamal Abdel Nasser have always exploited the average citizens for their own political gains, that Egyptians no longer trust the military or political Islam, to others that reframe the intersection of the romantic idealism of Arab nationalism and the sense of discontent and betrayal from the colonizer and the patron state [22]. Yet, others focus on "crisis informatics" or emergency information management during the political demonstrations and protests in Iran, Tunisia, and Egypt in June 2009, December 2010, and January 2011, respectively. Findings indicated that Twitter[®] filled a unique technology and communication gap at least partially. However, it recommends that social media and crisis research must be placed in the larger context of social media use in conditions of crisis [23].

Another study that attempted to understand the crisis communication of Egyptian workers' movements [24] revealed that the Egyptian government maintained an iron grip on power, harshly punished dissent, and played a central role in a system that keeps workers powerless and poor.

A study of tourists' perspectives before and after visiting Egypt following the Egyptian Revolution revealed that their perception of risk was affected by media and marketing communication messages [25]. Another study shows that young Egyptians, frustrated with the status quo, are engaged in online activism through social media to get their messages across [26].

These varied studies confirm that little is known about the cultural challenges to the core values of many Egyptians [27]. Clearly, cultural experience is related to social time and space on an individual level, but one can also distinguish certain collective cultural experiences related to certain crisis and risk discourses [28].

The Case of the Ousted Morsi, the Last Caliph-President of Egypt

Mohammed Morsi was the first democratically elected President in the post-Mubarak era. He was ousted in what was considered a coup orchestrated by the Egyptian military. Morsi's forced removal from power was perceived as both popular protest and a military coup. Such contrasting perceptions highlighted the cultural divide in Egyptian society. The political Islam camp under the Muslim Brotherhood perceived Morsi's ouster as illegitimate. The Muslim Brotherhood likened his removal to the Algerian Army's approach to purging Islamism from the country. On the other hand, the rest of the Egyptian society, which had grown up with the post-colonial state, favored decorated military officers whose legitimacy emanates from their war heroism [29]. In ousting Morsi, the military leaders said they were simply responding to concerns of a majority of Egyptians who feared they had come out of Mubarak's dictatorship into an Islamic dictatorship. They had good reason to be concerned as Morsi and the Muslim Brotherhood dominated the Egyptian legislature and suppressed the judiciary. Morsi also purged the top military leaders and transferred their powers to his office. He jailed opponents and suppressed the media and civil rights of Egyptians.

Public protests against Morsi started off with "Tamarod" (Rebel) Movement campaign that mobilized the streets (public opinion) to withdraw confidence from the president. Tamarod, together with "6 April" and other groups formed the "June 30 Front" [17]. The campaign collected 22 million signatures asking for Morsi's impeachment. At the same time, the National Alliance to Support Legitimacy, the backdoor of Muslim Brotherhood, refused any calls for negotiations with the army, calling any nonconstitutional step a military coup [30].

But the army and leading political and religious leaders, including the Coptic Orthodox Patriarch (Tawadros II); the Grand Imam of Al-Azhar (Ahmed El-Tayeb); a representative of the Salafist Nour Party (Mohamed ElBaradei); one of Tamarod campaign's founders (Mohamed Abdel-Aziz); and a senior judicial figure suspended the constitution temporarily and handed over power to the head of Egypt's High Constitutional Court [31].

The Muslim Brotherhood used hate speech on all platforms to promulgate false accusations about the role Christians played in the ousting of Morsi, and how they had declared a "war" on Islam. Such public discourse led to a deepening hatred of minorities, which resulted in a chaotic bloodbath [32].

Christians were subjected to continuous looting, vandalism, arson, kidnapping, torture, and murder. The trail of mayhem included looting and torching of 40 churches and destruction of another 23 churches by armed thugs. Over 160 Christian-owned buildings were attacked, and two security guards were burned alive while working on a tour boat owned by Christians [32].

The violence prompted an angry backlash across Egypt, causing the death of more than 300 people. Interim Prime Minister at the time, Hazem El-Beblawi, explained that the government had no choice but to order the crackdown to prevent further anarchy and deadly violence [33]. On July 3, 2013, the head of the *Egyptian Armed Forces*, Abdel Fattah El-Sisi, ousted President Mohamed Morsi from power and deployed Chief Justice Adly Mansour as Interim President.

What these series of events highlight is that the Egyptian cultural crisis is marked by unprecedented political shifts and hostility, highlighted by an increasing wave of terrorism and political violence which infringes on citizens' basic rights and worsens the country's human rights record. In order to address the numerous complex political and economic challenges in Egypt, there is an urgent need to prioritize the restoration of and support for the rule of law, by sticking to constitutional provisions.

Official Response of the Egyptian Government

The new Egyptian constitution that was passed in 2014 focused on achieving international human rights legislation and advocated the position of supporting and ratifying international rights and conventions [34]. The Egyptian government and parliament must therefore focus on passing these and making them part of domestic law. To serve this goal, the current parliament that was elected in 2015 must deal with several unresolved issues and ratify conventions to contribute to the human rights agenda and provide guarantees for basic constitutional rights [34]. While there has been no clear and specific communication regarding the goals of the government, we perceive that the following were goals that the government sought to achieve on the basis of actions taken.

Goal 1: To Restore Law and Order in an Out-of-Control Egypt

Objectives
- Contain mob reaction and protests. Law 107 of 2013 was signed to suppress the right to public gatherings, processions, and peaceful protests, though the law breaches Egypt's obligations under International Covenant on Civil and Political Rights to uphold freedom of assembly and respect the right to life.

Strategy
- Take actions that contain the violent situation and engender confidence among the Egyptian public.
- Utilize the law as a basis for preventing mass protests that could result in disorderly behavior.

Tactics
- Tried to enforce Law 107 of 2013, banning public gatherings, processions, and peaceful protests.
- Arrested and detained Mohammed Morsi, his aides and supporters, and all members of the Muslim Brotherhood.
- Suspended the Constitution.
- Dissolved the Shura or Consultative Council.
- Appointed Supreme Constitutional Court Justice, Adly Mansour, as Interim Head of State until elections and Mohammed El-Baradei as Vice President.
- Army appealed to Egyptians to desist from engaging in violence.

- Public Prosecutor ordered temporary freeze on assets of top leaders of Muslim Brotherhood and pro-Morsi groups.

Goal 2: To Restore Confidence in the Leadership and Governance by Supporting the Will of the Egyptian People via Early Presidential Elections

Objectives

- Reverse the current ongoing violence and decrease the political tensions in Egypt by ensuring political stability of the country and fighting government corruption.

Strategy

- Present a roadmap that will lead to the formation of a technocratic national government.
- Find solutions to the economic and social problems.

Tactics

- Declare early elections through the Constitutional Court.
- Form a technocratic, national government through popular demand.
- Secure and guarantee freedom of expression for all citizens.
- Take all necessary measures to empower youth and expand freedom of expression.

Goal 3: Improve and Restore the Economy and Create Opportunities for Egyptians

Objectives

- Short term: Achieve lower budget deficits, public debt and inflation, and adequate foreign exchange reserves.
- Long term: Achieve better standards of living with more jobs, less poverty, and better health and education systems.

Strategy

- Take actions that would spur the economy.

Tactics

- Cut fuel and food subsidies to spur growth and attract foreign investment.
- Initiated major public infrastructure projects to create jobs and spur structural reforms.

- Announced the development of the Suez Canal Special Economic Zone to attract investments and provide job opportunities.

Much of Egypt's economy is dependent on these areas: Gulf assistance, direct foreign investments, foreign remittances, and tourism. With the decline of oil prices, the Gulf countries are less likely to continue assistance in the way Egypt may have expected. Direct foreign investments are hampered by the dire security situation, highlighted by terrorist attacks at popular tourist destinations and the downing of the Russian charter plane at Sharm el Sheikh [35]. In addition to the perennially underperforming Egyptian economy, the suspension of General Motors operations, which manufactures 25% of Egypt's cars, due to a shortage of dollars [36], and the brutal killing of Italian doctoral student, Giulio Regeni [37, 38], who was conducting research on trade union activism in Egypt, have posed a challenge for the government in meeting this third goal.

Outcome of the Government's Response and Initiatives

On March 28, 2015, President Abdel Fattah El-Sisi gave a speech at the inaugural session of the 26th Arab Summit in Sharm el Sheikh, which purported to sum up the current situation in the Arab world, but which also essentially summed up Egypt's current situation as a microcosm of the wider MENA region. He noted that

> [t]he Arab nation is confronting various dangers that reached unprecedented limits with some of the crises escalating and expanding, threatening the present and future of all Arabs. Such plots are dismantling the texture of the societies from inside with the aim of dividing their unity on the basis of religion, race, sect, or doctrine. We have seen how the terrorists are making horrible and heinous attacks that exceed all limits regardless of any religious or ethical values with the aim of spreading panic and challenging the authorities of the countries, shaking confidence in them and showing up their powers to promote their extremist thoughts using religion to achieve their political goals. [39]

One of the problems is that the Egyptian authorities have been accused of presiding over the flagrant abuse of human rights with the claim of trying to restore stability [40, 41]. Hence, violence by different stakeholders of religious armed groups and the government have escalated in defense of their positions, not considering the cultural implications and the public's dire conditions. The patron state continues to engage in all sorts of abuse on a daily basis, including a lack of accountability for many killings of protesters by security forces, mass detentions, military trials of civilians, hundreds of death sentences, and the forced eviction of thousands of families in the

Sinai Peninsula [40]. Authorities governing by decree in the absence of an elected parliament and an impotent one, have shown no interest in stopping the abuses by the security forces and instead issued a raft of laws that severely curtail civil and political rights, effectively erasing the human rights gains of the 2011 uprising that ousted the longtime ruler Hosni Mubarak in 2011 [40, 42] and completely undermining the 2014 constitution's focus on championing human rights [34].

In addition, the national economy has received less attention as a result of the influx of financial support from Arab neighbors without addressing the entrenched problems. Hence, Egypt's economy is shaky and is continuously suffering from the threat of an insolvency crisis. In addition, the continuation of violence, political protests, and general political uncertainty along with the lack of vision and prevalence of incoherent economic policies have become a driving force for further repercussions. As such the Egyptian society is vulnerable and on the verge of a debilitating loop of more political instability, violence, and economic deterioration. In the face of such reality, the Egyptian society is exposed to an increasing chance of economic disaster and escalation of political turmoil; including mass demonstrations, harsher crackdowns, leadership struggles, and possibly the disintegration of state power.

Practical Suggestions or Action Plans for Resolving the Crisis

Since 2015, there has been greater awareness that the Egyptian government is inadequate and cannot be seen as a partner, not even when it comes to maintaining stability. So, regardless of the political ideology, class, gender, and economic status, there is a consensus on what is described as an "unprofessional approach" to resolving the prevailing crisis and violence in Egypt. Here are a few practical steps that may help to address the current insolvency situation.

- Promote the protection of human rights in all its aspects, and establish a safe place for dialogue between different constituents to fight against intolerance, discrimination, and to foster respect for citizenship.
- Enhance the use of information technology and communication in development and empowering the youth as alternative means of communication; this may result in general improvement of freedom and diversity.
- Reposition human rights issues on top of the societal agenda, particularly focusing on issues of equity and the notion of tolerance and acceptance of diversity in order to lessen agitations within the society.
- Mitigate the underlying economic problems that place Egypt at risk of an insolvency crisis by engaging civil society in discussions about how to deal with the

looming danger and alerting them to political consequences, should insolvency eventuate.

- Address the current societal challenges by eliminating institutional, regulatory, and administrative obstacles to create job opportunities and ultimately alleviate poverty.
- Enhance the effectiveness of media institutions and the public sphere to strengthen democracy and the rule of law, while consolidating independent and effective administration of justice for all.
- Strengthen cooperation on poverty reduction and social development through the strategic use of media and communication spaces, particularly in the areas of combating illiteracy, education reforms, upgrading vocational training, training systems, and offering better justice and socioeconomic inclusion.

Lessons to be Learned for Crisis Communication

Here are some valuable things to note for those seeking to communicate risk and crisis information or do business in Egypt.

1. As demonstrated in the above case study, crisis communication and response is influenced by the culture and contexts of the country where the crisis has unfolded. To, therefore, understand how Egyptians respond to a crisis—which is crucial when one is seeking to do business in Egypt—it is essential to comprehend the concerns of the majority of Egyptians, which are mainly about seeing tangible improvements to their economic opportunities/situation and determining the role that religion, particularly Islam, should play in politics and society [8].

2. Egypt is a country with ancient traditions that coexist seamlessly with a rapidly modernizing society. It also is a predominantly Islamic country situated in the MENA region and therefore is of immense interest to both Middle Eastern Islamic countries and western countries—all of which leave their impressions on the way the society is organized. Any crisis management strategy should take into consideration these influences for it to have any measure of success.

3. Egypt has a large number of Internet users who actively participate on social media platforms; any crisis management initiative must take this into account, particularly the fact that young Egyptians are using social media as an avenue for voicing their concerns and can therefore be easily reached through that means. A crisis response in Egypt, therefore, needs to be timely and must be mindful of various sociocultural factors.

To understand how Egyptians respond to a crisis—which is crucial when one is seeking to do business in Egypt—it is essential to comprehend the concerns of the majority of Egyptians, which is mainly about seeing tangible improvements to their economic opportunities/situation and determining the role that religion, particularly Islam, should play in politics and society.

Conclusion

The Egyptian crisis has had social, political, economic, and religious ramifications across the country and it is not surprising that millions of Egyptians poured out onto the streets, leading to the toppling of President Morsi. However, different actors and players have quickly moved their chess pieces in expectation of the momentous changes that were occurring, creating an ongoing unstable sociopolitical and cultural situation.

The political climate and cultural crisis can be tracked to many issues of economic failure and political stagnation. The main issue of concern here is this: Will Egypt continue to collapse into violence and disarray? Will Egypt's cultural insolvency be dealt with by the Army, or will the Army back just one side in a conflict that pulls the country apart rather than unifying it? In this confusing and fluid state of affairs, many of the issues relating to an "authentic" Egyptian identity need to be questioned. One of the main questions that needs to be asked and answered is this: Can Egyptian civil society participate in producing a political consensus in which civil and political freedoms may be legitimately sacrificed in the name of national unity and security?

It is thus pertinent here to look beyond the current events of harsh economic conditions, prevailing violence, and political agitations, to seek a more holistic approach that aims to address the hasty passage of the democratic transition in Egypt with its cultural crisis. In the end, it will be worthwhile to assess the impact of the crisis on governance from the point of view of the deeds of a regime rather than its discourse, and by differentiating between the success of a regime and the failure of a state.

In the end, it will be worthwhile to assess the impact of the crisis on governance from the point of view of the deeds of a regime rather than its discourse, and by differentiating between the success of a regime and the failure of a state.

Discussion Questions

2.1 Considering the specifics of Egypt's crisis, describe the main narrative that you might adopt that can be appealing to and also reflective of the different needs and demands of the various stakeholders in the Egyptian conflict? How will you tailor your message to multiple media platforms?

2.2 Knowing the sources from which information that has fueled the violence in Egypt have come from, what steps would you take to implement a crisis communication plan that integrates the three layers of social communication, namely face-to-face interaction, traditional mass media (such as TV, radio, and newspapers) and social media, as a student of communication or a PR practitioner?

2.3 Egypt has experienced turmoil since 2011, but the country has not been able to devise a crisis communication framework/strategy to talk about and combat the violence that has rocked the society. To address the existing gaps, develop a crisis communication plan which is meaningful in the Egyptian and the MENA context, keeping in mind the sociocultural, religious, and political factors.

2.4 In order to get citizens to stop engaging in violent acts, what are some suggestions that you can offer to do the following:

a. Provide peace-building education at the interpersonal level;

b. Create awareness about the impact of the violence on individuals and the wider community;

c. Build trust amongst various groups at the community and national levels.

2.5 Lack of understanding and cooperation among various stakeholders—specifically between the government and demonstrators—significantly affects the ability to end the demonstrations and bring about peace in Egypt. Suggest a plan to enhance understanding and cooperation among the various groups to effectively combat the violence.

References

1. Central Agency for Public Mobilization and Statistics. (2016, March 30). "The population time now" [Online]. Available: http://www.capmas.gov.eg/, March 30, 2016 (last date accessed).

2. S. A. Cook. (2014, April 9). "Egypt's Solvency Crisis (2014, April 9). *Contingency Planning Memorandum No. 20.*" Council on Foreign Relations [Online]. Available: https://www.cfr.org/report/egypts-solvency-crisis, May 20, 2016 (last date accessed).

3. R. Mokbel. (2015, February 20). "Egyptian tribes shift their approach to politics" [Online]. Available: http://www.al-monitor.com/pulse/tr/contents/articles/originals/2015/02/egypt-tribes-families-role-parliamentary-elections.html#, May 27, 2016 (last date accessed).

4. L. van Efferink. (2015, May 1). "Geopolitical review 2011: Egyptian uprising, regime change, Muslim brotherhood" [Online]. Available: http://www.exploringgeopolitics.org/publication_2011_egyptian_uprising_regime_change_muslim_brotherhood_reform_democracy_islamists_salafi_parties_human_rights_hosni_mubarak_ndp_ngos_crackdown/, May 30, 2016 (last date accessed).

5. I. Saleh, "Sitting in the shadows of subsidization in Egypt: Revisiting the notion of street politics," *Democracy and Security*, vol. 4, no. 3, pp. 245–267, 2008.

6. A. Bayat, "Activism and social development in the Middle East," *International Journal of Middle Eastern Studies (Cambridge Journals)*, vol. 34, no.1, pp. 1–28, 2002.

7. I. Saleh, "Street republic in Egypt: From bullets to ballots," *State craft in Africa, African Year Book of Rhetoric*, vol. 4, no. 1, pp. 62–72, 2012.

8. P. Manfreda. (2014, November 25). "Arab Spring impact on the Middle East: How did the uprisings of 2011 change the region?" [Online]. Available: http://middleeast.about.com/od/humanrightsdemocracy/tp/Arab-Spring-Impact-On-The-Middle-East.htm, May 26, 2016 (last date accessed).

9. I. Saleh, "When the sweet Arab Spring turns sour: The ties that bind," *INSIGHTS*, pp. 7–12, Winter, 2012.

10. R. El Shimi. (2013, August 22). "Egypt's culture sector fragmented on current political crisis" [Online]. Available: http://english.ahram.org.eg/NewsContent/5/35/79619/Arts–Culture/Stage–Street/Egypts-culture-sector-fragmented-on-current-politi.aspx, May 16, 2017 (last date accessed).

11. The World Bank. (2015, September 16). "An overview of Egypt" [Online]. Available: http://www.worldbank.org/en/country/egypt/overview, March 12, 2016 (last date accessed).

12. S. El-Sirgany. (2013, February 24). "Egypt's culture of violence" [Online]. Available http://www.al-monitor.com/pulse/originals/2013/02/egyptviolenceprotest.html, May 30, 2016 (last date accessed).

13. T. L. Friedman. (2013, July 23). "Egypt's three revolutions" [Online]. Available: http://www.nytimes.com/2013/07/24/opinion/friedman-egypts-three-revolutions.html, May 30, 2016 (last date accessed).

14. M. Salah, personal interview about the popular initiative to recover Egypt's looting funds from outside, *Egypt*, December, 2015.

15. R. Jan, personal interview about his detention, Egypt, December, 2015.

16. I. Saleh, "Crisis communication research in the Middle East and North Africa (MENA): Echoes of normalizing historical crisis," in *Handbook of International Crisis Communication Research, State of Crisis Communication Research Around the Globe*, A. Schwarz, M. Seeger, and C. Auer, Eds. New Jersey: Wiley-Blackwell, 2014.

17. I. Saleh, "365 days of Muslim brotherhood in Egypt: Contesting media, activism and power," *COSMOPOLIS: A Review of Cosmopolitics*, vol. 3, no. 4, pp. 53–71, 2013.

18. A. O'Sullivan, M Rey, and J. G. Mendez. (2011). "Opportunities and challenges in the MENA region" [Online]. Available: https://www1.oecd.org/mena/49036903.pdf, May 30, 2016 (last date accessed).

19. A. M. Ayish, "Communication research in the Arab world: A new perspective," *The Public*, vol. 5, no. 1, pp. 33–57, 1998.

20. D. Waymer and R. L. Heath, "Emergent agents: The forgotten publics in crisis communication and issues management research," *Journal of Applied Communication Research*, vol. 35, no. 1, pp. 88–108, 2007.

21. H. Musallam, "Communication strategies of crisis and conflict management in the public and private sectors in the state of Kuwait," PhD dissertation, Department of Mass Communication, University of Southern Mississippi, 2004. Paper 2342. [Online]. Available: http://aquila.usm.edu/theses_dissertations/2342/, May 21, 2016 (last date accessed).

22. M. Bahgat and M. Henry, "The Egyptian cultural identity crisis," M.A. thesis, Department of Political Science, American University, Cairo, Egypt, 2014.

23. A. Kavanaugh, S. Yang, L. T. Li, et al. (2011, May 12). "Microblogging in crisis situations: Mass protests in Iran, Tunisia, Egypt" [Online]. Available: https://www.princeton.edu/í jvertesi/TransnationalHCI/Participants_files/Kavanaugh.pdf, May 29, 2016 (last date accessed).

24. The Solidarity Center. (2010, February). "Justice for all: The struggle for worker rights in Egypt" [Online]. Available: https://www1.umn.edu/humanrts/research/Egypt/ The%20Struggle%20for%20Workers%20rights.pdf, May 30, 2016 (last date accessed).

25. D. Amara, A. El Samadicy, and M. Ragheb, "Tourists risk aversion and willingness to take risks: The case of tourists visiting Egypt after 25th January revolution," presented at the World Conference for Graduate Research in Tourism, Hospitality and Leisure, Fethlye, Turkey, 2012.

26. M. Awad and D. Zayed. (2011, January 25). "Egyptians rage against Mubarak's 30-year rule" [Online]. Available: http://www.reuters.com/article/ozatp-egypt-protest-idAFJOE70O00M20110125, May 30, 2016 (last date accessed).

27. A. Enander, O. Lajksjo, and E. L. Tedfeldt, "A tear in the social fabric: Communities dealing with socially generated crises," *Journal of Contingencies and Crisis Management*, vol.18, no. 1, pp. 39–48, 2010.

28. H. Harro-Loit, T. Vihalemm, and K. Ugur, "Cultural experience as a (critical) factor in crisis communication planning," *Journal of Contingencies and Crisis Management*, vol. 20, no. 1, pp. 26–38, 2012.

29. M. Lo. (2013, July 28). "Morsi, the last caliph-president of Egypt" [Online]. Available: http://mondoweiss.net/2013/07/morsi-the-last-caliph-president-of-egypt, May 30, 2016 (last date accessed).

30. M. Mourad. (2013, July 3). "Revolution part two: The fall of Mohammed Morsi" [Online]. Available: http://english.ahram.org.eg/NewsContent/1/64/75614/Egypt/Politics-/The-rise-and-fall-of-an-Egyptian-president.aspx, May 30, 2016 (last date accessed).

31. World Politics Journal. (July 4, 2013). "Mohamed Morsi, Egypt's first democratically elected president, has been ousted" [Online]. Available: http://worldpoliticsjournal.com/ world/africa/5095, May 31, 2016 (last date accessed).

32. S. A. Wood, A. D. Guerry, J. M. Silver, et al., "Using social media to quantify nature-based tourism and recreation," *Scientific Reports 3*, (October 17, 2013), Article number: 2976, doi:10.1038/srep02976 [Online]. Available: http://www.nature.com/articles/srep02976?wt.mc_id=fbk_ scireports, May 30, 2016 (last date accessed).

33. C. Gubash and A. Mohyeldin. (2013, August 15). "Egypt bloodshed: Death toll rises to 327 after troops clear pro-Morsi camps" [Online]. Available: http://www.nbcnews.com/news/other/egypt-bloodshed-death-toll-rises-327-after-troops-clear-pro-f6C10914454, May 30, 2016 (last date accessed).

34. Egyptian Initiative for Personal Rights. (2016, January 9). "On the parliamentary agenda: Nine issues to anchor democracy and the rule of law" [Online]. Available: http://eipr.org/en/pressrelease/2016/01/09/2493, May 31, 2016 (last day accessed).

35. G. Topham, M. Weaver, and A. Luhn. (2015, November 17). "Egypt plane crash: Russia says jet was bombed in terror attack" [Online]. Available: http://www.theguardian.com/world/2015/nov/17/egypt-plane-crash-bomb-jet-russia-security-service, May 30, 2016 (last date accessed).

36. Reuters. (2016, February 8). "GM suspends Egypt operations due to currency crisis: Company source" [Online]. Available: http://www.reuters.com/article/us-gm-egypt-idUSKCN0VH1YZ, May 31, 2016 (last date accessed).

37. D. Walsh. (2016, February 4). "An Italian's brutal death in Egypt chills relations" [Online]. Available: http://www.nytimes.com/2016/02/05/world/middleeast/italian-student-egypt-torture.html, May 31, 2016 (last date accessed).

38. K. Kirchgaessner and R. Michaelson. (2016, February 25). "Why was he killed? Brutal death of Italian student in Egypt confounds experts" [Online]. Available: http://www.theguardian.com/world/2016/feb/24/why-was-he-killed-brutal-death-of-italian-student-in-egypt-confounds-experts, May 31, 2016 (last date accessed).

39. State Information Service. (2015, March 30). "Sisi delivers Egypt's speech at 26th Arab Summit" [Online]. Available: http://allafrica.com/stories/201503300175.html, May 16, 2017 (last date accessed).

40. Ahram Online. (2015, June 9). "Egyptian government slams HRW 'abuses' statement as politicized" [Online]. Available: http://english.ahram.org.eg/NewsContent/1/0/132330/Egypt/0/Egyptian-government-slams-HRW-abuses-statement-as-.aspx, May 31, 2016 (last date accessed).

41. Ahram Online. (2015, June 8). "163 detained without questioning: Egyptian advocacy group" [Online]. Available: http://english.ahram.org.eg/NewsContent/1/0/132255/Egypt/0/-detained-without-questioning-Egyptian-advocacy-gr.aspx, May 31, 2016 (last date accessed).

42. P. Kingsley. (2014, February 22). "How did 37 prisoners come to die at Cairo prison Abu Zaabal?" [Online]. Available: http://www.theguardian.com/world/2014/feb/22/cairo-prison-abu-zabaal-deaths-37-prisoners, May 31, 2016 (last date accessed).

Ghana

3

Embarrassing the Nation to Pay Brazil: The Ghana Black Stars Player Revolt at the 2014 FIFA World Cup

Kwamena Kwansah-Aidoo

Chapter Preview

What was the official response when the pride and symbol of the nation of Ghana, the Black Stars, threatened to boycott their last group match against Portugal at the 2014 FIFA World Cup? The government, upon the orders of the president, adopted a rather unconventional approach to resolve the issue and avoid what was shaping up to be a crisis of gargantuan proportions. The approach ensured that the immediate issue of the boycott was resolved, but created major embarrassment for Ghana and Ghanaians all over the world. This singular event led to the nation's pride being unnecessarily bruised and left Ghanaians wondering how to regain the lost trust in their government after witnessing events that created unworthy news for the country on the world stage.

Culture and Crisis Communication: Transboundary Cases from Nonwestern Perspectives, First Edition.
Edited by Amiso M. George and Kwamena Kwansah-Aidoo.
© 2017 by The Institute of Electrical and Electronics Engineers, Inc. Published 2017 by John Wiley & Sons, Inc.

After reading this chapter, you will be able to

- *Understand the nature of and perception of crisis within the Ghanaian context*
- *Describe the unique role that culture plays in the definition and understanding of what constitutes crisis in the Ghanaian context*
- *Discuss the role that culture plays in the Ghanaian response to issues and potential crisis*
- *Appreciate the importance of trust and open communication in dealing with issues and potential crisis situations*
- *Appreciate the saying that "an issue ignored, is a crisis ensured," and therefore understand the importance of taking effective measures to deal with issues in order to prevent them from becoming crisis*
- *Understand the value of taking appropriate action before communicating in an attempt to avert crisis situations*
- *Appreciate the fact that when personal experience is pitted against cultural norms and expectations, personal experience will always win*

Introduction

Crisis communication, according to Fearn-Banks, is concerned with transferring information to persons who are significant (publics) in order to help avoid or prevent a crisis (or negative occurrence), help in the recovery process during a crisis, and to maintain or enhance reputation [1]. This chapter uses the Black Stars player revolt (hereafter; "The Revolt") at the 2014 Fédération Internationale de Football Association (FIFA, English: International Federation of Association Football) World Cup to show that the communication that occurred in this case did neither of what Fearn-Banks [1] suggests, resulting in the Black Stars returning to Ghana with their reputation and that of the government in tatters.

Within the Ghanaian culture, what constitutes crisis is not readily accepted.

The chapter will also reveal that within the Ghanaian culture, what constitutes crisis is not readily accepted, particularly when seen within the conceptual crisis framework of what constitutes a threat to the values that are core to, and help to sustain life in a community [2]. Finally, the chapter will demonstrate that within the context of Ghanaian cultural norms, while people can be persuaded to follow or uphold widely accepted societal priorities, cultural values, and traits, if these priorities, values, and traits go against their deeply held personal and experiential values, then societal priorities and cultural values will be undermined or jettisoned.

While people can be persuaded to follow or uphold widely accepted societal priorities, cultural values, and traits, if these priorities, values, and traits go against their deeply held personal and experiential values, then societal priorities and cultural values will be undermined or jettisoned.

The significance of this chapter lies in the fact that the crisis under discussion played out in the international media, and therefore the ramifications were far and wide and also clear for the international community to see; the international nature of the crisis makes any discussion of it pertinent in a transboundary sense. Also, as subsequent discussions will show, it reveals the universal (read: cross-cultural) human weakness of failing to learn from past crises.

Ghana: The People and Relevant Cultural Dimensions

With an estimated population of 26 million people, Ghana is made up of about 100 ethnic groups distinguished by culture, language, and myth of origin. Although the various ethnic groups inhabit different geographical areas, no one part of the country is ethnically homogenous. English, as the adopted official language, dominates as the language of communication in virtually all media, unless in isolated cases where media are specifically set up to operate in a given local language. As a nation state, Ghana is represented by such symbols as the national flag, national anthem, and national sporting teams, with the most significant sporting team being the senior national football team, commonly called the Black Stars. These national symbols, together with a common historical past of colonial rule provide the people with a focal point and a sense of belonging.

Ghanaians, like most people in the world, are influenced in their communication and their responses to situations by their culture and socialization and as a result, their different cultural traditions produce different attitudes. The Cultural Values Framework[1] [3, 4] is well respected and commonly used to measure societal differences [5] and this section will use aspects of it to discuss some Ghanaian cultural traits that are relevant to this chapter. Ghana can be classified as a relatively high context culture where respect for authority and the relationship between subordinates and their superiors are highly official in most cases [6]. Consequently, Ghanaians never call their bosses or superiors by their first name and using formal titles such as "Mr.," "Mrs.," "Madam," "Dr.," and "Professor" is the norm. Relationships are based on mutual respect and subordinates generally do not contravene the directions or orders of their superiors. Ghanaian culture is generally collectivist and Ghanaians can be said to practice vertical collectivism, defined as "a form of collectivism where individuals see themselves as a part of an in-group where there are differences in status" [7]. Ghana can be said to be culturally high on power distance; for example, this means that if the president of the country asked individuals or groups to do something, their culturally imbibed tendency would be to oblige.

Most Ghanaians adhere to some form of religion and the tenets of the various religions and those of Ghanaian culture largely result in an individual who is socialized to believe in reciprocity and the norms and expectations surrounding such cultural outlooks. A typical Ghanaian would be very respectful, especially of their superiors and older people, law abiding, refined, polite, and very considerate of others, as is the case in many high context cultures [8]. Ghanaians view time as elastic and so for many, time can change and be stretched to accommodate many of life's circumstances. Deadlines are not necessarily strictly adhered to and punctuality is not a most prized attribute, especially in social situations. This attitude toward time invariably influences the way officials respond to issues and events that might be classified as urgent and potentially crisis inducing in other settings.

Ghanaian business culture is cash centered and most transactions, particularly those involving individuals, are carried out in cash. Cash transactions dominate partly because of some distrust of banks and official sources; this is also true due to a large chunk of the population operating outside the banking sector.[2] There is also a distrust of national government, especially when it comes to financial matters. Finally, as a people, Ghanaians love football, which paradoxically serves as a major focal point of acrimony and harmony. As the Ghana Bar Association (GBA) rightly note

> There is no doubt that football transcends all other activities in bringing the nation together and helps alleviate the numerous problems our people face in their daily lives. The fact that football impacts on social cohesion and national pride cannot be overemphasized. [9]

These major cultural traits notwithstanding, Ghanaians can be said to be generally pragmatic as well, with a high tendency to exhibit flexibility and open-mindedness to new ideas, while being very accepting of creativity and innovations. As a result, it can be argued that Ghanaians have adopted many practices, which were hitherto classified as belonging to low context cultures, and Ghanaian culture, just like any other, can be said to be constantly evolving.

Ghanaian Culture and Crisis Communication

A comprehensive search for literature did not reveal a single published academic material specifically on crisis communication in Ghana. Nevertheless, personal observation and anecdotal evidence suggest a laissez faire attitude toward crisis and by extension crisis communication. Thus, one can argue that as a culture, crisis management does not feature high on the Ghanaian agenda and events or issues that might be seen as crises in other cultures, particularly in the western world, would simply pass unacknowledged or with very minimum fuss in the Ghanaian context. I will suggest here that the combined cultural traits of high power distance and respect for authority leads to the mindset that people in authority can get away with almost anything since they will hardly be questioned and their authority hardly challenged. As a result, people who are in positions of authority, particularly within public sector organizations tend to get away with communicating very little or communicating haphazardly in times of crisis. This attitude and approach to crisis is what influenced the handling of the Black Stars revolt during the 2014 FIFA World Cup.

"Show Us the Money or We Won't Play": When Trust Evaporates

On June 24, 2014, the Ghanaian media (and then the world's media) reported a revolt in the camp of the Black Stars at the ongoing FIFA World Cup. The cause was unpaid appearance fees—the players threatened to boycott their final game against Portugal on June 26 if their appearance fees and bonuses, amounting to $100,000 each, were not paid to them in cash. In an attempt to resolve the issue, the President of Ghana, John Dramani Mahama, called the players and pleaded with them to proceed as expected, promising he would ensure that the monies were paid in due course. The players refused to accede to the president's request and he was "forced" to promise to have the players paid in cash before the game. He then gave approval for USD3 million ($3 million) to be flown from Ghana to Brazil on a chartered flight to pay the revolting players. Upon arrival in Brazil, the money was dispatched to its intended destination by armed Brazilian police and military escort, all in full glare of television cameras and shown live on a prime time Brazilian TV. Subsequently, a picture of a Ghanaian player kissing a wad of cash appeared in various media around the globe and on social media. After receiving $100,000 each, it came to the fore that the players would have to pay taxes on the amount received in line with Brazilian law. Accordingly, 17% ($17,000) was deducted from the $100,000 given to each of the players and officials before they were allowed to take the money out of Brazil.

In the meantime, the Black Stars who were quarter-finalists in the 2010 edition of the FIFA World Cup lost the match against Portugal, ignominiously crashing out of the tournament at the group stages. This marked the first time that Ghana had failed to progress beyond the group stages at the FIFA World Cup in three appearances. In the ensuing commotion and the aftermath of this debacle, the government came under intense fire, resulting in the Minister of Sports and his deputy both being relieved of their posts and reassigned. The President also set up a three-member Commission of Inquiry to "look into issues concerning the preparation of the Black Stars, the cause of the team's exit from the competition, treatment of fans in Brazil as well as the remuneration for players and officials during the competition" [10]. FIFA also announced that it would take steps to ensure that similar pay disputes do not happen in future.

This incident (crisis)—the player revolt and the mode of resolution—made Ghana the subject of ridicule on the international scene,[3] and the picture of the player kissing a wad of cash became an enduring image of the crisis and a stark reminder of the ignominy of Ghana's world cup participation. While the Revolt and the mode of resolution revealed complex, multilayered issues in the management of the Black Stars and general football administration in Ghana, this chapter concentrates on one key area: communication strategy and the role that culture played in it.

Situational Analysis

Given the nature of the crisis, it is fair to say that the whole footballing world and everybody who was interested in the ongoing FIFA World Cup was a stakeholder. However, it is possible to delineate the following as the key stakeholders for this crisis:

- The ruling National Democratic Congress (NDC) Government (of Ghana)
- The Ministry of Youth and Sports in Ghana which has oversight of all sporting activities in Ghana and to which the Ghana Football Association (GFA) is accountable
- The Bank of Ghana which has the responsibility for dealing with monetary transactions on behalf of the National government
- The GFA which is responsible for managing everything concerning football in the country, at all levels, and therefore has oversight of all the national football teams
- The management committee of the Black Stars which has direct responsibility for dealing with everything concerning the Senior National Football Team (the Black Stars). This committee is a subcommittee of GFA
- FIFA as official organizers of the 2014 tournament
- The Government and people of Brazil as the host nation of the tournament
- The people of Ghana—including Ghanaians in the diaspora
- Mass media (local and international)
- The Portuguese national team and by extension all Portuguese nationals

Response to the Crisis

Given the lack of official acknowledgement of a crisis, it is difficult to imagine that there were any clearly stated formal goals and objectives and research did not reveal any officially set goals and objectives. Nonetheless, the following can be inferred from the communication that occurred during and after the crisis. In other words, based on how the government and the GFA communicated before, during, and after the crisis, the following can be deduced as goals and objectives, even if unstated:

Goals

- To prevent Ghanaians and the general public from finding out about what was going on inside the Black Stars camp
- To present the government's response as timely, and the most appropriate, under the circumstances

Objectives

- To create the impression that there was no trouble in the Black Stars camp
- To get the Black Stars to travel to Brasilia where the match with Portugal was going to be played
- To get the Black Stars to play the match against Portugal on June 26, 2014
- To convey to the various stake holders that the situation was being handled and that everything was under control
- To prevent sanctioning by FIFA for nonparticipation
- To convey to the Ghanaian public that the government's strategy for resolving the issue was the best and the only way

Strategies and Tactics

Strategy 1: Deny that there was any ferment in the Black Stars camp
Tactics

The initial strategy, which is very much in keeping with the Ghanaian culture of not planning for and/or acknowledging crisis and also exhibiting a laissez faire attitude toward crisis, was to deny that there was a problem in the Black Stars camp. Despite initial media reports that there was trouble brewing in the camp over nonpayment of bonuses and appearance fees, GFA officials travelling with the team continued to deny that there was any such thing happening, and even accused journalists of making things up. The following quote from a newspaper report, is illustrative

> A member of the Black Stars management committee, Wilfred Osei Palmer, says the decision by the FA to cover up reports of indiscipline and player revolts in the Stars camp in Brazil is partly to blame for the Stars' early exit. The FA's communications team mounted a strong denial of reports of player revolt in the Stars' camp and singled out Joy FM and its tournament correspondent Tony Bebli for criticism, accusing him of fabrication [11].

Strategy 2: Downplay the threat of boycott by the Black Stars players

Tactics

When the FA officials eventually accepted that there was trouble brewing in the camp, they downplayed the threat of the boycott, also in keeping with the Ghanaian cultural trait of not paying serious attention to issues that can potentially become crisis. As one commentator put it

> The Black Stars' behavior off the field overshadowed its three games in Brazil. The Ghana Football Association… suspended two of its top players for fighting and downplayed the threat of a boycott of the Portugal game. [12]

Strategy 3: Involve the president of the country and call on his authority (and culturally inherent persuasive powers), when the going gets tough

Tactics

In keeping with Ghanaian culture where there is respect for authority, the president of the country was contacted to speak to the players and to impress upon them to carry on as expected with a promise to ensure that the monies were paid in due course.

Strategy 4: Present the actual response—the decision to transport money to Brazil, which was heavily criticized—as nothing unusual—the way things have always been done—rather than due to individual and organizational failures

Tactics

When the decision to transport that huge amount of cash to Brazil was being heavily criticized, the GFA and government officials tried to present the very act of transporting the money as nothing unusual, very much in keeping with the Ghanaian cultural attitude to crisis and crisis communication. The media report below is illustrative.

> Ghana's football association on Wednesday defended its decision to charter a plane to carry $3 million in bonus money to players in Brazil, saying the country had done the same at the last two World Cups. [13]

Strategy 5: Blame the Black Stars players while positioning the actual response as necessary—the only reasonable thing for the government to do was to respond in the way they did.

Tactics

In the aftermath of the debacle of transporting that amount of money to Brazil, both the government and GFA defended their actions by seeking to present players as ill-disciplined and literally "forcing their hand" to respond the way they did. In one media report, the team Manager of the Black Stars, for example, was said to have lambasted the players stating that, "We gave them an inch and they took a mile. We had to adjust to the system or the behavior of the boys just to pick things from it" [14].

In the same report, a fellow management committee member of the Black Stars also condemned the players for indiscipline, stating

> I have not been long in this position as management member of the Black Stars but I never thought and never knew that there was so much indiscipline in the playing body. [14]

These statements sought to put the blame squarely on the players, absolving the management of any blame. Yet, there is evidence to suggest that the handlers of the Black Stars committed many errors in their preparations for the tournament, which ultimately brought matters to a head.

The government also sought to establish a narrative that presented its response as necessary and the only possible way the impasse could have been resolved. Various members of the government and the ruling NDC party were all cited in media interviews/reports as espousing such viewpoints as illustrated below.

> Mr. Yamin Deputy Minister of Youth and Sports explained that the Ministry wanted to use an e-banking transaction but the players insisted they wanted physical cash payments. The insistence by the players he said, forced the Ministry to "come back and mobilize the physical cash to be sent to them. [15]

> Mr. Allotey Jacobs called on Ghanaians to give President Mahama some breathing space... the President's decision to airlift the players' appearance fees in cash was crucial to the success of the team during the World Cup Group stages. "Why are we not sympathizing with the President in that situation, knowing very well that desperate situations call for desperate measures?" [16]

Despite such pronouncements, there was no shortage of statements from various sources condemning the government's response. The Council of Institute of Chartered Accountants, Ghana (ICAG), for example, condemned it as "inappropriate," stating that "the airlifting of cash to Brazil was ill-advised, contrary to established best practice and should not be contemplated again in future" [9].

Dancing to the Cultural Tune: How Culture Influenced the Response

There is no doubt that culture plays an important role in how people respond to situations and this was no different. First, the mindset of people in authority that they can get away with saying little about any situation, which is the result of the combined cultural traits of power distance and respect was at play here and influenced the initial response to the crisis, which was denial and then later downplaying it. The cultural attitude toward crisis and crisis communication, or rather noncrisis communication, was also in full force in the initial response.

Second, the call on the president to speak to the players was also influenced by Ghana's vertically collectivist culture, which emphasizes respect for elders and deferment to authority. In some quarters, the players were heavily criticized for not acceding to the pleas of the president. Also, the traits of vertical collectivism, where "inequality, hierarchical distinctions, and pressure to conform" are the norm and individuals are "expected to exhibit less voice" [7] can be seen in the way player agitation was handled.

Third, the actual response—the decision to transport that amount of cash to Brazil in contravention of the country's laws—was also culturally influenced. As indicated earlier, the twin cultural traits of power distance and respect for authority leads people in authority to think that they can do whatever they want and get away with it, and that mindset would have influenced the making of that decision, even if indirectly. I would argue that if the President believed that there would be serious and insufferable consequences for taking such a course of action, he would have thought twice about making such a decision.

Fourth, the announcement of the decision to send the money to Brazil was handled in the usual haphazard manner in which the Ghanaian cultural approach to crisis and crisis communication is carried out. There was no official press conference to announce the decision and to allow journalists to ask questions and to give the government an opportunity to attempt to make a convincing case for taking such a drastic measure. By doing so, they deprived themselves the chance to make a good case and also to frame the issue and influence the narrative and subsequent discourse in a way that would be conducive to their course. Consequently, the media—both national and international—presented it in their own way and influenced the narrative in whichever way they wanted.

Outcome of the Crisis

The immediate outcome of the crisis was that the threatened boycott of the game with Portugal was called off and the players took to the pitch against Portugal on June 26, 2014. In that sense, one can argue that the mode of resolution ensured a positive outcome as it staved off any future sanctions from FIFA. However, that was arguably the only positive outcome; the crisis itself and the mode of resolution spawned plenty of negative consequences. The pay dispute disrupted preparations for the match against Portugal, and Ghana lost, exiting the tournament with the least number of points in the group. Departing the tournament at that stage was in itself considered disastrous by the football-loving people of Ghana, but the manner in which it happened, made it even more difficult for people to take.

Also, the fallout from it within the media and in international circles was huge. Ghana made news headlines the world over, for all the wrong reasons, attracting international ridicule and becoming the butt of jokes by many a talk show host and program presenters in the western world.

> Ghana has become the butt of jokes in late night comedy shows in USA where the $3 million airlifted to the team has become an international scandal and an embarrassment to Ghanaians all over the world. [17]

Photographs of the convoy of vehicles ensuring the safe passage of the cash went viral on social media sites and as Jerome Valcke, Secretary General of FIFA commented, "The sight of a cavalcade with police support ferrying the cash to the hotel where Ghana's team was staying wasn't a good image" [18]. Also, social media sites were awash with disparaging comments from both Ghanaians and non-Ghanaians.

> This is worse than I thought... Government was actually able to speedily mobilize 3.5 million dollars in less than twenty four hours, bundle the cash in bags, charter a flight from Ghana to Brazil, hire 72 Military Police, 19 Municipal Guards, 26 Squadron Ground Force Military, 14 members of the Grupamento de Operacoes Especiais de Brasilia, One Aeronautical Policia (Air Force), 2 Highway Patrol Battalion and an Air Mobile Brasilia Group to send the $3.5 million through the streets of Brasilia to the players. Woow!!! Hahaha eih! [19]

The image of a Ghanaian player kissing a wad of cash caused even more discomfiture for the country, and became an enduring image of the crisis in the eyes of both foreign and Ghanaian media. That the said Ghanaian player also scored a goal against his own Black Stars team (an "own goal") in that fateful match against Portugal only made matters worse and served to accentuate the level of ridicule and embarrassment for Ghana and Ghanaians at large.

Locally, the NDC government came under intense fire with various groups and the opposition NPP party lambasting the government for the way they handled the crisis. The Institute of Chartered Accountants Ghana (ICAG) also accused the government of violating banking laws and noted that "The issue under reference has also brought the financial credibility of Ghana into disrepute and the damage is far-reaching" [20].

What Should Have Been Done: Learning for the Future

Open communication and honest communication is preferable to noncommunication or cover-ups. The management of the Black Stars should have come clean about what was happening in camp as part of managing the issue of nonpayment of bonuses and player agitation. As a management committee member of the FA puts it, "the strategy by the FA's communications to cover up backfired... When certain things happen in camp and we try to cover up... I don't think it helps anyone of us" [21].

As Fearn-Banks [22] points out, issues management and crisis communication go hand in hand. The two are inseparable because crises have the potential to create issues, and by the same token, issues, if not dealt with properly can lead to crises, and this is exactly what happened. Information suppressed in a situation like this always has a tendency to become public, thus giving credence to the saying that, an issue ignored is a crisis ensured.

Whatever the decision is, it is better to communicate it formally than not communicating it at all, or doing so through some informal means. Irrespective of the prudence of the decision to transport such a huge amount of money to Brazil, once the decision was made, there should have been an official press conference to announce it and to allow journalists to ask questions. This would have given the government the opportunity to actually make a convincing case for taking such a drastic measure. Instead of an official announcement, it was made known via an unusual means. As was reported, the deputy Minister of Youth and Sports, "phoned into a live program on Joy FM to announce that government had chartered a flight to send three million dollars ($3m) to the Black Stars in Brazil" [23]. By going about it in that way, government deprived itself the opportunity to make a good case and also to frame the issue and influence the narrative in a way that would be conducive to the official course. This oversight encouraged the media to develop a narrative that suited its own purposes.

Even in crisis situations, it is still important to do your homework and due diligence to ensure that your response does not create more problems or spawn ongoing issues after the crisis. The government should have done its homework well with the Brazilian authorities to be certain of the tax implications of individuals (the players) trying to take that much physical cash out of that country to prevent what later occurred with the loss of 17% of the said amount by each player. If communication around the decision had been transparent, perhaps it might have been picked up before the money arrived in Brazil.

During and after the crisis, it is imperative that those responsible for dealing with it speak with one voice. The key stakeholders who had responsibility for resolving the crisis should have spoken with one voice. The contradiction in the quotes below is illustrative

Mrs. Elly Ohene-Adu, Director of Banking Services at the BoG, could not fathom why the appearance fees had to be carried to Brazil by a chartered flight when the BoG had adopted a more effective mode of payment at the 2010 FIFA World Cup in South Africa. "In 2010, we had a challenge to pay players cash; we resisted fiercely and in the ensuing engagement, we finally succeeded in giving them cheques. ... in respect of the allowances, we actually transferred some funds to the Ghana Embassy in Pretoria for the team's accommodation, transportation, winning bonus and appearance fees." [24]

GFA president Kwesi Nyantakyi said airlifting cash to players was nothing new.

"In 2006 the same practice was adopted. Cash was carried from Ghana to Germany and paid to players," he said. "In 2010 ... cash was picked from Ghana to South Africa and paid to players—that is the practice." [13]

As the excerpts above show, even after the initial hullabaloo surrounding the crisis had died down, officials involved continued to give conflicting accounts and views about payment of appearance fees and bonuses for the Blacks Stars, thus ensuring that in some ways, the crisis continued. These officials should have had their story straight. They forgot a cardinal rule of crisis communication: "speak with one voice." **In a crisis situation, experiential antecedents may hold sway over cultural norms; potential influences from other cultures should not be ignored**. Although respect for elders/authority is a highly regarded tenet of Ghana's (high context) culture, the authorities ignored two key factors: (1) All but one member of the team played professional football outside Ghana, mostly in western low context cultures, where that was not readily the case and so these players would be acculturated to some extent; (2) the government/GFA had a history of not paying up or delaying payment. These would influence the decision of the players.

The lesson here is to note that people may be Ghanaian by birth, but could acquire other cultural traits in the course of their lives, either in Ghana or elsewhere, so care should be taken when dealing with them even within the local context. Also, when it comes to money, a history of nonpayment trumps all culturally imbibed sense of respect for authority.

Practical Suggestions for Interested Parties

On the basis of the discussion in this chapter, people interested in issues and crisis communication in Ghana should consider the following as suggestions that might be useful:

1. Ghanaians care about their reputation on the international stage and so what is seemingly a local crisis still needs to be handled with circumspection so that it does not spawn global/transboundary consequences. When a crisis has transboundary implications, it needs to be treated differently and communicative action especially needs to be well thought out and delivered appropriately.

> When the crisis is unfolding in full view of the international media,
> it is difficult to have full control over the framing of the issues and
> subsequently the narrative/s that are spawned.

2. When the crisis is unfolding in full view of the international media, it is difficult to have full control over the framing of the issues and subsequently the narrative/s that are spawned. Nonetheless, careful planning which outlines specific steps and processes to be followed and actions to be taken when a crisis strikes, and communication, using not just traditional media but social media as well, can help communicators provide meaningful input, and perhaps reduce the negativity that might arise without any well-thought-out strategy and response.

3. Ghana is a country that exhibits vertical collectivism, but journalists will seek and report the truth, particularly when it relates to matters that are extremely dear to the nation. Thus, denials of unrest (particularly in an area of endeavor that is almost the heartbeat of the nation) do not work, lending credence to the saying that "An issue ignored is a crisis ensured." It is better to accept, to be open, to be honest, and to provide information/focus attention on what is being done to resolve the situation.

4. Ghanaians exhibit high power distance and believe in respect for authority; however, such cultural knowledge is not enough and one needs to understand certain experiential antecedents. Ghanaians have a long history of distrusting public officials and national government when it comes to monetary dealings and that is important to know. In times of crisis, cultural traits may be pushed aside when what is at stake is seen to be more crucial and when there are highly vested personal interests involved. Addressing the key concerns of the players was the only way to resolve the issue. It is important to understand that Ghanaians regard mutual trust as a valuable element in their vertical collectivist culture.

5. In the Ghanaian context, just like any other, the age-old communication rule of "know your audience" still holds true. It is important to make the effort to understand the audience very well and not to take things for granted on the basis of known and/or expected cultural traits. If the handlers of the Black Stars knew their audience well, they would have appreciated the fact that most of them do not necessarily adhere strictly to the Ghanaian cultural norm of respecting your elders/authority irrespective of the situation.

6. Due to the high distrust of government, effective action should precede communication and in times of crisis appropriate actions need to be taken for communication to be effective. Indeed, it is usually an action or failure to act

that causes crisis and so it is only action that will resolve it. Irrespective of the prudence of the president's decision to fly the money to Brazil, it is only that action that resolved the initial impasse.

7. Ghana is a high context and high power distance culture with traits and expectations, such as respect for elders. Nevertheless, in the face of negative prior experience, such cultural traits will be jettisoned and no communication strategy will help. It is important to build trust with all stakeholders in order for such traits to manifest and work in one's favor in times of crisis. As a columnist for Ghanaweb aptly put it: "How come the Minister of Interior, Youth & Sports, GFA President, Technical bench and other dignitaries couldn't convince the boys to lessen their stance so as to avoid the shameful international ridicule? They say once bitten twice shy but in their case they've been bitten countless times and no amount of convincing was going to work" [25]. The handlers of the Black Stars should have known that given past history and the distrust of national government by sporting teams, acting on time to pay players their bonuses was the only way to prevent player agitation.

Conclusion

The revolt was a crisis not only for the handlers of the Black Stars and the Ministry of Youth and Sports, but also for the national government and some of its agencies, including the Bank of Ghana. The hullaballoo of the crisis and the revelations that came out during the sitting of the Commission of Inquiry that was set up in the aftermath showed that there were staid problems with the way the government and its agencies prepared for Ghana's participation in the tournament and also the way they responded. In addition to causing social, psychological, and financial uproar within the Ghanaian community, and to some extent internationally, the crisis and the way it was resolved also caused significant reputational and legitimacy issues for the government. And the communication that occurred in this case did not help avoid the crisis; it did not help in the recovery, and neither did it enhance the reputation.

For communications professionals and students, the sad truth is that many of the lessons to be learned were the same old problems, repeated again and again [26]. This was not the first time that players from an African country had threatened to boycott matches at a FIFA World cup, and steps should have been taken to avoid this whole kerfuffle. The warning signs were all over, yet no one bothered to think seriously about what could happen, let alone have a planned response; a clear case of the Ghanaian cultural attitude to (potential) crisis. Stocker suggests that the same situation is evident in many crisis situations when he aptly notes that, "when you look at the majority of crises which occur, what happened should have been on or near the top of the list of possible events." "Why," he asked, "wasn't anyone prepared?" [27] Indeed, Owusu-Barnes has observed that

[e]very single World Cup (WC) appearance has been wrought with some form of controversy—Germany '06 there was the alleged ticket connection scandal, South Africa '10 was the monies paid "ghost" journalists and this year the mother of all shames the bonus scandal that made Ghana a laughing stock on late night shows and in international media circles. The irony of this cyclicity of shame is that the same mistakes permeate every WC we've participated in which begs the question whether we are simply impervious to correction. [28]

While it would seem that different cultures understand and respond to crisis differently because of variations in the collective programming of the mind [29], there is a common thread that runs through crisis events in almost all settings, and that is the shared human trait of failing to learn from earlier crises, be it our own or that of our neighbors.

There is a common thread that runs through crisis events in almost all settings, and that is the shared human trait of failing to learn from earlier crises.

There are many lessons that can be learned from this Ghanaian case and many African countries can especially take a cue from this and learn first, what to do to avoid such a crisis, and second, what not to do should such a crisis eventuate.

For others who are interested in Ghana, either for business or pleasure, the value of this chapter lies in the details provided here about (a) the important Ghanaian cultural traits; (b) the general Ghanaian attitude toward crisis; (c) what works or does not work in times of crisis; and (d) how and what cultural traits may influence the success of communication in times of crisis. As Shrivastava has noted, the one thing more tragic than the crises which occur is the failure of organizations and organizational scholars to learn from them [30]. It is hoped that organizations and organizational scholars both within and outside Ghana can learn from the analyses and important observations made here and that these experiential antecedents can be generalized and incorporated into crisis communication preparedness in Ghana and elsewhere.

Discussion Questions

3.1 Assuming you were the communication director at the Office of the President, what would you have done in the first 24 hours after the president had been contacted to speak to the Black Stars players? Identify and describe five tasks that you think are the most urgent and important.

3.2 Given the vast array of people/groups that were interested in the situation, who do you think was the most important public? List five primary publics and prioritize them. Explain why you believe they are the most important in your chosen order and develop key messages for each of these publics.

3.3 If the Government of Ghana had held a press conference and announced the course of action, do you think it would have helped in the way both the media and citizen groups responded? Do you think the president would have had any luck convincing people that the course of action he was about to embark on was the right one to deal with the situation? Give reasons for your answer.

3.4 The earliest sign of trouble in the Black Stars camp was reported by a journalist and the immediate reaction of the Black Stars management group was to deny that there was ferment in the camp. Do you think that an initial frank admission of trouble brewing in the Black Stars camp would have altered the way events unfolded eventually? What are the reasons for your answer?

3.5 The "threatened boycott and the way it was handled by the government" not only affected the reputation of Ghana, but also the way the President and the ruling NDC government were perceived. Imagine that you are the communication director at the presidency, what kinds of image recovery strategies would you develop to recover both the President's and the government's damaged image? Suggest one short-term and one long-term image restoration program.

Notes

1. This is well respected and commonly used to measure societal differences [30]. Hofstede's framework initially consisted of four dimensions: power distance, uncertainty avoidance, individualism/collectivism, and masculinity/femininity, with a fifth added later: short-term/long-term orientation [31, 32].
2. While there are no recent figures, a 2005 Ghana News Agency (GNA) report cited by Kwansah-Aidoo and Owusu-Hemeng stated that 70% of cash in the country was circulating outside of the banking sector at the time [33].
3. I personally watched and read many discussions about the events as they unfolded, and they were, in my opinion, very unflattering.

References

1. K. Fearn-Banks, *Crisis Communications: A Casebook Approach*. New Jersey and London: Lawrence Erlbaum Associates, 2007.
2. A. Enander, O. Lajksjo, and E. L. Tedfeldt, "A tear in the social fabric: Communities dealing with socially generated crises," *Journal of Contingencies and Crisis Management*, vol. 18, no. 1, pp. 39–48, 2010.

3. G. Hofstede, *Culture's Consequences: International Differences in Work-Related Values* (Abridged ed.). London: Sage Publications, 1980.

4. G. Hofstede, *Cultures and Organisations: Software of the Mind.* New York: McGraw-Hill, 1991.

5. C. J. Robertson, "The global dispersion of Chinese values: A three-country study of Confucian dynamism," *Management International Review,* vol. 40, pp. 253–268, 2000.

6. G. Hofstede, "Cultural constraints in management theories," *The Executive,* vol. 7, pp. 81–94, 1993.

7. R. Tajaddini and B. G. Mujtaba, "Stress perceptions and leadership orientation of Malaysians: Exploring their similarities and differences with Americans," *Chinese Business Review,* vol. 8, no. 8, pp. 26–42, 2009.

8. H. M. Dahlan, "Local values in intercultural management," *Malaysian Management Review,* vol. 1, pp. 45–50, 1991.

9. "Gov't set a bad precedent with $3m – GBA" (2014, June 27) [Online]. Available: http://www.ghanaweb.com/GhanaHomePage/NewsArchive/artikel.php?ID=314621, February 23, 2016 (last date accessed).

10. "Gov't sets up committee to probe 2014 World Cup" (2014, July 4) [Online]. Available: http://www.ghanaweb.com/GhanaHomePage/NewsArchive/Gov-t-sets-up-committee-to-probe-2014-World-Cup-315510, January 15, 2016 (last date accessed).

11. "GFA covered up players' indiscipline – FA management member" (2014, June 29) [Online]. Available: http://www.ghanaweb.com/GhanaHomePage/SportsArchive/artikel. php?ID=314808, January 15, 2016 (last date accessed).

12. "$3M was to stop player agitations – Mahama" (2014, June 28) [Online]. Available: http://www.ghanaweb.com/GhanaHomePage/NewsArchive/artikel.php?ID=314732, January 15, 2016 (last date accessed).

13. "Airlifting cash to WC players common practice – GFA" (2014, July 4) [Online]. Available: http://www.ghanaweb.com/GhanaHomePage/SportsArchive/artikel.php?ID=315403, January 15, 2016 (last date accessed).

14. "We gave players an inch and they took a mile" (2014, July 2) [Online]. Available: http://www.ghanaweb.com/GhanaHomePage/SportsArchive/artikel.php?ID=315095, February 23, 2016 (last date accessed).

15. "Gov't airlifts $3m for Black Stars – Joseph Yamin" (2014, June 24) [Online]. Available: http://www.ghanaweb.com/GhanaHomePage/NewsArchive/artikel.php?ID=314129, February 23, 2016 (last date accessed).

16. "Allotey Jacobs appeals to Mahama to dissolve GFA" (2014, July 4) [Online]. Available: http://www.ghanaweb.com/GhanaHomePage/NewsArchive/artikel.php?ID=315472, February 23, 2016 (last date accessed).

17. "Flying $3M to Brazil has made Ghana a laughing stock – Pratt" (2014, June 27) [Online]. Available: http://www.ghanaweb.com/GhanaHomePage/NewsArchive/artikel. php?ID=314598, February 23, 2016 (last date accessed).

18. "Jerome Valcke: Ghana cash row must never happen again'' (2014, June 28) [Online]. Available: http://www.ghanaweb.com/GhanaHomePage/SportsArchive/artikel.php?ID= 314683, February 23, 2016 (last date accessed).

19. "Flying $3.5M to Brazil is worse than I thought – Hammer" (2014, June 29) [Online]. Available: http://www.ghanaweb.com/GhanaHomePage/entertainment/artikel. php?ID=314833, February 23, 2016 (last date accessed).

20. "Airlifting $3m to Brazil violates banking law – ICAG" (2014, July 5) [Online]. Available: http://www.ghanaweb.com/GhanaHomePage/NewsArchive/artikel.php?ID=315638, February 23, 2016 (last date accessed).

21. "GFA covered up players' indiscipline – FA management member" (2014, June 29) [Online]. Available: http://www.ghanaweb.com/GhanaHomePage/SportsArchive/artikel. php?ID=314808, February 23, 2016 (last date accessed).

22. K. Fearn-Banks, "Crisis communication: A review of some best practices," *in Handbook of Public Relations*, R. L. Heath, Ed. London and New Delhi: Sage, 2002, pp. 479–485.

23. "Black Stars fiasco in Brazil: Blame Afriyie-Ankrah – Yamin" (2014, July 4) [Online]. Available: http://www.ghanaweb.com/GhanaHomePage/NewsArchive/artikel.php?ID= 315473, February 23, 2016 (last date accessed).

24. "Bank of Ghana released $4m for Black Stars appearance fees" (2014, August 15) [Online]. Available: http://www.ghanaweb.com/GhanaHomePage/soccer/321397/, February 23, 2016 (last date accessed).

25. C. Owusu-Barnes. (2014, July 4). "The aftermath – part I" [Online]. Available: http://www.ghanaweb.com/GhanaHomePage/NewsArchive/artikel.php?ID=315374, February 23, 2016 (last date accessed).

26. C. Galloway and K. Kwansah-Aidoo, "Victoria burning: Confronting the 2009 catastrophic bushfires in Australia," in *Crisis Communication: International Perspectives on Hits and Misses*, A. George and C. B. Pratt, Eds. London/New York: Routledge/Taylor Francis, 2012, pp. 279–292.

27. K. P. Stocker, "Strategic approach to crisis management," *in The Handbook of Strategic Public Relations and Integrated Communications*, C. L. Caywood, Ed. New York: McGraw Hill, 1997, pp. 189–203.

28. C. Owusu-Barnes. (2014, July 5). "The aftermath – part II" [Online]. Available: http://www.ghanaweb.com/GhanaHomePage/NewsArchive/artikel.php?ID=315375, February 23, 2016 (last date accessed).

29. G. Hofstede, *Culture's Consequences: International Differences in Work-Related Values* (Abridged ed.). London: Sage Publications, 1980.

30. P. Shrivastava, "Industrial crisis management: Learning from organizational failures," *Journal of Management Studies*, vol. 25, no. 4, pp. 283–284, 1988.

31. G. Hofstede and M. H. Bond, "The Confucius connection: From cultural roots to economic growth," *Organizational Dynamics*, vol. 16, no. 4, pp. 5–21, 1988.

32. G. Hofstede and G. J. Hofstede, *Cultures and Organizations Software of the Mind: Intercultural Cooperation and Its Importance for Survival*, 2nd ed. Sydney: McGraw-Hill, 2005.

33. K. Kwansah-Aidoo and B. Owusu-Hemeng, "'I will never allow any of my children to choose it': Ghanaian Bank Managers' views about public relations," *Asia Pacific Public Relations Journal*, vol. 7, no. 1, pp. 155–176, 2006.

Nigeria 4

Containing Ebola in Nigeria: Lessons in Effective Risk and Crisis Communication

Amiso M. George

Chapter Preview

How did Nigeria beat the Ebola virus disease (EVD) with few deaths in only 3 months when other West African countries struggled to contain the deadly virus with devastating and fatal results? The Nigerian government acted swiftly to implement effective strategies and tactics that co-opted existing health infrastructures and personnel, effective communication, technology to trace and track, while quarantining and treating Ebola-infected patients and contacts. A concerned, but patient, public complied with new government directives; religious, traditional, opinion leaders and local and international health organizations cooperated and collaborated with the government in an unprecedented manner to bring what would have been a nightmare, to a quick end.

After reading this chapter, you will be able to

- *Describe the Nigerian political and belief system as a basis for understanding Nigerians' response to the crisis*

Culture and Crisis Communication: Transboundary Cases from Nonwestern Perspectives, First Edition.
Edited by Amiso M. George and Kwamena Kwansah-Aidoo.
© 2017 by The Institute of Electrical and Electronics Engineers, Inc. Published 2017 by John Wiley & Sons, Inc.

- *Analyze the goals, objectives, strategies, and tactics of the Nigerian government in educating and persuading the public in its fight against the Ebola virus*
- *Understand the role of technology and social media in the anti-Ebola campaign*
- *Outline the role of international health partners in combating a transboundary crisis situation like Ebola*
- *Comprehend the role of culture in the Nigerian government's response to the Ebola crisis*

Background on Nigeria

Nigeria is Africa's most populous country with a population of 181.5 million [1]. Located on the west coast of Africa, the country is composed of more than 250 ethnic groups, with the largest being Hausa/Fulani (29%), Yoruba (21%), Igbo/Ibo (18%), Ijaw (10%), Kanuri (4%), Ibibio (3.5%), Tiv (2.5%), and others. About 50% of Nigerians classify themselves as Muslims, 40% as Christians, and 10% claim belief in indigenous religions. English is the official language, but Hausa, Yoruba, and Igbo are major regional languages. Additionally, there are over 500 indigenous languages [2].

Before Nigeria became a country, it was a collection of independent states on the west coast of Africa. It formally came under British colonial rule from 1900 to 1960 when Lord Frederick Lugard was appointed high commissioner and commander-in-chief of the British Protectorate of Northern Nigeria. Lagos, then a colony, was joined to the protectorate of Southern Nigeria and the duo became the Colony and Protectorate of Southern Nigeria. Lord Lugard was subsequently appointed governor of Northern and Southern Nigeria and tasked with uniting both protectorates into what is present-day Nigeria. This amalgamation occurred in 1914. However, the name Nigeria was proposed by a British journalist, Flora Shaw, in 1897 and named for River Niger, which runs through the country and several other West African countries [3].

Britain gave Nigeria graduated autonomy after World War II; however, the country gained her independence in 1960 and was named the Federal Republic of Nigeria. Since then, hostilities between the south and the north, two regions divided by ethnicity and religion, escalated because of perceived unequal access to shared national resources. Political parties clearly identified with specific regions and ethnic groups. This uneasy union continued, but lurking underneath were political skirmishes that threatened the newly independent nation. The hostilities escalated, leading to a series of military coups that altered the political power balance. The Federal Military Government, then led by Gen. Yakubu Gowon, a Northerner, sought to engender unity by creating, by decree, 12 states from the former regions: North, West, East, and Midwest. The military leader of the former Eastern region, Lt. Col. Chukwuemeka Odumegwu Ojukwu, a Southerner, felt the government's creation of the states without consultation was unconstitutional. He declared the former Eastern region, the Republic of Biafra. Following a series of abortive meetings to resolve the crisis, a civil war erupted on July 6, 1967. The bloody and vicious war lasted for 3 years, with both forces supported by outside western powers—the Federal Government by United States and Britain and Biafra by France. The war ended in 1970 with Ojukwu fleeing to Ivory Coast and the commanding officer of the Biafran forces surrendered to the Federal Government [4,5]. Even now, the unease remains as is evidenced by agitation by a group from the former Eastern Nigeria seeking secession from Nigeria [6].

A succession of military rulers, interspersed with brief civilian heads of state, governed Nigeria until 1999 when a new constitution was adopted and the country elected a former military leader, Gen. Olusegun Obasanjo, as the first civilian head of state in the Fourth Republic. Obasanjo's peaceful transition of power to late President Musa Yar'Adua, ushered in a relatively peaceful time in Nigeria. On 29 May 2015, the country elected an opposition party leader, Muhammadu Buhari, also a former military leader, as the fourth president in Nigeria's 4th Republic [7].

Today, the country faces an ongoing challenge by the Islamist terror group, Boko Haram, which has caused thousands of civilian and military deaths and the destruction of property, while leading to the largest internal displacement of civilians. Coupled with this is the sharp drop in oil prices, a major source of revenue, which has affected the pace of development in the country [8].

In the midst of all these, came Ebola, a nightmare that fortunately was not allowed to fully manifest.

Background of Crisis Communication Research/Practice

Since independence, Nigeria has experienced a series of crises—a civil war that lasted 3 years, several spates of political and religious crises, natural disasters, the ongoing Boko Haram terrorism, and the recent Ebola crisis. These crises justify the need for research that would inform the planning, management, and communication of crisis. However, there is negligible research on crisis communication in Nigeria. The few journal articles and book chapters [9–13] examine corporate crisis to media coverage of crisis. What are in abundance are blogs, opinion pieces, and news articles on various crisis cases. This chapter adds to the body of work on the subject. An encouraging development is the establishment, in July 2015, of a Centre for Crisis Communication in Nigeria's capital, Abuja. According to the website, the organization would be "engaged in research and publication of crisis information management in Nigeria" [14].

Role of Culture in Crisis Communication Practice in Nigeria

Culture is a group of behaviors, values, and beliefs held by a group that defines how that group conducts life. Culture is variously defined as "the collective programming of the human mind that distinguishes the members of one human group from those of another" [15], "a complex web of information that a person learns and which guides each person's actions, experiences, and perceptions" [16]. Culture can be thought of as a common identity that is pervasive yet hidden or "layered" as Schein describes it [17]. The top is visible and observable through behavior; bottom is invisible and often impossible to observe. Schien notes that the invisible layer of values or beliefs is the most difficult to change. Nigeria, an amalgam of distinct and diverse ethnic and religious entities, each with its own unique cultural values, illustrates Schien's argument. While Nigerians identify as Nigerians, they generally tend to identify most closely as members of their ethnic groups first; hence it is not unusual for Nigerians, on meeting for the first time to ask where each other comes from. Often times, the name would identify the ethnic origin of the individual. This ethnic identification sometimes provides access to employment and political power. It also makes it difficult for them to criticize a kinsman's wrongdoing. Concurrently, this ethnic and religious identification also makes people more likely to believe information sources with whom they share a similar background.

Thus, in crisis situations, people sometimes tend to believe information from sources they know and trust, without bothering to confirm the accuracy of the message. Rumors thrive when there is mistrust between the society and its government. When rumors are not stemmed, the consequences could be deadly. Examples abound—the polio vaccination campaign was halted in some of the northern states in Nigeria in 2003 and 2004, because of rumors buoyed by pronouncements of religious and traditional rulers that the vaccinations were western plot to sterilize their children [18]. Rumors about the existence or origin of Ebola in West Africa led many to believe the disease was a western plot designed to decimate the population; hence, local residents in Sierra Leone prevented health workers from removing bodies of Ebola victims for burial. Nigeria sought to stem such occurrence by communicating to its population the risks associated with Ebola. Such communication enlisted spokespersons who are trusted and appeal to the major ethnic and religious groups in Nigeria.

For a majority of Nigerians, traditional African remedies for physical and spiritual ailment are preferred over western medicine. Some assume that Western ailments do not affect them because they've been naturally immunized as a result of their ability to survive and thrive in their environment.

For many, their ethnic, religious and cultural beliefs influence how they perceive, assess and make decisions on risk, crisis and the attendant communication. Nigerians' perception of risk and crisis is filtered through the lens of cultural compassion, such as solidarity or standing by a family or community member who is sick or has experienced bad luck. For instance, people care for their sick, hug and touch them. When someone dies, they perform rituals in which the body is touched and, in some cases, kissed by family members and friends, as they prepare the body for burial. They may stay in the same room for the wake, often with an open casket or the body laid out on a bed and help in other ways that are needed. These cultural practices were obviously hazardous to life and health in the wake of the deadly Ebola crisis. Communicating these risks in ways that upend long-held cultural practices is a challenge. It is no surprise that when Ebola first hit, it was difficult for health care workers and the government to get people to understand that these practices must stop in order to contain the spread of the disease.

Case Study: The Ebola Crisis

Ebola virus disease (EVD) erupted in West Africa in December 2013 and by April 2015, it had killed 10,689, infecting over 25,791 [19]. News outlets, such as Reuters, state that the deaths were over 11,000 [20]. It spread across large swaths of the region, affecting countries, most with poor health care facilities that struggled to contain the virus.

Ebola in Nigeria took on an unprecedented urgency when Liberian government official, Patrick Sawyer, arrived in the commercial capital, Lagos, on 20 July 2014, and collapsed at the airport. News reports indicated that the Liberian government cleared him to travel to Nigeria to seek medical help, although Liberian President Ellen Johnson Sirleaf denied that. Given the privilege accorded to foreign diplomats, he was whisked to a private clinic in Lagos, tested, and days later, was found to have the Ebola virus. He died 5 days after diagnosis. Nineteen health care professionals, including a doctor who had treated him, were infected. Of these, seven subsequently died.

The Nigerian health authorities immediately sought out all persons who had been in contact with Sawyer because they knew that if those persons were not found and quarantined, the spread of Ebola in the teeming metropolis of Lagos, a city of approximately 21 million, would be disastrous.

Sawyer's colleague, who was also infected, escaped to the southeastern city of Port Harcourt. There he sought help from a local doctor who treated him in his hotel room. The doctor contracted Ebola and died.

Quick and robust coordinated risk and crisis management efforts by Nigeria's Federal Government, Lagos, and Rivers State governments and supported by international partners, like the World Health Organization (WHO), UNICEF, Centers for Disease Control (CDC), and Médecins Sans Frontières (MSF) or Doctors Without Borders, were instrumental in stopping the epidemic in its track. Among the risk and crisis management measures taken by the Nigerian government when Ebola arrived in Nigeria were to set up emergency operations centers; find, monitor, and quarantine persons identified as having the virus; close all schools; enforce strict and aggressive border control; use effectively mobile technology; and set strict public health behavior supported by massive national multimedia health and risk communication campaign. The campaign incorporated elements of the local culture, cooperation with opinion leaders, religious leaders, and traditional leaders. Forty-two days after the last Ebola outbreak with no new case reported, the WHO

TABLE 4.1. Key Dates in the Ebola Crisis in Nigeria

July 20, 2014	Patrick Sawyer (Liberian) arrives in Lagos, collapses at airport, and is rushed to a private hospital.
July 25, 2014	Sawyer dies. Cause of death: Ebola. He becomes the first diagnosed Ebola victim in Nigeria.
August 8, 2014	WHO declares Ebola an international health emergency.
August 10, 2014	Dr. Stella Adadevoh, Lagos physician who treated Patrick Sawyer, dies from Ebola.
August 22, 2014	Dr. Iyke Enemuo, a Port Harcourt physician who treated the ECOWAS diplomat travelling with Patrick Sawyer, dies.
August 27, 2014	Doctors Without Borders calls WHO's response to Ebola "irresponsible" and "slow and derisory." WHO criticizes politicians' empty promises.
October 20, 2014	WHO declares Nigeria Ebola-free.
November 2015	WHO's "slow response" to Ebola criticized in a joint report sponsored by the Harvard Global Health Institute and London School of Hygiene and Tropical Medicine.

declared Nigeria free of Ebola on October 20, 2014. In a statement released to mark the declaration, WHO commended the "Nigerian Government's strong leadership and effective coordination of the response" to the Ebola crisis and declared Nigeria's response a "spectacular success" [21]. This was a transboundary case that could have gone awry; however, the major stakeholders had the same goal—contain and terminate the Ebola virus disease in Nigeria as quickly as possible to avoid possible transmission to other West African countries.

Stakeholders

The Nigerian Public

Given the power of Nigeria's rumor mill as illustrated by the refusal of some Northern Nigerian states to allow immunization of children against polio because of rumors that it is designed to sterilize their children, the Nigerian government knew it had to act fast to inform, persuade the public, and contain what could possibly turn to a pandemic.

Health Care Professionals

These are the first responders and thus, the most likely to contract the Ebola virus. Some of these professionals had experience in dealing with public health issues such as polio and AIDS, but none had encountered Ebola, which is transmitted through direct contact with bodily fluids of someone who has the virus. The public health professionals had to be trained as well as private health professionals who were recruited to join the cause.

Foreign Businesses, the Diplomatic Corps

The Nigerian government wanted to ensure that its swift action to contain Ebola would indicate to the foreign representatives that Nigeria is a country in which they can live and continue to do business.

Neighboring Countries

Nigeria is a member of the Economic Community of West African States (ECOWAS) whose treaty guarantees unrestricted travel between member countries. Given that Ebola had devastated some West African countries, such as Liberia and Sierra Leone, the Nigerian government wanted to assure other neighbors that it was doing everything possible to contain the crisis by enforcing strict border controls.

International Health Partners

Nigeria's willingness to cooperate and coordinate with international partners such as WHO, MSF, CDC, and UNICEF indicates that it was serious about stopping Ebola in its track. This international cooperation also highlights the transboundary nature of the response to the crisis.

Nigerian Government Response

The overall goal of the Federal Government was to *contain the Ebola virus as quickly as possible to ensure that it did not spread to the rest of Lagos and potentially, the rest of the country, and neighboring countries.*

Although the government did not appear to have a timetable within which to contain and eradicate Ebola, it was clear from the urgent actions taken that the government wanted it to be fast and effective.

Therefore, the objectives appeared to be as follows:

1. To thoroughly and quickly trace, track, and isolate all potential Ebola patients and contacts
2. To enact a strict border control to monitor everyone coming into or leaving the country
3. To use humans and technology to strictly monitor all of the contacts and educate the public
4. To use multimedia and opinion leaders to educate and allay fears of public

The government's strategies and tactics were laid out in numerous articles written by local Nigerian media, international news organizations, interviews with Lagos State Health Commissioner and Rivers State Ministry of Health officials, and an op-ed written by the former president of Nigeria, Goodluck Jonathan, and published in *USA Today* [22]. In it, he noted that the government executed a well-coordinated emergency management strategy that identified, quarantined, and treated those infected quickly. The government also identified and monitored persons exposed to the virus as a result of their contact with Patrick Sawyer or health care professionals who treated him.

Objective 1: To thoroughly and quickly trace, track, and isolate all potential Ebola patients and contacts (contact tracing)

The government did this through a coordinated strategy with domestic and foreign partners.

Nigeria's health minister and commissioners of health for Lagos and Rivers states, the epicenters of the Ebola scare, noted that early preparation for a potential Ebola outbreak and the government's coordinated response and partnerships with local and international health organization partners made the difference in containment of the virus. This coordinated effort resulted in specific government tactics.

- An immediate Ebola emergency was declared.
- All schools and tertiary institutions were closed.
- Trained doctors and health workers were rapidly deployed to handle Ebola cases.
- Agencies effectively tracked, traced, and monitored Ebola patients and all who have treated them.
- The government converted an Incident Management Center to an Emergency Operations Center in Lagos, and, subsequently, Port Harcourt.
- The government activated an already existing Infectious Disease Hospital in Lagos as the primary place to quarantine and treat Ebola patients. In Port Harcourt, a former Model Primary Health Care center was repurposed for use for confirmed Ebola cases and suspected Ebola cases.
- Six Ebola testing centers nationwide were established.
- Medical professionals used services of an already existing medical lab in Lagos to ensure rapid test results of infected persons.
- The government established an Ebola Treatment and Research Group tasked with researching the Ebola virus.
- The transportation of corpses was banned; special medical burial teams were formed to bury dead bodies properly and in a culturally sensitive manner.

- The government used technology and communication campaign to educate the population about Ebola.

As the Nigerian Federal Government mobilized health care workers in its fight against Ebola, it also provided incentives, such as life insurance, that attracted health care professionals from the private sector to supplement the public health officials. It must be noted that the Lagos State Government, under the leadership of Governor Babatunde Fashola, played a pivotal and decisive role in containing Ebola in Lagos. The Lagos State Government, already a veteran of the polio campaign, with established and effective virology facilities at Lagos University Teaching Hospital (LUTH), set the stage for an aggressive medical response to Ebola. The facilities were simply repurposed for the fight against the Ebola virus. Once it was clear that the second Ebola patient had traveled to Port Harcourt, the government dispatched a medical team to get Port Harcourt ready to respond as rapidly and effectively to the Ebola crisis.

Specifically, Lagos State health authorities tracked and monitored more health care professionals and others who came in contact with the late Sawyer; they also tracked, monitored and quarantined family members of health professionals who treated Sawyer. Reports indicate that the success rate was 100%. As well, in Port Harcourt, the other epicenter of Ebola in Nigeria, health officials monitored more than 400 persons suspected of contact with a Port Harcourt doctor who died from Ebola in Port Harcourt and quarantined them for the 21-day incubation period of the virus. Success rate for Port Harcourt was 99% [23].

Objective 2: To enact a strict border control to monitor everyone coming or leaving the country

The strategy was to institute and enforce strict border control. Health professionals, supported by customs officers and military personnel were posted to all international airports, seaport, and land border crossings and authorized to set up Ebola testing stations. This ensured that all persons entering the country were screened for symptoms of the virus.

Tactics included the following:

- The temperature of everyone entering the country was checked by health care professionals. Persons found to have a high fever were immediately transported to the Infectious Disease Hospital for further testing and monitoring. Refusal to obey was not an option.
- Hand sanitizers were made available to everyone entering the country at any of the border crossings.
- Every passenger was given a pamphlet about Ebola symptoms with instructions on what to do if symptoms were detected.

- Posters about Ebola in English, Pidgin English, and the major languages were prominently displayed at airports and all border crossings.
- The same process was repeated in Port Harcourt.

Objective 3: To use humans and technology to strictly monitor all of the contacts and educate publics

A strategy was the use of technology, specifically mobile communication. Major carriers in Nigeria reported that at the end of 2013, approximately 87% of Nigerians had 2G phone coverage and 49% had 3G coverage [24]. Given that a majority of Nigerians tend to rely more on their smartphones to access the Internet and to conduct commercial and personal activities, it made sense for the government to harness this tool to help in the fight against Ebola. The government partnered with local and international technology companies to develop or improve communication among location-based services, share information, and monitor the Ebola virus among persons identified as having been exposed to the virus.

The government partnered with Ebola Alert, a (Nigerian) nonprofit firm that "applies design thinking and appropriate technology to solve health and health-related problems" to reach millions of Nigerians who own smart phones [25].

The government also allied with outside organizations, including "eHealth & Information Systems Nigeria," a California-based research company experienced in working with health professionals in the polio eradication campaign in Northern Nigeria, and others that helped to develop a real-time reporting Android app was also used to contain the spread of the virus. The phone app mobile technology was used to track persons who may have been exposed to the virus, disseminate health information quickly to first responders in the field, access medical records, replacing outdated and often missing patient medical files, and teaching health care workers how to use technology to counter myths about the Ebola virus prevention and cure.

Social media technology was used in the following manner:

- Ebola Alert used Facebook®, Twitter®, and blogs to educate Nigerians about the Ebola virus.
- Google® Inc.'s Nigeria trained news reporters on how to use Google Trends to recognize and categorize important questions about the virus to which Nigerians wanted responses.
- Specially trained "contact tracers" conducted 18,500 home visits to check on persons suspected to have been exposed to Ebola [26]. As the name implies, the "contact tracers" tracked and identified persons who had come in contact with anyone diagnosed with the disease.
- Health workers reached 100% of all known Ebola contacts in Lagos, the initial site of outbreak, and nearly 100% at Port Harcourt, the nation's second outbreak site [26].

- Specially trained health workers used Android phone app to report times of infection. The apps reduced reporting times by 75% [27].
- Health workers "scanned test results to tablets and uploaded to emergency databases, and (location-based) field teams got text message alerts on their phones informing them of the results" [28].

Objective 4: To use multimedia and opinion leaders to educate and allay fears of public

A strategy was the development of a robust national multimedia risk communication campaign on multiple media platforms. The government mobilized all the resources in its communication arsenal, and with help from its international partners, cooperation with traditional, religious, community leaders, and popular stars of the entertainment industry, developed and executed a risk communication campaign that helped to minimize fear or counter misinformation about the Ebola virus. This campaign, which was in English, Pidgin English, and major local languages, not only informed but also persuaded people on what actions to take if they suspected someone had the virus. The campaign took on various forms.

Tactics included the following:

- House-to-house information (conversation) campaigns were enacted, using trained health care workers to educate those in close proximity to persons identified as having contracted the virus.
- Ebola prevention messages were broadcast on local radio stations and in multiple local dialects.
- Ebola prevention messages on national television and all commercial stations were broadcast.
- Ebola prevention messages were promoted by popular entertainers.
- Ebola prevention billboards and posters in multiple local dialects were posted in public offices, markets, public notice boards, and places of worship. See Figure 4.1.
- Town hall or village meetings and dialogs educated communities and answered questions about Ebola prevention. These meetings were often presided over by community leaders and traditional rulers and supported by health care professionals.
- Ebola prevention messages were disseminated by religious leaders in their various places of worship.
- Ebola prevention messages were disseminated via multiple social media platforms like Twitter, Facebook, blogs, and YouTube®.

FIGURE 4.1. Ebola poster, English version. Posters such as this were released in affected countries. This photo came to the author courtesy of Dr. Ngowari Okara, Braithwaite Memorial Hospital, Port Harcourt, Rivers State, Nigeria. Similar versions for download can be found online at the United States' Center for Disease Control, where many versions of Ebola posters and outreach can be located (http://www.cdc.gov/vhf/ebola/resources/posters.html). UNICEF also has a version of this poster (https://www.unicefusa.org/stories/how-unicef-helps-prevent-ebola-liberia/19036).

Culture's Influence on the Response

Nigerians are skeptical and superstitious by nature. They are skeptical of their government, politicians, and the myriad of unfulfilled promises; they are skeptical of persuasive messages from sources they do not trust or share commonalities with. Most Nigerians are religious, but also quite superstitious; hence, there is a tendency to believe information from a trusted religious, community (shares same ethnicity), or opinion leader or a close family or friend. Thus, when Ebola arrived in Nigeria courtesy of Liberian Patrick Sawyer, some Nigerians bought into a hoax that circulated on social media urging people to consume excessive amounts of salt water to avoid contracting the Ebola virus [29].

To mitigate such hoaxes, skepticism, and superstitious nature of Nigerians, and to minimize the potential damage that Ebola could cause to the health and economy of Nigeria, the government had to clearly and repeatedly communicate the threat and impact of the Ebola virus if the public did not adhere to the strict health guidelines and other strategies and tactics adapted by the government at the height of the crisis. The government also used religious, traditional, and opinion leaders who could relate to various sociocultural segments of society.

The government had to communicate its message in a way that allayed the public's anxiety, fear, and concern about the potential for contracting and possibly dying from Ebola. It also had to communicate the risk messages in ways that consider the sociocultural and religious sensitivities of the public; hence, the tracking of persons exposed to Ebola was limited to those who lived in close proximity to confirmed Ebola patients.

In a statement released to mark the declaration, WHO commended the "Nigerian Government's strong leadership and effective coordination of the response" to the Ebola crisis. This was a truly transboundary case whose major stakeholders had the same goal—contain and terminate the Ebola virus disease in Nigeria.

Another concern was the handling of the dead, as traditionally, preparation of the body for burial is a ritual performed by family members of the deceased. Ebola temporarily changed that, by government decree. The Nigerian government trained special teams of health workers who were charged with the task of disposing of dead bodies in a respectful and culturally acceptable manner. The public accepted this unusual change because of the high risk of contracting Ebola. The government had to sensitively handle superstitious beliefs of potential desecration of the dead body of a family's loved one by strangers—hence the use of health professionals, trained health personnel, and traditional rulers to communicate the message to the public about adherence to government restrictions even when it was inconvenient to them.

Other cultural and social norms were discarded in the wake of the Ebola virus— so hugging and receiving Holy Communion wine from the same goblet were temporarily discontinued.

Outcome of the Ebola Crisis Communication Campaign

The Nigerian Government declared victory over the Ebola virus, when on October 20, 2014, a mere forty-two days following the last outbreak of Ebola in Nigeria, the WHO declared the country free of the virus. The government was singled out for its "strong leadership and coordinated response" [30]. This was a truly transboundary case whose major stakeholders had the same goal—contain and terminate the Ebola virus disease in Nigeria.

As of February 2016, the World Health Organization (WHO) reported that there have been 28,603 recorded cases of Ebola virus disease worldwide. Of this number, 11,301 died from the disease [31].

Nigeria's containment of Ebola was not by chance. Granted, some critics may say Nigeria was lucky; however, it was a combination of several circumstances combined with effective and robust implementation of strict health measures that contributed to the containment. The leadership of the Lagos State Government, the Nigerian Federal Government, and the Rivers State Government, coupled with the financial and material support of private entities like the Dangote Foundation and international health partners, made a profound difference in stopping Ebola in its tracks. The cooperation of the Nigerian public was equally instrumental in containing the virus.

While Nigeria got help from international partners, it ensured that the campaign was tailored to its population—a campaign that considered the sociocultural, religious, and political norms that govern the society. This consideration was evident in the choice of messengers to disseminate the Ebola message to different audiences through multiple media platforms. The country used technology in an efficient manner to help health workers in identifying and recording medical information and tracking patients with Ebola. Technology also enabled the government to educate average Nigerians with cell phones about the Ebola virus.

Positive Lessons

WHO praised Nigeria's speedy remarkable success in containing the Ebola virus for good reason. With an estimated 2015 population of 181.5 million [1], a teeming Lagos metropolis with a population of 21 million [32], and Port Harcourt with a population of 1.14 million [33], Nigeria recorded only 19 Ebola cases with a fatality of 7. This spectacular success was made possible by the quick action of the Nigerian Federal, Lagos and Rivers State governments, repurposing and using existing medical facilities, a compliant public, and partnerships that enabled superb epidemiological investigation that traced all the virus outbreak to one man—Patrick Sawyer of Liberia.

Here is a list of practical suggestions or action plans for those seeking to communicate risk and crisis information or do business in that region/country/countries.

- *Prepare in advance.* Recognize that risk and crisis are no longer confined to one country or region. They are transboundary. An air passenger from Liberia introduced the Ebola virus to Nigeria. Had Nigeria not responded as aggressively as it did, the outcome could have been disastrous for Nigeria and neighboring countries.

- *A crisis/risk communication plan must be developed.* The Federal Government of Nigeria, the governments of Lagos and River States, having had some experience with public health outbreaks such as AIDS and polio, appeared to have a crisis and risk communication plan which they executed effectively and aggressively.

- *Establish partnership with relevant organizations within the country before they are needed.* Cooperation from international and local organizations and businesses in Nigeria have been evident in many previous natural disasters like floods and crises such AIDS; so in the Ebola crisis, these same organizations eagerly stepped in to support the Nigerian government and to fulfill their social responsibility to the communities in which they operate.

- *Establish partnerships with relevant international organizations before they are needed.* Nigeria already had excellent working relationships with the major international health organizations, including MSF, WHO, UNICEF, and others.

- *Test the efficacy of communication technology in simulated environment.* The Ebola crisis illuminated the crucial role of communication technology in reaching a vast number of people scattered in a wide geographic area. Most important, the technology must be tested to ensure it would work during a crisis.

- *Ensure the ability to activate and enforce strict measures that would ensure success of such a campaign.* The ability of the Federal Government of Nigeria to close its borders, close schools, order quarantine of infected and potential Ebola patients and appropriate already existing facilities like the infectious disease hospitals and primary health care centers to house isolated Ebola patients contributed to the containment of the Ebola virus.

- *Sociocultural, religious, and political norms are important.* The Ebola response in Nigeria has highlighted the important role of community, religious, and traditional leaders to champion or reinforce key messages in a communication campaign.

Conclusion

When Ebola arrived in Nigeria via Liberian-American civil servant, Patrick Sawyer, on July 20, 2014, strict measures were immediately set in motion once he was diagnosed. The government repurposed already existing medical infrastructures and with expert assistance from international partners, including WHO, United States Centers for Disease Control and Prevention (CDC), Médecins Sans Frontières (MSF), UNICEF, and others, the Federal Government of Nigeria instituted and enforced measures that helped to contain the spread of the virus. First, the government closed all schools, enforced border controls, and set strict public health behavior supported by a massive multimedia risk communication campaign. This robust campaign engaged religious, traditional, and community leaders as well as popular entertainers to spread the message about Ebola prevention. The Lagos State Government, which played a pivotal role in the fight against Ebola, dispatched specially trained health workers to track, monitor, and quarantine persons who have been identified as having the virus. Health authorities tracked and monitored more than 400 persons who were suspected of contact with health care workers who treated Sawyer in Lagos, and subsequently, his colleague who fled to the southern city of Port Harcourt. The Rivers State Government, with cooperation from the Lagos and Federal governments and international partners, tracked and quarantined all who came in contact with the doctor who treated Sawyer's colleague and then died from Ebola in Port Harcourt.

The government's rapid response and unprecedented cooperation with non-governmental organizations within and outside the country, swift deployment of health personnel, and use of existing health and crisis management facilities, including an Incident Management Center which was repurposed as an Emergency Operations Center, and a vigorous risk communication campaign, ensured that the Ebola virus was quickly contained, with only 9 deaths. On October 20, 2014, 3 months after the arrival of the virus in Nigeria, the WHO praised the country's "spectacular success," and declared Nigeria Ebola free.

Discussion Questions

4.1   You are the head of the crisis team in the Ministry of Health, Lagos, when you get a text message from the hospital where Mr. Sawyer had been taken that he has been diagnosed with Ebola. What would be your action in the next 1 hour? What other actions would you take in the next 24 hours?

　　　a. Write out the three key messages you would post on your website, Twitter, and Facebook.

　　　b. Craft the wording you would send out as a press release to the media and highlight in your first press conference about the diagnosis.

4.2   You have international partners (WHO, MSN,) and local partners (tech companies) who are eager to help. Describe how you would assign tasks to ensure that their expertise is used effectively and efficiently.

4.3   Describe how you would balance the need for cultural sensitivity in your messaging and the need to ensure that the public understands the profound nature of the risk message.

4.4   Given the diverse nature of Nigerian society, who would you use to disseminate your risk message and on what media platforms?

4.5   Working with a team, list a quick and easy crisis plan that addresses an effective response to the Ebola crisis.

4.6 You are the chief speechwriter for former President Goodluck Jonathan. Write out a brief speech that he would give to the nation at the onset of the Ebola crisis.

References

1. CIA. (2015). "The world factbook: Populations-Nigeria" [Online]. Available: https://www.cia.gov/library/publications/the-world-factbook/fields/2119.html, November 10, 2015 (last date accessed).

2. CIA. (2015). "The world factbook: Ethnic groups-Nigeria" [Online]. Available: https://www.cia.gov/library/publications/the-world-factbook/fields/2075.html, November 10, 2015 (last date accessed).

3. Hogarth-Blake Ltd. (2008). "Flora Shaw gives the name Nigeria," transcribed from an article printed by *The Times of London*, January 8, 1897. [Online]. Available: http://www.hh-bb.com/flora-shaw.pdf, November 10, 2015 (last date accessed).

4. A. Atofarati, "The Nigerian civil war: Causes, strategies and lessons learned," U.S. Marine Command and Staff College. [Online]. Available: http://www.globalsecurity.org/military/library/report/1992/AAA.htm, November 10, 2015 (last date accessed).

5. H. B. Momoh, *The Nigerian Civil War, 1967–1970: History and Reminiscences*. Ibadan, NG: Sam Bookman Publishers, 2000.

6. I. Okonta, "Biafra of the mind: MASSOB and the mobilization of history," *Journal of Genocide Research*, vol. 16, nos. 2–3, pp. 355–378, 2014. [Online]. Available: http://www.tandfonline.com/doi/abs/10.1080/14623528.2014.936710, November 10, 2015 (last date accessed).

7. F. Owete, "After 30 years, Buhari returns to power as Nigeria's elected president," *Premium Times*, May 29, 2015. [Online]. Available: http://www.premiumtimesng.comfrom: /news/183962-after-30-years-buhari-returns-to-power-as-nigerias-elected-president-2.html, November 10, 2015 (last date accessed).

8. C. Stein, (2016, February 9). "Budget woes hit Nigeria amid oil price crash," Voice of America. [Online]. Available: http://www.voanews.com/a/rocky-year-ahead-for-nigeria-amid-oil-price-crash/3183020.html, February 20, 2016 (last date accessed).

9. T. O. S. Owolabi and C. O. Ekechi, "Communication as critical factor in disaster management and sustainable development in Nigeria," *International Journal of Development and Economic Sustainability*, vol. 2, no. 3, pp. 58–72, 2014.

10. G. H. Ezeah and C. E. Asogwa, "A study of crisis communication management programmes of Shell Petroleum Development Company in the Niger Delta," *Swiss Journal of Research in Business and Social Science*, vol. 1, no. 1, pp. 11–37, 2014. [Online]. Available: http://www.srjbss.com, November 10, 2015 (last date accessed).

11. A. M. Hamid and I. M. Baba, "Resolving Nigeria's 'Boko Haram' insurgence: What role for the media?" presented at the International Conference on Communication and Media 2014 (i-COME'14)—Communication, Empowerment and Governance: The 21st Century Enigma, *Procedia—Social and Behavioral Sciences*, vol. 155, pp. 14–20, November 2014. [Online]. Available: http://www.sciencedirect.com/science/article/pii/S1877042814057152, November 10, 2015 (last date accessed).

12. I. W. Udomisor and A. A. Sonuga, "Handling communication crises in media organiza-tion: The case of Africa Independent Television," *Research on Humanities and Social Sci-ences*, vol. 3, no. 2, 2013, pp. 62–71. [Online]. Available: http:// www.iiste.org, November 10, 2015 (last date accessed).

13. W. Adamolekun, K. Ogedengbe, and C. B. Pratt, "Crisis in Nigeria's banking and finan-cial industry: Government actions reassure skittish, jittery publics," in *Case Studies in Crisis Communication: International Perspectives on Hits and Misses*, A. M. George and C. B. Pratt, Eds. New York/London: Routledge, 2012, pp. 81–112.

14. Centre for Crisis Communication (CCC), Abuja. [Online]. Available: http://www.cccnigeria.org, November 26, 2016 (last assessed date).

15. G. Hofstede, *Cultures and Organizations: Software of the Mind*. London: McGraw-Hill, 1997.

16. D. E. Campbell, *Choosing Democracy*, 2nd ed. Englewood Cliffs, NJ: Prentice–Hall, 2000, p. 38.

17. E. H. Schein, *Organizational Culture and Leadership*. San Francisco, CA: Jossey-Bass Publishers, 1985.

18. I. Ghinaj, C. Willott, I. Dadari, et al., "Listening to the rumours: What the Northern Nige-ria polio vaccine boycott can tell us ten years on," *Global Public Health*, vol. 8, no. 10, pp. 1138–1150, December 2013.

19. Ebola Situation Report [29 April 2015]. http://apps.who.int/ebola/current-situation/ebola-situation-report-29-april-2015. World Health Organization, May 29, 2017 (last date accessed).

20. K. Kelland, Global health experts accuse WHO of 'egregious failure' on Ebola ..." Reuters, November 22, 2015. [Online]. Available: http://www.reuters.com/article/us-health-ebola-response-idUSKBN0TB10K20151122, May 29, 2017 (last date accessed).

21. World Health Organization. (2014, October 20). "Nigeria is now free of Ebola virus transmission,". Ebola Situation Assessment. [Online]. Available: http://www.who.int/mediacentre/news/ebola/20-october-2014/en/, February 20, 2016 (last date accessed).

22. G. Jonathan, "Nigeria president: How we beat Ebola," *USA Today*, January 23, 2015. [Online]. Available: http://www.usatoday.com/story/opinion/2015/01/23/eradicating-ebola-nigeria-president-jonathan/22056513/, January 15, 2016 (last date accessed).

23. Rivers State Government, "Fighting Ebola epidemic in Rivers State," 2014 Annual Report, Rivers State Primary Healthcare Management Board, Port Harcourt, Rivers State, 2014, pp. 72–79.

24. GSM Mobile Economy Africa, "Network infrastructure and policy," *The Mobile Econ-omy Sub-Saharan Africa*, 2014, p. 31. [Online]. Available: http://docplayer.net/5471903-The-mobile-economy-sub-saharan-africa-2014.html, May 29, 2017 (last date accessed).

25. Ebola Alert. Ebola Emergency Operations Centre, Central Public Health Laboratory, Lagos. [Online]. Available: http://ebolaalert.org/index.php/contact/, January 15, 2016 [last date accessed].

26. Centers for Disease Control and Prevention. (2014, October 3). "Ebola virus disease outbreak—Nigeria, July–September 2014" [Online]. Available: http://www.cdc.gov/mmwr/preview/mmwrhtml/mm6339a5.htm, January 15, 2016 (last date accessed).

27. Y. Ibikun, "Nigeria uses Android App with Facebook to beat Ebola," *Bloomberg News*, October 7, 2014. [Online]. Available: http://www.bloomberg.com/news/articles/2014-10-07/nigeria-uses-android-app-with-facebook-to-beat-ebola, February 20, 2016 (last date accessed).

28. E. McCann, "WHO credits mHealth app with helping Nigeria get rid of Ebola," *mHealth News*, October 24, 2014. [Online]. Available: http://www.mhealthnews.com/news/who-credits-mhealth-app-helping-nigeria-get-rid-ebola, January 15, 2016 (last date accessed).

29. L. Neporent, "Nigerian Ebola hoax results in two deaths," *ABC News*, September 30, 2014. [Online]. Available: http://abcnews.go.com/Health/nigerian-ebola-hoax-results-deaths/story?id=25842191, January 15, 2016 (last date accessed).

30. World Health Organization. (2014, October 20). "WHO declares end of Ebola outbreak in Nigeria" [Online]. Available: http://www.who.int/mediacentre/news/statements/2014/nigeria-ends-ebola/en/, February 20, 2016 (last date accessed).

31. World Health Organization. (2016, February 17). "Ebola situation report" [Online]. Available: http://www.who.int/ebola/current-situation/ebola-situation-report-17-february-2016, February 20, 2016 (last date accessed).

32. World Population Review. (2016). "Lagos population 2016" [Online]. Available: http://worldpopulationreview.com/world-cities/lagos-population/, March 20, 2016 (last date accessed).

33. Port Harcourt Population. (2016). [Online]. Available: http://www.geonames.org/maps/google_4.777_7.013.html, March 20, 2016 (last date accessed).

South Africa 5

Killing in the Name of "Stolen" Jobs: The April 2015 Xenophobic Attacks in South Africa

Kwamena Kwansah-Aidoo and Ibrahim Saleh

Chapter Preview

In April 2015, and not for the first time, South Africans experienced xenophobic attacks on immigrants living in their midst. On the basis of the country's violent history and also previous incidents, this was a crisis that should have been foreseen. So, how did the ruling African National Congress (ANC) government respond to this crisis? The legacy of apartheid has made it easy for South Africans to be suspicious of, and often antagonistic to, people who are different, and in times of difficulty such feelings blow up, manifesting in physical and psychological violence directed at foreigners. This makes xenophobia in South Africa a matter of grave concern and raises some very important questions. Do these xenophobic attacks represent a deep-seated suspicion of other people and/or an in-bred intolerance of others? Are there multiple causes that simmer under the surface, and from time to time explode violently? Do the South African media report on foreigners in ways that perpetuate stereotypes and invariably encourage xenophobia? This chapter

Culture and Crisis Communication: Transboundary Cases from Nonwestern Perspectives, First Edition.
Edited by Amiso M. George and Kwamena Kwansah-Aidoo.
© 2017 by The Institute of Electrical and Electronics Engineers, Inc. Published 2017 by John Wiley & Sons, Inc.

seeks to examine the way the government responded to the 2015 attacks while trying to interrogate the culture of xenophobia in South Africa and the validity of claims against foreigners. This case ultimately reveals the complex nature of South African society and the dynamics of the relationship between South Africans as hosts, and foreigners who live in their midst, particularly those foreigners from north of the River Limpopo.

After reading this chapter you will be able to

- *Understand how South Africa's history of apartheid and violence has bred distrust and affected the way foreigners are viewed*
- *Discuss how the South African government attempted to deal with the April 2015 xenophobic attacks*
- *Discern the different stakeholders and how they were situated during the 2015 xenophobic crisis in South Africa*
- *Explain how the rest of the world, particularly African countries, responded to the April 2015 xenophobic attacks*
- *Understand the role of language and interpretation in the understanding of the different terms assigned to foreigners*
- *Interpret the role played by the South African media in fomenting xenophobia amongst South Africans*

Introduction: South Africa and Its Culture

Located at the southernmost tip of the African continent, South Africa is home to over 52 million people. The country is immensely diverse in landscape, ecosystems, and its people. It is made up of nine provinces and has three capitals: Cape Town (legislative), Pretoria (administrative), and Bloemfontein (judicial). In 1994, South Africa attained political freedom from apartheid and a new era of political and democratic dispensation began where for the first time all citizens, irrespective of their race/color, were allowed to vote in the national elections. The African National Congress (ANC) won the elections and has been in power since then.

South Africa has one of the leading economies on the African continent and is also a member of an elite group of developing nations that includes Brazil, Russia, India, and China. With 11 official languages, a multitude of religions and traditions, South Africa has a rich and diverse culture which has survived the brutal apartheid regime. The country also plays host to people from many other African nations and from other countries around the world, particularly Asia—India, Bangladesh, Pakistan, and China. As a people, South Africans are very proud of their culture which is often expressed in clothing, music, and food, as well as observing various ceremonies and festivals throughout the year.

The Apartheid System, "not only left a deep legacy of white-against-black racism by forcefully ghettoising ethnic groups, those with different shades of skin or languages, it also left a legacy of not only interracial group and color prejudice, but also prejudice against Africans from outside the country."

—William Gumede

Though there have been major developments and successes since the end of apartheid, problems of inequality and unemployment still persist, with unemployment rates hitting their highest in 2014–2015. Equally, in other sectors such as health and infrastructure, much progress has been made but the country still faces several challenges. Another aspect of South African society and culture is its violence. Gumede points out that South Africa "is a deeply violent society" and explains that the culture of violence can be traced back to the violence of colonialism and apartheid—and the oppressed peoples' counter-violence in response [1]. Gumede further argues that South Africa is not just one of the world's most diverse societies, but also one "where different communities are often deeply intolerant of others" [1]. According to him, the apartheid system "not only left a deep legacy of white-against-black racism by forcefully ghettoising ethnic groups, those with different shades of skin or languages, it also left a legacy of not only interracial group and color prejudice, but also prejudice against Africans from outside the country" [1]. The result of all of this, as Gumede surmises, is that South Africans generally—both black and white—are "deeply suspicious of Africans from north of the Limpopo. African immigrants are violently attacked because perpetrators believe the police will not prosecute them with the same zeal because the victims are foreign, not 'like us'" [1].

Consequently, one of its most recent challenges has been the reoccurrence of xenophobic violence. The first outbreak occurred in 2008, in which 62 people died. In April 2015, another series of xenophobic attacks spread across the country, leaving death and destruction to property in its wake. This chapter focuses on that April 2015 outbreak of xenophobic violence in South Africa, the government's response to it, and the role that culture played in that response.

Culture and Crisis Communication

As in many other parts of the world, communication in South Africa is entrenched in and influenced by cultural context, hence there is the need to work toward integrating these aspects into corporate strategies and public relations research in order to avoid the "disconnectedness of communications from culture" [2]. In South Africa, it can be said that the spirit and practice of communication (public relations) coincides with traditional communitarian values of African humanism (*ubuntu*) and a harmonious society [3]. Thus, the African cultural and normative premium of cultivating amicable relationships is a quintessential precursor to doing business in South Africa [2].

Research by Van Heerden found that in Africa "the main purpose of public relations pertains to understanding society" [4] and this influences the role that public relations plays in top management's decisions regarding organizational behavior and how to become good corporate citizens [4]. This observation shows a high concern for societal issues, which requires a more authentic approach to the practice of public relations in the African context [4]. This also means that in a crisis situation, a genuine attempt is made to deal with the crisis and to connect with the people at a level that will gain their understanding.

In South Africa it can be said that the spirit and practice of communication (public relations) coincides with traditional communitarian values of African humanism (*ubuntu*) and a harmonious society. Thus, the African cultural and normative premium of cultivating amicable relationships is a quintessential precursor to doing business in South Africa.

In that same spirit of authenticity, the South African government, at the national level, attempted to take serious steps toward crisis communication by adopting a disaster risk reduction paradigm [5] with the aim of matching global trends by integrating risk reduction methodologies into developmental initiatives to build resilience in households, communities, and areas known to be at risk [6]. This framework emphasized the disaster risk reduction concepts of disaster prevention and mitigation as the core principles to guide disaster risk management in South Africa [7]. The South African National Disaster Management Framework (SANDMF) places specific focus on communication and communication flow during incidents by identifying this aspect as one of the three enablers of the SANDMF [7]. Communication responsibilities are even assigned to the Provincial Disaster Management Centre (DMC) and Municipal DMC [7].

Case Study: Pack Your Bags and Go Home

Over a period of about 3 weeks in April 2015, South Africa experienced a resurgence of anti-immigrant violence. The attacks were allegedly sparked by a statement reportedly made by the Zulu king, Goodwill Zwelithini, that foreign-born Africans should pack up their bags and go home. However, some observers [1] believe that xenophobic statements by other national leaders prior to April 2015 were a contributory factor. For example, President Jacob Zuma was reported to have said in 2014 that South African blacks should not behave as if they were "typical" blacks from "Africa." The

African National Congress (ANC) general secretary, Gwede Mantashe, also supposedly blamed "foreigners" for instigating unrest in South Africa's platinum belt [1], while Small Business Development Minister Lindiwe Zulu also reportedly said that "[f]oreigners need to understand that they are here as a courtesy and our priority is to the people of this country first and foremost... They cannot barricade themselves in and not share their practices with local business owners" [8]. Sometime in January of the same year (2015), Nomvula Mokonyane, the Minister of Water and Sanitation, was also said to have commented on Facebook® that, in Kagiso, Gauteng province "[a]lmost every second outlet (spaza) or even former general dealer shops are run by people of Somali or Pakistan origin (sic)... I am not xenophobic fellow comrades and friends but this is a recipe for disaster" [8].

The attacks on individuals and businesses which started in Isipingo in the KwaZulu-Natal province quickly spread from Durban to other major cities [9]. They involved destruction of property and resulted in many injuries, while claiming a minimum of seven lives [10]. More than 5000 people were displaced, and shops looted and razed. According to the United Nations High Commissioner for Refugees (UNHCR) most of those affected were "refugees and asylum seekers who were forced to leave their countries due to war and persecution" [10]. These events made world headlines and media images showing the killing of a Mozambican immigrant, Emmanuel Sithole, in Alexandra Township in Johannesburg became one of the sad and enduring reminders of the brutality of the attacks as well as a photographic representation of the violence that ensued during those shameful 3 weeks.

Situational Analysis

There were a number of key stakeholders, and these are outlined below.

The South African Government—As the government in power, it was the responsibility of the ruling African National Congress (ANC) Government led by President Jacob Zuma to ensure that the violence was brought under control and that lives and property were kept safe and people, especially foreign nationals, did not feel threatened. They also had a responsibility to assure foreign governments that their nationals in South Africa were safe and would be treated with dignity.

Immigrants—The estimated number of foreign nationals in South Africa ranges from 2–5 million, among a population of more than 51 million [11]. Many of them have settled in townships across the country, operating small businesses among the poorest South Africans and were major targets of the violent attacks.

King Goodwill Zwelithini—Comments made by him to the effect that foreigners should go back to their home countries supposedly sparked the attacks in April 2015. This made him an important stakeholder in the crisis.

Perpetrators of the violence—Though not necessarily a single and/or well-organized group, South African citizens who were randomly attacking foreigners (African immigrants) were themselves an important public that needed to be addressed.

Civil society organizations—As in the case of the 2008 xenophobic attacks, the civil society sector was vocal in condemning the violence in 2015. Thirty-one organizations wrote to the Chairperson of the African Union, Dr. Nkosazana Dlamini Zuma, urging her to pressure the South African government to speedily address the situation [12].

Foreign governments—All foreign governments, particularly African and Asian, who had nationals living and working in South Africa constituted an important public and many of them voiced their concerns.

Xenophobia or Not? How the South African Government Responded to the Attacks

Before considering the government's response, it is worth pointing out that the South African government was criticized in certain quarters for its tardiness in responding to the xenophobic attacks. One South African commentator, for example, wrote that as the xenophobic violence spread across the country like wild fire, "instead of sending in the army to the affected communities, the government remained stuck in denial, leaders claimed it was not xenophobic and was made up of "isolated" incidents" [1]. The government did respond eventually though, but it did not state any clear objectives. What has been provided here in this section, then, is deduced from the way the government responded, both in action and communication.

Objective 1: Stop the attacks on foreigners as quickly as possible
Strategy/Tactics: Once the government got over its initial denials, it sought to create the impression that it was ready and willing to act to put a quick end to the violent attacks. Specific actions taken included the following:

- President Jacob Zuma cancelled a state visit to Indonesia to deal with the crisis. He visited a camp in the Durban suburb of Chatsworth, where there were more than a thousand foreign nationals sleeping in tents and depending on volunteers for food. Many of these foreign nationals were said to be boarding buses to return to Malawi, Zimbabwe, and other home countries [11].
- President Zuma assigned the Ministers of Home Affairs (Mr. Malusi Gigaba), Police (Mr. Nathi Nhleko), and State Security (Mr. David Mahlobo) to stop the violence. This included the establishment of an Inter-Departmental Task Team to coordinate the response.

- A Panel of Experts was set up under the leadership of the former United Nations High Commissioner for Human Rights, Judge Navi Pillay, to advise the Government on the integration of foreigners into the local communities on an ongoing basis.
- Additional law enforcement officers were mobilized from around the country and deployed to the affected areas to enforce the law and prevent further attacks.
- All District Disaster Management Centers were placed on high alert.
- A 24-hour Call Center was established and remained accessible in the event of further xenophobic attacks happening in future.
- Shelters were set up to accommodate displaced foreign nationals and basic amenities such as water, sanitation, and healthcare were being provided.
- The South African Government began to work closely with the United Nations High Commissioner for Refugees (UNHCR), United Nations Children's Fund (UNICEF), International Organization for Migration (IOM), as well as nongovernmental organizations to provide food, psychosocial, and other support to those affected. [13]

While taking all these measures, the government in its communication tried to demonstrate a willingness to be tough, all the time stressing that perpetrators would be brought to book.

> The South African Government views the attacks on foreign nationals as a criminal offence that will not be tolerated… No one has the right to take the law into their own hands. The South African Government will enforce the laws of the country and will not hesitate to act against criminal activity or those found to incite violence. [13]

Accordingly, regular updates on arrests made were provided so as to deter would-be perpetrators. The police arrested 307 suspects, some of whom were accused of using social media to spread fear. The report said: "They have been sending out fictitious SMS and WhatsApp messages with fictitious and photoshopped images warning people of imminent attacks" [10]. When after almost 3 weeks the violence had not stopped completely, the army was deployed in areas assessed as still volatile [14].

Objective 2: Convince perpetrators and South Africans, generally, that the attacks were bad for South Africa on the economic/social front
Strategy/Tactics: The government adopted a narrative that sought to convince citizens that the economic (and to an extent social) interests of South Africa were in jeopardy with the xenophobic attacks. For example, Jeff Radebe, Minister in the Presidency,

pointed out in a speech that the country's companies that operate in the rest of Africa could be at risk of reprisals. "The impact of these attacks has far-reaching implications for our economic and social relations with the continent and the world," he said, adding that "South African companies who are running successful businesses on the continent who help to contribute to our revenue and sustaining our economy may suffer the same fate" [11]. Other references were made to South African artists who were suffering the consequences of the attacks, outside of South Africa: "Recently, South African artists who were to showcase their craft outside the borders of our country, such as Big Nuz in Zimbabwe, Kelly Khumalo and Cassper Nyovest in London, have had their concerts cancelled as a result of these attacks" [11]. The Deputy Minister for Trade and Industry, Mzwandile Masina, also stated that, "Since the start of the attacks, our country has lost billions of rands in export foreign revenue" [15].

Objectives 3: Prevail on foreign governments that it was safe for their nationals to be in South Africa, while trying to convince those foreign nationals in South Africa that they are welcome and would be protected
Strategy/Tactics: The South African government hastily convened a meeting of African ambassadors and high commissioners where it tried to provide reassurance that the government was taking their concerns seriously. At this meeting, the Minister of International Relations and Cooperation, Maite Nkoana-Mashabane, outlined actions taken by the government thus far, and gave assurances foreigners are welcome in South Africa:

> Inspired by the spirit of Pan-Africanism, the motive force of our liberation struggle, South Africa's foreign policy is driven by the vision to achieve a united African continent that is peaceful, democratic, non-racial, non-sexist, prosperous and which contributes to a world that is just and equitable. South Africa pursues this vision, informed by the values of Ubuntu (Humanity). Ubuntu is the central concept of social and political organization in the African global outlook, it consists of the principles of sharing and caring for one another. This means, generally speaking, that to be human is to affirm one's humanity by recognizing the humanity of others and establish mutually respectful relations with them. .... I can therefore state with utmost conviction that the spirit of Ubuntu is tightly woven in South Africa's moral fiber, more especially in our interaction with fellow Africans and the international community in general. South Africa stands unwaveringly against all intolerances such as racism, xenophobia, homophobia and sexism. [13]

President Jacob Zuma in an address to a crowd of foreign nationals also said that those who wanted to go home would be helped, and then said, to those who want to remain: "We are firstly going to stop the violence and then allow them to stay here in peace" [11]. He further explained

It is not every South African who says go away, not at all. It is a very small number who say so. We don't want countries in the region where the citizens are going to look at each other in a hostile manner. We want to live as sisters and brothers. [11]

Ubuntu is the central concept of social and political organization in the African global outlook, it consists of the principles of sharing and caring for one another. This means, generally speaking, that to be human is to affirm one's humanity by recognizing the humanity of others and establish mutually respectful relations with them.

Objective 4: Stave off revenge attacks on South Africans and South African businesses in other parts of the world, particularly in Africa
Strategy/Tactics: The meeting with African ambassadors and high commissioners in which assurances of dealing swiftly with the situation were provided was also meant to assure the home countries of these ambassadors and high commissioners that the situation was being dealt with and to prevent similar revenge attacks on South Africans across the continent. Across the continent, reports had started filtering in about acts of aggression toward South Africa and South Africans. In another effort to placate foreign nationals and their governments, the Minister of International Relations and Cooperation, Maite Nkoana-Mashabane, apologized on behalf of the government and people of South Africa with "a deep sense of pain, shame, and regret" [16].

Enter King Goodwill Zwelithini, the Zulu Chief

One other strategy that was perhaps aimed at helping achieve all the objectives stated above was getting King Goodwill Zwelithini involved. The influential monarch was accused of sparking the attacks and so political pressure was brought to bear on him to explain himself and help end the attacks. In response, the King and his defenders claimed that his remarks, which were made in the Zulu language, had been misconstrued and that he was only referring to the deportation of illegal immigrants [10]. Addressing an anti-xenophobia gathering at Durban's Moses Mabhida stadium, King Goodwill Zwelithini said: "Most of the things that are being said about me are not true. I understand that most of the people I am talking to understand the Zulu language well" [10]. In rallying the people together to help stop the violence, he said:

We need to make sure no more foreigners are attacked. We must stop these vile acts. I called you all here today so we can start a real war which is needed now. The war I am referring to is to ensure that all foreign nationals in South Africa, regardless of which country they come from, are protected. [10]

Although some commentators condemned the king for using the speech to blame the media and also for being utterly defensive, his gesture in calling on his people to help stop the attacks can be seen as a positive step in the fight against the xenophobic attacks.

Outcome of the Government's Response

After about 3 weeks of violence and the actions taken by the government, the situation quietened down and the violent attacks stopped. In that 3 week period, however, local South Africans had looted shops belonging to foreigners and attacked immigrants in general. These attacks literally forced many immigrants to relocate to places such as police stations, where they believed they would be safe. In the meantime, authorities in Malawi started to repatriate their nationals, while a number of other concerned foreign governments also announced that they would evacuate their citizens [17]. More than 300 people were arrested [18]. Four suspects were arrested after *The Sunday Times* published photographs of the murder of the Mozambican street vendor Emmanuel Sithole in the township of Alexandria [19–21]. At the end of it all, 7 people had been killed, all of them in KwaZulu-Natal [22]. The image of South Africa took a battering on the international scene. As one commentator put it

> It will probably take a while for the country to restore its image … From now on, visits to South Africa by foreign nationals may be marred by concern about when the next xenophobic violence might erupt, the same way some people say they are afraid to visit Nigeria because of Boko Haram. [23]

Transboundary Reactions

Given the nature of the crisis and the violent nature of the attacks, it is worth noting how other countries, especially across the African continent, reacted to the unfolding events. The xenophobic mayhem sharpened a sense of "us and them," causing bitterness among nations that hosted thousands of South African exiles during the struggle against apartheid [10]. In many places, citizens of affected countries sought to apply tit-for-tat measures. In Mozambique, South African vehicles were pelted with stones and demonstrators blocked the road for half an hour, refusing to allow cars with South African registration plates to pass. Again in Mozambique, Sasol, an energy and chemical company, evacuated 340 South Africans over fears for their safety and in Zambia, a privately owned radio station stopped playing South African music in protest. Reports from Nigeria said that South African companies there were threatened with closure. Across the continent, protests were held at various South African embassies and several South African musicians were forced to cancel concerts abroad [10].

In the Zimbabwean capital Harare, the police clashed with more than a 100 people who marched outside the South African embassy with a petition that said, "We, the people of Zimbabwe standing in solidarity with our brethren in Africa, strongly condemn and denounce the cruel, senseless and gruesome xenophobic slaughter of foreign nationals and the looting of their properties in South Africa" [10]. The president of the Zimbabwe National Students' Union, Gilbert Mutubuki, was also quoted as saying: "Right now we have South African businesses such as Pick n Pay operating freely here, but our brothers are being butchered in South Africa … It's high time we should do the same to all South African businesses here until they stop all this nonsense" [10]. The Economic Community of West African States also condemned the "barbaric, criminal and xenophobic murder of innocent foreigners" [10], and there were protests and calls in Malawi, Zimbabwe, and other nations for boycott of South African goods.

How Culture Influenced the Government's Response

Looking at the way the government responded, one can detect traces of cultural influence in those responses. First was the tardiness or the refusal of the government to immediately acknowledge that the attacks were xenophobic; the same thing happened in 2008. This confirms Gumede's view that perpetrators believe "the police will not prosecute them with the same zeal because the victims are foreign, not 'like us'" [1]. Also, if one considers the earlier cited statements by government officials directed against foreigners, it can be argued that the government's feet-dragging was the result of deeply held/shared beliefs about the victims and their place in the South African society. As indicated earlier, the army was sent in almost 3 weeks after the violence started.

The involvement of traditional authority, that is, the Zulu king Zwelithini was also very much a cultural response. Whether the violence started because of his words or not, as an influential traditional leader with followers who would listen to him, it was a good decision to get him to add his voice to the government's in admonishing the perpetrators to stop their violent attacks.

Sending in the military after almost 3 weeks could also be seen as influenced by culture. Given the history of violence in South Africa, especially the running battles that different groups had with the police and military in the apartheid era, it is possible to surmise that the reluctance to send in the military was actually influenced by culture in the form of past history. Even when the decision was taken to send in the military, there was some hesitance, and the Minister of Defense Nosiviwe Mapisa-Nqakula, had to go on the defensive, noting that: "There will be those who will be critical of this decision but the vulnerable will appreciate it" [14].

Also, the apology rendered by the Minister of International Relations and Cooperation, on behalf of the Government and people of South Africa, was in line with the spirit if *ubuntu* which espouses the traditional communitarian values of African humanism and a harmonious society [3]. Thus, in line with putting a premium on cultivating amicable relationships as an essential precursor to doing business [2], the government's apology sought to appease those affected and their governments, to pave the way for continued good economic/business relationships. The strategy of communicating the business/economic consequences of the attacks on the South African economy fits very well with this line of thinking.

Xenophobia in South Africa: A Disconnect Between Perception and Reality?

Wilkinson points out that "with every outbreak of xenophobic violence in South Africa, the refrain is the same: "The *kwerekwere* [foreign nationals] are stealing our jobs." Yet when one looks at the facts, the situation is anything but what is perceived. The reasons why this perception exists are varied. First, is government rhetoric. As cited earlier, pronouncements by national leaders in the past have fueled tensions and set up a view/discourse of "us and them."

The second reason is economic. Each wave of xenophobic violence is preceded by or happens within the context of tough economic times. The 2008, attacks occurred at the height of the global financial crisis and before the April 2015 attacks, finance minister Nhlanhla Nene had stated in his budget speech earlier that the South African economy was again at a "crossroads" [1]. In a situation of difficult economic times, competition for jobs gets keener between poor blacks and African immigrants at the township level. Given that most African immigrants are likely to be better educated and more resourceful than the locals, the locals then resort to violence to try and get rid of the competition. Research about attitudes toward foreigners in Europe has identified that negative views about foreigners are higher among people who are socially and economically vulnerable and hold conservative political ideologies [24].

A third is what Gumede [1] calls a crisis of government and of politics. According to him, the country's existing party political system, its parties, and leaders are not responding to the needs of the majority of voters which is causing disillusionment among many of the citizens and a subsequent withdrawal from politics or refusal to vote. Although the ANC won 62% of the vote in the last election, it is believed to be losing its hold over black society and there is nothing to replace it yet [1]. Gumede argues that democratic institutions, such as parliament, are being perceived as failing poor black South Africans. The result, he says, is that, "people increasingly seek answers in populist, tribalist, ethnic and fundamentalist solutions." They look for scapegoats, whether "capitalists," "settlers," or "foreigners" [1]. In sum, South Africa in 2015 was facing two crises simultaneously: the government was not delivering effective public services to the poor, and the economy was in a slump with job losses in both the private and public sectors [1].

Fourth is media discourse. According to Nelson, Clawson, and Oxley [25], media exercise subtle influence on people's reasoning and attention about divisive issues. In

South Africa, the situation is not different and research shows that the media have been a source of unflattering reports about foreigners. In 2003, the South African Media Institute released a report on racism and xenophobia in the South African media published by Media Monitoring Africa (MMA). The report provided insights into stereotypes and positions present in South African media reporting on foreigners. It describes racism and xenophobia as supporting each other and sharing discriminatory discourses as they both operate on the same basis of profiling people and making negative assumptions [26]. In the case of racism, profiling is on the basis of race, while in the case of xenophobia it is done on the basis of nationality [26]. It is worth noting that the Zulu king Zwelithini had accused the media of misrepresenting what he said in his speech.

> It is unfortunate that we have to face this difficulty because of misreporting of what I said. There are many vile things that are being written in newspapers about me and you, the Zulu people ... I am saying to you, Zulu people, peace must be first and foremost. [10]

The King said he had written to the South African Human Rights Commission asking for it to examine the role of the media regarding violence against foreign nationals. The importance of the media's role in creating these perceptions is underlined by the fact that an interaction session on xenophobia was held between them and Members of Parliament (MPs) of various committees and ministers. At the close of the session, Small Business Development Committee chairwoman Ruth Bhengu, noted that

> The media... has a right to report on issues. The media has a responsibility to think about the possible consequences of the angle that they take when they report on issues. Before you become a reporter in the media, you are a South African. Before you focus on selling the news, you must think there are consequences. [27]

The Reality on the Ground

Professor Loren Landau, director of the African Centre for Migration and Society (ACMS) at Wits University, has observed that "The claim that 'foreigners' are taking jobs from South Africans is an argument that is always made," yet the true state of affairs, as borne out by statistics, paints a very different picture and shows that there is "a disconnect between perception and reality" [1]. According to a report issued by Migrating for Work Research Consortium (MiWORC), in 2014, 82% of the working population aged between 15 and 64 were "nonmigrants," 14% were "domestic migrants" who had moved between provinces in the past 5 years and only 4% could be classed as "international migrants" [1, 28]. A racial breakdown of the statistics reveals that 79% of international migrants were African, 17% were white, and around 3% were Indian or Asian. These findings show clearly that there were serious misconceptions about the size of the international migrant community in South Africa [1].

According to the research, migrants play a positive role in South Africa's economy, noting that international migrants are far more likely to run their own businesses. It found that 11% of migrants are "employers" and 21% are classed as "self-employed" [28]. By comparison, only 5% of nonmigrants and domestic migrants were employers, and only 9% of nonmigrants, and 7% of domestic migrants were self-employed. On the whole, the evidence shows that migrants make a major contribution to the South African economy by providing jobs, paying rent, paying VAT, and providing affordable and convenient goods [1].

Lessons Learned and Practical Suggestions

For those wanting to do business in South Africa and communicate during crisis times, there are a few lessons that can be learned that will also come in handy when dealing with future crisis.

Denial and/or Tardiness: Even though Coombs [29] suggests that denial is a valid crisis response strategy, it is not always appropriate. Particularly in situations where precious lives are lost, adopting a strategy of denial does not help resolve the crisis and only serves to alienate key stakeholders and aggravate the situation. In this particular case, the initial denial that the violence was xenophobic and the insistence that the attacks were isolated incidents only served to encourage the perpetrators and give fillip to a situation that was fast getting out of hand. An early and honest acknowledgement of the situation and its severity would have greatly aided the process of dealing with the crisis and enhanced success. As Benoit [30] rightly points out, an organization's success in dealing with a crisis is partly dependent on what it *says* (communication) after the crisis erupts. This means that in this particular situation, the right thing had to be said, and the right thing was not denial. In an African context that requires an authentic approach to the practice of public relations, denial in clear-cut situations like this is not helpful and that initial strategy, was costly; it caused a major dent in the image the South African government on the African continent and across the world [1].

In this particular case, the initial denial that the violence was xenophobic and the insistence that the attacks were isolated incidents only served to encourage the perpetrators and give fillip to a situation that was fast getting out of hand.

Language: South Africa has many languages, including 11 that are used officially. Thus, there are situations where information presented in one language will be translated into another or many other languages. This presents opportunities/risks for significant misinterpretations or for meanings to change or get lost in translation. In the case discussed here, the Zulu king Zwelithini, insisted that his words were misinterpreted and the government, through Police Minister Nathi Nhleko, supported that assertion. An Eye Witness News Report quoted Nhleko as saying

> If you're in the country illegally, effectively you need to be deported. That's essentially the long and short of what the king said. I then don't understand why the whole thing was turned around. [31]

In another case, President Jacob Zuma was reported to have allegedly criticized Christianity and suggested that it is responsible for orphans and old-age homes. The then-Presidential spokesperson Mac Maharaj defended Zuma, saying, "The president speaks in deep Zulu on occasion and his message is often lost in translation" [32]. In dealing with reporters and media in different languages, and especially in times of crisis it would be perhaps crucial to provide transcripts and get experts to verify that the translations are accurate. Also, if possible, in media relations engage the media using mainly the language that they will publish/broadcast in to avoid possible misinterpretations.

Violence: South Africa has a deeply violent past and an existing culture of violence. In such an environment, it does not take much for violence to erupt and so communicators need to be careful with their choice of words and exactly what they communicate in public, both in normal and in crises times.

Ubuntu: The spirit of *ubuntu* which prioritizes the building of harmonious social relations, makes a heartfelt apology an acceptable means of making amends when a person or an entity is in the wrong. Consequently, honestly acknowledging and facing up to one's mistakes is an acceptable strategy in dealing with crisis situations. In the wake of the xenophobic attacks, one South African commentator suggested that

> President Zuma must go to the victims, and be seen embracing them, apologising as a president for the sickening violence meted out against them. Zulu King Zwelithini must also publicly apologise and be seen to go to the affected African migrant communities. [1]

In this context, apology as a crisis communication/management strategy as suggested by Coombs' situational crisis communication theory [33], is acceptable.

Perception versus Reality: There is a huge disconnect between perception and reality when it comes to views about employment and particularly employment of foreigners. It is important for companies to take note of this in their activities and their communication and to do all in their power not to be seen as either directly or indirectly confirming the myth of the foreigner stealing the job of the local. Wherever and whenever companies can, activities and communication should portray and encourage an all-embracing culture that upholds the building and maintaining of harmonious relationships among all groups, just as public relations in the South African cultural context is supposed to do.

Tradition: The custodians of the nation's culture—the traditional leaders—are important and do wield some influence and so it is worthwhile to get them on one's side where necessary. They are important stakeholders in many issues and it is crucial to have open lines of communication with them if possible. Traditional leaders also present an opportunity to engage directly with communities at the Town Hall gathering level where assurances can be given, myths can be dispelled, and people can be influenced for good.

Conclusion

The wave of deadly xenophobic attacks against, particularly, foreigners of African descent, both shamed the South African government and presented it with an opportunity to address an issue that is fast becoming a problem of major concern. The problem of xenophobia smolders under the surface and occasionally manifests in a violent explosion that affects many and hardly benefits anyone [1]. In this instance, the government needed to act and act fast to end the violence, but its initial response was one of sluggishness—manifested in a denial discourse that only served to encourage the perpetrators and resulted in the spread of the violence to other cities. In terms of crisis communication, the initial nonacknowledgment amounts to a denial which was not the best strategy to adopt at the time.

Looking at the April 2015 attacks, one has to acknowledge that many of the lessons to be learned were actually lessons that should have been learnt earlier, given that this was not the first time such violence was occurring against foreigners. From the point of view of any keen observer, there were clear warning signs all over, yet the government seemed to have been caught unprepared. As one South African commentator observed

The previous wave of xenophobic attacks and the government's uninterested response was one of the factors that dislodged Thabo Mbeki. This current round of xenophobic violence, and likely negative effect on the fragile economy, our relations with other African countries, and the shame of our complicity, may be the harbinger of the beginning of the end of the Zuma presidency also. [1]

Given that the image of a burning African immigrant during the 2008 xenophobic attacks still haunts the collective consciousness of many South Africans and makes xenophobia a matter of critical concern [34,35], it is clear that what happened should have been on or near the top of the list of possible crisis events for the government, yet it seems that was not the case; one has to wonder why no one was prepared [36].

Discussion Questions

5.1 The initial denial that the violence constituted xenophobic attacks caused great concern among many African governments and resulted in a hastily arranged meeting with African ambassadors and high commissioners. Imagine that you are the communication director at the Ministry of International Relations and Cooperation; what are some of the key messages you would come up with for this specific meeting?

5.2 The perpetrators of the xenophobic violence represent a particular group of people, perhaps with a certain mindset. Develop a communication strategy with key messages that you would use to address these people both during and after the crisis. Apart from mass media channels, which other communication channels and/or methods would you use to get your messages across?

5.3 Imagine that you work in the Office of the South African President as Director of Communication, what would you have done in the first 24 hours after the attacks against foreigners broke? Identify and describe five tasks that you think are the most urgent and important.

5.4 Given the different stakeholders in the situation, both within and outside of South Africa, who do you think was the most important public? List five primary (internal) publics and three secondary (external) publics, and prioritize them. Explain why you believe they are the most important in your chosen order and develop key messages for each of these publics.

5.5 Given that the Zulu king was supposedly at the heart of this crisis, what communication strategies would you suggest should be used in dealing with him and his followers and what message(s) would you seek to pass on to them in the aftermath of the crisis to try and prevent any such thing from reoccurring?

References

1. W. Gumede. (2015, April 20). "South Africa must confront the roots of its xenophobic violence" [Online]. Available: http://www.theguardian.com/commentisfree/2015/apr/20/south-africa-xenophobic-violence-migrant-workers-apartheid, April 18, 2016 (last date accessed).

2. C. B. Pratt and W. Adamolekun, "The People's Republic of China and FAPRA: Catalysts for theory building in Africa's public relations," *Journal of Public Relations Research*, vol. 20, no. 1, pp. 20–48, 2008.

3. W. Visser, "Corporate social responsibility in developing countries," in *The Oxford Handbook of Corporate Social Responsibility*, A. Crane, A. McWilliams, D. Matten, J. Moon, and D. Siegel, Eds. Oxford: Oxford University Press, 2008, pp. 473–479.

4. G. Van Heerden, "The current status of the practice of public relations in Africa," unpublished Master's dissertation, Department of Marketing and Communication Management, University of Pretoria, South Africa, 2004.

5. C. Skinner and R. Rampersad, "A revision of communication strategies for effective disaster risk reduction: A case study of the South Durban basin, KwaZulu-Natal, South Africa," *Jàmbá: Journal of Disaster Risk Studies*, vol. 6, no.1, pp.1–10, 2014.

6. P. Reid and D. Van Niekerk, "A model for a multi-agency response management system (MARMS) for South Africa," *Disaster Prevention and Management*, vol. 17, no.2, pp. 244–255, 2008. [Online]. Available: http://dx.doi.org/10.1108/09653560810872541, March 25, 2016 (last date accessed).

7. South Africa. (2005), "The National Disaster Management Framework," Notice 27534 of 2005, Government Printer, Pretoria. [Online]. Available: http://www.gov.za/sites/www.gov.za/files/35427gen448_a.pdf, March 26, 2016 (last date accessed).

8. K. Wilkinson. (2015, April 20), "South Africa's xenophobic attacks: Are migrants really stealing jobs?" Africa Guardian Network. [Online]. Available at: http://www.theguardian.com/world/2015/apr/20/south-africa-xenophobic-violence-migrants-workforce, April 19, 2016 (last date accessed).

9. A. Egan, "Xenophobia in South Africa," *America*, vol. 212, no. 16, pp. 11–15, 2015.

10. D. Smith. (2015, April 21). "Zulu leader suggests media to blame for South Africa's xenophobic violence" [Online]. Available: http://www.theguardian.com/world/2015/apr/20/south-africa-xenophobic-violence-zulu-king-goodwill-zwelithini, April 19, 2016 (last date accessed).

11. D. Smith. (2015, April 19). "South Africa faces backlash over xenophobic attacks on migrant workers" [Online]. Available: http://www.theguardian.com/world/2015/apr/18/south-africa-migrant-workers-protests, April 19, 2016 (last date accessed).

12. Corruption Watch. (2015, June 11). "Civil society unhappy with government's xenophobia efforts," Corruption Watch.Org. [Online]. Available: http://www.corruptionwatch.org.za/civil-society-unhappy-with-govts-xenophobia-efforts/, March 24, 2016 (last date accessed).

13. M. Nkoana-Mashabane. (2015, April 19). "Xenophobia: We apologise to Africa - Maite Nkoana-Mashabane" [Online]. Available: http://www.politicsweb.co.za/politics/xenophobia-we-apologise-to-africa–maite-nkoanamas, April 25, 2016 (last date accessed).

14. Africa Guardian Network. (2015, April 22). "South Africa sends army to stop xenophobic attacks" [Online]. Available: http://www.theguardian.com/world/2015/apr/21/south-africa-deploys-army-xenophobic-attacks-foreigners, April 18, 2016 (last date accessed).

15. Business Teck. (2015, April 23). "Xenophobic attacks cost SA billions in revenue" [Online]. Available: http://businesstech.co.za/news/government/85822/xenophobic-attacks-cost-sa-billions-in-revenue/, April 25, 2016 (last date accessed).

16. S. Ebrahim. (2015, April 17). "SA apologises for xenophobia shame" [Online]. Available: http://www.iol.co.za/news/africa/sa-apologises-for-xenophobia-shame-1846914, April 22, 2016 (last date accessed).

17. Los Angeles Times. (2015, April 17). "Attacks on foreigners spread in South Africa; weekend violence feared" [Online]. Available: http://www.latimes.com/world/africa/la-fg-south-africa-foreigners-20150417-story.html, April 20, 2016 (last date accessed).

18. BBC News. (2015, April 19). "South African anti-immigrant violence: Hundreds held" [Online]. Available: http://www.bbc.com/news/world-africa-32372501, April, 20, 2016 (last date accessed).

19. T. Beauregar and J. Oatway. (2015, April 19). "The brutal death of Emmanuel Sithole" [Online]. Available: http://www.timeslive.co.za/local/2015/04/19/the-brutal-death-of-emmanuel-sithole1, April 20, 2016, (last date accessed).

20. S. Brent. (2015, April 21). "Xenophobic killing in South African township caught by photographer" [Online]. Available: http://edition.cnn.com/2015/04/20/africa/south-africa-xenophobia-killing-photos/, April 20, 2016 (last date accessed).

21. K. Dipa and G. Makhafola. (2015, April 21). "These are the four Sithole suspects" [Online]. Available: http://www.iol.co.za/news/crime-courts/these-are-the-four-sithole-suspects-1848086#.VTy8YiGqqko, April 20, 2016 (last date accessed).

22. E. Ferreira. (2015, April 28). "Sithole murder not xenophobic: Mahlobo" [Online]. Available: http://www.iol.co.za/news/crime-courts/sithole-murder-not-xenophobic-mahlobo-1851253#.VUIbM_mqqko, April 20, 2016 (last date accessed).

23. A. T. Nwaubani. (2015, May 7). "Xenophobic violence: South Africa's identity crisis" [Online]. Available: http://www.bbc.com/news/world-africa-32580807, April 20, 2016 (last date accessed).

24. M. Semyonov, R. Raijman, and A. Gorodzeisky, "Foreigners' impact on European societies," *International Journal of Comparative Sociology*, vol. 49, no.1, pp. 5–29, 2008.

25. T. Nelson, R. Clawson, and Z. Oxley, "Media framing of a civil liberties conflict and its effect on tolerance," *The American Political Science Review*, vol. 91, no.3, pp.567–583, 1997.

26. Media Monitoring Africa (MMA). (2015, April 21). "Xenophobia and the media" [Online]. Available: http://www.mediamonitoringafrica.org/index.php/news/entry/xenophobia_and_the_media/, March 27, 2016 (last date accessed).

27. M. Merten. (2015, April 29). "Xenophobia puts focus back on media" [Online]. Available: http://www.iol.co.za/news/crime-courts/xenophobia-puts-focus-back-on-media-1.1851940#.VhPZDZd3VdQ, April 22, 2016 (last date accessed).

28. Migrating for Work Research Consortium (MiWORC). (2014). "Migration and employment in South Africa: An econometric analysis of domestic and international migrants" [Online]. Available: http://www.miworc.org.za/docs/MiWORC-Report-6.pdf, April 19, 2016 (last date accessed)

29. W. T. Coombs, *Ongoing Crisis Communication: Planning, Managing, and Responding.* Thousand Oaks, CA: Sage, 2012.

30. W. L. Benoit, "Image repair discourse and crisis communication," *Public Relations Review*, vol. 23, no. 2, pp. 177–186, 1997.

31. L. Isaacs. (2015, April 16). "Hate speech charge laid against Zulu King" [Online]. Available: http://ewn.co.za/2015/04/16/Sandu-lays-a-charge-of-hate-speech-against-Zulu-King, April 22, 2016 (last date accessed).

32. Mail and Guardian. (2011, December 21). "Zuma's Christianity comments 'misinterpreted'" [Online]. Available: http://mg.co.za/article/2011-12-21-maharaj-zumas-christianity-comments-misinterpreted. April 22, 2016 (last date accessed).

33. W. T. Coombs. "Protecting organization reputations during a crisis: The development and application of situational crisis communication theory," *Corporate Reputation Review*, vol. 10, no. 3, pp. 163–176, 2007.

34. J. Crush, "The dark side of democracy: Migration, xenophobia and human rights in South Africa," *International Migration*, vol. 38, no. 6, pp. 103–133, 2001.

35. B. Dodson, "Locating xenophobia: Debate, discourse, and everyday experience in Cape Town, South Africa," *Africa Today*, vol. 56, no.3, pp. 2–22, 2010.

36. K. P. Stocker, "Strategic approach to crisis management," in *The Handbook of Strategic Public Relations and Integrated Communications*, C. L. Caywood, Ed. New York: McGraw Hill, 1997, pp. 189–203.

Asia/Euro-Asia

China and Taiwan

6

One Crisis, Two Responses: A Transboundary Analysis of the Melamine-Tainted Milk Powder Crisis in China and Taiwan

Yi-Hui Christine Huang and Joanne Chen Lyu

Chapter Preview

Most theories of crisis communication have been developed in western societies, yet many rapidly developing eastern societies are prone to crises from which we can draw valuable new lessons for both crisis response and scholarship. The melamine-tainted milk powder crisis was one of the most serious transregional crises of the twenty-first century in Greater China. This chapter illustrates the role played by traditional Chinese culture and various institutions, especially political and media systems, through a comparative analysis of the form and content of crisis communication strategies (CCSs) used to mitigate public anger over the contaminated milk powder. The ultimate aim of this chapter is to develop a holistic approach for examining crisis communication practice and its effects in the Chinese context. Additionally, this chapter motivates theory advancement by using a Chinese perspective to enhance the cultural and contextual sensitivity needed for crisis communication practitioners and policy makers in various Chinese regions.

Culture and Crisis Communication: Transboundary Cases from Nonwestern Perspectives, First Edition.
Edited by Amiso M. George and Kwamena Kwansah-Aidoo.
© 2017 by The Institute of Electrical and Electronics Engineers, Inc. Published 2017 by John Wiley & Sons, Inc.

After reading this chapter, you will be able to

- *Understand the role played by traditional Chinese culture in responding to crisis*
- *Perceive the role that other institutions, especially political and media systems play in the formulation of crisis response strategies on both China and Taiwan*
- *Appreciate the form and content of CCSs*
- *View the importance of developing a holistic approach to examining crisis communication practice and its effects in the Chinese context*
- *Recognize the importance of looking at cases from a comparative/transboundary perspective*
- *Appreciate the need for cultural and contextual sensitivity in crisis communication practice and policy making in various Chinese regions*

Background and Purpose

In 2011, food safety surpassed traffic safety, environmental safety, and general public safety as the chief public safety concern of Chinese people [1]. The years 2012 and 2013 also saw the food and beverage industry ranked by the Chinese public as "the least trusted industry" [2]. Public concern for food safety in China goes beyond hygiene to include the use of chemical fertilizers, pesticides, hormones, steroids, preservatives, flavor enhancers, and colorants [3]. The stakes are high; the Chinese public's distrust of the food industry has risen to levels that suggest a threat to the broader public trust in institutional competence.

In order to deeply understand crisis communication in a nonwestern context, it is necessary to revise the cultural and institutional assumptions adopted by the majority of current theories developed in western democratic societies.

Due to economic globalization, crisis events are seldom confined to one region. This chapter focuses on the melamine-tainted milk powder crisis, one of the most serious transregional crises of the twenty-first century in Greater China. We hold that in order to deeply understand crisis communication in a nonwestern context, it is necessary to revise the cultural and institutional assumptions adopted by the majority of current theories developed in western democratic societies. Exploring how companies from Mainland China and Taiwan dealt with the crisis in terms of the contextual factors (i.e., traditional culture and institutional factors) that influenced the crisis response will provide insight into the practice and effect of crisis communication in the Chinese context.

This chapter is based upon Lyu's [4] comparative study of the CCSs adopted by companies from Mainland China and Taiwan in the melamine-contaminated milk powder crisis. The chapter illustrates and theorizes the complex interrelations that exist among Chinese traditions and their various institutional contexts, especially their political and media contexts, and elaborates upon the contextual factors that influence CCSs in order to develop a holistic approach to the study of crisis communication in the Chinese context. More specifically, it seeks to do the following:

1. **Motivate theory advancement:** Most theories of crisis communication originated in western societies where organizations influence public opinion by building mass media agendas [5]. CCS does not develop under exactly similar conditions in China. Using a case study, this chapter explains how the various power relations among media, corporations, and the government influence Chinese crisis communication practice, providing another approach to understanding the diversity of crisis communication practices in nonwestern cultures.

2. **Enhance cultural and contextual sensitivity:** Cross-regional research enhances the understanding of differences in crisis communication between Mainland China and Taiwan. At the same time, recognizing a trend of cross-regional economic activity in Chinese societies will help enhance the cultural and contextual sensitivity of crisis-response practitioners working in various Chinese regions. This chapter therefore answers calls in existing scholarship for a more context-sensitive approach to crisis communication [6, 7].

3. **Provide practical crisis communication guidelines:** Practically, this project provides guidelines for crisis management and CCSs to makers of local public policy. This contributes to the development of more regionally specific CCSs in Chinese societies. Besides, this chapter also aims to benefit the individuals and organizations that want to do business in China or with the Chinese. A better understanding of Chinese crisis communication practices and the reasons behind the behavior may help to increase the communication effectiveness of their crisis handling in the Chinese context.

A Brief Background of Mainland China and Taiwan

Mainland China and Taiwan are living laboratories of crisis communication practice. Although they share a common cultural heritage, they are situated in different political, legal, and media systems.

Mainland China, commonly known as the People's Republic of China, has been administered by a single-party (i.e., Chinese Communist Party, CCP henceforth) authoritarian political system [8] since 1949. The ruling party in China is seemingly omnipotent, projecting supreme power toward its subjects, while Taiwan, commonly known as the Republic of China, is a democracy with several active political parties

[9]. Compared with Mainland China, the political landscape in Taiwan is diverse, and political debate is fierce.

Compared with Mainland China, the political landscape in Taiwan is diverse, and political debate is fierce. Together with this major difference in political systems, media ecology in the two places varies as well.

Together with this major difference in political systems, media ecology in the two places varies as well. Taiwan possesses a liberal media system [9]; under this system, media competition is intense, and media outlets are allowed to monitor or even criticize the government. In contrast, Mainland Chinese media are mouthpieces of the government and CCP. Although media reform in the 1990s provided Chinese media with more freedom than before, most Chinese media still operate under the principle of "regulated marketization," which means that media organizations have partial economic autonomy while still being required to obey party control [10].

Chinese Culture and Crisis Communication

Culture plays a strong role in shaping the decision-making function of organizations [11]. One previous study showed that Taiwanese care strongly about saving face and therefore tend to avoid high risk communication [12]. Moreover, Yu and Wen [12] hold that traditional assumptions, values, and norms of Chinese culture tend to be unsettled by crisis communication. In order to understand the practice of Chinese crisis communication, then, Chinese culture should not be ignored.

Traditional assumptions, values, and norms of Chinese culture tend to be unsettled by crisis communication.

Hofstede's [13] individualism–collectivism framework, which is widely used to compare western and eastern communication modes [14], takes China as paradigmatic of collectivist culture (see [15]). While individualistic cultures tend to employ low context communication, Chinese emphasize the context of a communication [16]. In Chinese communication, "most of the information is either in the physical context or internalized in the person, while very little is in the coded, explicit, transmitted part of the message" [17]. Huang, Lin, and Su [18] empirically supported this propensity for contextual communication among the Chinese. They conducted a survey of Taiwanese public relations and public affairs managers in order to examine actual crisis-handling experiences. Apart from the four CCSs that already existed in western theories, new strategies with cultural implications emerged from the data. That most important new category to emerge was "diversion," consisting of strategies that try to put the issue "to rest." Such strategies can include distraction of the public through creation of a different issue and easing public anger by showing regards (without apologizing). Huang, Lin, and Su [18] concluded that the contextual and indirect communication and the orientation toward the future characteristic of Chinese culture [19] may explain the Chinese emphasis on diversion.

Huang et al. [18] developed a comprehensive CCS typology with more Chinese characteristics, integrating Benoit and Brinson's [20] and Benoit's [21] strategy categorization, and including strategies such as expression of regard and building new agendas, which emerged from several case studies conducted in the Chinese context. The five main types of CCSs, plus substrategies and their definitions, are listed in Table 6.1.

Traditional Chinese culture not only influences the content of crisis communication (i.e., CCS) but also exerts impact on its form. Western scholarship prescribes a crisis response that is timely, consistent, and active [22]. Sillince [23] held that the unpredictable state of an event under crisis conditions requires a timely response. A timely response to a crisis can benefit the organization by fostering trust among stakeholders [24] and enhancing satisfaction across stakeholder groups [25]. Consistent responses helped increase credibility and accountability [26, 27] and further improve trust [22]. Similarly, active responses indicated that the organization cared about its stakeholders and was capable of controlling the situation. Inactivity or passivity is likely to create an indifferent and uncontrollable impression, as people tend to think organizations deliberately hide information [28]. Despite the positive effects mentioned, timely and active responses to crises face great obstacles in the Chinese society due to certain aspects of the deeply rooted traditional culture.

Traditional Chinese culture not only influences the content of crisis communication (i.e., CCS) but also exerts impact on its form.

For centuries, the dominant culture in Chinese societies was Confucian, a tradition that emphasizes hierarchical authority and justifies an unequal distribution of power and wealth. Authority, order, harmony, and the strict rules governing interpersonal relationships, all key concepts in the philosophy of Confucianism, help explain some of the nuances of communication practice and public relations in Chinese societies [9]. For traditional, devout Confucian Chinese, both the universe and human societies are hierarchically structured. Five classes of superior roles or stations exist in this worldview. They are, in descending order of authority, heaven, earth, the emperor, parents, and teachers. In fact, each of these serve the role of "father figure" to all of the orders or roles beneath it, compounding the flow of force and authority in a single direction and structuring inherently one-sided power relationships among people, as well as between people and their social and natural environments [29]. Respect for authority and the rigid order of authority lead to the mindset that, during crises, organizations should wait for commands from senior authorities and should not take action without authorization from the organizational power structure. The lower levels of organizational autonomy and proactivity produced by this mindset mean that

TABLE 6.1. Comprehensive Typology of Crisis Communication Strategies (CCSs) Developed by Huang, Lin, and Su, with More Chinese Characteristics.

CCS	Strategy Definition	Substrategy	Substrategy Definition
Denial	Statements that deny the occurrence or existence of the questionable event, or deny that the person is the cause of the event	Simple denial	Statements that deny the occurrence or existence of the questionable event, or deny that the person is the cause of the event
Excuse	Statements that argue that the accused person should not be held responsible for the occurrence and/or impact of the questionable event because certain factors limited the person's control over the occurrence and/or impact of the event. (Statement that attempts to evade responsibility for the offensive act)	Provocation	Statements that claim that the offensive act was a reasonable response to someone else's offensive act
		Defeasibility	Statements that claim that the actor did not have the knowledge, ability, or control to avoid committing the offensive act
		Good intentions	Statements that claim that the act was performed with good intentions
Justification	Statements that imply that, even though the accused person could be somewhat responsible for the questionable event, the standards being used by the accusers to evaluate the impact of the questionable event are inappropriate	Bolstering	Statements that emphasize a person's (or an organization's) former positive record or good deeds
		Minimization	Statements that suggest that the act in question is not as offensive as it seems
		Suffering	Statements that claim that the rhetor is a victim
		Attacking accuser	Statements that confront the person or groups who claim the accused caused the act or crisis
		Reframing	Statements that attempt to justify the act by reframing the facets within the same issue but in a larger and more favorable context

(Continued)

TABLE 6.1. (*Continued*)

CCS	Strategy Definition	Substrategy	Substrategy Definition
Concession	Statements that agree that the questionable event did occur or that the accused organization caused the event, apologized, and expressed the willingness for remediation, rectification, and proactive works, changed corporate policy, and provided adaptive and/or instructive information	Admission of fault/apology	Statements that agree that the questionable event did occur or that the accused person caused the event. Also, statements that the person apologizes, asks for forgiveness
		Compensation	Compensation offers the victim money, goods, or services to help mitigate the negative feelings toward the rhetor
		Corrective/ proactive works	Statements that involve a commitment to repair the damage from the offensive act and/or attempts to restore the state of affairs before the offensive act or preventing the recurrence of the offensive act or to prevent a repeat of the crisis
		Changing corporate public policy	Statements that involve a commitment to change an organization's corporate public policy
		Instructive information	Statements that instruct people how to react to a crisis in terms of actual behaviors
		Adaptive information	Statements that educate people on how to adapt to the occurrence in terms of psychological aspects

(*Continued*)

TABLE 6.1. (Continued)

CCS	Strategy Definition	Substrategy	Substrategy Definition
Diversion	Strategies that try to put the issue "to rest" or distract public or media attention by creating a different issue or temporarily easing public anger by showing regards (while not apologizing)	Showing regards/ sympathy	Statements that show regards and/or sympathy without apologizing. Statements that express feelings and regards, e.g., "I feel a pity that...."
		Building a new agenda	Statements that create a new issue in order to switch or distract the media focus or public attention
		Differentiating	Statements that attempt to distinguish the act from other similar but more offensive actions. In comparison, the act performed by the rhetor may not seem so bad

Source: Huang et al. 2005 [18]. Reproduced with permission of Springer.

the form of Chinese crisis communication rarely follows the prescriptions of western theories, especially those theories that call for timely and active CCSs.

Traditionally, the government in power is the most senior authority; however, as the political systems currently adopted by Mainland China and Taiwan differ, the relationship of governmental authority to the entire social power structure varies as well. The differentiation of the status of political authority influenced the forms of crisis communication taken by organizations in the two Chinese societies. We found that the two factors (i.e., traditional culture and institutional factors, especially political systems) twist together, revealing the specific characteristics of Chinese crisis communication. In the following section, we use the tainted milk powder crisis as a case study to illustrate this viewpoint.

Background to the Melamine-Tainted Milk Powder Crisis

In 2008, the melamie-tainted milk powder crisis, became the biggest food safety crisis that has ever happened in mainland China. On September 11, 2008, the *Oriental Morning Post* reported kidney stones and other medical problems arising in babies after they were fed Sanlu infant formula milk powder. Other media outlets reported more victims in the following days, and Sanlu milk powder soon became the focus of scrutiny across the country. In Taiwan, several major dairy producers were found to have imported creamer (a main ingredient of milk product) from the mainland, thereby contaminating their milk powder as well.

In the following section (case study), we examine the two leading dairy companies that suffered from the melamine crisis (Sanlu from Mainland China and KingCar® from Taiwan). This allows us to compare the similarities and differences of their CCSs. The influence of Chinese culture, politics, and media is analyzed as well.

Case Study

To represent how the melamine crisis developed, Wisenews was used to access news coverage about the situation and its corporate handling. Using the keywords "Sanlu" and "KingCar" for each region revealed the major actions taken by the two corporations. The types of CCS adopted by Sanlu and KingCar were identified according to Huang et al.'s [18] typology of CCS. More detailed information is available in Tables 6.2 and 6.3.

TABLE 6.2. Major Events in the Melamine-Tainted Milk Powder Crisis Tabulated Against the Crisis Communication Strategies (CCSs) Adopted by Sanlu.

Time, Year 2008	CCS	Major Actions
11 Sept	Denial	At 19:00, Cui Yanfeng, Director of Sanlu's media department, said, "We can assure the consumers that we don't have any problematic products at all" [30].
	Corrective action	On the night of Sept 11 (at 20:50), Sanlu released an announcement, recalling the Sanlu milk powder produced before August 6, 2008 [31].
12 Sept	Provocation	At 14:00, on the 12th, Sanlu said that it was the milk providers who added melamine to fresh milk, which led to nephrolith of infants [32].
	Bolstering	At 14:00, on the 12th, Sanlu also claimed that through self-inspection, the conclusion had been made as early as on August 1 that it was the milk providers who added melamine to fresh milk, which led to nephrolith of infants. At that time they instantly reported the results to related departments and announced a recall of the problematic infant milk powder through the Ministry of Health [32].
	Defeasibility	At 15:00, on the 12th, Su Changsheng, Director of the Brand Management Department of Sanlu, claimed that since the protein level in Sanlu's dairy products was measured through the quantity of azote, the milk providers added melamine to raise the azote level. Due to the lack of monitoring standards for melamine levels, Sanlu carried no special inspection of melamine [33].
15 Sept	Apology	Vice President of Sanlu bowed three times to apologize to the public, during the press conference held in Hebei, expressing their sincerest apology for the serious harms on the victim infants and their families [34].

Source: Lyu 2012 [4]. Reproduced with permission of Springer.

TABLE 6.3. Major Events in the Melamine-Tainted Milk Powder Crisis Tabulated Against the Crisis Communication Strategies (CCSs) Adopted by KingCar.

Time, Year 2008	CCS	Major Actions
21 Sept	Apology	KingCar held an emergency press conference. Li Yuding, the Deputy Manager, bowed and apologized to the public on behalf of KingCar Group, saying that "the inspection by the Food Industry Development Research Institute showed that some of our products using milk creamer imported from Chinese mainland do not meet health standards, which had caused worries among consumers. I sincerely apologize in the name of KingCar" [35].
	Compensation	If consumers have any concerns about the products, they can ask for an exchange or refund [36].
	Suffering	KingCar claimed that the problematic batch was produced between April 9 and September 12, 2008. The cost of manufacturing the tainted product and the expense of recall added up to a loss of at least 500,000,000 New Taiwan Dollars (approximately 166 million USD) [35].
	Corrective action	KingCar expressed that over 20,000 cases of three in one instant coffee have been recalled, and the new products will be introduced to the market with new packaging [37].
22 Sept	Minimization	KingCar claimed that the 120,000 cases of problematic products had been recalled to the factory in Taoyuanping County. No illnesses had been reported so far [38].
23 Sept	Attack accuser	Mainland Duqing Company, the milk creamer provider of KingCar, claimed no melamine was present in any of its products. In response, KingCar said that Duqing had admitted that some casein in the milk creamer was imported from Mainland China after April. KingCar believed that Duqing's claim was intended to confuse the public, and KingCar said that it might sue Duqing or ask for compensation [39].
28 Sept	Provocation	Li Yuding, Deputy Manager of KingCar, said to the press, "Though we are aware that it is the dealers from Mainland China who should be responsible, KingCar will accept its own responsibility by absorbing any damages without complaint..." [40].

Source: Lyu 2012 [4]. Reproduced with permission of Springer.

The two tables above demonstrate that companies from the two societies both used excuse, justification, and concession, with diversion being the chief strategy taken by KingCar and denial being used as the chief strategy by Sanlu. This echoed the findings of Huang, Wu, and Cheng's [41] study that a prominent crisis-response strategy in Mainland China is to deny the existence of the crisis by covering up. The tendency to cover up partly derives from the traditional face-saving mindset. More recently, covering up can be seen as resulting from the insistence of the central government in China that economic development and social stability are top national priorities [42]. This creates a larger incentive to cover up scandals.

A prominent crisis-response strategy in Mainland China is to deny the existence of the crisis by covering up. The tendency to cover up partly derives from the traditional face-saving mindset.

Though difference in CCSs exists, especially in substrategies, in general, Taiwanese and Chinese communication practitioners alike tend to express apology and take corrective action. Also observed was the fact that they incline toward reasoning or explaining in order to justify wrongdoing. The selection of these strategies may be influenced by the severity and nature of the crisis itself. When a crisis threatened or harmed public safety, corrective action, apology, and, if possible, explanation were the best ways of achieving understanding and forgiveness.

Responses to the Crisis

Besides the specific CCSs used, the difference in the form of crisis response between Sanlu and KingCar deserves more attention. According to western scholarship, crisis response should be timely, consistent, and active. In Sanlu's case, however, timely and active crisis response was not directed to a public that urgently needed information but to the political authorities in a proactive manner. As Sanlu claimed, the company knew its milk had been tainted in early August. But the company did not recall the problematic milk or release the information to the public. Instead, the company reported the situation to the government and waited for instructions on what to do. This behavior may be explained by the fact that Sanlu is partly state owned. With Sanlu being the pillar enterprise in the local province, it is also reasonable to infer that Sanlu expected some kind of protection from the government.

Given the holistic perspective that the Chinese tend to hold, it is also necessary to take the social context into consideration to understand Sanlu's crisis response. In August, when Sanlu claimed it discovered the contamination, China was hosting the Beijing Olympics. A traditional Chinese proverb states that "the ugly things in the family should not go public." Saving face, coupled with narrow obedience to the

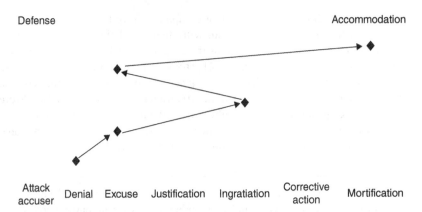

FIGURE 6.1. Graphic depiction of the Crisis Communication Strategies (CCSs) adopted by Sanlu. Sanlu's strategies started off with denial, provocation, bolstering, defeasibility, before ending up with an apology. Sanlu's first strategy was to deny the accusation leading to inconsistency in their crisis response. This diminished both the credibility of Sanlu's arguments and the public's trust. Overall, Sanlu's reaction to the crisis was typically passive. *Source*: Lyu 2012 [4]. Reproduced with permission of Springer.

national agenda, derived from the traditional collectivistic culture, intensified the tendency to cover up the crisis in its beginning phase. Being a totally private enterprise, KingCar demonstrated the more timely and active crisis response. The company held an emergency press conference to recall the product, briefing concerned citizens and the mass media.

Sanlu and KingCar also differed in the sequence of the CCSs they adopted. On September 11, 2008, China's Ministry of Health said that Sanlu infant milk powder might be tainted. Sanlu's strategies were denial, provocation, bolstering, defeasibility, and apology, taken in that order. According to CCS definitions in Coombs' [43] defense–accommodation continuum, the strategies adopted by Sanlu moved from defense to accommodation (see Figure 6.1). Contrary to Sanlu, KingCar's CCS moved from accommodation to defense (see Figure 6.2).

The sequence is illustrative of what the two corporations did in the same phase of the crisis. When the crisis was revealed by the media, Sanlu's first strategy was to deny the accusation and "assure the consumers that we don't have any problematic products at all" [30]. This denial also led to the inconsistency of the crisis response when examined from a longitudinal perspective, which diminished both the credibility of Sanlu's arguments and the public's trust. From the first to the last of its crisis responses, Sanlu demonstrated a typically passive reaction to the crisis. In contrast, KingCar began handling the crisis by accomodatively holding an

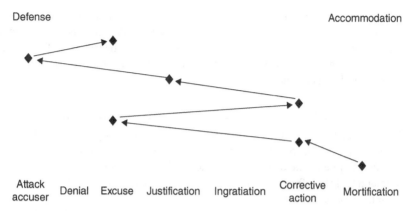

Defense   Accommodation

Attack accuser Denial Excuse Justification Ingratiation Corrective action Mortification

FIGURE 6.2. Graphic depiction of the Crisis Communication Strategies (CCSs) adopted by KingCar. KingCar's strategies moved from accommodation to defense in contrast to Sanlu. KingCar began handling the crisis by being proactive and holding an emergency media conference. This was viewed by the public as taking ownership of and responsibility for the crisis, with the company's performance being praised by the media and recognized by the public. *Source*: Lyu 2012 [4]. Reproduced with permission of Springer.

emergency conference. Compared with Sanlu's passivity, KingCar's reaction was proactive and viewed by the public as taking ownership of responsibility for the crisis. KingCar's performance during the crisis was praised by the media and recognized by the public.

Power Relations that Influence the Practice of Crisis Communication

As mentioned, Confucian traditions dominate Chinese culture. Confucianism emphasizes the order of authority. In the past half-century, Mainland China and Taiwan developed separately under distinct political systems. Different institutions determined each society's hierarchies of authority. In Mainland China, the top of the power structure is occupied by the CCP. In contrast, as a democratic society, Taiwan's government is not that omnipotent and is monitored by the media. Different relationships among government, media, and corporation lead to the difference in handling corporate crisis between Mainland China and Taiwan. In spite of the difference, Chinese crisis communication, either in Mainland China or Taiwan, reflects the respect for authority, which is inherent in the Confucian culture.

The government in Mainland China has the power to not only control the media, but also to interfere with the operation of corporations. Less autonomy and more dependence on the government led to Sanlu's lagging responses. There was almost no action or active response from Sanlu apart from its initial denials. The public had to rely on mass media and the government rather than Sanlu for instructive information, even though conventionally the involved companies should bear the responsibility of informing the public about how to react to crises.

Different relationships among government, media, and corporation lead to the difference in handling corporate crisis between Mainland China and Taiwan. In spite of the difference, Chinese crisis communication, either in Mainland China or Taiwan, reflects the respect for authority, which is inherent in the Confucian culture.

In Taiwan, the media are empowered to monitor government behavior, but in Mainland China, the government and mass media are in a highly asymmetrical relationship [44]. Specifically, media organizations must stand ideologically on the same side as the government and the Party; otherwise, they are deprived of the right to survive [45]. This imbalanced power relationship between media and government helps explain why there was no negative voice criticizing the government's slow reaction to Sanlu's report. According to Sanlu's statement as below, they had known that some of their milk powder contained melamine as early as August 1 2008. Upon learning this, they instantly reported it to relevant government departments and announced the recall of the problematic product through the Ministry of Health. Once the contamination was revealed, all media critique pointed to the Sanlu Group, criticizing it for late responses and covering-up. However, if the Sanlu Group had told the truth, the government would have had a compelling obligation to deal with the incidents immediately, which in fact did not happen. No media outlets challenged the government's dereliction of duty at that time. Conversely, the media praised the authority for its quick response after the incident was widely known by the public.

The Health Ministry, the General Administration of Quality Supervision, Inspection, and Quarantine of the PRC (AQSIQ), and the State Administration for Industry and Commerce of the PRC have taken emergency actions to investigate the incident and have strengthened inspections of infant milk powder in the market. The incident has also been reported to the WHO and other impacted countries. These all represent a responsible attitude towards public health. [46]

The relationship among government, media, and corporations in Taiwan is different from that in Mainland China. The government seldom directly interferes with corporations. When corporations face crises in Taiwan, the government tends to give them implicit support rather than direct them or take charge of the situation. For example,

> Jin Chuan, director of Taiwan's Department of Health, said that "it will be decided by KingCar. If KingCar requires, the Department of Health will ask for compensation from the Association for Relations Across the Taiwan Strait." [47]

Therefore, compared with Sanlu, KingCar enjoyed more autonomy in dealing with the crisis and behaved more actively and flexibly. Without waiting for orders from the authorities or reporting to government officials before responding to the crisis, KingCar took action immediately when company officials knew some of their products did not meet public health standards.

Furthermore, Taiwanese media are more independent than their Chinese counterparts. They play a role in monitoring both the government and corporations. The liberal media system grants the media in Taiwan the right to challenge or even criticize the government. While media outlets in Mainland China often function as government mouthpieces, Taiwanese media seem to stand independently and voice objective public concerns over the abuses and oversights committed by authority figures. After September 23 2008, the media began praising KingCar's responsible behavior as an example not only for other corporations to follow but also as an example for the government to emulate. KingCar's active response was also compared favorably to the government's incompetence in responding to the crisis, questioning the government's inefficiency and obliviousness, which almost turned the fiasco into a government crisis.

In short, traditional Chinese culture, in conjunction with the power relationships that exist among government, media, and corporations (see Figures 6.3 and 6.4),

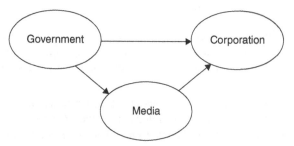

FIGURE 6.3. Relationships among government, media, and corporations in Taiwan. In Taiwan (the government) seldom directly interferes with corporations or the media. Taiwanese media are more independent and play a role in monitoring both the government and corporations. The Taiwanese government tends to give corporations implicit support when they face crises rather than direct them or take charge of the situation.

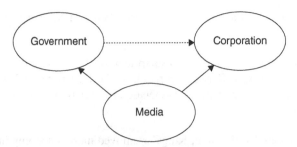

FIGURE 6.4. Relationships among government, media, and corporations in Mainland China. Media outlets in Mainland China lack independence and autonomy and often function as government mouthpieces. Corporations also tend to be tightly controlled by the government, which means that during times of crisis, they tend to wait for the government to take the lead or to direct them in how to respond to the crisis, making it impossible to be proactive.

helps explain why companies from Mainland China and Taiwan adopted different ways of dealing with the melamine crisis in terms of CCS selection and the specific form of crisis response. Confucianism, the dominant philosophy underpinning Chinese culture, advocates respect for authority. The different positions of government and corporations, relative to one another, in each of the two Chinese societies, helped determine which CCSs were selected as well as how proactive and timely crisis responses were.

Practical Implications

The practical implications of this study are twofold.

- First, it is important to take into consideration both traditional Chinese culture and modern institutional systems when analyzing Chinese crisis communication. Culture and institutions interactively influence the content and form of Chinese crisis response.
- Second, when western scholars talk about the Chinese, they tend to take them as a whole; however, as demonstrated in this study, Chinese living and working within different institutional contexts are likely to respond to crises in different ways.

Thus, on the one hand, this study confirms the critical role of culture in crisis communication; on the other hand, it highlights other important factors (i.e., media and political system in this study) for understanding the practice and effects of crisis communication within a specific cultural context.

Discussion Questions

6.1 Chinese communication is featured with high context communication. How do you think this style of communication may influence the effectiveness of crisis communication? Is there any other CCSs you identified from the Chinese crisis communication practice, in addition to the substrategies included in diversion?

6.2 This chapter demonstrated the different ways companies from Mainland China and Taiwan dealt with crises. Besides cultural and institutional factors, how do you think the nature of the crisis, such as severity of crisis, crisis type, and scope of influenced area, etc. may influence the Chinese crisis handling?

6.3 Given the traditional culture, political, and media systems in Mainland China and Taiwan, how can foreign companies survive well from crises in the two Chinese societies? What is the similarity and difference in the effective ways?

6.4 What do you think will be the impact of new media, one of the characteristics of which is instant information dissemination, on the form of crisis response in Mainland China (i.e., inactive and untimely response in this case)? Do you think the new media have the potential to change the way how the Chinese deal with crises?

Acknowledgment

We developed this book chapter based on Lyu [4]. Case materials and relevant arguments were adopted and rewritten accordingly.

References

1. H. Ouyang, "Five top safety issues of Chinese in 2011," *Insight China*, vol. 7, pp. 50–54, 2011.
2. Edelman (2014, September 3). "Edelman trust barometer 2013 annual global study- China findings" [Online]. Available: http://www.slideshare.net/DJECHINA/2013-edelmantrustbarometerchinadecken?related=1, May 19, 2017 (last date accessed).
3. Y. Yan, "Food safety and social risk in contemporary China," *The Journal of Asian Studies*, vol. 71, no. 3, pp. 705–729, 2012.
4. J. C. Lyu, "A comparative study of crisis communication strategies in Mainland China and Taiwan: The melamine-tainted milk powder crisis in the Chinese context," *Public Relations Review*, vol. 38, no. 5, pp. 779–791, 2012.
5. B. K. Berger, "Power over, power with, and power to relations: Critical reflections on public relations, the dominant coalition, and activism," *Journal of Public Relations Research*, vol. 17, no.1, pp. 5–28, 2005.

6. Y. Choi and G. T. Cameron, "Overcoming ethnocentrism: The role of identity in the contingent practice of international public relations," *Journal of Public Relations Research*, vol. 17, no.2, pp. 171–189, 2005.

7. K. G. Corley, C. V. Harquail, M. G. Pratt, et al., "Guiding organizational identity through aged adolescence," *Journal of Management Inquiry*, vol. 15, pp. 85–99, 2006.

8. C. J. F. Hung and Y. R. Chen, "Public relations in China in the era of change," in *Public Relations in Asia: An Anthology*, K. Sriramesh, Ed. Singapore: Thomson Learning, 2004, pp. 29–62.

9. B. Sha and Y. H. Huang, "Public relations on Taiwan: Evolving with the infrastructure," in *Public Relations in Asia: An Anthology*, K. Sriramesh, Ed. Singapore: Thomson Learning, 2004, pp.161–185.

10. Y. Z. Zhao, "From commercialization to conglomeration: The transformation of the Chinese press within the orbit of the Party State," *Journal of Communication*, vol. 50, no. 2, pp. 3–26, 2000.

11. G. L. Pepper, *Communicating in Organizations: Cultural Approach*. New York: McGraw-Hill, 1995.

12. T. Yu and W. Wen, "Crisis communication in Chinese culture: A case study in Taiwan," *Asian Journal of Communication*, vol. 13, no. 2, pp. 50–64, 2003.

13. G. Hofstede, *Culture's Consequences: International Differences in Work-Related Values*. Newbury Park, CA: Sage, 1980.

14. D. Oyserman, M. H. Coon, and M. Kemmelmeier, "Rethinking individualism and collectivism: Evaluation of theoretical assumptions and meta-analysis," *Psychological Bulletin*, vol. 128, pp. 3–72, 2002.

15. M. H. Bond, *Beyond the Chinese Face*. New York: Oxford University Press, 1991.

16. W. B. Gudykunst and S. Ting-Toomey, *Culture and Interpersonal Communication*. Newbury Park, CA: Sage, 1988.

17. E. T. Hall, *Beyond Culture*, New York: Doubleday, 1976.

18. Y. H. Huang, Y. H. Lin, and S. H. Su, "Crisis communicative strategies in Taiwan: Category, continuum, and cultural implication," *Public Relations Review*, vol. 31, pp. 229–238, 2005.

19. G. Gao and S. Ting-Toomey, *Communicating Effectively with the Chinese*. Thousand Oaks, CA: Sage, 1998.

20. W. L. Benoit and S. L. Brinson, "AT&T: Apologies are not enough," *Communication Quarterly*, vol. 42, pp. 75–88, 1994.

21. W. L. Benoit, "Image repair discourse and crisis communication," *Public Relations Review*, vol. 23, no. 2, pp. 177–186, 1997.

22. Y. H. Huang, "Trust and relational commitment in corporate crises: The effects of crisis communicative strategy and form of crisis response," *Journal of Public Relations Research*, vol. 20, pp. 297–327, 2008.

23. J. A. A. Sillince, "A model of the strength and appropriateness of argumentation in organizational contexts," *Journal of Management Studies*, vol. 39, pp. 585–618, 2002.

24. C. Moorman, R. Deshpande, and G. Zaltman, "Factors affecting trust in market research relationships," *Journal of Marketing*, vol. 57, pp. 81–101, 1993.

25. K. C. Strong, R. C. Ringer, and S. A. Taylor, "The rules of stakeholder satisfaction (timelines, honesty, empathy)," *Journal of Business Ethics*, vol. 32, no. 3, pp. 219–230, 2001.

26. L. Barton, *Crisis in Organizations: Managing and Communicating in the Heat of Chaos.* Cincinnati, OH: South-Western, 1993.

27. A. P. Garvin and R. I. Berkman, *The Art of Being Well Informed.* Garden City Park, NY: Avery, 1996.

28. J. E. Grunig, "Communication, public relations, and effective organizations: An overview of the book," in *Excellence in Public Relations and Communication Management*, J. E. Grunig, Ed. Hillsdale, NJ: Lawrence Erlbaum Associates, Inc., 1992, pp.1–30.

29. C. Y. Shih, "National role conception as foreign policy motivation: The psychocultural bases of Chinese diplomacy," *Political Psychology*, vol. 9, no. 4, pp. 599–631, 1988.

30. "Sanlu recalls 700 tons of problematic milk powder," *Southern Metropolis Daily*, September 12, 2008.

31. "The number of 'nephrolith infants' is increasing: One baby died," *Oriental Morning Post*, September 12, 2008.

32. "Sanlu replied to its consumers: Self-inspection found the problem sources," *Southern Metropolis Daily*, September 13, 2008.

33. "Sanlu claimed the milk provider adulterated melamine into fresh milk," (2008, September 12) [Online]. Available: http://news.sina.com.cn/c/2008-09-12/152216281741.shtml, October 3, 2016 (last date accessed).

34. "Vice president of Sanlu bowed to apologizing three times," *Beijing Evening News*, September 13, 2008.

35. Z. Ye and X. Hu, "Coffee powder was found problematic, KingCar apologized, and 1.2 million boxes were recalled," *China Times*, September 22, 2008.

36. Y. Yang, Z. Luo, R. Li, et al., "KingCar recalled 21.6 million packages of brewing beverage products," *Liberty Times*, September 22, 2008.

37. Y. Yang, "KingCar three in one coffee is introduced to the market with new packaging," *Liberty Times*, September 23, 2008.

38. Z. Ye, "KingCar recalled 75%, new products enter into markets today," *China Times*, September 23, 2008.

39. D. Chen, "Duqing denied responsibility, KingCar said it obscured the issue," *United Daily News*, September 24, 2008.

40. J. Pan and H. Wu, "KingCar stops losing profit quickly after the melamine milk powder crisis," *Apple Daily*, September 29, 2008.

41. Y. H. Huang, F. Wu, and Y. Cheng, "Crisis Communication in Context: Cultural influence and institutional impact underpinning Chinese public relations practice," presented at Association for Education in Journalism and Mass Communication 2014 Annual Conference, Montréal, Canada, August, 2014.

42. Y. Huang and C. C. M. Leung, "Western-led press coverage of Mainland China and Vietnam during the SARS crisis: Reassessing the concept of 'media representation of the other,'" *Asian Journal of Communication*, vol. 15, no. 3, pp. 302–318, 2005.

43. W. T. Coombs, "An analytic framework for crisis situations: Better responses from a better understanding of situation," *Journal of Public Relations Research*, vol. 10, no. 3, pp. 177–191, 1998.

44. C. C. Lee, Z. He, and Y. Huang, "Party-market corporatism, clientelism, and media in Shanghai," *The Harvard International Journal of Press/Politics*, vol. 12, no. 3, pp. 21–42, 2007.

45. Z. Pan, "Improvising reform activities: Interpreting China's journalism reforms," in *Power, Money, and Media: Communication Patterns in Cultural China*, C.C. Lee, Ed. Evanston: Northwestern University Press, 2000, pp. 68–111.

46. B. Chen, "Baby kidney stone incident must be thoroughly investigated," *Beijing News*, September 12, 2008.

47. S. D. Lee, "Toxic baby formulas seeking compensation in Mainland China, government to assist," *United Daily News*, October 17, 2008.

India

7

They Came by Boat: The 2008 Terrorist Attack on Mumbai

Soumitro Sen and Uttaran Dutta

Chapter Preview

How did the Indian government respond to the terrorist attacks that took place in November 2008 in Mumbai? This crisis had a transnational impact as it affected not only the immediate citizens of Mumbai, but also foreign nationals who were at certain venues of the attacks, including business houses, public places, a hospital, and a Jewish center that were targeted during the period of a few days. The unprecedented continuous live coverage of the crisis on mainstream television channels coupled with pressure from international and local stakeholders—among numerous other social factors—prevented the Indian government from taking prompt action which, in turn, exacerbated the crisis.

After reading the chapter, you will be able to

- *Understand the role of culture in handling of crises situations*

Culture and Crisis Communication: Transboundary Cases from Nonwestern Perspectives, First Edition.
Edited by Amiso M. George and Kwamena Kwansah-Aidoo.
© 2017 by The Institute of Electrical and Electronics Engineers, Inc. Published 2017 by John Wiley & Sons, Inc.

- *Learn about a case of transnational terrorism, its scope, and how a government entity responded to it amid myriad national and international constraints*
- *Identify the strengths and weaknesses of the response of the Indian government to the crisis*
- *View the role of traditional and social media within the matrix of a crisis situation and their impact on crisis response*
- *Know that crisis communication is not a linear or a simple process, but rather multilayered, and influenced by numerous sociocultural factors, which need to be taken into account while planning any crisis response*

Background: India and Its Immediate Neighbor, Pakistan

The geopolitical landscape of Southeast Asia is dominated in particular by the presence of two—out of Asia's three—nuclear powers, who also are neighbors—and rivals. Carved out of what was once British-ruled India, mainly on the basis of religion (Pakistan and East Pakistan had a Muslim majority, while India remained a secular state with a Hindu majority), the two nation-states, since their genesis in 1947, have clashed on issues of boundaries, religious problems, and most important on the controversy surrounding the North Indian region of Kashmir, which Pakistan lays claim to. Incorporating Kashmir—with its Muslim majority—within its boundaries "is a basic national aspiration [of Pakistan] bound up in its identity as an Islamic state" [1]. For India, having Kashmir as a part of it is "vital to its identity as a secular, multiethnic state" [1].

Since the 1980s, militancy in Kashmir has been a particular source of discord between India and Pakistan [1]. According to the Council on Foreign Affairs, the three major terrorist groups active in Kashmir include Harakat ul-Mujahideen, which was held responsible for hijacking an Indian airliner in December 1999; Jaish-e-Mohammed, a group blamed for attacking the Indian Parliament in 2001; and Lashkar-e-Taiba, the group that was pointed out as having carried out the bombings on Mumbai's trains in July 2006 as well as the Mumbai attacks in 2008.

The Mumbai attacks were unique for a number of reasons: (i) collectively, as a coordinated act of terrorism, it caused a transnational crisis, claiming not only Indians but also people of various nationalities who were especially targeted in the attacks [2]; (ii) the attacks were perpetrated on multiple high profile, elite locations in Mumbai, including two renowned five-star hotels; (iii) the attacks unfolded live on television over a number of days; (iv) the attacks were carried out by terrorists under the close guidance of handlers in Pakistan who were "monitoring the situation in Mumbai through live media, and delivered specific and situational attack commands through satellite phones" [2] to the attackers; and (v) social media—especially Twitter—were leveraged by the public to share information about the attacks as the events were unfolding. These twitter feeds in turn were providing information to the mainstream global media.

However, before we delve into the specifics of the 2008 Mumbai attacks, we first want to discuss how the culture of India influences the way the country usually responds to crisis situations in general.

Culture and Crisis Communication

Although public relations firms in India today offer crisis communication services for clients, there is limited scholarly literature on crisis communication research or practice in India. Also, within the larger purview of crisis communication research, there is a dearth of scholarship that assesses the role of culture in crisis communication practice. The closest reference one can draw is from international public relations [3] which posits that the culture of a country indeed plays a role in its public relations practice, through their examination of public relations in India, Japan, and South Korea. Given the close relationship between crisis communication and public relations—both of which deal with the communication processes between an organization and its stakeholders albeit under different circumstances—it might be worthwhile to discuss how culture then plays a role in the way a country responds to crises in general. But analyzing the history of crises response in a country of such great antiquity as India would itself demand a chapter, if not an entire book. We therefore touch upon certain cultural values that are embedded within the Indian psyche that might play a role in the way in which the country handles crises.

In an interview recorded around 1971, prior to India's military conflict with Pakistan, then-prime minister of India, Mrs. Indira Gandhi, was asked by a television journalist if India might attack Pakistan in light of the political turmoil that was unfolding then in East Pakistan (former name of Bangladesh). Mrs. Gandhi replied: "I hope not. India has always tried to be on the side of peace and negotiations and so on. But of course we can't endanger our security in any way" [4].

Indians are generally patient people, broad-minded with a high threshold for accepting the unexpected; but at the same time, they display a preference for a more long-term, pragmatic culture.

One might argue that Prime Minister Indira Gandhi's response encapsulates the Indian approach to conflict in general, which is typified by tolerance tempered with caution. According to the Hofstede Center, "India is traditionally a patient country where tolerance for the unexpected is high ... People generally do not feel driven and compelled to take action-initiatives and comfortably settle into established roles and routines without questioning" [5].

To put it simply, as most tourists from western countries visiting India would notice early in their sojourn, Indians are generally easy-going people who live life at a more relaxed pace than the people, say, in the United States, do. Scoring high on "long-term orientation"—one of the six dimensions of national culture as enunciated by Hofstede [6]—Indian society displays a preference for a more long-term, pragmatic culture [5]. "Societies that have a high score on pragmatism typically forgive lack of punctuality, a changing game-plan based on changing reality, and a general comfort with discovering the fated path as one goes along rather than playing to an exact plan" [5]. This relaxed perspective on life is perhaps why response to a crisis situation in India often takes longer than it would elsewhere. For example, "during the first hours of the [2008 Mumbai terrorist] attack the police forces were in a state of confusion ... Nobody knew what was going on, or what to make of the fragments of information they were receiving" [7].

Given the numerous occasions when Mumbai had experienced bombings in the past, one would expect that law enforcement would have been better prepared for a crisis arising from a terrorist attack.

Given the numerous occasions when Mumbai had experienced bombings in the past (we will discuss these in greater detail in the next section), one would expect that law enforcement would have been better prepared for a crisis arising from a terrorist attack. But when two terrorists, Ismail Khan and Ajmal Amir Kasab, entered Chhatrapati Shivaji Terminus at about 9:20 p.m. on November 26 and started firing and throwing grenades into the crowds of passengers, "poorly equipped and ill-prepared police and security guards could do little other than hide behind the columns" [7]. We also know that commandos at the Oberoi Hotel—one of the five-star hotels which was attacked—were able to kill two assailants at that venue after 42 hours of siege [7]. At yet another venue of attack, Khan and Kasab—who had first massacred victims at the railway station—encountered a police vehicle and were able to kill six out of the seven policemen in the police jeep [7]. All of the above pieces of information indicate that security personnel and law enforcement agencies were not prepared well enough for a terrorist attack. This lack of alertness and preparedness for action is symptomatic of the relaxed approach to life in India, which we mentioned earlier.

In the next section, we provide an overview of the attacks and also situate them within the matrix of past terrorist attacks in Mumbai as well as terrorist attacks that had taken place in other Indian cities in 2008, before the Mumbai attack. In addition, we discuss (in subsequent sections), how India—here the main entity against whom the acts of terror were precipitated—responded to the crisis, the cultural influences on the response, the outcome, and the lessons learned from the case.

Case Study: 2008 Mumbai Terrorist Attacks

On November 23, 2008, a group of 10 Pakistani young men left the port metropolis of Karachi by boat, sailing southeast for Mumbai, the commercial capital of India on the Arabian Sea coast [8]. En route, they hijacked a fishing trawler, killing its captain and crew, and finally reached Mumbai on November 26 [8]. Once on shore, they broke up into five pairs [7] and unleashed terrorist attacks using machine guns and grenades on seven locations around Mumbai [8], killing approximately 173 people and injuring 293 [9] over the next 3 days. The locations were some of the busiest in the city of around 21 million residents [10]—including the Chhatrapati Shivaji Terminus railway station—as well as some of the most elite, such as the iconic Taj Mahal Palace and Tower Hotel overlooking the touristy Gateway of India and the Oberoi Trident Hotel, located at Nariman Point, Mumbai's central business district. Terrorist attacks also took place at the Leopold Café—a destination especially popular among international tourists, the Metro Cinema, the Cama and Albless Hospital, and Nariman House, also known as Chabad House, which was a guest house purchased by an orthodox Jewish organization called Chabad Liberation Movement of Hasidic Jews [7].

This, however, was not the first time terrorist attacks had been carried out in Mumbai by Islamic extremist groups. Twelve bomb attacks had taken place in and around Mumbai between 1993 and 2008, claiming 544 lives and injuring 1774 [11]. Some of the more prominent ones on the list—especially in terms of the number of casualties—included seven explosions which took place on July 11, 2006, within a period of 15 minutes on various commuter trains in Mumbai's suburban railway system—one of the busiest in the world—during evening rush hour [12]. The attacks killed nearly 200 people and injured 900, according to the National Counterterrorism Center in Washington DC. In September 2015, after an 8-year-long trial, 12 men were found guilty for their roles in the bombings [12]. Lashkar-e-Taiba, an Islamic militant group backed by Pakistan, was blamed for the attack, although Pakistan denied the allegation [12].

Earlier, on August 25, 2003, two bombs planted in taxis killed at least 44 people and injured nearly 150 [13]. Incidentally, one of the blasts took place near the Gateway of India, as one of the taxis was parked outside the Taj Mahal Hotel—the most prominent location of the 2008 attacks [13]. Two men and a woman—all of whom were members of Lashkar-e-Taiba—were sentenced to death by an Indian court in August 2009 because of their roles in the bombings [14].

The highest number of casualties, however, occurred in the terrorist attacks which rocked Mumbai on March 12, 1993 [11]. This time, Islamic terrorists detonated devices at 13 different locations around the city killing 257 people and injuring 700 [11]. One of the masterminds behind the attacks was Dawood Ibrahim, a well-known organized crime leader [11], who, India suspects, lives in Karachi [15] and is still at large. India convicted 100 of 123 suspects for their roles in the attacks [16]. Yakub Memon, one of the key players in the attacks, was hanged in July 2015 [16].

While the above incidents recall the deadliest attacks that have taken place in Mumbai since the early 1990s, it is also worth noting that in 2008 itself, prior to the Mumbai attacks in November, terrorist bombings by Islamic extremists groups had taken place in other Indian cities. On May 13, 2008, six blasts ripped through the city of Jaipur, a popular tourist destination in the western state of Rajasthan, killing more than 60 people [17]. Later, on July 25, 2008, seven explosions killed two individuals in Bengaluru in Southern India [17]. The following day, July 26, a total of 21 bomb blasts within a period of 70 minutes killed 56 and wounded 200 people in Ahmedabad in Western India [17]. Indian Mujahideen, a terrorist group, claimed responsibility for the May attacks in Jaipur and the July bombings in Ahmedabad [17].

What, however, set apart the Mumbai attacks in November 2008 from the others in the past, was the vast number of foreigners who were among the casualties—which in turn drew the attention of the international media to the attacks. The other important factor was how the attacks unfolded on live mainstream television over 3 days, and also how ordinary citizens used smartphones and social media "to post a constant stream of information to websites that were accessed by people locally and around the globe [18]. Thus, it has been claimed that for the first key hours of the attacks, Flickr rather than the New York Times or BBC World had more detailed and relevant information" [18]. While bloggers reported "first-hand information from e-mail, tweets and uploaded photos posted by people who were close to the attacks, Twitter updates fed a steady stream of live coverage of events as they occurred on the scene" [18].

At the end of the 3-day mayhem that had turned the entire city of Mumbai into "an undifferentiated 'enemy space' in which nobody could feel safe," [7] all but one of the terrorists had been killed. Ajmal Kasab, a 21-year-old terrorist, was arrested and later sentenced to death. He was hanged on November 21, 2012 in Pune, India, after his plea for clemency was rejected by the Indian President Pranab Mukherjee.

The 2008 Mumbai attack, therefore, was a terrorist-created crisis like India had never faced before. It unfolded over 3 days at multiple locations in India's financial capital, in full view of the world media, and it impacted people from multiple nations. According to Raman [2], the terrorists targeted the specific locations to fulfill a three-pronged political agenda, which was anti-India, anti-Israel and anti-Jewish, and anti-US and anti-NATO.

The 2008 Mumbai attack was a terrorist-created crisis like India had never faced before. It unfolded over 3 days at multiple locations in India's financial capital, in full view of the world media, and it impacted people from multiple nations.

The anti-India agenda was accomplished by targeting busy public places such as the Chhatrapati Shivaji railway station as well as the Taj and Oberoi Trident hotels and the Leopold Cafe, which are frequented by international visitors, whose faith in the security of life and property in India would be shaken [2]. The anti-Israel and anti-Jewish agenda was served by attacking Nariman House, a Jewish center [2]. The anti-US and anti-NATO agenda was served as terrorists particularly targeted foreigners—12 out of the 25 killed—from countries which had contributed troops to the NATO in Afghanistan [2].

In the subsequent sections, we discuss the stakeholders who were impacted in the attacks as well as examine the strategies and tactics adopted by some of those stakeholders as response to the crisis.

Stakeholders

This unprecedented terrorist-initiated crisis impacted numerous stakeholders including the common citizens of Mumbai (of various religions, age groups, socioeconomic classes, and castes), foreigners (tourists, business executives, and religious personnel) at the venues of attacks, the business houses which were targeted (the Taj Mahal Palace and Tower Hotel, Oberoi Trident Hotel, and Leopold Cafe), the Indian nation state as a whole (this included police and security officials who were killed and injured; infrastructural facilities which were damaged; and the desecration of the overall image of India as a secure nation), as well as countries and international organizations.

Responses of the Indian Government

The attacks drew multiple responses from the Indian government and certain prominent international entities such as the United Nations as well as nations like the United States. As we demonstrate below, the responses were unilateral (from India's side alone), bilateral (from India and Pakistan), multilateral (involving international organizations and nations), and nongovernmental.

Goals and Objectives of the Indian Government

- To stop the siege as soon as possible.
- To assure citizens—including affected families—of the government's commitment to subduing the crisis.
- To ensure such terrorist attacks never happen again by forming a federal investigative agency.
- To communicate India's strong anti-terrorist stance to neighboring nations.
- To display India's commitment to transnational peace building by refraining from taking hasty military action against pro-terror nations and organizations.

Unilateral Strategies and Tactics Deployed by the Indian Government

- **Indian Prime Minister's immediate reaction**. The crisis marked a particular high point in the tensions between India and Pakistan. In his address to the nation on November 27, 2008, Prime Minister Dr. Manmohan Singh addressed the worst-hit stakeholders in the attacks—the common people of Mumbai. He offered his condolences to the families of the deceased and sympathies to the injured [19] and promised that the government would "take all necessary measures to look after the well-being of the affected families, including medical treatment of the injured" [19]. But more importantly, to assure the nation, he promised that the government would take "the strongest possible measures to ensure that there is no repetition of such terrorist acts. We are determined to take whatever measures are necessary to ensure the safety and security of our citizens" [19].

- **Call to the nation and future actions**. Asserting potential actions by the Indian government, Prime Minister Dr. Manmohan Singh said: "We will take up strongly with our neighbors that the use of their territory for launching attacks on us will not be tolerated, and that there would be a cost if suitable measures are not taken by them" [19]. He also proposed a number of other actions, which included tightening existing laws to ensure no terrorist could escape the law [19]; setting up a Federal Investigation Agency to investigate acts of terrorism and bring the guilty to justice [19]; strengthening the police and intelligence authorities; restricting the entry of suspects into the country; and ensuring that perpetrators, organizations, and supporters of terrorism are punished irrespective of their affiliation or religion [19]. And finally, to ensure that the attacks did not ignite communal hostilities between the Hindu and Muslim communities, he urged people to remain peaceful so that the "enemies of our country" do not succeed in their "nefarious designs."

- **Nation-level anti-terrorist initiative**. In a meeting with major political parties on November 30, 2008, the Indian Prime Minister reiterated his intention to "establish a federal investigative agency, strengthen maritime and air security, and set up a number of new bases for commando forces" [7] since the attacks were carried out in a commando style. Subsequently, on December 17, 2008, the Indian Parliament passed the National Investigation Agency Act 2008 to establish the National Investigation Agency to investigate and prosecute acts of terrorism [7].

Governmental Bilateral and Multilateral Strategies and Tactics

- **Temporary suspension of bilateral initiatives**. According to Javaid and Kamal [9], "the Mumbai mayhem on November 26, 2008 proved to be the sunset of the ongoing Indo-Pak peace dialogues" [9], which had been gaining momentum since 2003. Once the attacks took place, all the secretary-level talks on trade, Siachen, and Sir Creek were suspended. The cricket tour of Pakistan and the meeting of Indian Pakistan Joint Commission on Environment were cancelled. In addition, the Indian visa issuance process for Pakistani nationals was restricted [9].

- **Multilateral anti-terrorist steps**. The attacks also put India and Pakistan on high alert in terms of the possibility of a war breaking out [9]. However, diplomatic pressures from the United States helped to avert the possibility of war [9]. India, nevertheless, demanded a ban on Jamaat-ud-Dawa (JuD)—a front organization of Lashkar-a-Taiba, which was later banned by the United States in 2014 [20]—to the UN Security Council [7]. Pakistan subsequently launched an operation against a JuD complex near Muzaffarabad and detained several people including Zakiur Rehman Lakhvi, a mastermind behind the Mumbai 2008 attacks [7]. In addition, in January 2009, Pakistan officially accepted that Ajmal Kasab was its citizen and that parts of the Mumbai attacks had been planned in Pakistan [9]. Lakhvi, however, was released from Rawalpindi's high security Adiala jail on bail in April 2015 because of dearth of evidence from the Pakistani government to continue his detention [21]. His release was decried in India as an "insult" to those killed in the Mumbai attacks in 2008 [21].

Nongovernmental Actions

Nongovernmental stakeholders in the attacks—the businesses and the Jewish center which had been attacked—all subsequently resumed functioning as usual after staying closed for varying periods of time.

- Leopold Café resiliently resumed its normal business just 4 days after the attack, on November 30, 2008 [22].
- The Taj Mahal Palace reopened its doors on August 15, 2010—India's 63rd independence day [23].
- The Nariman House reopened its doors in August 2014, where its new co-directors, Rabbi Yisroel Kozlovsky and his wife Chaya Kozlovsky, carry on the work begun by Rabbi Gabi and Rivka Holtzberg, who were slain in the Mumbai attacks [24].

Relationship Between Culture and Crisis Response

The response of the Indian people as well as that of the Indian government to the Mumbai attacks exposed certain deficiencies that exist within the fabric of the Indian society and disadvantage Indian masses. Since there is no substantial emphasis on crisis communication pedagogy in the Indian education system, there is little awareness even among educated urban Indians—not to speak of those who are illiterate—on how to respond in a crisis situation. In addition, there is a lack of infrastructure and resources that would allow people to communicate, organize themselves, and act quickly during a crisis. For instance, the number of police personnel for 100,000 citizens is 129 in India [25]—nearly a third of the corresponding number in the United States [26]. This deficiency accentuates the communication gap between the masses and the government machinery. Further, at the time of the attack, there was no emergency response system in India that corresponds to, say, the 911 or 000 emergency call system in the United States and Australia, respectively.

The coordination between government departments also was weak and that decelerated the crisis response. This can partly be attributed to the hierarchical nature of the Indian administrative structures as well as the bureaucratic hurdles. In this particular crisis situation, there was also a massive intelligence failure in anticipating and responding to the attacks. The local law enforcement was taken unawares which exacerbated the impact of the crisis.

The sensitive bilateral political situation between India and Pakistan also might have hindered an immediate response to the attacks on the part of India. As stated earlier in this chapter, both India and Pakistan are nuclear powers which might have prompted India to handle the situation with extra caution.

Positive and Negative Lessons Learned

Long-term conflicts and prolonged tensions between India and Pakistan over the years have created an atmosphere of mistrust and suspicion in the South Asian region. The Mumbai terror attacks in 2008 contributed to escalating the existing animosity between the two nation-states. While the lack of preparation and/or failure of state intelligence (on India's part) might have allowed the attacks to take place, a dearth of coordination between government officials and leaders of India and Pakistan decelerated the processes of timely and meaningful actions/rebuttal against the terrorists. Moreover, unprecedented media attention over a considerable period of time might have awakened intense emotions and expectations among the public as well as put governmental stakeholders in a dilemma.

The lessons that can be learned from the incident are subdivided into three categories, namely unilateral—the Government of India's perspective; bilateral—the context of Indo-Pakistani relationship; and multilateral—the transnational or global point of view.

Unilateral Aspects

In order to resolve conflicts and build peace in South Asia, the Government of India needs to identify its weaknesses and shortcomings, and reflect on culturally and contextually meaningful measures to prevent reoccurrence of such incidents. We believe some of the pointers mentioned below are worth paying attention to.

a. As noted earlier, an arena of mistrust is considered a barrier to building a healthy relationship between two neighboring countries. The Government of India should pay active attention to reducing/eradicating distrust and enhancing intercultural competence among leaders and bureaucrats as well as common citizens to ensure more coordination and cooperation in combating terrorism.

b. Roles of religious intolerances/conflicts and geopolitical tensions are crucial in the Indo-Pakistan terrorism context. Paying attention to religious harmony and initiating a strategy of inclusion of religious and other minorities in counter-terrorist initiatives would be meaningful in co-creating dialogic spaces. In other words, by going beyond the binary rhetoric (i.e., us vs. them) and narrow ethnocentric discourses, the state as well as the citizens could take appropriate initiatives in strengthening peace-building activities and efforts in the South Asian region.

c. Creation of awareness about terrorism and its sinister implications, as well as communication of India's commitment to fight terrorism in the broader global platforms is an important step for the government of India to take to clarify its intentions. Such efforts would be instrumental in building consensus among leaders [27] and forming international coalitions to counter terrorism and to bolster global peace-building processes.

Bilateral Aspects

Terrorism is a transnational phenomenon; in the South Asian context, both India and Pakistan need to pay sincere attention and take meaningful steps to combat terrorists and their activities. A transboundary crisis such as the 2008 Mumbai terror attacks calls for exploring some of the following issues:

a. Notions of mistrust and reluctance to bridge communicative gaps prevent both the nation-states from combating terrorism and to come up with a mutually agreed-upon crisis communication initiative. An effort at restoring communicative avenues would be helpful in building meaningful bilateral crisis communication strategies.

b. Frequent terrorist activities have increased the sense of suspicion and lack of trust, especially among the trade and business sectors of the two nations. In an era of globalization, such negative impressions can greatly affect opportunities for economic growth between the two nations. Bilateral initiatives for restoring and sustaining trade and transportation services are important for the financial health of both nations.

c. Sincere engagement in bilateral peace-building dialogues is important in combating cross-national terrorism activities. More involvement of the two nations in conflict resolution initiatives would be beneficial for the Indo-Pakistani political relationship. For instance, high level summits can be organized, or joint declarations can be signed in this regard.

d. To combat a crisis such as the 2008 Mumbai attacks, coordination between the nations needs to be seamless both diplomatically as well as in the context of the judiciary. Joint actions against terrorism, including conducting joint search and expediting transparent judicial processes, are the needs of the hour.

e. The 2008 Mumbai attacks affected the cultural exchange processes between the two nation-states. Promotion of cross-cultural activities and exchange of ideas and artifacts would create a positive and hopeful environment. For instance, organizing sports events such as Indo-Pak cricket series would contribute to reducing tensions between the two nations.

Multilateral Aspects

As terrorism impacts the lives of multiple stakeholders, multilateral measures are often useful in combating such incidents and preventing them from recurring.

a. Scholars have argued that interventions of the developed world could have been useful to minimize terrorism in the South Asian region. They opine that third-party interventions such as imposing economic sanctions and pressurizing Pakistan to expedite judicial processes and counterterrorism activities can be instrumental in reducing terrorist activities. Markey notes that, "Washington could also prepare tools for coercing and inducing New Delhi and Islamabad away from military escalation" [28]. From an Indian perspective, such measures could potentially threaten the sovereignty of both India and Pakistan if taken unilaterally by the economically and politically powerful nations and/or international organizations such as the United Nations.

b. Transnational and multiparty interventions could be meaningful in promoting peace-building dialogues and cooperation among the South Asian countries. Such dialogic spaces need to be created both at strategic and tactical levels as long-term and short-term crisis communicative praxis, respectively. In addition, opening up track-two dialogic spaces among various stakeholders of both nation-states is necessary for meaningful communication between political leaders, military personnel, representatives of civil societies, and other key decision-makers of India, Pakistan, and other international players. Multilateral cooperation and collaboration against terrorism would strengthen various global counterterrorist and peace-building initiatives. Diplomatic ties and formulating multilateral strategies using various global platforms would also help to collaboratively counter the acts and/or politics of terrorism.

c. South Asian culture, especially its legacy of religious tolerance and peaceful coexistence, would potentially show us meaningful avenues to bring about peace and effectively negotiate crises created by terrorism. Hinduism, Islam, and Buddhism are some of the major religions in the region; teachings of these religions inspire and influence the majority of the South Asian population. Over the years, followers of these religions (as well as the followers of Sikhism, Jainism, and Christianity) embraced the values and teachings of these religions in their everyday lives. All the aforementioned religions put heavy emphasis on peace and peace-building processes to counter crisis created by hatred and violence. For instance, Hinduism pays attention to human qualities like truthfulness (*satyagraha*) and nonviolence (*ahimsa*) [29], Islam emphasizes forgiveness, mercy, and compassion [30], while Buddhist teachings value conquering worldly desires [31].

Gandhi, one of India's greatest political leaders, followed the principles of *satyagraha* and *ahimsa* in his life and work. His commitment to embracing the truth and practices of nonviolence was inspired by the teachings of the Upanishads. For example, according to Ishavasya Upanishad, "when a person sees the self in all people and all people in the self, then he hates no one" [36]. Similarly, in the teachings of Islam, "forgiveness and mercy are recommended as virtues of the true faithful" [30]; principal texts of Islam such as the Quran and the Hadith emphasize brotherhood, social justice, tolerance, and compassion, thereby actively encouraging its followers to engage in peace-building processes [30]. Again, the teachings of Buddha, one of the greatest religious teachers of ancient India, taught the principles of the eightfold middle path, which emphasizes right thoughts, right speech, right action to conquer human greed and desires [37]. The aforementioned religious teachings are therefore relevant in fighting crises caused by terrorism as we see in contemporary societies. Reflexively engaging with the principles and praxis of South Asian religions is important for creating contextually and culturally appropriate crisis communication strategies to combat acts of terror in the long run.

Grounded in the above discussion, we might consider a few future-centric culturally meaningful action plans.

- Scholars have argued that awakening of critical collective consciousness is essential for fighting against acts of violence, including cultural violence [32]. Accordingly, culturally appropriate long-term initiatives can be initiated and promoted in the South Asian region through policy formulation and implementation as well as through preparing communities to respond effectively in crisis situations.

- While explaining the essence of dialogic processes, Sorrells noted, "the process of dialogue invites us to stretch ourselves—to reach across—to imagine, experience, and creatively engage with points of view, ways of thinking and being and beliefs different from our own…" [33]. Such critical dialogic interactions among various stakeholders are important in the context of crisis communicative praxis. Therefore, bilateral and multilateral peace-building dialogues among and within various stakeholder groups are necessary for creating a more positive and nonviolent South Asia.

- A meaningful and effective coordination and collaboration among regional and international stakeholders such as nation-states, international organizations (including nongovernmental organizations and media organizations), transnational corporations, and civil societies in developing new strategies for promoting peace and bolstering counterterrorist alliances to combat terrorism in South Asia (and around the world). Such efforts would help stakeholders build more effective crisis communication strategies, well-coordinated intelligence, as well as effective technologies (both hardware and software) in combating terrorism.

- As a long-term measure, educational initiatives would be meaningful for creating awareness and enhancing preparedness among citizens of both countries. So, critical and reflective counterterrorism education starting from the primary level through to adult-education level would be helpful in shaping public opinion, increasing alertness, and encouraging citizen-level vigilance to fight terrorism.

Practical Suggestions

1. As demonstrated in the above case study, crisis communication is influenced by the culture and contexts of the country where the crisis has unfolded. Therefore, to understand how Indians respond to a crisis—which is crucial when one is conducting business in India—it is essential to comprehend the Indian psyche and worldview.

2. India is a country with ancient traditions that co-exist seamlessly with a rapidly modernizing society. It also is a diverse country with 780 different languages [34], 705 ethnic groups [35], and multiple religions—all of which leave their impressions on the Indian worldview. Any crisis management strategy should take the above-mentioned nuances into consideration for it to have any measure of success.

3. India has one of the largest number of Internet users in the world who actively participate on social media platforms; any crisis management initiative needs to take this into account. A crisis response in the Indian context, therefore, needs to be timely as well as reflective and mindful of various sociocultural factors. In the case of the Mumbai attacks, for instance, we discussed how people at the venues of the attacks were constantly sharing information via Twitter. This constant engagement with social media is typical of urban Indians.

Discussion Questions

7.1 India has experienced terrorism several times in the last few decades. So far, the country has not been able to devise a crisis communication framework/ strategy to combat terrorism. To address the existing gaps, develop a crisis communication plan which is meaningful in the Indian and South Asian context, keeping in mind the social, cultural, and political factors.

7.2 In order to prepare citizens against terrorist attacks, what are some suggestions that you can offer to do the following:

a. Provide peace-building education at the interpersonal level;

b. Create awareness about terrorism at the community level;

c. Building trust at the national and international levels.

7.3 Lack of coordination and synergy among various stakeholders—specifically between the Indian and Pakistani governments—significantly affected countert-errorist measures (in a timely fashion) during the 2008 Mumbai attacks. Suggest a plan to enhance bilateral cooperation and coordination between nations to combat terrorism effectively.

7.4 In a diverse country such as India where there are numerous local languages, different religions and ethnicities, what are some challenges that one is likely to face while putting together a crisis communication plan? What suggestions would you offer to address those challenges?

7.5 As a student of communication or a PR practitioner, what steps would you take to implement a crisis communication plan that integrates the three layers of social communication, namely face-to-face interaction, traditional mass media (such as TV, radio, and newspapers) and new media?

References

1. J. Afridi. (2009). "Kashmir militant extremists," Council on Foreign Relations. [Online]. Available: http://www.cfr.org/kashmir/kashmir-militant-extremists/p9135, March 13, 2016 (last date accessed).
2. O. Oh, M. Agrawal, and H. Raghav Rao, "Information control and terrorism: Tracking the Mumbai terrorist attack through Twitter," *Information Systems Frontiers*, vol. 13, no. 1, pp. 33–43, 2011.
3. K. Sriramesh, Y. Kim, and M. Takasaki, "Public relations in three Asian cultures: An analysis," *Journal of Public Relations Research*, vol. 11, no. 4, pp. 271–292, 1999.
4. M. Rajasthan. (2013, June 29). "Indira Gandhi's interview on India Pakistan War in 1971" [YouTube video]. Available: https://www.youtube.com/watch?v=_MATAqeiL-4, March 13, 2016 (last date accessed).

5. "What about India?" (n.d.). The Hofstede Center [Online]. Available: http://geert-hofstede.com/india.html, May 20, 2017 (last date accessed).

6. "National culture" (n.d.). The Hofstede Center [Online]. Available: http://geert-hofstede.com/national-culture.html, May 20, 2017 (last date accessed).

7. A. Kolas, "The 2008 Mumbai terror attacks: (Re)constructing Indian (counter) terrorism," *Critical Studies on Terrorism*, vol. 3, no. 1, pp. 83–98, 2010.

8. "Mumbai terror attacks fast facts," *CNN.com*, 2015. [Online]. Available: http://www.cnn.com/2013/09/18/world/asia/mumbai-terror-attacks/, May 20, 2017 (last date accessed).

9. U. Javaid and M. Kamal, "The Mumbai Terror '2008' and its impact on the Indo-Pak relations," *South Asian Studies*, vol. 28, no. 1, pp. 25–37, 2013.

10. United Nations Department of Economics and Social Affairs Population Division. (2014). "Population facts" [Online]. Available: http://www.un.org/en/development/desa/population/publications/pdf/popfacts/PopFacts_2014-2.pdf, May 20, 2017 (last date accessed).

11. S. M. Beebe and R. H. Pherson, *Cases in Intelligence Analysis: Structured Analytic Techniques in Action.* Thousand Oaks, CA: SAGE, 2012.

12. M. Rao, "Mumbai blasts 2006: India court finds 12 men guilty," *BBC*, September 11, 2015. [Online]. Available: http://www.bbc.com/news/world-asia-india-342183 96d, May 20, 2016 (last date accessed).

13. "2003: Bombay rocked by twin car bombs" (n.d.). *On this day. BBC.* [Online]. Available: http://news.bbc.co.uk/onthisday/hi/dates/stories/august/25/newsid_3921000/3921475.stm, May 20, 2016 (last date accessed).

14. "Trio given death penalty for 2003 Mumbai terror attacks," *The Guardian*, August 6, 2009. [Online]. Available: http://www.theguardian.com/world/2009/aug/06/india-mumbai-terror-attacks-2003, May 20, 2016 (last date accessed).

15. S. Chowdhury, "Dawood Ibrahim's new residence in Karachi near Bilawal's residence," *The Indian Express*, August 23, 2015. [Online]. Available: http://indian express.com/article/india/india-others/india-has-evidence-of-dawood-ibrahim-living-in-pakistan-report/, May 20, 2016 (last date accessed).

16. P. Armstrong and H. S. Singh, "Mumbai bomber Yakub Memon hanged after long battle for mercy," *CNN*, July 30, 2015. [Online]. Available: http://www.cnn.com/2015/07/30/asia/mumbai-bomber-yakub-memon/, May 20, 2016 (last date accessed).

17. "Counterterrorism guide: Historic timeline" (n.d.). National Counterterrorism Center. [Online]. Available: http://www.nctc.gov/site/timeline.html, May 20, 2016 (last date accessed).

18. C. Kaplan, "The biopolitics of technoculture in the Mumbai attacks," *Theory, Culture and Society*, vol. 26, nos. 7–8, pp. 301–313, 2009.

19. "Prime Minister Dr. Manmohan Singh's address to the Nation," Embassy of India, Washington DC (2008) [Online]. Available: https://www.indianembassy.org/archives_details.php?nid=952, May 20, 2016 (last date accessed).

20. "U.S. blacklists Pakistan's Jamaat-ud-Dawa," *Al-Jazeera*, June 26, 2014. [Online]. Available http://www.aljazeera.com/news/asia/2014/06/us-blacklists-pakistani-islamic-charity-20146261127191358.html, May 20, 2016 (last date accessed).

21. D. Nelson, "Mumbai terror mastermind release in Pakistan causes anger in India," *The Telegraph*, April 10, 2015. [Online]. Available http://www.telegraph.co.uk/news/

worldnews/asia/india/11528185/Mumbai-terror-mastermind-release-in-Pakistan-causes-anger-in-India.html, May 20, 2016 (last date accessed).

22. "Mumbai's Leopold Café reopens," *The Sydney Morning Herald*, November 30, 2008. [Online]. Available http://www.smh.com.au/world/mumbais-leopolds-cafe-reopens-20081130-6ns9.html, May 20, 2016 (last date accessed).

23. B. Mansukhani, "Taj Palace hotel reopening in Mumbai: Fortress for a week, landmark forever," *CNN Travel*, August 31, 2010. [Online]. Available http://travel.cnn.com/mumbai/visit/taj-palace-wing-reopens-mumbai-689379, May 20, 2016 (last date accessed).

24. H. L. Julian, "Chabad of Mumbai opens Nariman House in Mumbai," *The Jewish Press.com*, August 24, 2014. [Online]. Available http://www.jewishpress.com/news/breaking-news/chabad-of-mumbai-reopens-nariman-house-in-india/2014/08/24/, May 20, 2016 (last date accessed).

25. M. Vyawahare, "India's police force lags much of the world," *The New York Times*, January 16, 2013. [Online]. Available http://india.blogs.nytimes.com/2013/01/16/india-has-one-of-the-lowest-police-population-ratios-in-the-world/, May 20, 2016 (last date accessed).

26. U.S. Department of Justice, Office of Justice Programs. (2008). "Federal law enforcement officers, 2008" [Online]. Available http://www.bjs.gov/content/pub/pdf/fleo08.pdf, May 20, 2016 (last date accessed).

27. M. J. Canel and K. Sanders, "Crisis communication and terrorist attacks: Framing a response to the 2004 Madrid bombings and 2005 London bombings," in *Handbook of Crisis Communication*, T. W. Coombs, Ed. Oxford, UK: Blackwell, 2010, pp. 449–466.

28. D. Markey, *Contingency Planning Memorandum No. 6*. New York: Council on Foreign Relations, 2010.

29. J. Senehi, S. Ryan, and S. Byrne, "Introduction: Peacebuilding, reconciliation, and transformation," *Peace and Conflict Studies*, vol. 17, no. 1, pp. 1–42, 2010.

30. M. Abu-Nimer, "A framework for nonviolence and peacebuilding in Islam," *Journal of Law and Religion*, vol. 15, no. 1/2, pp. 217–265, 2001.

31. D. Keown, "The role of deterrence in Buddhist peace-building," *Journal of Buddhist Ethics*, vol. 21, pp. 655–678, 2014.

32. P. Friere, *Pedagogy of the Oppressed*. New York: Bloomsbury Academic, 1970.

33. K. S. Sorrells, *Intercultural Communication: Globalization and Social Justice*. Thousand Oaks: SAGE Publications, 2013.

34. "780 languages spoken in India, 250 died out in last 50 years," *Hindustan Times*, July 17, 2013. [Online]. Available: http://www.hindustantimes.com/books/780-languages-spoken-in-india-250-died-out-in-last-50-years/story-Y3by8ooYbXRA77xP2AEWKN.html, May 20, 2016 (last date accessed).

35. Office of the Registrar General and Census Commissioner, India. (2011). "Primary census abstract for total population, Scheduled Castes and Scheduled Tribes" [Online]. Available: http://censusindia.gov.in/Census_And_You/scheduled_castes_and_sceduled_tribes.aspx, May 20, 2016 (last date accessed).

36. P. Dhakal, "Hindu vision of nonkilling," in *Nonkilling Spiritual Traditions*, J. E. Pim and P. Dhakal, Eds. Honolulu, Hawaii: Center for Global Nonkilling, 2015, pp. 151–162.

37. D. J. Christie, R. V. Wagner, and D. A. Winter, *Peace, Conflict and Violence: Peace Psychology for the 21st Century*. Englewood Cliffs, NJ: Prentice-Hall, 2001.

Indonesia

8

Power Distance, Uncertainty Avoidance, and *Rukun*: Managing the Transboundary Haze Crisis in Indonesia

Reidinar Juliane Wardoyo and Augustine Pang

Chapter Preview

How did Indonesia respond to the forest fires that led to the transboundary haze crisis in 2013? The Indonesian government at the national and local level responded to the crisis differently. While the local government showed ignorance over the issue by taking the haze crisis lightly, the national government's responses varied according to the respective institutions: Some Indonesian ministry officials responded with denial and evasion of responsibility while some others responded in a more progressive and corrective way. Some of these responses were influenced by the Indonesian cultural characteristics as described by the Hofstede and the GLOBE studies, mainly the high power distance, weak concern about uncertainty avoidance, high in-group collectivism, and low institutional collectivism.

After reading this chapter, you will be able to

- *Understand the differences of strategies deployed by the government at different levels due to varying interests*

Culture and Crisis Communication: Transboundary Cases from Nonwestern Perspectives, First Edition.
Edited by Amiso M. George and Kwamena Kwansah-Aidoo.
© 2017 by The Institute of Electrical and Electronics Engineers, Inc. Published 2017 by John Wiley & Sons, Inc.

- *Describe how culture may or may not influence the government's response during crisis*
- *Discern that there are other factors (such as corruption and personal interests) that influence crisis communication responses*
- *Appreciate the importance of appropriate message dissemination using one voice and synchronization of messages in times of crisis*

Brief Overview of Indonesia and Its Culture

Indonesia is the largest archipelago in the world with a population of over 200 million [1]. In 1999, following the fall of the then-President Suharto, Indonesia embarked on a reform of government decentralization, devolving power from the central government to the provincial units. This decentralization entailed separate responsibilities between the local and national governments and empowered the regional autonomy initiative. The revised governmental structures were in sharp contrast to the centralized government in the Suharto era where political power was concentrated in the hands of the national government. It was proposed that decentralization would enable the local government to deliver services most needed by the local people. However, the downside was the clash of interests between the national and local governments that occurred frequently [2].

In such a diverse and geographically large country as Indonesia, there may be no single word to describe the cultural values of the Indonesian people. Indonesia is home to more than 200 ethnicities who speak more than 300 local languages [3]. The Javanese are the largest ethnic group in Indonesia, making up to nearly 42% of the population, followed by Sundanese (15.5%), Batak (3.6%), Sulawesi (3.2%), and others [4]. Each ethnic group displays different cultures and behaviors, highlighting the importance of cultural understanding when communicating in Indonesia. Despite these highly diverse ethnics, Indonesians show national pride as they bear the motto of "Unity in Diversity" [5].

Studies have attempted to define Indonesian's national culture, most notably the GLOBE project [5] and Hofstede's [6] study which categorized Indonesia based on three cultural dimensions—power distance, uncertainty avoidance, and individualism/collectivism. Hofstede [6] identified Indonesia as having a high power distance, indicating a greater acceptance of the unequal power distribution between superiors and subordinates. The GLOBE study indicated a higher score in uncertainty avoidance whereas Hofstede [6] identified Indonesia as having lower score on this dimension. That is, Indonesians have a great tolerance for ambiguity and show a strong preference toward the Javanese culture that avoids getting too directly to the point [7].

Indonesia has also been identified as a collectivist society, suggesting that Indonesians place emphasis on loyalty, relationships, and collective responsibility

[8]. Collectivism is linked to a Javanese cultural trait called *rukun*, which refers to the importance of maintaining collective peace and social harmony with each other [9]. Although originating from Java, the *rukun* culture has been identified with Indonesians in general because the Javanese have been recognized to be culturally and politically dominant in Indonesia [10]. Not only is Javanese the largest ethnic group in Indonesia, but also all Indonesian presidents have been Javanese.

Even with the many studies identifying Indonesia as a collectivist society [9,10], the GLOBE study went further by segregating collectivism into two dimensions—institutional collectivism and in-group collectivism—to better differentiate the types of collectivism [8]. Institutional collectivism refers to a society's preference for group goals and rewards, meaning that individuals have obligations to the greater society goals [11,12]. For instance, in an institution or region where institutional collectivism is high, the leaders have to prioritize the welfare of all members of the institution or region. By contrast, in-group collectivism refers to loyalty, pride, and responsibility to families [11,12]. Hence, the leaders who uphold strong in-group collectivism will concentrate on the goals of their own close people rather than on those of the general society.

Indonesia scores high on the in-group collectivism dimension according to the GLOBE study [5]. The fact that many Indonesians live in big families or clans, who then become the focus of the primary loyalties of individuals, presumably drives this. In such a society, living up to those loyalties, fulfilling obligations to the families and taking care of each other are powerful motivators, leading to strong in-group collectivism [13].

Background of Crisis Communication in Indonesia

There is limited published literature about crisis communication in Indonesia. Those that are published have discussed the role of media and communication in the context of disasters (e.g., volcano eruption, Tsunami) [14,15], conflict (e.g., civil war) [16], terrorism (e.g., Bali bombing) [15], and corporate crisis [17].

In disasters, for instance, past studies have examined the role of conventional and new media in reaching the affected communities, the national policies that affect the local practice and the key factors in disaster communication [15–18]. In terrorism, studies have explored the governments' conflict of interests in handling crisis communication resulting from terrorism, and the impact it has on tourism [15–19].

Despite the limited studies, organizations in Indonesia practice crisis communication widely in response to emerging crises. In the corporate sector, a number of organizations have been embroiled in major crises. For instance, an Indonesian oil and gas company, Lapindo Brantas, was involved in causing a mudflow disaster in Sidoarjo, East Java, due to an error in its drilling activities [17]. Crises also hit Indonesia's airlines, Garuda Indonesia in 2007, killing 23 out of 133 passengers on board [20] and the Adam Air plane that disappeared with 102 passengers and crew on board [21]. In the public sector, the complication that was frequently found in the Indonesian government's response to crisis was the lack of coordination between government officials [15].

Role of Culture in Crisis Communication Practice in Indonesia

The Hofstede study has been used to explain corporate response in crisis communication context [22–24] but studies on culture and crisis communication in government institutions are few and far between [25]. Specifically, there are only few studies that examine the role of culture in crisis communication in the Indonesian context. While Hofstede and GLOBE cultural dimensions are useful in discerning cultural characteristics of a specific country, it may result in an overgeneralization, especially in a country like Indonesia with its varied ethnic groups.

This chapter examines how Indonesian cultural characteristics surfaced in the face of government's crisis response in the 2013 transboundary haze crisis when forest fires that raged in Riau, Indonesia, caused the haze to spread to its neighboring countries including Singapore and Malaysia, hitting high levels of air pollution in those countries. The subsequent subsections explain the haze crisis and Indonesian government's response. In the analysis, we examine how Hofstede and GLOBE cultural dimensions were at play in various situations at different governmental levels. Finally, we offer practical suggestions for those seeking to communicate crisis or do business in Indonesia.

Case Study: The 2013 Transboundary Haze Crisis

Situational Analysis

Transboundary haze has been a serious problem in Southeast Asia since 1985 [26]. The first long and severe haze episode took place back in 1997–1998 in Riau, Indonesia, causing huge damage to not only Indonesia but also neighboring countries, including Singapore and Malaysia [27, 28]. In 2013, the haze returned and badly shrouded Riau, disrupting flights, schools, and raising health concerns in Riau. The 2013 haze episode also blanketed Singapore and Malaysia, leading to concerns and pleas for the Indonesian government to tackle the problem.

The fires and haze in Riau persisted due to the confluence of factors such as illegal logging practices, weak law enforcement in the forestry sector, and Indonesia's peatlands and drought season. Corruption was also evident as companies took advantage of the weak law enforcement to deliberately clear land for oil-palm plantations. These were reported to be the major causes of the haze [29]. According to the

Indonesian National Disaster Mitigation Agency (BNPB), more than 90% of forest and peat swamp fires in Riau were deliberate [30].

The key to tackling the fires in Riau was for the government to determine the cause of the fires, and enforce the law by prohibiting the firms and farmers from burning the forests and peat lands. However, the degree of urgency with which the local and national governments tackled this problem differed. The haze was perceived as a crisis by the local (Riau) government as the fires took place within its territory. The national government, however, had different prerogatives. It considered the 2013 haze crisis as one that badly impacted neighboring countries. The national government's response was in part exacerbated by the multiple demands of the world media and the governments of the neighboring countries [31, 32]. See Table 8.1.

The subsequent section discusses the Indonesian government's response and shows how Indonesian cultural characteristics identified by Hofstede and the GLOBE study may or may not have influenced the Indonesian government's response to the 2013 haze episode.

TABLE 8.1. Key Players in the Crisis

	Stakeholder	Responsibility
Local government	Riau governors	Finding out the cause of the haze and preventing it from recurring
National government	Then-President Yudhoyono	Main spokesperson in dealing with neighboring countries
	Ministry of Foreign Affairs	Main spokesperson in dealing with neighboring countries
	Ministry of Forestry	Tackling the fires to reduce the haze
	Ministry of Environment	Tackling the fires to reduce the haze
	Ministry of Agriculture	Tackling the fires to reduce the haze
International	Government of Singapore Environment and Water	Mitigating the haze in their region
	Resources Ministry Foreign and Law Ministry [31– 33]	Spokesperson in dealing with Indonesia
	Government of Malaysia Natural Resources and	Mitigating the haze in their region
	Environment Ministry [34] Foreign Ministry [35]	Spokesperson in dealing with Indonesia

Adapted from Chua 2013 [31], Channel News Asia 2015 [33], ABC 2015 [34], Wulandari and Cho 2015[35].

Response by the Local and National Governments

Local Government

The governor was reportedly irresponsible and showed minimal efforts in tackling the fires. The governor acknowledged the existence of the fires and the haze but minimized the local government's responsibility by handing the haze matter over to God. The governor said, "We let God take care of the haze" [36].

Local government officials showed their ignorance over the issue by taking the haze crisis lightly [36, 37]. Many local leaders were not convinced that maintaining forest sustainability would lead to development; hence, many initiatives that provided incentives for the local government to preserve its forests failed to gain momentum [37].

National Government

As suggested by Benoit and Pang [38], there are five strategies deployed by nations to restore their image: denial, evasion of responsibility, reducing offensiveness, corrective action, and mortification.

- *Denial* involves two variants, that is, simple denial or shifting the blame to another party to position the accuser as victim.
- *Evasion of responsibility* includes four variants, that is, provocation—where a nation reacts by responding it was egged on to do so, defeasibility—when a nation argues its case on the basis of lack of information and control, accident—where the "accused" states that the accident happened unintentionally, and good intention—where a nation argues that the offensive act was done with good intentions.
- *Reducing offensiveness* can be done by five strategies, that is, minimization strategies can be used to reduce the severity of the situation, differentiation strategies seek to reduce offensiveness by suggesting that the act was less offensive than perceived, transcendence strategies seek to place the situation at a higher level with more important concerns, attacking the accuser seeks to reduce the credibility of the accusations, and compensation strategy is where those responsible decide to offer something of value to the victims.
- *Corrective action* aims to reassure stakeholders that such crisis situations would not reoccur.
- *Mortification* is when one admits mistake and seeks forgiveness.

In line with the strategies elaborated by Benoit and Pang [38], the national government's responses varied according to the respective institutions. Some Indonesian ministry officials exhibited a denial response and argued over who was to blame for the haze, with some even shifting the blame to Malaysia and Singapore. A Ministry of Forestry official said the slash-and-burn technique that caused the fires was the cheapest land-clearing method and was used by palm oil investors including Singaporean and Malaysian companies [39]. In a similar move, the Indonesian environment minister highlighted the fact that Malaysian companies were involved in the fires [40]. The coordinating minister for people's welfare worsened the situation through aggressive comments, shifting the blame to nature and chiding Singapore by stating that: "Singapore should not be behaving like a child and making all this noise" [41]. Agung Laksono, the minister coordinating Indonesia's response, told reporters, "This is not what the Indonesian nation wants, it is because of nature" [41].

However, two other ministers who were directly involved in the crisis, the Minister of Forestry, Zulkifli Hasan, and the Minister of Agriculture, Suswono Asyraf, showed restraint. They said that the government would not tolerate companies that used slash-and-burn to clear land in Riau and that companies who were proven to do so would be dealt with firmly [40, 42]. Indonesia's Foreign Affairs Minister, Marty Natalegawa, also showed corrective response by stating that the government would do everything it can to tackle the problem and prevent it from recurring, although he insisted that Indonesia would not issue an apology to Singapore. In contrast to some of his ministers, the then-President Yudhoyono accepted responsibility by issuing a full apology to Singapore and Malaysia.

"For what is happening, as the president, I apologize to our brothers in Singapore and Malaysia," Yudhoyono said. He asked for their understanding and said Indonesia is working hard to fight the fires. [43]

He also conveyed his displeasure with the negative comments made by some government officials by saying that he had instructed officers to not give such statements [44].

How Culture Influenced the Indonesian Government's Response

Local Government

According to Hofstede and the GLOBE studies, the higher power distance and the weaker concerns about uncertainty avoidance in Indonesian society would condition Indonesian leaders to use a defensive strategy in response to crisis. In this culture, Indonesians are accustomed to accepting the role of power and ambiguity. These cultural traits were visible in the evasion of responsibility strategy employed by the local government, in which they were less visible and less involved in the crisis. In this case, some government entities also avoided assuming responsibility by shifting the blame onto nature and companies that were based in Singapore and Malaysia.

This evasion of responsibility strategy was in part influenced by the weak capacity of the local government to handle the fires. For instance, it did not have the adequate monitoring system, technology, and funds to finance necessary projects to fight the fires [45, 46]. This strategy was further exacerbated by the in-group collectivism practices. While Hofstede [6] identified Indonesia as a collectivist society which generally shows great willingness to engage in pro-social behavior for the good of the society, the recurrence of the haze since 1985 clearly showed that the local government did not put the issue as its priority agenda despite the danger that the haze caused.

Instead, the local government's interest in granting illegal access for companies to burn the peat to clear land for lucrative oil-palm planting in return for bribes received by local government officials showed that in-group collectivism practices were salient. That is, the local government gave the goals of the in-group a higher priority than the goals of the public.

> Indeed, as it became clear that the bulk of the burning was taking place in Riau province, analysts were quick to point out that its governor—Mr. Rusli Zainal—is the leading suspect in a case involving illegal logging permits. [37]

In fact, some studies have shown that in-group collectivism culture is associated with high levels of corruption [47, 48]. Corruption has long been rooted in Indonesia's forestry industry and became more pervasive during the Suharto regime [2, 37]. Suharto gave concessions to his inner circle of political advisors and families. As a result, foreign investors wishing to do business in Indonesia had to seek a partner among Suharto's political elite [49]. With the devolution of power from national to the local level and the implementation of regional autonomy, provincial and local governments were empowered to grant illegal logging permits, and thus a culture of corruption remains very much ingrained [26].

In sum, in-group collectivism practices, rather than institutional collectivism practices, from the Suharto era have devolved to the provincial level and that has triggered corrupt practices. These individuals interpret laws, rules, and regulations for the benefit of their groups and close friends. Consequently, three Riau governors were sentenced to jail for corruption [50].

National Government

Similar to the local government, high power distance, low uncertainty avoidance, and low institutional collectivism characteristics were apparent in the response of some officials at the national level. These cultural dimensions, however, were not reflected in President Yudhoyono's response toward the transboundary haze crisis. As a leader, President Yudhoyono assumed personal responsibility and apologized to Singapore and Malaysia following a string of negative comments from his ministers directed at the two countries.

Interestingly, President Yudhoyono reportedly apologized in 2013 only when the haze badly impacted Indonesia's neighbors. He did not apologize to the people in Riau for the haze that had been taking place since 1985 [51]. This response suggests that Hofstede's cultural characteristics were only relevant in domestic, but not international, settings. There are several possible reasons for this difference in stances. First, with Indonesia being highly decentralized, different interests exist between the local and national governments. The national government's interest is to respond to the international community; hence, President Yudhoyono took the lead by apologizing to neighboring countries.

Second, President Yudhoyono was arguably trying to position himself as a leader on the world stage. Thus, he may have felt the need to address the concerns from Singapore and Malaysia by issuing a formal apology, a gesture that he never extended to his own people. Third, President Yudhoyono is a former military officer whose approach focused heavily on fostering both national and regional (i.e., Association of South-East Asian Nations, ASEAN) resilience. Hence, maintaining solidarity and preventing conflict with neighboring countries became the main emphasis of his leadership [52].

There was also a clash between President Yudhoyono and his ministers in which some ministers were unwilling to apologize to Singapore and Malaysia for the haze. This indicated that President Yudhoyono ignored the positions of some of his ministers, a prerogative that he exercised far less frequently in domestic affairs [53]. In the haze crisis, President Yudhoyono overruled Foreign Minister Marty Natalegawa by issuing a formal apology one day after Natalegawa mentioned that Indonesian government would not apologize to the neighboring countries [54].

The haphazard way in which information was disseminated through various centers did not augur well for the country and caused confusion among its stakeholders.

This crisis showed that the Indonesian government did not exhibit collectivist culture as it did not achieve consensus before making a decision and disseminating messages, in contrast to Hofstede's [6] study that would have suggested otherwise [5]. The haphazard way in which information was disseminated through various centers did not augur well for the country and caused confusion among its stakeholders: Whose version should one believe in? It is important for organizations to speak with one voice, particularly in times of crises [55]. Failure to do that creates confusion and leaves an information vacuum [56], which will be filled by sources other than the organization's voice. Attempts to synchronize messages would be advised.

However, in this case, political realities appear to take precedence. President Yud-hoyono's military background that focused on regional resilience and avoidance of confrontation with neighboring countries was not in line with his civilian ministers whose interest and aspirations were different. It is likely that these different inter-ests, along with the lack of coordination, made it impossible for the government to undertake a centralized and consistent approach in this crisis communication. Con-sequently, the mixed responses on Indonesia's part were seen as incoherent and con-fusing to its neighbors.

With regard to the relations with the local government, President Yudhoyono was also reported to have clashed with Riau's governor [57]. This was driven more by the anger of neighboring countries rather than the need to respond to the negative impact of the fires on the people of Riau.

In sum, cultural dimensions of high power distance, low uncertainty avoid-ance, and low institutional collectivism appeared to influence President Yudhoyono's response only in the domestic setting. These cultural dimensions were less visible in the transboundary crisis communication due to his background and political inter-ests. Additionally, the collectivism cultural dimension was not visible in the relations among the stakeholders at the national government as well as the communication between the national and local governments.

Outcome of the Transboundary Haze Crisis

In addition to the negative impact that the haze had on people (e.g., twofold increase of acute respiratory infection among people in Riau [58], 20% hike of basic com-modities' price due to the disruption of distribution [59]), the transboundary haze strained diplomatic relations between Indonesia and its neighbors—Malaysia and Singapore—as some Indonesian government officials played the blame game and avoided assuming responsibility. Relations improved when President Yudhoyono issued a formal apology to the neighboring countries. To overcome the transbound-ary haze crisis, the ASEAN Agreement on Transboundary Haze was enacted in 2003. Indonesia had stalled in ratifying it. This suggests the lack of willingness on the part of Indonesian government to enforce its own law against irresponsible farming. The 2013 transboundary haze episode, however, pressured Indonesia to ratify the haze agreement with ratification finally occurring in September 2014 [60].

Lessons Learned and Practical Suggestions

The case study showed that Hofstede and the GLOBE's study identifications of Indonesian culture did not always apply, particularly in the transboundary cri-sis communication setting. High power distance and low uncertainty avoidance were reflected in the defensive response of local government and some national government officials, except President Yudhoyono, whose response in the trans-boundary crisis rejected Hofstede and the GLOBE's characterization of its cultural characteristics.

For those interested in crisis communication in Indonesia, it is important to understand how culture works differently in various situations at different levels.

One of the most important discussions following this is probably to question Indonesia's collectivist culture. The case study rejected Hofstede's identification of Indonesia as a collectivist and *rukun* society because both local and national governments seemed to be incapable of tackling the fires that have occurred since 1985. Instead, the Indonesian government's response, particularly the local government, in the transboundary haze showed low institutional collectivism and high in-group collectivism, leading to corrupt practices in return for illegal access to land clearing.

For those interested in crisis communication in Indonesia, it is important to understand how culture works differently in various situations at different levels.

- First, each government institution in Indonesia has conflicting interests, thus the messages and stands may be different. Communicators must identify influential people in related government positions to understand the respective institutions' interests and cultural values, so that they can adjust communication strategies accordingly and communicate crisis in an accurate manner.
- Second, some Indonesian government officials have a sense of belonging and loyalty to particular closed individuals or social groups, and much of the work in Indonesia is very much relationship led. Hence, building strong relationship with key officials is necessary to secure local respect.
- Third, some national government officials showed a defensive strategy when asked to be responsible for the haze by neighboring countries. This response was influenced by a strong power distance and this would suggest that Indonesian leaders greatly emphasize the importance of roles in crisis communication [5]. Government officials might not like to be instructed by other countries on how to handle the fires because they perceived the haze as a domestic affair and thus it was their role and power to decide on the policy without outside intervention. Hence, external parties should deploy a subtle approach when dealing with crisis in Indonesia irrespective of where the blame may lie.

Some countries in the ASEAN, of which Indonesia is a part, had attempted to exert influence on Indonesia through this regional body since it affected at least 3 of the 10-member coalition. However, at that time, Indonesia was still not ready to ratify the "ASEAN Agreement on Transboundary Haze Pollution" [61]. Arguably, it was rather the personal influence of the respective countries' leaders on Indonesia's leaders that mattered more. Understanding government's respective roles is equally important for a greater probability of successful communication outcomes.

External parties should deploy a subtle approach when dealing with crisis in Indonesia irrespective of where the blame may lie.

Discussion Questions

8.1   What are the other factors that can possibly override cultural characteristics in crisis communication responses?

8.2   The case study showed that Indonesia's in-group collectivism has possibly triggered corrupt practices, which influenced some of the government officials' response to crisis. Do you think in-group collectivism can also have positive impact on the government's response to crisis? Justify your answer with evidence.

8.3   In what other ways can one capture Indonesia's cultural characteristics? Are Hofstede's and the GLOBE's cultural identification of Indonesia still relevant?

8.4   How do you perceive the differences in the President's responses in the internal and the transboundary haze crisis? If you were the communication team member for the President, how would you have advised the President in responding to both types of crises?

8.5   How do you perceive the clash between the government (e.g., the President and his ministers) in their response to the crisis? How do you think Indonesia's diverse stakeholders (e.g., companies, local, and national government) can work together to solve this problem? How can communication of haze be centralized so that the country speaks with one voice instead of from multiple centers as it is doing today?

References

1. "Indonesia profile," *BBC*, September 7, 2015. [Online]. Available: http://www.bbc.com/news/world-asia-pacific-14921238, December 28, 2015 (last date accessed).
2. E. Pisani, "Indonesia in pieces: The downside of decentralization," *Foreign Affairs*, July/August 2014. [Online]. Available: http://www.foreignaffairs.com/articles/141481/elizabeth-pisani/indonesia-in-pieces, December 28, 2015 (last date accessed).

3. Indonesia Ministry of Tourism. (n.d.). "Discover Indonesia" [Online]. Available: http://www.indonesia.travel/en/discover-indonesia#tab1, December 28, 2015 (last date accessed).

4. Indonesia Central Statistics Agency. (2010). "Kewarganegaraan, suku bangsa, agama, dan bahasa sehari-hari penduduk Indonesia" [Citizenship, ethnics, religions, and daily languages of Indonesians], [Online]. Available: http://demografi.bps.go.id/phpfiletree/bahan/kumpulan_tugas_mobilitas_pak_chotib/Kelompok_1/Referensi/BPS_kewarganeg araan_sukubangsa_agama_bahasa_2010.pdf, December 28, 2015 (last date accessed).

5. N. H. Gray, "Bahasa, batik, and bargaining: An exploratory study of the negotiation styles and behaviors of Indonesian managers," *Journal of Transnational Management*, vol. 15, no. 3, pp. 215–228, August 2010. doi:10.1080/15475778.2010.504490

6. G. Hofstede, *Culture's Consequences: Comparing Values, Behaviors, Institutions, and Organizations Across Nations*. London: Sage Publications, 2001.

7. G. Hofstede and G. J. Hofstede, *Cultures and Organizations: Software of the Mind, Intercultural Cooperation and Its Importance for Survival*. New York: McGraw-Hill, 2005.

8. R. J. House, P. J. Hanges, M. Javidan, et al., Eds., *Culture, Leadership and Organisations: The GLOBE Study of 62 Societies*. London: Sage Publications, 2004.

9. V. Murphy-Berman and J. J. Berman, "Cross-cultural differences in perceptions of distributive justice: A comparison of Hong Kong and Indonesia," *Journal of Cross-Cultural Psychology*, vol. 33, no. 2, pp. 157–170, March 2002.

10. D. W. Irawanto, P. L. Ramsey, and J. C. Ryan, "Tailoring leadership theory to Indonesian culture," *Global Business Review*, vol. 12, no. 3, pp. 355–366, October 2011.

11. M. Javidan, P. W. Dorfman, M.S. De Luque, et al., "In the eye of the beholder: Cross cultural lessons in leadership from Project GLOBE," *The Academy of Management Perspectives*, vol. 20, no. 1, pp. 67–90, February 2006.

12. D. Waldman, M. de Luque, N. Washburn, et al., "Cultural and leadership predictors of corporate social responsibility values of top management: A GLOBE study of 15 countries," *Journal of International Business Studies*, vol. 37, pp. 823–837, November 2006.

13. G. Hofstede, "The cultural relativity of the quality of life concept," *Academy of Management Review*, vol. 9, no. 3, pp. 389–398, July 1984.

14. É. De Bélizal, F. Lavigne, J. C. Gaillard, et al., "The 2007 eruption of Kelut volcano (East Java, Indonesia): Phenomenology, crisis management and social response," *Geomorphology*, vol. 136, no. 1, pp. 165–175, January 2012.

15. E. K. Dougall, J. S. Horsley, and C. McLisky, "Disaster communication: Lessons from Indonesia," *International Journal of Strategic Communication*, vol. 2, no. 2, pp. 75–99, April 2008.

16. L. Trijono, "Peran komunikasi dalam konflik dan untuk perdamaian," in *Media, Militer, Politik: Crisis Communication: Perspektif Indonesia dan Internasional*, L. S. Ispandriarno, T. Hanitzsch, and M. Loeffelholz, Eds. Yogyakarta: Friedrich Ebert Stiftung, pp. 125–141, 2002.

17. R. Kriyantono, "Measuring a company reputation in a crisis situation: An ethnography approach on the situational crisis communication theory," *International Journal of Business and Social Science*, vol. 3, no. 9, May 2012.

18. M. Abud, "Indonesia: Crisis communication channels, case studies in humanitarian communication preparedness and response," *Internews*, November 4, 2013. [Online]. Available: https://internews.org/research-publications/indonesia-crisis-communication-channels, December 28, 2015 (last date accessed).

19. J. C. Henderson, "Terrorism and tourism: Managing the consequences of the Bali bombings," *Journal of Travel and Tourism Marketing*, vol. 15, no. 1, pp. 41–58, November 2003.

20. D. Prasetyo, "Indonesia plane crash kills 23, scores escape," *Reuters*, March 7, 2007. [Online]. Available: http://www.reuters.com/article/2007/03/07/us-indonesia-plane-idUSSP23854920070307, December 15, 2014 (last date accessed).

21. "Indonesia jet explodes on landing," *BBC*, March 7, 2007. [Online]. Available: http://news.bbc.co.uk/2/hi/asia-pacific/6425419.stm, December 28, 2015 (last date accessed).

22. A. Haruta and K. Hallahan, "Cultural issues in airline crisis communications: A Japan–US comparative study," *Asian Journal of Communication*, vol. 13, no. 2, pp. 122–150, January 2003.

23. M. K. Pinsdorf, "Flying different skies: How cultures respond to airline disasters," *Public Relations Review*, vol. 17, no. 1, pp. 37–56, May 1991.

24. E. K. Wertz and S. Kim, "Cultural issues in crisis communication: A comparative study of messages chosen by South Korean and US print media," *Journal of Communication Management*, vol. 14, no. 1, pp. 81–94, February 2010.

25. Y. Low, J. Varughese, and A. Pang, "Communicating crisis: How culture influences image repair in Western and Asian governments," *Corporate Communications: An International Journal*, vol. 16, no. 3, pp. 218–242, August 2011.

26. A. Gill and T. S. Bin, "Transboundary haze: How might the Singapore government minimise its occurrence?" Available: http://lkyspp.nus.edu.sg/wp-content/uploads/2014/01/Transboundary-Haze.pdf, December 28, 2015 (last date accessed).

27. ADB (Asian Development Bank) and BAPPENAS (National Development Planning Agency), "Causes, extent, impact and costs of 1997/98 fires and drought," Final Report, Annex 1 and 2. Planning for Fire Prevention and Drought Management Project. Asian Development Bank TA 2999-INO July 1998–March 1999. Jakarta, Indonesia. Fortech, Pusat Pengembangan Agribisnis, Margueles Pöyry, 1999.

28. E. Quah, "Transboundary pollution in Southeast Asia: The Indonesian fires," *World Development*, vol. 30, no. 3, pp. 429–441, March 2002.

29. N. Siger, "Haze risk will remain high," *The Jakarta Post*, July 17, 2013. [Online]. Available: http://www.thejakartapost.com/news/2013/07/17/haze-risk-will-remain-high.html, December 15, 2014 (last date accessed).

30. W. D. Basorie, "Canal blocking: One solution to stop peat fires," *The Jakarta Post*, September 1, 2014. [Online]. Available http://www.thejakartapost.com/news/2014/09/01/canal-blocking-one-solution-stop-peat-fires.html, December 15, 2014 (last date accessed).

31. G. Chua, "Singapore urges Indonesia to take immediate measures over worsening haze," *The Straits Times*, June 17, 2013. [Online]. Available: http://www.straitstimes.com/the-big-story/the-haze-singapore/story/haze-sumatra-worsens-psi-cusp-unhealthy-levels-20130617#sthash.LFgLG7P5.dpuf, January 7, 2015 (last date accessed).

32. S. A. Shaikh, "No quick solution to haze woes," New Straits Times, August 30, 2013. [Online]. Available: http://www.asiaone.com/malaysia/no-quick-solution-haze-woes, May 21, 2017 (last date accessed).

33. "Strong comments from Foreign Minister K. Shanmugam over Indonesia's shocking statements," *Channel News Asia*, September 26, 2015. [Online]. Available: http://www.straitstimes.com/asia/strong-comments-from-foreign-minister-k-shanmugam-over-indonesias-shocking-statements, October 21, 2015 (last date accessed).

34. "Indonesian fires cannot be put out, says Malaysian minister, with rainy season seen as only saviour," *ABC*, October 19, 2015. [Online]. Available: http://www.abc.net.au/news/2015-10-19/indonesian-fires-can-not-be-put-out-says-malaysian-minister/6867480, October 21, 2015 (last date accessed).

35. F. Wulandari and S. Cho. (2015, October 2011). "Singapore, Malaysia fly in planes to fight Indonesia's haze" [Online]. Available: http://www.bloomberg.com/news/articles/2015-10-11/singapore-malaysia-fly-in-aircraft-to-fight-indonesia-s-haze, October 21, 2015 (last date accessed).

36. U. Maharadja, "Pemerintah Riau dinilai membiarkan kabut asap" [Riau government let the haze occur], *Sinar Harapan*, March 11, 2014. [Online]. Available: http://sinarharapan.co/index.php/news/read/33713/pemerintah-riau-dinilai-membiarkan-kabut-asap.html, December 15, 2014 (last date accessed).

37. S. Schonhardt, "How corruption is fuelling the haze," *The Straits Times,* June 25, 2013. [Online]. Available: http://www.straitstimes.com/st/print/1238669, December 15, 2014 (last date accessed).

38. W. L. Benoit and A. Pang, "Crisis communication and image repair discourse," in *Public Relations: From Theory to Practice*, T. Hansen-Horn and B. Neff, Eds. Boston, MA: Pearson Allyn & Bacon, 2008, pp. 244–261.

39. "Haze: PSI remains in unhealthy range," *Channel News Asia*, June 19, 2013. [Online]. Available: http://www.channelnewsasia.com/news/specialreports/mh370/news/haze-psi-remains-in/713592.html, December 15, 2014 (last date accessed).

40. A. Abdussalam, "Malaysian firms suspected to have sent haze home," *Antara News*, June 23, 2013. [Online]. Available: http://www.antaranews.com/en/news/89491/malaysian-firms-suspected-to-have-sent-haze-home, December 15, 2014 (last date accessed).

41. "Indonesia chides Singapore over reactions on haze situation," *Channel News Asia*, June 21, 2013. [Online]. Available: http://www.channelnewsasia.com/news/specialreports/mh370/news/indonesia-chides/717798.html, December 15, 2014 (last date accessed).

42. "Indonesia to punish firm burning forest," *People's Daily*, June 21, 2013. [Online]. Available: http://en.people.cn/90777/8293264.html, December 15, 2014 (last date accessed).

43. "Indonesia formally apologizes for smoky haze," *The Jakarta Post*, June 25, 2013. [Online]. Available: http://www.thejakartapost.com/news/2013/06/25/indonesia-formally-apologizes-smoky-haze.html, December 15, 2014 (last date accessed).

44. "The haze: Another Indonesian minister slams S'pore," *Asia One*, June 27, 2013. [Online]. Available: http://news.asiaone.com/print/News/Haze/Story/A1Story20130626-432342.html, December 15, 2014 (last date accessed).

45. S. E. Pinuji. (2015, September 15). "Masyarakat dan penanggulangan asap" [Public and haze mitigation], [Online]. Available: http://nasional.kompas.com/read/2015/09/15/15000051/Masyarakat.dan.Penanggulangan.Asap?page=all. September 27, 2015 (last date accessed).

46. W. Soeriaatmadja. (2015, September 26). "Jokowi orders canal network to be built immediately," Available: http://www.straitstimes.com/asia/jokowi-orders-canal-network-to-be-built-immediately. September 27, 2015 (last date accessed).

47. N. Mazar and P. Aggarwal, "Greasing the palm: Can collectivism promote bribery?" *Psychological Science*, vol. 22, no. 7, pp. 843–848, July, 2011.

48. A. Seleim and N. Bontis, "The relationship between culture and corruption: A cross-national study," *Journal of Intellectual Capital*, vol. 10, no. 1, pp. 165–184, January, 2009.

49. A. K. J. Tan, "Asean agreement on transboundary haze pollution: Prospects for compliance and effectiveness in post-Suharto Indonesia," *The NYU Environmental Law Journal*, vol. 13, p. 647, 2005.

50. R. Novitra, "Disaster, 3 Riau governors arrested," *Tempo*, September, 2014. [Online]. Available: http://www.tempo.co/read/news/2014/09/26/078609868/Musibah-Besar-3-Gubernur-Riau-Berakhir-di-KPK, December 17, 2014 (last date accessed).

51. "Riau diterjang asap, warga kecam pemerintah pusat" [Riau shrouded with smog, people condemn national government], *JPNN*, March 13, 2014. [Online]. Available: http://www.jpnn.com/read/2014/03/13/221797/Riau-Diterjang-Asap,-Warga-Kecam-Pemerintah-Pusat-, December 15, 2014 (last date accessed).

52. M. Leifer, *ASEAN and the Security of South-East Asia*. New York: Routledge Revivals, 2013.

53. A. L. Connelly. (2014, October). "Indonesian foreign policy under President Jokowi," Lowy Institute. [Online]. Available: http://www.lowyinstitute.org/files/indonesian-foreign-policy-under-president-jokowi_0.pdf, December 29, 2015 (last date accessed).

54. "Ministers respond coolly to Yudhoyono apology," *The Jakarta Post*, June 25, 2013. [Online]. Available: http://www.thejakartapost.com/news/2013/06/25/ministers-respond-coolly-yudhoyono-apology.html, January 7, 2015 (last date accessed).

55. A. Pang and A. Diers, "Organization speaking with one voice during crisis: The diffusion of BP's message through mediated channels during the Gulf Coast disaster," 77th Annual International Convention of the Association for Business Communication, Honolulu, HI, 2012.

56. A. Pang, "Dealing with external stakeholders during the crisis: Managing the information vacuum," in *The Handbook of Research on Crisis Leadership in Organizations*, A. J. DuBrin, Ed. Northampton, MA: Edward Elgar Publishing, 2013, pp. 209–229.

57. "SBY apologizes to Singapore and Malaysia for haze," *The Jakarta Globe*, June 24, 2013. [Online]. Available: http://thejakartaglobe.beritasatu.com/news/sby-apologizes-to-singapore-and-malaysia-for-haze/, December 15, 2014 (last date accessed).

58. "Dampak kabut asap terburuk di Dumai" [Worst haze impact in Dumai], *BBC*, June 23, 2013. [Online]. Available: http://www.bbc.com/indonesia/berita_indonesia/2013/06/130623_asap_dumai, December 25, 2015 (last date accessed).

59. A. Ny and A. Teresia. (2013, June 26). "Ini dampak ekonomi kabut asap" [Economic impact of haze], Available: bisnis.tempo.co/read/news/2013/06/26/092491252/ini-dampak-ekonomi-kabut-asap/2, December 25, 2015 (last date accessed).

60. M. S. Aritonang, "RI ratifies haze treaty," *The Jakarta Post*, September, 2014. [Online]. Available: http://www.thejakartapost.com/news/2014/09/17/ri-ratifies-haze-treaty.html, December 15, 2014 (last date accessed).

61. "Hazing rituals," *The Economist,* September 12, 2015. Available: http://www. economist.com/news/asia/21664231-after-all-meetings-and-promises-smog-south-east-asia-still-proves-ineradicable-hazing, December 25, 2015 (last date accessed).

Japan

9

Culture as Crisis Communication: Tokyo Electric Power Company and the Fukushima Daiichi Nuclear Power Plant Disaster

Cornelius B. Pratt and Ronald Lee Carr

Chapter Preview

Japan's worst nuclear disaster occurred in 2011; yet, its transboundary effects continue to reverberate across the globe, particularly as new, more troublesome revelations become public in Japan. At the center of the whirlwind of revelations are the culture and communication practices of Tokyo Electric Power Company (TEPCO), which operates the world's largest nuclear power plant. TEPCO's management's cultural expectations of employee loyalty and of harmony with stakeholders have resulted in public ire. This chapter examines TEPCO's failure to demonstrate consistently high standards in its crisis management protocol and its failure to be transparent with its stakeholders, particularly the everyday public. Therefore, this chapter proposes a communication plan, which, if launched, has the potential to restore the company's public image and to reduce the growing public disaffection with it over its perception of TEPCO's mishandling of a major nuclear

Culture and Crisis Communication: Transboundary Cases from Nonwestern Perspectives, First Edition.
Edited by Amiso M. George and Kwamena Kwansah-Aidoo.
© 2017 by The Institute of Electrical and Electronics Engineers, Inc. Published 2017 by John Wiley & Sons, Inc.

crisis. It also presents proactive elements that can help organizations develop crises-prevention plans and invoke upfront crises-prevention activities.

After reading this chapter, you will be able to

- *Identify the main events that led to a crisis of confidence in the general public over TEPCO's handling of the nuclear power plant disaster*
- *Connect the significance of culture (e.g., loyalty and harmony) to institutional responses to the March 2011 Tōhoku earthquake*
- *Understand Japanese management style, ringi, and its impact on TEPCO's approach to crisis management*
- *Discuss the importance of transparency among governmental and private institutions and general public in maximizing the impact of effective crisis management*
- *Discuss the implications of the special relationship between Japanese government and utility companies with regard to safety regulations of nuclear power plants*
- *Appreciate the role of female activists on the sociopolitical landscape of the post-March 11 triple disaster*
- *Recognize the importance—and the influence—of local governments in Japan*

***

... in Japan, 60 to 80 percent of fish caught in Japanese waters each month are found to contain radioactive cesium ... So many lessons ignored by the powers that be. Why should we want to attempt to continue to harness a form of energy over which we can't control?

—Kimberly Roberson [1]

Introduction

Japanese corporate culture indicates three overarching elements: (A) a majority of Japanese companies—large and small—use a decision-making process called *ringi* to arrive at a group consensus before implementing decisions [2]; (B) social capital—bonding, bridging, and correcting forms—guides Japanese business expectations of individuals in interactions (or in alliances) and between social units such as organizations and institutions [3]; and (C) indigenous, collectivistic social values emphasize the corporate notion of protecting one's own in-group [4]. In essence, then, the world's third largest economy has a corporate—as well as a societal—culture that emphasizes the virtues of (surface) harmony, of group loyalty among all citizens and corporate stakeholders, and of reverence for one's (chronological) age. Japan's business culture does not embrace the word "no," even when a strategic response requires the negative, because that would interfere in the harmony between organizations [5]. That culture frames communication practices that are uniquely Japanese, even as they are also relevant to the corporate landscape of much of Southeast Asia.

Corporate loyalty, for example, frames communications in Japan. That loyalty is indicated in two ways: an employee takes much pride in being tethered to a company's current and future well-being, while management responds similarly to the employee. That concept, generally dubbed *lifetime employment*, is, however, being eroded in an economy that, from the late 1980s through the 1990s, experienced high unemployment, an increase in public debt, a banking system saddled with high risk loans, political instability, and failures in foreign policy, all of which resulted in what had been dubbed a "lost decade" to the people and government of Japan [6–9]. And Prime Minister Shinzo Abe's government's increase in the sales tax from 5% to 8% in April 2014 has proved to be an albatross on a sluggish economy.

The transboundary significance of this chapter is indicated in the International Atomic Energy Agency annals, in which only two accidents have had a "Level 7" nuclear-disaster rating, the highest possible, on the International Nuclear and Radiological Event Scale: the first, on April 26, 1986, was the Chernobyl Nuclear Plant accident in Ukraine, then part of the Soviet Union; and the second was on March 11, 2011, with the Fukushima nuclear meltdown in Japan. Both accidents have a common dimension; their massive human and environmental toll evoked major public concerns, particularly among national, regional, and global health agencies [10–16,]. Such effects engender antinuclear protests and movements in Canada [17]; Japan [18, 19]; Taiwan [20, 21]; the United States [19, 22]; and elsewhere [22, 23].

This chapter presents a culture-based crisis-communication plan that TEPCO, which operates the world's largest nuclear power plant, could have launched within seconds of learning of the human and environmental destruction that began on March 11, 2011, the day of a seeming apocalypse to millions of citizens, particularly those in the country's worst-hit prefectures: Aomori, Chiba, Fukushima, Ibaraki, Iwate, and Miyagi.

Culture and Crisis Communication

Culture affects *all* social interactions. Because Japan is a close-knit society, one is better able to understand how government infrastructure works in a disaster. The Japanese company illustrates the inner workings of disaster communication. Traditionally, Japanese companies lack the transparency common in the West [24]. This may be an outcome of the relationship between company and employee. Think of the Japanese company as an extended family in which allegiance and loyalty are unquestioned. For example, the majority of Japanese companies hold intensive training secessions for new employees. For large companies, this may involve a week or more, and require recruits to live in dormitories.

Meetings are more than approaches to strategy, and they entail some level of harmonizing employees to work as one cohesive, bonded unit. Differences of opinion are discussed until consensus is reached. New employees are not just hired but, figuratively speaking, adopted into their new family. One example of this cohesion is the company Work Rules or *shū gyō kisoku*. Full-time employees have a say in how the company treats their employees to some extent. The Work Rules not only adhere to Ministry of Labor regulations, but also attempt to customize the rules to the employees' needs. Before the Work Rules are submitted to the ministry office, each full-time employee is given the opportunity to revise them. A final copy is submitted to the labor office only after each full-time employee has had an opportunity to contest the rules. One's identity and the company are powerfully linked.

This can also affect government offices, as well. On the heels of the Kobe earthquake of January 17, 1995, for example, the bureaucracy of adjacent wards and communities hindered the flow of disaster-related communication among them. Outside assistance also had communication roadblocks in aid-receiving communities. Even though the prefecture did ultimately accept US military assistance such as blankets, tents, and water, it refused other resources such as aircraft and tractors. Trained rescue dogs, flown from Switzerland, were stuck in quarantine at Kansai Airport. Why? At first glance, it seemed inconceivable for an organized, functioning nation like Japan to allow bureaucratic pettiness to block the flow of desperately needed goods and services offered to victims of a major disaster. On closer investigation, however, one realizes that cultural context determines communication patterns—that is, how, with whom, and to whom one communicates, hence the bureaucratic impasse.

In Japan, the responsibility for responding to disasters follows a strict trajectory: the local government, the prefecture, the national government. Contemporary Japanese society supports autonomous governance that gives preference to local issues. Essentially, two tiers exist: prefectures and municipalities [25]. Prefectures are regional authorities overseeing municipalities, which are local entities that have strong, direct ties to their citizens. Japan has 47 municipalities, including Tokyo. Tokyo comprises 23 wards, or local entities. Each ward addresses various needs of its citizens, often dealing with daily and long-term needs. This rigidly enforced sequence of responsibility places the burden of crisis management on the shoulders of those most proximate to the disaster and to its victims.

Even though such a management hierarchy is rational within the village context, natural disasters like those of the Kobe and Tōhoku earthquakes affect directly hundreds of thousands of people across several prefectures. As noted in the introduction, *ringi* permeates Japanese decision-making process. Group consensus inherently takes more time than does the western upper-management-centered style where decisions are either reached quickly at the zenith of power or are delegated to subordinates. In the aftermath of the Kobe earthquake, wards, not used to working together, had distinct bureaucratic responsibilities. Communications were based on traditional practices. Each bureaucracy must reach an internal consensus before any actions are taken. Kobe earthquake victims waited for specific instructions while the affected wards attempted to reach a consensus among themselves.

The everyday practice of public relations in Japan is as a medium of public hearing, hence, its two-way asymmetric characteristic; and as marketing and press-agency tactical tools, with the sole purpose of attracting media attention to a company or its products [26].

Against those accepted practices in Japan, then, it behooves Japan's crisis communication practitioners to use (tactical) media relations, framed in cultural contexts, when communicating during a crisis. Because cultural influences loom large in Japan's crisis communication, they were brought to the fore in the aftermath of charges by both consumers and the Osaka City Hall that Snow Brand Milk Products Co., Ltd., of Japan, sold poisonous milk products in 2000 [27]. But the inflexibility of company's culture, fueled in large measure by societal practices of high power distance, high levels of uncertainty avoidance, harmonious interpersonal relationships, and group solidarity, prevented open communication about the issue and stifled warnings from employees about a possible problem with the product. Embedded in such cultural contexts are opportunities for communicating effectively during crises—issues to which we now turn. Cooper-Chen and Tanaka [28] note that Japan's collectivistic culture, which embraces *wa* (harmony), *amae* (trust), *enryo* (conformity), and *ittaikan* (oneness), contributes to the country's "slow [corporate] reactions to crisis situations" (p. 104).

Opportunity and Problem Statements

The communication practices presented in the preceding section point to the importance of three key players—national and local governments, TEPCO, the public—in managing this nuclear crisis primarily by reducing significantly the growing public disaffection with the company over the public's perception of TEPCO's *mis*handling of the fallout. Those culture-based communication practices frame the nature of exchanges among them—particularly the form of communications that TEPCO *should* use to assuage its stakeholders and their pent-up passions.

Opportunity Statements
OS 1: TEPCO's in-house communication professionals have the wherewithal to steer their company to a new, desired direction to engage and assuage stakeholders. The rationale for this statement is that "... TEPCO and its leadership had been in the forefront of developing, disseminating, and expanding 'best practices' in corporate communications in Japan" [29]. The company uses strategic research to investigate ways in which corporations can better communicate in Japan and to develop management structures in an increasingly globalizing business environment.

OS 2: TEPCO is committed to protecting the interests of its strategic publics: Residents of the worst-hit prefectures. The rationale for this statement is the unanimous concerns among all interest groups over the health risks associated with the fallout from the nuclear disaster and their attempt to "eliminate the curatorial hand" [30] in reporting the sanitized views of the powers that be. Because women, for example, seem particularly vulnerable to the fallout from natural disasters, they tend to play active environmental roles [31]. As Enarson [32] notes, "Typecast as hapless women awaiting strong-armed male rescuers, many women are in fact active disaster responders as well as particularly vulnerable to disaster impacts" (p. 158).

There have also been major concerns about the communication conduct, particularly the disclosure policy, of TEPCO, the operators of the plant. Japanese women are a major resource in Japan's political landscape vis-à-vis their responses to the knock-on effects of the disaster.

OS 3: TEPCO's partnership with the Japanese government and with interest groups are a medium for engaging them and for responding strategically to their environmental and health concerns. This statement is based on the notion that engagement can serve as a vehicle of mobilization, validation, and legitimization—all of which are crucial to establishing corporate credibility and understanding of the dire nature of the challenges TEPCO faces.

OS 4: TEPCO's communication staffers have the professional resources for strategic public engagement. The rationale for this statement is that the professionalism that TEPCO's communications operation has developed over the years can be a viable medium for disseminating and sharing powerful, transformative narratives on sociopolitical and economic issues while at once connecting them to the news media. Such engagement can enhance the company's public impact in that it can be perceived as an alternative medium of social impact on society by intervening in and actively building public spheres and fomenting social change.

Problem Statements

1. Nuclear-meltdown-related messages are uncoordinated and inconsistent.
2. TEPCO's information-gathering and disseminating operations leave much to be desired by a public skeptical—and critical—of TEPCO's behavior.
3. TEPCO is rattled by public concerns that the radioactive contamination from the March 2011 meltdown could be active for 300 years.

Outcomes of the Crisis

All these dimensions are manifested increasingly in the growing public cavalcade from the fallout of the March 11 disaster and in the expanding impact that they have on Japan's political life. Public outrage over TEPCO's handling of the fallout from the transboundary environmental and human disaster continues to reverberate across the globe, particularly as new, more troublesome revelations become public in Japan. The significant public role, particularly that of Japanese women, in the antinuclear movement following the Fukushima Daiichi nuclear disaster [18]; the list of movies on a subject that constitutes an all-but-instant subgenre; and the long, growing list of documentary films on the disaster, all

> [speak] to any number of factors: the convenience of digital recording tech-nology, the velocity of today's 24/7 news cycle, the scale of the catastrophe (which killed thousands and ... displaced many more) and the perceived need to counter government positions and news media reports (which have come under scrutiny and criticism). [30]

Particularly noteworthy is that for a culture immanently high context, it is important—if not imperative—that such manifestations serve as pointers to an evolving political and social landscape that is assuming characteristics at cross-purposes to cultural practices and to a national mind-set.

As a consequence of the public outcry over nuclear meltdown, at least 25 nuclear-energy lawsuits have been filed in 20 district courts and court branches across Japan [33]. Sixteen of those lawsuits are pending, as of this writing. And Prime Minister Shinzo Abe's cabinet embraces nuclear power even though there is growing public opposition to using that form of energy [34–36]. Particularly in nuclear-energy-dependent Japan, communication practices of the nation's largest utility company raise umpteenth questions, some of which are examined in this chapter.

In the aftermath of Japan's Fukushima disaster, antinuclear protests have coa-lesced around the female voice—that is, Japanese mothers were so riled and agonized by the meltdown that they have been taking to task the government and the company that manages the nuclear plant. There is so much distrust, discontent, apprehension, and disgust on all sides of the nuclear issue that citizen groups are now rallying to vent their feelings and wrest control of a slippery issue from two strange bedfellows: government agencies and TEPCO. In light of the preceding analysis, this chapter pro-poses a crisis-focused communication plan as a much-needed strategic response to the nuclear meltdown. The following proposals are directed to the appropriate local and prefectural government offices. It is the authors' opinion that the most effective platform for change is through local municipalities working within their prefectures as these institutions work with local residents on a daily basis. For funding, both national resources and allocations from TEPCO would be used. In essence, this cam-paign is developed as an effective response to the communication gap engendered by TEPCO's response to the disaster.

Proposed Goals

1. To increase understanding of the government and corporate role in the crisis.
2. To inform various interest groups of TEPCO's substantive actions during and after the crisis.
3. To bring leaders of social movements up to date on TEPCO's evolving actions.
4. To demonstrate a palpably compassionate and caring TEPCO.

Proposed Objectives

1. To facilitate, during the next 12 months, a number of dialogues and town-hall meetings on TEPCO's actions to date coordinated by local and prefectural government offices.
2. To present publicly, during the next 12 months, TEPCO's accomplishments vis-à-vis the crisis. Such forums will be handled through local ward offices acting as watchdog committees.
3. To demonstrate to lawmakers and the public, during the next 12 months, that TEPCO has significantly improved its transparency and its public trustworthiness.

Proposed Strategies and Tactics

Strategy 1: To encourage a public understanding of the importance of corporate-initiated public safety

Local municipalities would implement the following tactics, drawing funds from government allocations and TEPCO. Each ward, through its main government office, would follow a uniform procedure, agreed upon by its members, arriving at viable proposals. The authors suggest that prefectural government representatives oversee the review-and-disbursement process.

- Tactic 1: Disseminate information on the importance of self-help in protection from environmental hazards—especially for residents of the worst-hit prefectures.
- Tactic 2: Establish a community-based oversight committee comprising members of the hardest-hit communities and safety experts who will ascertain the immediate safety hazards that exist.
- Tactic 3: Arrange ongoing meetings among the oversight committee, TEPCO, and local municipal government agencies to evaluate proposals to determine those that are potentially feasible.
- Tactic 4: Enact into policy those policies mandated under Tactic 3 (immediately above).

Strategy 2: To ensure organizational transparency

- Tactic 1: Local ward office will establish an independent committee made up of major shareholders in the community and local government to evaluate present practices of major utility companies and Ministry offices with regard to the kinds of improprieties that led to the deflation of TEPCO's reputation after the March 2011 disasters.

- Tactic 2: Present to government legislative branch policy suggestions on eliminating nepotism between TEPCO and government agencies.
- Tactic 3: Ensure that TEPCO agree to adopt policies that re-establish its corporate autonomy and public trustworthiness.

Strategy 3: Revamp TEPCO's public relations machine
- Tactic 1: Local wards would coordinate meetings between TEPCO management and an independent legislative body to rigorously re-evaluate its public relations tactics.
- Tactic 2: Mandate changes as determined by TEPCO legislative body.
- Tactic 3: Establish a well-integrated (and coordinated) public relations strategy that informs the public on TEPCO's international changes in an attempt at image repair and restoration.

Outcomes Assessment

As of this writing, TEPCO had publicly announced plans to establish a decade-long Fukushima renewal, a major internal restructuring, and an expanded compensation for those affected by the nuclear disaster. In a January 21, 2014 TEPCO report, President Naomi Hirose announced an "effort that will address the human, environmental, and economic challenges that lie ahead" [37]. The new plan is coordinated within the framework of a consortium of financial institutions that will provide "credit and liquidity" over the next several years [37]. The company plans to cut an additional ¥1.4 trillion (US$11.5 billion) in expenses and to invest ¥750 billion (US$6.2 billion) during the next decade in safety technologies.

On April 1, 2014, Fumio Sudo took over as CEO of TEPCO. In the company's April 2014 *Prompt Report*, Sudo said, "The most important mission I must address before anything else is to carry out the commitments to Fukushima" [38]. Regardless of how positively TEPCO attempts to portray itself to the public, it is still wedged in the vortex of its own improprieties. It has been taken to task by the nation's government nuclear watchdog for its failure to disclose information on radioactive rainwater leaking into the sea [39]. Such occurrences are not rare for TEPCO as was the company's announcement that its operations to remove spent and melted nuclear fuel from the No. 1 reactor would be delayed by 2–5 years [40].

Given that TEPCO plans to get its nuclear power plants running again, there is an urgent need for shareholders to leverage the utility giant into undertaking reforms. TEPCO President Naomi Hirose told *The Wall Street Journal*® that the utility giant was making progress in persuading local community members to "accept" the restart of the Kashiiwasaki–Kariwa nuclear power plant [41]. TEPCO has acknowledged that starting two of the seven newest reactors would increase profit by about ¥30 billion ($250 million). TEPCO's need for profit is clear: estimates for compensation of those eligible due to the Fukushima accident exceed ¥5 trillion ($41.3 billion) [37].

Lessons Learned

This case study attempts to uncover the reasons for TEPCO's failure to fulfill Milton Freedman's classic view of corporate responsibility. TEPCO's flagrant disregard for clear and direct communication with shareholders allowed for obfuscation of vital and necessary information. The first lesson is one that is crucial to basic social responsibility: the willingness to address the public in a forthright, open manner. In the case of TEPCO, there was an unwillingness to speak forthrightly to the press about the initial explosions at Fukushima. TEPCO executives first addressed the press and public 4 days after the earthquake. Why wait so long, and risk losing both respect before the public and attract ridicule in the press, even as the government is ordering evacuation of local citizens?

The answer to that question leads to a possible second lesson learned, in that approaches to crisis management are cloaked in cultural norms. Considering Japan's tendency toward demonstrating the dimensions of a high context society that emphasize, for example, loyalty to the group rather than to oneself, TEPCO's executives meander through a multilayered causeway of decision-making based upon rules regarding public and private face. Even though Japan is certainly a democracy, its corporate structures are bound by the same rules that apply to the Japanese public in general. Whereas in low context United States and Britain, communication is likely to be direct, in a society like Japan, where the expectation of responsibility may follow even the most random event, there is less willingness to reveal information. Such considerations are paramount for crisis management considerations.

Overcoming cultural barriers in a high context society such as Japan is a daunting task. In the case of the Fukushima disaster, what seems to have worked to some degree is activism by shareholders and by mothers in social movements. As noted in a preceding paragraph, one of the most effective platforms for change was radical action taken by the mothers of Fukushima and of those in surrounding areas. Their resistance to government whitewashing and refusal to accept the mostly tepid response to vital needs by TEPCO rallied locals to take action themselves. These locals insisted on removing contaminated dirt from kindergarten schoolyards, demanded using radiation checks in areas affected by the blasts, and, most important, connected with one another by creating networks of mothers through the region [42,43].

Emotional reactions ran high, particularly as anger and outrage encouraged people to join and commit themselves to social movements [44,45]. The possibility of a child contracting thyroid cancer because government bureaucracy hindered the few hours it took for a digger to remove contaminated dirt from a school sandbox angered the mothers to such an extent that they ultimately removed the dirt themselves with spades [46]. This by-hook-or-crook approach worked well to counterbalance Japan's orderly society. One problem is that the same tight, internal mechanisms that maintain social order can quickly fail during crisis situations when time demands are intense and malleable, and continuous actions are required.

Discussion Questions

9.1 What were the major chronological errors made by TEPCO in its failure to inform the press about events at its Fukushima plant after March 11, 2011?

9.2 How did TEPCO's communication practices fail residents living close to the plant?

9.3 What improprieties did TECPO allow for, in its relationship to the press that may have influenced proper reporting?

9.4 In what ways can TEPCO improve its relations with local residents whose lives have been upended by the Fukushima disaster?

9.5 What are the limitations of the communication plan presented in this chapter in re-establishing TEPCO in the good graces of its stakeholders?

References

1. K. Roberson, *Silence Deafening: Fukushima Fallout … A Mother's Response*, 2nd ed. Playa Del Rey, CA: VisionTalk, 2013, p. 8.
2. B. M. Hawrysh and J. L. Zaichkowsky, "Cultural approaches to negotiations: Understanding the Japanese," *International Marketing Review*, vol. 7, no. 2, pp. 28–41, 1990.
3. S. Slater and M. J. Robson, "Social capital in Japanese-Western alliances: Understanding cultural effects," *International Marketing Review*, vol. 29, no. 1, pp. 6–23, 2012.
4. T. Matsui, T. Kakuyama, Y. Tsuzuki, and H. S. You, "Joint effects of corporate positions and prospects on perceptions of business ethics among Japanese students: A reflection of collectivistic cultures," *Journal of Social Psychology*, vol. 39, pp. 624–633, 2009.
5. N. Oikawa and J. F. Tanner Jr., "The influence of Japanese culture on business relationships and negotiations," *Journal of Services Marketing*, vol. 6, no. 3, pp. 67–74, 1992.
6. H. Dobson, "Review "Rethinking Japan's 'lost decade'," *Global Society: Journal of Interdisciplinary International Relations*, vol. 19, pp. 211–223, 2005.
7. C. W. Hughes, *Japan's Security Agenda: Military, Economic and Environmental Dimensions*. Boulder, CO: Lynne Rienner, 2004.
8. T. Inoguchi, Ed., *Japan's Asian Policy: Revival and Response*. Basingstoke: Palgrave Macmillan, 2002.

9. H. Yoshikawa, *Japan's Lost Decade*. Tokyo: Trust/International House of Japan, 2001.

10. M. Baba, "Fukushima accident: What happened?" *Radiation Measurements*, vol. 55, pp. 17–21, 2013. doi: 10.1016/j.radmeas.2013.01.013

11. F. Gralla, D. J. Abson, A. P. Møller, et al., "The impact of nuclear accidents on provisioning ecosystem services," *Ecological Indicators*, vol. 41, pp. 1–14, 2014. doi: 10.1016/j.ecolind.2014.01.027

12. S. M. L. Hardie and I. G. McKinley, "Fukushima remediation: Status and overview of future plans," *Journal of Environmental Radioactivity*, vol. 133, pp. 75–85, 2014.

13. D. Kinley, Ed., *Chernobyl's legacy: Health, environmental and socio-economic impacts*. The Chernobyl Forum. International Atomic Energy Agency Report #IAEA/PI/A.87 REV2/06-09181, 2006.

14. V. Kortov and Y. Ustyantsev, "Chernobyl accident: Causes, consequences and problems of radiation measurements," *Radiation Measurements*, vol. 55, pp. 12–16, 2013. doi: 10.1016/j.radmeas.2013.01.013

15. G. Steinhauser, A. Brandl, and T. E. Johnson, "Comparison of the Chernobyl and Fukushima nuclear accidents: A review of the environmental impacts," *Science of the Total Environment*, vols. 470–471, pp. 800–817, 2014. doi: 10.1016/j.scitotenv.2013.10.029

16. G. Steinhauser, A. Brandl, and T. E. Johnson, "Erratum to 'Comparison of the Chernobyl and Fukushima nuclear accidents: A review of the environmental impacts' [*Science of Total Environment*, vols. 470–471, pp. 800–817, 2014]," *Science of the Total Environment*, vol. 487, p. 575, 2014.

17. M. Leeming, "The creation of radicalism: Anti-nuclear activism in Nova Scotia, c. 1972–1979," *The Canadian Historical Review*, vol. 95, no. 2, pp. 217–241, 2014. doi: 10.3138/chr.1945

18. A. Ogawa, "Demanding a safer tomorrow: Japan's anti-nuclear rallies in the summer of 2012," *Anthropology Today*, vol. 29, pp. 21–24, 2013.

19. H. L. Angelique and M. R. Culley, "To Fukushima with love: Lessons on long-term antinuclear citizen participation from Three Mile Island," *Journal of Community Psychology*, vol. 42, pp. 209–227, 2014. doi: 10.1002/jcop.21605

20. "Taiwan stops construction of nuclear plant" (2014, April 28) [Online]. Available: http://www.wsj.com/articles/SB10001424052702303939404579529103578288372, April 28, 2016 (last date accessed).

21. J. W. Hsu, "Taiwan police forcefully repel antinuclear protesters; police in Taipei used water cannons to evict thousands of antinuclear protesters" (2014, April 28) [Online]. Available: http://www.wsj.com/articles/SB10001424052702304163604579529050283575632, April 28, 2016 (last date accessed).

22. B. P. Taylor, "Thinking about nuclear power," *Polity*, vol. 45, pp. 297–311, 2013. doi:10.1057/pol.2013.3

23. W. van der Zeijden, "A Dutch revolt? The salience of the nonstrategic nuclear weapons issue in Dutch politics," *European Security*, vol. 23, no. 1, pp. 45–57, 2014. doi: 10.1080/09662839.2013.856302

24. P. Figueroa, "Nuclear risk governance in Japan and the Fukushima triple disaster: Lessons Unlearned," in *Disaster Governance in Urbanising Asia*, M. A. Miller and M. Douglass Eds. Singapore: Springer, 2016, pp. 263–282.

25. The structure of the metropolitan government (TMG), Tokyo Metropolitan Government, (2015) [Online]. Available: http://www.metro.tokyo.jp/ENGLISH/ABOUT/ STRUCTURE/structure01.htm. April 28, 2016 (last date accessed).

26. K. Sriramesh, Y. Kim, and M. Takasaki, "Public relations in three Asian cultures," *Journal of Public Relations Research*, vol. 11, pp. 271–292, 2009. doi: 10.1207/ s1532754xjprr1104_01

27. B. J. Wrigley, S. Ota, and A. Kikuchi, "Lightning strikes twice: Lessons learned from two food poisoning incidents in Japan," *Public Relations Review*, vol. 32, pp. 349–357, 2006.

28. A. Cooper-Chen and M. Tanaka, "Public relations in Japan: The cultural roots of *kouhou*," *Journal of Public Relations Research*, vol. 20, pp. 94–114, 2007. doi: 10.1080/ 10627260701727036

29. C. B. Pratt and A. Yanada, "Risk communication and Japan's Fukushima Daiichi Nuclear Power Plant meltdown: Ethical implications for government-citizen divides," *Public Relations Journal*, vol. 8, no. 4, 2014. [Online]. Available: http://www.prsa.org/intelligence/ PRJournal/Vol8/No4/. March 18, 2015 (last date accessed).

30. D. Lim. (2012, March 18). "Post-traumatic filmmaking in Japan," [Online]. Available: http://www.cnbc.com/id/46755977, April 28, 2016 (last date accessed).

31. L. Gordon, "Preserving family and community: Women's voices from the Christchurch earthquakes," *Disaster Prevention and Management*, vol. 22, pp. 415–424, 2013. doi: 10.1108/DPM-10-2013-0175

32. E. Enarson, "Through women's eyes: A gendered research agenda for disaster social science," *Disasters*, vol. 22, no. 2, pp. 157–173, 1998.

33. AJW.Asahi.com. (2015, May 5), "Plaintiffs soon to exceed 10,000 in lawsuits against TEPCO seeking extra compensation," *The John Wells Program*, May 5, 2015. [Online]. Available: https://caravantomidnight.com/plaintiffs-soon-to-exceed-10000-in- lawsuits-against-tepco-seeking-extra compensation/?doing_wp_cron=1495503746.6333 210468292236328125, May 23, 2017 (last date accessed).

34. M. Fackler. (2014, February 7). "2 former premiers try to use Tokyo election to rally public against nuclear power" [Online]. Available: http://www.nytimes.com/2014/02/08/ world/asia/2-former-premiers-try-to-use-tokyo-election-to-rally-public-against-nuclear- power.html, April 28, 2016 (last date accessed).

35. M. Fackler. (2014, March 20). "Warily leading Japan's nuclear reawakening" [Online]. Available: http://www.nytimes.com/2014/03/21/world/asia/warily-leading-japans- nuclear-reawakening.html. April 28, 2016 (last date accessed).

36. J. Kingston. (2014, June 28). "Abe's nuclear renaissance ignores stiff opposition" [Online]. Available: http://www.japantimes.co.jp/opinion/2014/06/28/commentary/abes- nuclear-renaissance-ignores-stiff-opposition/}.U8a4tUtOUeF, September 14, 2015 (last date accessed).

37. TEPCO, Recent topics: TEPCO announces sweeping new plan with government for Fukushima renewal, compensation, and reorganization, (2014, January 21) [Online]. Available: http://www.tepco.co.jp/en/press/corp-com/release/2014/1233729_5892.html. April 28, 2016 (last date accessed).

38. TEPCO, Recent topics: Fumio Sudo takes over as TEPCO chairman, pledges commitment to Fukushima and to company reform, (2014, April 1) [Online]. Available: http://www.

tepco.co.jp/en/press/corp-com/release/2014/1235237_5892.html. June 11, 2015 (last date accessed).

39. "Radioactive water detected again at Fukushima plant, source unknown," *Japan Bullet*, May 6, 2015. [Online]. Available: http://www.japanbullet.com/news/radioactive-water-detected-again-at-fukushima-plant-source-unknown, May 23, 2017 (last date accessed).

40. "TEPCO to postpone nuclear fuel removal at Fukushima No. 1 reactor," ENENEWS, November 4, 2013. [Online]. Available: http://enenews.com/postponed-fuel-removal-attempt-at-fukushima-unit-4-delayed-possibly-for-weeks-govt-safety-agency-wants-tests-conducted, May 23, 2017 (last date accessed).

41. M. Iwata. (2013, September 27). "Cash-strapped TEPCO seeks approval for nuclear startup" [Online]. Available: http://www.wsj.com/articles/SB10001424052702304526204579102003745190652, November 14, 2014 (last date accessed).

42. A. Mizhuo. (2012, January 4). "Mothers first to shed food-safety complacency" [Online]. Available: http://www.japantimes.co.jp/news/2012/01/04/national/mothers-first-to-shed-food-safety-complacency/}.VPr6LWYx5xI, January 4, 2015 (last date accessed).

43. J. Watts. (2011, May 2). "Fukushima parents dish the dirt in protest over radiation levels" [Online]. Available: http://www.theguardian.com/world/2011/may/02/parents-revolt-radiation-levels, February 27, 2014 (last date accessed).

44. J. M. Jasper, "The emotions of protest: Affective and reactive emotions in and around social movements," *Sociological Forum*, vol. 13, pp. 397–424, 1998.

45. J. M. Jasper and J. D. Poulsen, "Recruiting strangers and friends: Moral shocks and social networks in animal rights and anti-nuclear protests," *Social Problems*, vol. 42, pp. 493–512, 1995.

46. H. Tabuchi. (2011, May 25), "Angry Parents in Japan Confront Government Over Radiation Levels". *The New York Times*. [Online] Available: http://www.nytimes.com/2011/05/26/world/asia/26japan.html, May 23, 2017 (last day accessed).

Kazakhstan 10

Understanding the Zhanaozen Crisis Through the Intercultural Lenses of Eurasianism in Kazakhstan

Elena Kolesova and Dila Beisembayeva

Chapter Preview

This chapter analyzes the conflict between the oil workers, the KazMunaiGas oil company, and the local government authorities that took place between May and June 2011 in Zhanaozen, a small town in the Republic of Kazakhstan. The culmination point of this conflict was the unrest at the central square on December 16, 2011. According to official reports, 17 civilians were killed with many more wounded. However, social media reports indicate that at least 100 people died as a result of the clash with local police. Kazakhstani government and President Nursultan Nazarbayev initially denied the possibility of conflict/crisis in the region. However, ongoing reports of some journalists and bloggers from Zhanaozen and the continuous unrest in the region forced Nazarbayev to acknowledge the existence of the conflict and move toward finding some solution to end it. This chapter analyzes the Zhanaozen conflict/crisis through cultural lenses. The national ideology of

Culture and Crisis Communication: Transboundary Cases from Nonwestern Perspectives, First Edition.
Edited by Amiso M. George and Kwamena Kwansah-Aidoo.
© 2017 by The Institute of Electrical and Electronics Engineers, Inc. Published 2017 by John Wiley & Sons, Inc.

Eurasianism provides a useful framework for understanding the role of culture in the communication of the Zhanaozen conflict/crisis.
After reading this chapter, you will be able to

- *Discuss the role of social media in the Zhanaozen crisis/conflict*
- *Describe the national ideology of Eurasianism as a useful framework for understanding the Zhanaozen conflict/crisis*
- *Analyze the official response to the Zhanaozen conflict/crisis according to the nine strategies described in the chapter (attack the accuser, denial, scapegoat, excuse, justification, compensation, apology, reminder, and ingratiation)*
- *Understand the role of the local Kazakhstani culture in the official response to the Zhanaozen crisis/conflict*

A Brief Overview of Kazakhstan and Kazakhstani Culture

Kazakhstan, officially the Republic of Kazakhstan, one of the post-Soviet successor states, is located in Central Asia and occupies a territory as large as all of Western Europe, which makes it the ninth largest country in the world by area. Geographically, it is the largest country in Central Asia, sharing borders with Russia, China, Kyrgyzstan, Uzbekistan, Turkmenistan, and the Caspian Sea. Its population of approximately 17 million makes Kazakhstan the 62nd most populated country in the world [1].

Under the Soviet regime, Kazakhstan became home to a large number of ethnic/cultural groups who were often forcefully relocated by the State, making it one of the most diverse Soviet republics. There were more than 140 different ethnic groups living on the territory of Kazakhstan as of 2015. According to the latest statistics, among the population of Kazakhstan, 63.3% are Kazakh, 23.5% are Russian; the remaining 13.2% is composed of Germans, Tatars, Ukrainians, Uzbeks, Uighurs as well as much smaller numbers of Byelorussians, Koreans, Poles, and other ethnic groups [2]. In Kazakhstan, the majority group's (Kazakhs) share of the total population is the lowest of all post-communist states (with the exception of Latvia) [3].

Historically, the Russian or Slavic population was concentrated in the North Kazakhstan and East Kazakhstan regions, while Germans dominated the Karaganda region. More Russians reside in the southeast in and around Almaty, the largest city in Kazakhstan. Almaty was the capital of Kazakhstan during the Soviet era until it lost its status to Astana in 1997. One of the main reasons for relocating the capital to the north was to strengthen Kazakh presence in the northern part of the country, which is traditionally dominated by Russians and Russified Kazakhs. Additionally, the Kazakhstani government actively encourages the repatriation of Kazakhs from Russia, China, Mongolia, Turkey, Uzbekistan, and Turkmenistan to Kazakhstan, first of all, to the regions traditionally populated by Russians.[1] The Kazakhs who return to Kazakhstan are called "Oralmans" which means "returnees" in the Kazakh language. According to the report by the Commission on Human Rights (under the President of the Republic of Kazakhstan) 860,400 Kazakh individuals immigrated to Kazakhstan from 1991 until October 1, 2011 [4]. This is a significant proportion for a country with a population of approximately 17 million people.

The growing Oralmans' presence strongly contributes to the cultural makeup of today's Kazakhstan society. Oralmans make a strong contrast to the local Kazakhs as they speak Kazakh language more fluently, and have a greater awareness of the traditional culture, including food, music, folklore, family rituals, and behavior patterns. Local Kazakhs had lost this cultural knowledge under the Soviet regime. However, Oralmans equally brought some unacceptable practices to Kazakhstan due to their cultural differences that separated them from the majority of Kazakhs in Kazakhstan and which will be discussed further in this chapter. As a result of such a government policy that encourages relocation of the ethnic Kazakhs back to Kazakhstan, the proportion of ethnic Russians is steadily decreasing, while the proportion of ethnic Kazakhs is on the rise.

The complex ethnic and cultural composition of the Kazakhstani population creates challenges for developing national identity and constructing the Kazakhstan nation.

The complex ethnic and cultural composition of the Kazakhstani population creates challenges for developing national identity and constructing the Kazakhstan nation. Nursultan Nazarbayev, Kazakhstan's first president who continues to hold this position in 2017, faces the task of moving away from the national and cultural politics promoted by the former Soviet Union which had a strong emphasis on "russification of the masses," toward constructing a new state identity of the Republic of Kazakhstan based on promotion of authentic Kazakh culture and language. At the same time, Nazarbayev tries to avoid antagonizing his northern neighbor, Russia, by making an effort not to alienate ethnic Russians in Kazakhstan. Nazarbayev also does not support the exodus of Russian speakers from Kazakhstan, as they play an important role in the country's economy.

But relations with Russia and the Russian population in Kazakhstan are not the only challenges Nazarbayev faces with his task of constructing Kazakhstani national and cultural identity. Other challenges are associated with the multiethnic, multicultural reality of the country. Kazakhstan and the Kazakh people historically have never been united or constructed as a homogenous group. The historical division was and still remains among the three main zhuz (tribal confederations or clans). These tribes are the Great Horde (Uly Zhuz), Middle Horde (Orta Zhuz), and Small Horde (Kishi Zhuz), with further subdivisions within these three zhuz [3].

Although kinship is often invisible, at least to outsiders, it plays a very important role in Kazakhstani society today influencing strongly its political life.

These kinship-based groups or networks facilitate initial social relations and are based on trust and mutual support. A number of authors contributed toward research on clans in Kazakhstan and the implication of such relations for modern political, social, and economic structures [5, 6]. Edward Schatz, who published extensively on modern clan politics in Kazakhstan, argues that although kinship is often invisible, at least to outsiders, it plays a very important role in Kazakhstani society today, influencing strongly its political life [6]. For the majority of people in Kazakhstan, kinship provides the initial social relationship based on mutual trust. Schatz suggests that the kinship/clan relations are even more complicated than ethnic differences due to their invisibility, which is also linked to the lack of transparency at the official or government level in Kazakhstan [6]. These kinship/clan relationships constitute one of the important cultural characteristics of Kazakhstan, hard to detect, but strongly present.

Nazarbayev has addressed such cultural and ethnic complexity through his policies. As early as 1995, Nazarbayev created an *Assembly of the People of Kazakhstan*. This new assembly brought together more than 800 ethnic and cultural associations who elected nine members to the Majilis (lower house of parliament in Kazakhstan) [3]. This was one of the first of Nazarbayev's attempts to construct a unified nation through legitimization of different ethnic and cultural groups.

Culture and Crisis Communication: The Concepts of Eurasia and Eurasianism

In 2008, the new Law on the Assembly of the People of Kazakhstan was promulgated to assist with institutionalizing interethnic relations and prevention of potential interethnic and intercultural conflicts [3]. In 2009, the Doctrine of National Unity further promoted the strengthening of interethnic harmony. Such a focus on interethnic and intercultural coexistence was crafted around the concept of Eurasia and Eurasianism, or to be more accurate, President Nazarbayev's interpretation of the two concepts at the time.

The concepts of Eurasia and Eurasianism have been in use for more than a century; however, there is no agreement among academics and politicians about the meaning of both of these concepts. The origins of the category of Eurasia can be tracked to the British geographer Sir Halford Mackinder who used the term Eurasia in 1904 when defining the new concept of "geo-politics," discussing at the same time the categories of "pivot" and "heartland [8]." Mackinder pointed out the importance of the territories east of the Ural Mountains for the geopolitical future, suggesting that those who controlled this land would control global politics. Nearly a century later, the concept of Eurasia attracted the first Kazakhstani president in his attempt to position Kazakhstan on the global map.

Golam Mostafa, who conducted research on the development of the concepts of Eurasia and Eurasianism in Kazakhstan, points out the highly illusive, contested, and debatable nature of this category. In his own words

> It [Eurasia] has two apparent meanings and dimensions: geographical and politico-philosophical-ideological; where the first one deals with space and location meaning Eurasia is a place (space) which is located both in Asia and Europe; the other is more complex and complicated with multiple views and perceptions, often conflicting and contradictory, probably with one common feature that the concept of Eurasia first emerged and evolved in imperial Russia. [9]

Consequently, scholars found defining the concept of Eurasianism an even harder task. Eurasianism belongs to the category of politico-ideological and philosophical concepts that is conveniently used by government authorities, intellectuals, and media in different historical and geographical contexts to promote a particular ideology.

For Nazarbayev, the concept of Eurasianism became the flagship of his governance, the foundation for his nation-building exercise. Many scholars, journalists, and policy makers assisted Nazarbayev with the task of developing their own (Kazakhstani) version of Eurasianism. The aim was to help construct peaceful and harmonious relations within 140 ethnic groups that resided in Kazakhstan, and between members of the three main zhuz (clans) that divide Kazakhs themselves, and also to help build cooperation with other countries. In the words of Nazarbayev himself:

> There are individuals who like to make a link between Kazakhstan and Europe; and there are those who also like to see Kazakhstan to be in close tie with the Asian "Tigers"; still there are others who want to consider Russia as our strategic partner, while suggesting not to ignore the Turkish model for development. Paradoxically, they are all right in their own way, since they have felt the issue from different angles. In reality, Kazakhstan, as a Eurasian state that has its own history and its own future, will have a completely different path to travel down the road. Our model for development will not resemble other countries; it will include the achievements from different civilizations. [10]

Consequently, the idea of a peaceful and harmonious coexistence between and beyond different ethnic groups in Kazakhstan provides the foundation for the national ideology of Eurasianism and eliminates any opportunity for conflict or crisis. Under this ideological framework, recognizing any form of political, economic, or social unrest/conflict/crisis is impossible as it threatens Nazarbayev's ultimate goal of building a happy and prosperous multiethnic and multicultural Republic of Kazakhstan around Eurasia. This rejection of any conflict or crisis became a cultural characteristic of Kazakhstan that influences crisis communication practice. The ideology of Eurasianism complements the clan/kinship culture with its lack of transparency and also contributes toward constructing a conflict/crisis free environment, at least on the surface. In kinship-based groups or networks, the power distance is usually high, which manifests itself through face-saving behavior when the person who possesses the highest authority is never expected to reveal any weaknesses, such as the acknowledgment of possible mistakes, and moreover apologize for any wrongdoings.

The ideology of Eurasianism complements the clan/kinship culture with its lack of transparency, and it also contributes toward constructing a conflict/crisis free environment, at least at the surface.

The conflict between the oil workers, the KazMunaiGaz oil company, and local government authorities, which took place in Zhanaozen between May 2011 and June 2012, seriously challenged Nazarbayev's rhetoric on Eurasianism and Kazakhstan as a center of Eurasia. This conflict is the most dramatic crisis of the post-Soviet era in Kazakhstan, resulting in dozens of people dead and hundreds arrested according to official sources [11].

Crisis Time: The Zhanaozen Uprising

Before we analyze the Zhanaozen crisis and Nazarbayev's response to it, we will provide the definition of "crisis" that will be used in this chapter, as communication scholars have difficulties agreeing on the definition. Herein, we define crisis as *a turning point when the status quo gets challenged and certain changes have to follow when the system cannot ignore these challenges.* "Crisis" is equivalent to an emergency that results in instability and possible chaos.

Scholars identify the three phases of crisis communication including a pre-crisis phase, when the crisis can be avoided or at least the preparation for the crisis can be made. The second phase includes the crisis response phase when the organization(s) involved respond to the crisis. The third and final phase deals with managing the effects of the crisis in the longer term after the immediate crisis has been resolved [12]. In this chapter, we will mainly discuss the first and the second phases of crisis communication.

W. T. Coombs, an expert in crisis communication research, argues that often only a proportion of the total crisis story can reach the public, while most of the crisis remains hidden from the public view. He encourages researchers to analyze the crisis well beyond the "official" interpretation of the crisis [13]. Following Coombs's recommendation, we aim to provide an analysis of the Zhanaozen crisis beyond the official interpretation, with particular focus on the role of culture in this crisis.

Zhanaozen is a single-industry town located in the Mangistau region to the southeast of the city of Aktau in Western Kazakhstan. The town was founded in 1964 following the discovery of an oil field there. The original name of the settlement was Novy-Uzen. In 1993, it was renamed Zhanaozen, according to an official attempt to change Russian geographical names into Kazakh names. Life in this town resembles many other industrial settlements in Kazakhstan or anywhere else in the former Soviet Union and is far from paradise. The continental climate means very hot summers with temperatures in the mid-30°C range, occasionally reaching the mid-40s, only to be replaced by low subzero temperatures during the long winter. The land is not suitable for agriculture. Food and all other goods have to be transported across great distances to reach Zhanaozen, and the living costs are generally very high. This creates a paradox as oil workers are usually well paid; however, because of living costs that are higher than in many other places in Kazakhstan, their salaries do not compensate for all the hardship they and their families face. Ecological problems are another contributing factor to very harsh living conditions when residents are permanently exposed to chemical vapors and fumes from the oil refineries. But in spite of all these hazards, in the past decade many Oralmans have chosen to move to Zhanaozen, attracted by work opportunities [14].

The main company and employer in Zhanaozen is OzenMunaiGaz, a subsidiary of KazMunaiGaz, which produces the bulk of its oil. KazMunaiGaz, Kazakhstan's national oil and gas company, was established in 2002 and since then has attempted to reacquire stakes in petroleum companies that were sold off to foreign investors when the country gained independence in 1991. KazMunaiGaz also owns 50% in JSC KarazhanbasMunai—an oil company that explores and develops the Karazhanbas oil field [15].

In 2011, oil workers of OzenMunaiGaz started raising concerns over decreases in pay. In April of that year, a number of workers attempted to get the attention of both the management of OzenMunaiGaz and government officials by sending a number of letters outlining their inadequate salary and difficult living conditions. In response, the Department of Labour and Social Protection responded that the demands of the oil workers were not justified [15]. Oil workers continued sending individual letters outlining their concerns over the decreased pay and social injustice that would eventually lead to a hunger strike. Again, the management of the oil company ignored workers' demands. Instead of negotiating with the workers, the management of OzenMunaiGaz, together with the local government authorities, announced that their demands were "unjustified and illegitimate" [15].

In late May 2011, thousands of workers went on a peaceful strike as the company failed to address the workers' concerns. In response, authorities fined a number of workers who participated in this strike and those who supported them. Some of them were charged on grounds of organizing mass unrest, and others were arrested on charges of "initiating social disorder" [16]. Many workers remained on strike for approximately 8 months until December 16 when violent clashes occurred at Zhanaozen's main square in the center of town, during the celebrations of the 20th anniversary of Kazakhstan's independence.

Situational Analysis: The Different Voices

CaspioNet (this is the English version of *Khabar*, which is the state owned largest news company in Kazakhstan) reported that in the morning of December 16, 2011, around 800 people who acted aggressively gathered in the main square in Zhanaozen. There were 120 police in the same square whose task was to ensure that the demonstration went well.

According to the official interpretation of the events provided by the journalists of CaspioNet, only one police officer had a gun. The same journalists reported that the clash between police and protesters was initiated by one of the "hooligans," a word which Nazarbayev later referred to when asked who was responsible for the bloody events in Zhanaozen [17]. Following the official narrative, this led to a number of "aggressive" people from the crowd attacking the police van, the decorated Christmas tree, yurts (traditional Kazakh houses used as a decoration at the square) as well as a few spectators who joined the celebration. It was later confirmed by the police that the rioters then moved to the office of OzenMunaiGaz, the local hotel, and the local city council [18].

Such reporting by the official media separates the riots on December 16 from the long lasting protests over oil issues. It presents the crisis as a random "hooligans' attack," rather than the highest point of an 8-month conflict between OzenMunaiGaz employees and the company management, including the government officials who fully supported the management and ignored the demands of the employees.

Immediately after December 16, a new video of the event was uploaded on YouTube® before all forms of communication were cut off in Zhanaozen on December 17. The video showed the police shooting civilians in the square and then beating injured people to death. When Kazakhstani officials found out about this video, they quickly removed it from the web [19]. It is important to remember that anyone can make a request to remove a video. If the government got hold of the person who uploaded this video on YouTube, then the video could be easily removed. This video presented a very different picture to the official version of the events, with police acting as aggressive and merciless killers attacking peaceful protestors. This challenged the official narrative and forced OzenMunaiGaz employers and government officials to eventually reassess their crisis communication strategy.

The Prosecutor General Office reported that 97 people were injured and 14 died on December 16 [20]. On the same day, Nazarbayev declared a state of emergency and a curfew, which were both supposed to last 20 days and end on January 5, 2012.

However, these were extended until January 31, 2012 [16]. According to Nazarbayev, these measures were intended "to restore the economy of Zhanaozen, restore all buildings, and most importantly, to ensure the safety of all citizens" [21]. By imposing the state of emergency, Nazarbayev legitimized the ban on radio, television stations, internet, and even copy machines, and stopped information being disseminated about the Zhanaozen crisis.

The arrests of oil workers involved in the protests and members of their families then followed. Russian journalists, who managed to come to Zhanaozen a day after the violent clashes, reported in Novaya Gazeta, one of the most liberal newspapers in Russia, on a number of instances of ill-treatment and torture of civilians who were not even oil workers and were not involved in the oil strikes [22]. Local authorities used the situation to punish members of opposition movements, such as the People's Front, and also those who strongly criticized the regime and openly supported the oil workers.

The trials of the protesting oil workers started on March 27, 2012 and ended on June 4, 2012. The outcome was rather predictable—the Aktau City Court found 37 defendants guilty of various crimes, which included "organization and participation in mass unrest" and theft. They were all sentenced to 5–8 years in prison. None of the members of the police who shot the civilians were charged with murder or homicide [23].

The Official Response to the Zhanaozen Crisis

The official response to the Zhanaozen crisis was quick and protective of the government officials and the OzenMunaiGaz management. Coombs organizes crisis response strategies in nine categories, placing them on a scale from defensive and accommodating, to rebuilding and bolstering [13]. Defensive strategies are used to protect the organization while accommodative responses address concerns of the victim(s). These nine strategies include the following: *attack the accuser, denial, scapegoat, excuse, justification, compensation, apology, reminder, and finally ingratiation.* Next, we will analyze the official response to Zhanaozen crisis using these nine strategies through cultural lenses.

Nazarbayev in his initial response to the December 16 riots denied the existence of the crisis and accused the "hooligans" of organizing mass disorder. "Hooligans" were used as scapegoats in his response [21]. He also blamed the opposition for initiating this conflict which sadly led to the shooting of the civilians by the police [24]. Such a response reflected an *attack the accuser* strategy.

It is important to remember that OzenMunaiGaz, the local government, and the central government failed to recognize the existence of unrest and the oil workers' demands for 8 months before the events of December 16. This meant that the pre-crisis stage, which provided an opportunity to avoid or prevent the crisis, or at least to prepare for it, was totally missed in Zhanaozen.

Nazarbayev *denied* knowledge of the conflict. He announced that he was not informed by his advisors of the severity of the conflict [25]. The officials, Nurdaulet Suindikov, a spokesperson for the Kazakhstani Prosecutor General's Office in particular, also insisted that weapons were used only after several police officers suffered very serious injuries [26].

However, after the initial denial, Nazarbayev also acknowledged that the employees' demands were quite reasonable and that "employers should not forget that these are our citizens ... and that it is important to listen to them and to support them if at all possible, which unfortunately did not happen in this case" [25]. Here the President moves to the *excuse* stage where, by acknowledging the crisis, he removes himself and his government from the responsibility by making the employer (OzenMunaiGaz) responsible for the negligence. He also refers to the feelings of employees by stating that they are "our citizens" and suggests that the employers should listen to their demands. At this stage, Nazarbayev did not name anyone specifically from Ozen-MunaiGaz or the local authorities, who might be responsible for the bloodshed and used the general terms "employers" and "police."[2] This tactic helped the President to escape from taking responsibility for the crisis. By not naming the actual people who are responsible for the crisis/conflict, understanding of the crisis is robbed by the human agency.

In spite of the authorities' attempts to block radio, internet, and television communication channels between Zhanaozen and the rest of the world, when the state of emergency was declared on December 16, the presence of Russian journalists from Novaya Gazeta and the Youtube video depicted aggressive actions by police in shooting unarmed civilians. The interest of local bloggers in the crisis prevented Nazarbayev and his government from completely removing this crisis from public view. Furthermore, the government even realized the need to use social media to support the official version of the crisis. Karim Massimov, the Prime Minister at the time, sent a group of pro-governmental bloggers to Zhanaozen to report about the crisis. The group was called "the bloody bloggers" by the Kazakhstani blogosphere for their support of the regime and reporting from the pro-Nazarbayev and pro-government position. They either blamed the political opposition, the west, the Islamists, and in some cases, the Oralmans for the crisis [27]. This is the *scapegoat* strategy in this crisis. This strategy also means denouncement when the bloody bloggers tried to blame the external agents for the crisis. The Oralmans were a different story, they were "local," but the bloody bloggers by identifying them as the initiators of the conflict drew the line between the Oralmans as outsiders and the rest of the population in Zhanaozen.

Nazarbayev went even further by firing his son-in-law, Timur Kulibayev, from the position of Chairman of the National Welfare Fund, which owns KazMunaiGaz amongst other major state enterprises. He also fired KazMunaiGaz EP Chief Executive Officer, Askar Balzhanov, and replaced the head of parent company KazMunaiGaz National Co., Bolat Akchulakov [28]. He also replaced the Mayor of the Mangistau region. According to Kazakhstan's prominent political analyst Dossym

Satpayev, Kulibayev's firing was a showcase to prove that even members of the President's family must take responsibility for Zhanaozen, and that none were untouchable [25]. Such actions indicate that Nazarbayev tried to dissociate himself from the clan politics.

The *justification* strategy was present at the early stage of the crisis response when OzenMunaiGaz officials, together with government authorities, tried to downplay the severity of the conflict and simply tried to use censorship for all the information coming to and from Zhanaozen.

The firing of a few key figures from top management positions in the region was as close to an *apology* strategy as Nazarbayev ever got. According to the parliamentary elections that took place on January 15, 2012, 1 month after the crisis in Zhanaozen, Nur Otan Party led by Nazarbayev, received an overwhelming majority and Nazarbayev continued his reign as the leader of the nation. Arguably, the crisis in Zhanaozen could have provided Nazarbayev with a reason to postpone the elections. However, Nazarbayev was confident in his crisis communication strategy. One of the main characteristics of Kazakhstani culture, as mentioned earlier, which follows from high power distance is the respect of authority.

Nobody in Kazakhstan expected a personal apology from Nazarbayev for the bloodshed in Zhanaozen and the arrests of oil workers and some other civilians that followed. Public apology by the national leader would mean showing weakness and could result in losing face. Nazarbayev's reelection also demonstrated that the ideology of Eurasianism that promotes coexistence between different ethnic and cultural groups, as well his crisis management strategy, were supported by the majority of voters. Although the Kazakhstani people may disagree with Nazarbayev's harsh policies and the lack of democracy in the country, when it comes to stability, prosperity, and the existing balance amongst all cultures and ethnicities, Nazarbayev, over the years, has proven that he is capable of keeping the majority of the Kazakhstani political and military elite under control [31]. The Kazakhstani people voted for such stability [30]. Nazarbaev's victory in the January elections further cemented his position.

Not only was an apology absent from the crisis response strategy in Zhanaozen, but there was little financial *compensation* for the oil workers either. Mourning for the dead during the crisis did not happen and left families of the deceased very unhappy. The trials of the arrested oil workers that started in March 2012 resulted in almost all of them being sentenced to at least 4 years in prison [27]. Bloggers reported instances of violations of human rights including the use of torture against arrested members of the opposition [32]. As previously mentioned, none of the police officers involved in the shooting of the civilians were put on trial. Again, such an official response was accepted in Zhanaozen for the same reason as Nazarbayev won the parliamentary elections. The high power distance in Kazakhstan means that the general public does not hold many democratic rights, such as freedom of expression. Kazakhstani people feel very insecure and vulnerable in the face of authorities, be it their president or local authorities including the police. Although the presence of social media forced Nazarbayev finally to acknowledge the existence of the crisis, it did not greatly influence the actual response to the crisis.

The last two crisis response strategies proposed in this chapter, *reminder* and *ingratiation*, also could be traced to the Zhanaozen crisis. The reminder is usually associated with reminding about the good work performed in the past by the organization(s) involved. It is hard to trace such direct reminders in the official response, but the ideology of Eurasianism that promotes harmony and stability was a powerful tool in reminding Kazakhstani citizens about the "good" work which the government does for its people. Ingratiation strategy appeared softly when Nazarbayev said that employers should not forget that "these are our citizens..." and that it is important to listen to them. This is far from praising stakeholders but at least it is a recognition, possibly only at the surface, of the interests of the people involved in this crisis.

Outcome of the Crisis: Oralmans' Problem

The biggest changes that followed from the crisis related to the government policy toward Oralmans. Government officials and OzenMunaiGaz managers suspected that Oralmans played a key role in organizing the protests in Zhanaozen. Nazarbayev's political advisor, Yermukhamet Yertysbayev, proposed that "What was happening in Zhanaozen is absolutely not typical of the Kazakh mentality. Kazakhs would never go against the authorities, never ... Those who were protesting originally come from Uzbekistan, and Turkmenistan and have just recently got their Kazakhstani citizenship. They haven't quite figured out the Kazakh mentality yet" [27]. These words reinforce again the national ideology of Eurasianism that is constantly promoted to the Kazakh people, and who, as we know already from the results of the January 2012 parliamentary elections, were happy to support Nazarbayev to preserve the political status quo. The Zhanaozen crisis showed that Oralmans tried to challenge this ideology and the government decided to reassess the repatriation policy.

Oralmans highlighted yet another problem in Kazakhstan. Although they have a superior knowledge of traditional Kazakh culture and Kazakh language, they mostly lost kinship-based networks due to the fact that their ancestors left Kazakhstan over a century ago. As was suggested earlier in this chapter, the initial social relationship in a kinship network is based on trust which is constantly reinforced by the members of such a network. Oralmans, by not belonging to the primary clans, have difficulties trusting people around them including officials, neither can they be trusted by other Kazakhs. This is what Yertysbayev means when he says that "What was happening in Zhanaozen is absolutely not typical of the Kazakh mentality..." He separates Oralmans from the "real" local Kazakh, constructing the "us-other" dichotomy, which points to the trans-boundary nature of the Zhanaozen crisis.

In early 2013, the repatriation program was reopened after a short shut down during the previous year under the new title "Business Road Map - 2020" [33]. Before introducing the new program, government officials tried to meet with Oralmans to hear their concerns. According to the new program, Oralmans are now eligible for educational grants [34]. The houses built for Oralmans are carefully checked by officials to ensure that they meet certain government standards [34]. Salamat Amanbayev, head of the Migration Committee has also stated that newly developed migration legislation will incorporate the principles of the similar programs from both Germany and Israel. Therefore, the Oralmans will be provided with options for settlement in the country upon their arrival depending on the needs of a particular region.

On the one hand, the new repatriation program allows for better integration of Oralmans into Kazakhstani society through providing education opportunities, better living conditions, and even better job opportunities. But on the other hand, these measures also indicate a tighter control on Oralmans to prevent the possibility of further social unrest. This indicates that the government learnt a certain lesson from the Zhanaozen crisis and tried to establish preventive measures that include not only improving the living standards of Oralmans, but also tightening its control over them. This also relates to the cultural characteristics of Kazakhstan such as tight censorship and governmental control over the people. It is also part of crisis management strategy as it works to prevent the crisis in the first place.

Conclusion: Lessons Learned

In conclusion, the analysis of the Zhanaozen crisis identified the presence of nearly all nine strategies in crisis communication response. The direct apology is the only strategy that was missing, as neither President Nazarbayev nor any government officials, or KazMunaiGaz managers expressed their apologies for the crisis and for the shootings on December 16 and the arrests that followed. The cultural characteristic that derives from the national ideology of Eurasianism promoted by Nazarbayev and the kinship-based networks that reinforce the high power distance, resulted not only in the absence of the apology from authorities, but also the fact that the majority of Kazakhstani people supported Nazarbayev's official response to the crisis. Because there were no apologies, there was no recognition of wrongdoing by government officials, and therefore there was no direct compensation to the people who suffered during the crisis and from police actions.

Apologies and compensations are regarded as a weakness in Kazakhstan. The Kazakh people prefer to see their national leaders as strong figures and apologies do not contribute to such an image.

Apologies and compensations are regarded as a weakness in Kazakhstan. The Kazakh people prefer to see their national leaders as strong figures and apologies do not contribute to such an image. However, the replacement of a few key figures in the government who "missed" the opportunity to recognize the crisis at the pre-crisis stage did occur. In addition, changes in policies toward Oralmans demonstrated that the government learned its lesson and responded by improving the living standards of Oralmans, who make up a high proportion of the oil workers in Zhanaozen.

At the same time, the government tried to establish tighter control over Oralmans and all Kazakhstani citizens to prevent future conflict and crises. In view of the current Kazakhstani government led by President Nazarbayev, the ideology of Eurasianism, which promotes a peaceful coexistence among all ethnic and cultural groups in Kazakhstan and beyond, should prevail. This ideology successfully hides power structures in Kazakhstan based on kinship/clan networks. History will show how long such an ideology will keep President Nazarbayev and his government in power.

Practical Suggestions

For those seeking to communicate crisis information or conduct business in the Republic of Kazakhstan, below are a few suggestions that may be of help.

- Kazakhstan is one of the high context culture countries. Personal relations and belonging to a group (e.g., Zhuz) play an important role as such relationships lead to trust among members of the group. Make sure that you understand the complexity of such human relations and try to establish long term relations based on mutual respect and trust.
- Kazakh people regard "face-saving" as an important interpersonal skill. Make sure that you understand the situation and try to avoid making any damage to anybody's "face."
- Learn and understand the country's culture. The Kazakhstani government is trying to become a powerful country in its own right and not to be in the shadow of Russia. Respect and understand the attempts of the Kazakhstani government to construct its own independent identity and national ideology.

Discussion Questions

10.1 What was the official response to the Zhanaozen crisis?

10.2 Why do you think the apology strategy was missing in the official response to the Zhanaozen crisis?

10.3 What was the role of culture in the official response to the Zhanaozen crisis?

10.4 If you were the Communications Director for KazMunaiGaz, what would you have done in the period prior to the Zhanaozen uprising on December 16, 2011? During the actual uprising? In the following week after the uprising?

10.5 In what ways can Kazakhstani government improve its crisis management strategy?

Notes

1. The initiative for members of Kazakh diaspora to "come home" was started by Kazakh government officials in the last years of the Soviet regime. This was done in an attempt to reverse the situation where Kazakh had a minority status in their own country with steady Russification or Sovietization among the Kazakhs themselves. For more details on Oralmans in Kazakhstan [5].
2. It is important to understand that in Kazakhstan, President Nazarbayev holds tight control over the central government and the local government. KazMunaiGaz, as a national oil and gas company, remains under the control of the central government. It is no surprise that the response to the crisis by these three institutions, (central government lead by president Nazarbayev, KazMunaiGaz managers, and local authorities) was interchangeable.

References

1. Central Intelligence Agency. (2015, September 24). "The World Factbook: Kazakhstan" [Online]. Available: https://www.cia.gov/library/publications/the-world-factbook/geos/kz.html, October 1, 2015 (last date accessed).
2. L. Kennedy, "International migration in central Asia," in Migration in Central Asia: Challenges and Prospects, Conference Report, F. Coxshall, Ed. UNESCO, 2005, pp. 72–74, [Online]. Available: http://unesdoc.unesco.org/images/0015/001579/157974eo.pdf, May 31, 2017 (last date accessed).
3. J. Melich and A. Adibayeva, "Nation-building and cultural policy in Kazakhstan," *European Scientific Journal*, vol. 2, pp. 265–280, 2013.
4. N. Oka. (2013, March). "A note on ethnic return migration policy in Kazakhstan: Changing priorities and a growing dilemma" [Online]. Available: https://ir.ide.go.jp/dspace/bitstream/2344/1218/1/ARRIDE_Discussion_No.394_oka.pdf, October 1, 2015 (last date accessed).
5. N. E. Masanov, "The role of clans in Kazakhstan today," *Prism*, vol. 4, no. 3, February 1998. [Online]. Available: http://www.jamestown.org/single/?no_cache=1™tx_ttnews[tt_news]=20207™tx_ttnews[backPid]=220}.Vg4glRDnnbM, October 1, 2015 (last date accessed).
6. E. Schatz, *Modern Clan Politics: The Power of "Blood" in Kazakhstan and Beyond.* Seattle, WA: University of Washington Press, 2013.
7. N. Nazarbayev, "Об Ассамблее народа Казахстана" [On the Assembly of the People of Kazakhstan], Казахстанская Правда [*Kazakhstan Pravda*], October 21, 2008. Quoted

in: J. Melich and A. Adibayeva, "Nation-building and cultural policy in Kazakhstan," *European Scientific Journal*, December 2013, special edition, vol. 2, pp. 265–279.

8. H. J. Mackinder, "The Geographical Pivot of History", *The Geographical Journal*, Vol. 23, no.4, (April 1904), 421–437.

9. G. Mostafa, "The concept of 'Eurasia': Kazakhstan's Eurasian policy and its implications," *Journal of Eurasian Studies*, vol. 4, no. 2, pp. 160–170, 2013.

10. N. Nazarbayev, "Евразийский союз: идеи, практика, перспективы. 1994–1997". [The Eurasian Union: ideas, practices, perspectives. 1994–1997], *Фонд содействия развитию социальных и политических наук* [Fund for cooperation and development in social and political science], Moscow, 1997.

11. Radio Azattyq. (2011, December 22). "Officialnyi spisok postradavshih v besporyadkah v Zhanaozene" [Online]. Available: http://rus.azattyq.org/content/injured_people_zhanaozen/24461284.html, October 2, 2015 (last date accessed).

12. W. T. Coombs, "Parameters for crisis communication," in *The Handbook of Crisis Communication*, W. T. Coombs and S. J. Holladay, Eds. Wiley-Blackwell, 2010, pp. 17–53.

13. W. T. Coombs, "Conceptualizing crisis communication," in *The Handbook of Risk and Crisis Communication*, R. L. Heath and H. D. O'Hair, Eds. New York: Routledge, 2009, pp. 99–119.

14. Japan International Cooperation Agency and Local Government of Mangistau Oblast Government of the Republic of Kazakhstan, "Master plan study on integrated regional development for Mangistau Oblast in the Republic of Kazakhstan," 1994, pp. 1–2.

15. Human Rights Watch. (2012, September 12). "Striking oil, striking workers. Violations of labor rights in Kazakhstan's oil sector" [Online]. Available: https://www.hrw.org/report/2012/09/10/striking-oil-striking-workers/violations-labor-rights-kazakhstans-oil-sector, October 1, 2015 (last date accessed).

16. Amnesty International. (2012, March 21). "Kazakhstan: Progress and nature of official investigations called into question 100 after violent clashes between police and protesters in Zhanaozen" [Online]. Available: https://www.amnesty.org/download/Documents/.../eur570012012en.pdf, October 1, 2015 (last date accessed).

17. M. Assenova. (2012, March 16). "37 on trial in Zhanaozen violence, journalist released" [Online]. Available: http://www.jamestown.org/programs/edm/single/?tx_ttnews percent5Btt_news percent5D=39149&cHash=ddc4a2e9e42ee6bc36b2f2563978932c#.VgzY4mSqpBc, October 1, 2015 (last date accessed).

18. Vesti. (2011, December 16). "Besporyadki v Kazahstane: v gorode Zhanaozen nachalis pogrom i moroderstvo" [Online]. Available: http://www.vesti.ru/doc.html?id=663345&tid=94954, October 2, 2015 (last date accessed).

19. Gazeta. (2011, December 21). "Na YouTube opublikovano video, na kotorom kazakhstanskie policeiskie rasstrelivayut tolpu v Zhanaozene" [Online]. Available: http://www.gazeta.ru/news/lenta/2011/12/21/n_2143018.shtml, October 1, 2015 (last date accessed).

20. Zakon. (2011, December 22). "Generalnaya prokuratura opublikovala spisok lic, postradavshih v resultate massovih besporyadkov v Zhanaozene" [Online]. Available: http://www.zakon.kz/4463979-generalnaja-prokuratura-opublikovala.html, October 1, 2015 (last date accessed).

21. C. Riedel. (2011, December 24). "Kazakhstan's clashes: Most violent and deadly since the country's independence" [Online]. Available: http://foreignpolicyblogs.com/2011/12/24/kazakhstans-clashes-most-violent-and-deadly-since-the-countrys-independence/, October 1, 2015 (last date accessed).

22. E. Kostyuchenko. (2011, December 23). "Zhanaozen – neftyanaya reka" [Online]. Available: http://www.novayagazeta.ru/society/50247.html, October 1, 2015 (last date accessed).

23. N. Schenkkan. (2012, December 20). "Kazakhstan: One year after Zhanaozen" [Online]. Available: https://freedomhouse.org/blog/kazakhstan-one-year-after-zhanaozen, October 2, 2015 (last date accessed).

24. S. Gunaev. (2011, December 22). "Glava fonda "Samruk-Kazyna" budet otpravlen v otstavky - Nazarbayev" [Online]. Available: http://ria.ru/world/20111222/523566526.html, October 1, 2015 (last date accessed).

25. RosBiznesKonsulting. (2011, December 24). "N. Nazarbayev: Pogromshikov v Zhanaozene pered buntom napoili" [Online]. Available: http://top.rbc.ru/politics/24/12/2011/631597.shtml, October 1, 2015 (last date accessed).

26. Interfax. (2011, December 21). "Kazakh police used weapons amid riots only after colleagues were injured – prosecutor's office" [Online]. Available: https://www.timesca.com/index.php/news/13269-kazakh-police-used-weapons-amid-riots-only-after-colleagues-were-injured-prosecutors-office, May 31, 2017 (last date accessed).

27. D. Beisembayeva, "Exploring the impact of online political activism on political processed in Kazakhstan," Master of International Communication thesis, Department of Communication Studies, Unitec, Auckland, 2016.

28. "KazMunaiGas EP oil output drops as labor strikes curb operations," Bloomberg, January 9, 2012. [Online]. Available: http://www.bloomberg.com/news/articles/2012-01-09/kazmunaigas-ep-oil-output-drops-as-labor-strikes-curb-operations, September 29, 2015 (last date accessed).

29. The Bertelsmann Stiftung's Transformation Index. (2014). "Kazakhstan Country Report" [Online]. Available: http://www.bti-project.org/reports/country-reports/pse/kaz/index.nc, October 2, 2015 (last date accessed).

30. "Kazakh leader gains crushing election victory," *BBC News*, April 27, 2015. [Online]. Available: http://www.bbc.com/news/world-asia-32471428, October 2, 2015 (last date accessed).

31. S.N. Cummings, *Power and the Elite*. London: I.B. Tauris, 2005.

32. D. Shyolokov. (2012, January 3). "Kak zakalyalsya blogging" [Online] Available: https://78ds.wordpress.com/2012/01/03/blogging-zhanaozen/, May 30, 2017 (last date accessed).

33. "Об утверждении Дорожной карты занятости 2020" [On establishing the Business Road Map -2010] (2015, March 31) [Online] Available: https://tengrinews.kz/zakon/pravitelstvo_respubliki_kazahstan_premer_ministr_rk/trud/id-P1500000162/, May 30, 2017 (last date accessed).

34. Реализация программы «Дорожная карта занятости 2020» [Realisation of the Programme "Business Road Map -2020]. (2015, March 1). [Online]. Available: http://egov.kz/cms/ru/articles/zanyatost_2020, May 30, 2017 (last date accessed).

Malaysia   11

"Almost Without a Trace": Missing Flight MH370, Culture and Transboundary Crisis Communication in the Era of Social Media

Kwamena Kwansah-Aidoo and Amiso M. George

Nobody saw this coming, nobody knows why it happened, and nobody knows precisely where it is. That, essentially, is the story of Flight MH370— at least for now

—Najib Razak, 2014 [1].

Chapter Preview

On March 8, 2014, Malaysia experienced what its Prime Minister, Dato' Seri Najib Tun Razak, at the time described as, the most extraordinary event ever to befall the country—the disappearance of a Malaysia Airlines Boeing 777 (Flight MH370) on a routine flight from Kuala Lumpur to Beijing, China. Precisely 327 days (on

---

Culture and Crisis Communication: Transboundary Cases from Nonwestern Perspectives, First Edition.
Edited by Amiso M. George and Kwamena Kwansah-Aidoo.
© 2017 by The Institute of Electrical and Electronics Engineers, Inc. Published 2017 by John Wiley & Sons, Inc.

Thursday January 29, 2015) after the flight literally vanished without a trace, Malaysia officially declared that the disappearance of the aircraft was an accident and added that it presumed all the flight's passengers and crew were dead. The announcement was necessary in order to allow Malaysia Airlines to pay compensation to families. However, many of the relatives of the 239 people on board were furious with the decision by the Malaysian authorities. This was because some of them actually believed in the possibility that their loved ones could still be alive. Several said they could not accept the decision. The search for the aircraft continued though, until it was called off on January 17, 2017, almost 3 years after it went missing. The close to 3 years search, yielded no significant clues as to the whereabouts of the aircraft; only some aircraft parts were found washed up on the beach, in far-flung places such as Reunion Island. Thus, this remains an unresolved crisis for the Malaysian government.

But how did the Malaysian government respond to the vanishing of Flight MH370 and how did it communicate with the relatives of people who were on board the flight and their governments, given that it was an international flight? Did culture in anyway influence initial responses and communication, and if so, how? What role did social media play in the unfolding crisis and its handling thereof? What are the lessons, both positive and negative, that can be learned from the way Malaysia responded to this crisis? This chapter seeks to examine the various aspects of the Malaysian response through the lenses of communication, culture, and social media within the context of transboundary crisis. This case ultimately reveals the complex nature of transboundary crisis and the dynamics of the relationship between communication, crisis, and culture in an era of widespread social media use that knows no geographic and/or communicative boundaries.

After reading this chapter you will be able to

- *Understand the circumstances surrounding the disappearance of flight MH370*
- *Appreciate the crisis communication surrounding the disappearance*
- *Understand the role of social media in crisis communication, and in particular, this crisis*
- *Appreciate the transboundary nature of modern crisis*
- *Understand the role of culture in the initial Malaysian communication response to the crisis*

Introduction and Background

Malaysia is a Southeast Asian country occupying the Malaysian Peninsula and part of the island of Borneo. It covers a total landmass of 329,847 square kilometers (127,355 square miles) and is known for its beaches and rainforests. Its capital, Kuala Lumpur, is the hub of both commercial and political activities. It is the headquarters of Malaysia Airlines which is at the center of the crisis discussed in this chapter. It is also home to the iconic 451 m tall Petronas Twin Towers. [2, 3].

Malaysia is a federation that consists of 13 states and 3 federal territories. It is a multicultural country and in 2016 was estimated to have a total population of 31.7 million, consisting of three main ethnic groups as follows: ethnic Bumiputera (68.6%), Chinese (23.4%), Indians (7%), and others (1%). The percentage of non-Malaysian citizens in 2016 was at 10.3% out of total population in Malaysia [4].

A heterogeneous society, Malaysia has a mixture of languages with Bahasa Malaysia as the official language. Various Chinese dialects such as Cantonese, Hakka, Hokkien, and Mandarin are widely spoken by Chinese Malaysians. Tamil is spoken by Indian-Malaysians. English is also widely spoken, especially in the big cities. While Malaysians are free to practice any religion of their choice, Islam is enshrined in the country's constitution as the official religion, practiced by over 60% of the population. The second most practiced religion is Buddhism, followed by Taoism, Christianity, Hinduism, and other minor traditional religions. In recent years, Malaysia has faced profound political, economic, social, and technological challenges such as falling oil prices, a dip in the value of the currency, the Ringgit, and a slowing down in the rate of economic growth, to mention a few [4–6].

Cultural Context and Crisis Communication

Despite the varying ethnicities, Malaysia can be categorized as a high context culture [5]. As a collectivist culture, the group is the primary unit of social organization among all the different ethnicities (Malaysian culture) and living in extended families is usually the norm especially among the Chinese populations [5]. According to Tajaddini and Mujtaba [5], Asian collectivism is analogous to vertical collectivism which is described as "a form of collectivism where individuals see themselves as a part of an in-group where there are differences in status" [5, 7]. Such a group is exemplified by norms such as inequality, hierarchical distinctions, and pressure to conform and individuals are generally expected not to say much in such settings [5,7].

In Hofstede's [8] study of 50 countries, Malaysia scored the highest on the Power Distance Index, showing that hierarchy is given very high prominence in Malaysian society. As a result, hierarchy and inequality between managers and employees or people in authority and underlings is usually the case, just as in most collectivist societies. Religion plays an important part in the Malaysian culture with religious concepts of Islam and Buddhism (the most practiced religions in Malaysia), being at the forefront. These religions especially provide norms and expectations where the principles of mutuality and of reciprocity are concerned; values that tend to prefer win–win outcomes over winner-takes-it-all outcomes. [5, 9]. Dahlan [10] suggests that the aforementioned cultural attributes work together to produce a certain type of person who is typified by refinement, politeness, and consideration of others and generally seeks approval from others.

> Within the Malaysian context, developing relationships—rather than exchanging facts and information—tends to be the prime purpose of communication and this is mainly because all relationships (social and business) are considered personal and based on trust.

In Malaysia, just as in many high context cultures like Ghana, as (discussed in Chapter 3) meaning is often more implicit and less direct, implying that one needs to pay more attention to other aspects of the communication context such as voice tone, body language, eye contact, and facial expressions [5, 10, 11]. Also, as Tajaddini and Mujtaba [5] note, within the Malaysian context, developing relationships rather than exchanging facts and information tends to be the prime purpose of communication and this is mainly because all relationships (social and business) are considered personal and based on trust.

This bears a direct relationship to the cherished cultural values of courtesy, tolerance, harmony, and saving face. Consequently, people tend to avoid providing direct answers, particularly negative ones, in order to prevent disagreement and preserve harmony, two very important aspects of Malaysian culture [5]. In this regard, and as a corollary to power distance, respect for authority characterizes most formal relationships, especially between subordinates and their superiors. Thus, for example, in situations where a highly placed official is speaking at a press conference, the individual would not expect to be grilled by journalists/reporters or be asked difficult questions; those may elicit answers that would possibly create disharmony. As a country, Malaysia generally scores high on trust and customer orientation than other Asian nations [12].

Storz [13] points out that both the Chinese and the Malay view the experience of time as a subjective and holistic notion, meaning that they do not view any time-related concepts, such as, punctuality and deadlines, in absolute terms. "Rubber time" is a common term used by Malaysians to describe their practice of punctuality, giving the impression that time is both changeable and stretchable, consequently making deadlines not absolute but mobile [5]. As would be expected, such cultural traits are bound to influence communication and action, even in a crisis situation and the subsequent discussion illustrates this concept.

Crisis Communication in Malaysian Culture

Our search for research on crisis communication in Malaysia revealed limited academic literature on the subject. A few were primarily case studies. However, the MH370 disappearance has spurred the publication of a few articles, thesis, and many nonacademic publications, including blogs by western observers and crisis experts. The only published critical material we found was, *Flying Through Crisis*

MH370: Lessons in Crisis Communication, a book co-authored by David Kirkham and Malaysian journalist Krishnamoorthy Muthaly [14], available in Malaysia. This book acknowledges the issue of "face-saving" as an important aspect of maintaining harmony in the Malaysian culture [14]. Muthaly acknowledged that he was cautioned not to "write anything that will hurt our leaders, the Government, or the airlines" [14]. He noted that he had e-mailed top officials in charge of communication during the crisis, but got no response. This corresponds with our experience, as we also contacted an official directly in charge of crisis communication, but got no response. While the publication provides an excellent documentation of the crisis based on eyewitness and Malaysian media coverage, it is not necessarily critical of the government's response, but provides advice on effective crisis communication to protect an organization's brand image.

Personal observations, informal conversations with some public relations practitioners in Malaysia, and anecdotal evidence suggest an attitude toward crisis, and by extension crisis communication, that is largely driven by social and political culture in Malaysia. Therefore, one can contend that crisis communication is not high on the Malaysian agenda as it might in western cultures. What may be considered a scandal or crisis in the West may be met with little or no concern in the Malaysian setting. This may be attributed to the combined cultural trait of high power distance and deference to authority. This reverence is evident in interactions between journalists and people in high positions of authority, where by extension, such person's authority may be unchallenged. Consequently, people in high positions, especially those in public institutions, get off with little, arbitrary, or no communication at all during a crisis. This approach to crisis communication was evident in the first few hours of the disappearance of Malaysia Airlines Flight 370.

Background of Malaysia Airlines

Malaysia Airlines Berhad (MAB) (*Penerbangan Malaysia Berhad* in Malay) was founded in 1937 as Malaysian Airline System Berhad (MAS) (*Sistem Penerbangan Malaysiain* in Malay). Since then, it has gone through many iterations. In 1947, operating as Malayan Airways Limited, it flew its inaugural commercial flight. It changed its name to Malaysian-Singapore Airline (MSA) following the independence of Malaysia from Great Britain. However, after the post-independence split from Singapore in 1972, the airline reconstituted itself as Malaysian Airlines System (MAS). In 2015, it rebranded itself as Malaysia Airlines Berhad (MAB), now fully owned by the Malaysian Government through its sovereign wealth fund, Khazanah Nasional [15].

MAB is the national (flagship) carrier of Malaysia and operates out of its main hub of Kuala Lumpur International Airport. An award-winning airline, MAB is a member of the One World Alliance. MAB has two subsidiaries, Firefly and

MASwings [15]. MAB had been lauded for its safety record since its founding. Until the dual tragedies of 2014 (MH 370 which disappeared and MH17, which was shot down over Ukrainian territory), the airline had experienced only three crashes [16]. For the purposes of this analysis, we shall use the acronym MAS throughout the chapter, as the MH370 disappearance occurred before the rebranding of the airline company.

Into Thin Air: The Disappearance of Flight MH370

On March 8, 2014, Malaysia Airlines flight MH370 departed from Kuala Lumpur International Airport at 12:41 a.m., Malaysian time, bound for Beijing Capital International Airport, China. The routine flight was scheduled to arrive in Beijing at 6:30 a.m. on the same day. The flight was carrying 227 passengers from 14 different countries and a 12-member all-Malaysian crew. A majority of the passengers were Chinese [17]. At 1:07 a.m, the plane sent its last ACARS—an acronym for Aircraft Communications Addressing and Reporting System, a computer communication system that allows an onboard computer to communicate short messages with on-ground computers. Shortly thereafter, the ACARS fell dead. According to Malaysia Airlines, the plane lost contact with ground control less than an hour after takeoff. Airline officials said the last recorded communication between the plane and Malaysian Air Traffic Control was at 1:19 a.m. with the words: "Good night Malaysian three seven zero" [18] possibly uttered by the pilot or copilot. Shortly after that, the plane's transponder, which communicates with ground radar, stopped as the airplane left Malaysian airspace and flew into Vietnamese airspace.

A few minutes later, exactly at 1:21 a.m., officials of the Vietnamese Civil Aviation Authority reported that MH370 failed to communicate with them as was expected [18]. While there have been contradictory reports as to when the last actual electronic communication occurred, it is documented that at 7:24 a.m., local Malaysian time, nearly 6 hours after the confirmation of loss of contact from the Vietnamese authorities, Malaysian Airlines issued a statement that MH370 was missing [19]. This was followed at 7:39 a.m. by a similar statement by China's Xinhua News Agency. Meanwhile anxious family members were waiting for their loved ones at the Beijing Airport. There was no distress signal or message sent before the plane went missing [20]. At 9:05 a.m., Malaysia Airlines acknowledged the loss of the aircraft [19].

Search and Rescue Efforts Commence

The morning of March 9, as news of the missing aircraft filled up social media, a full-scale multinational search and rescue effort commenced in the body of waters between Vietnam and Malaysia. In addition to Malaysian Air Force planes, navy ships, coast guard vessels, and satellites, countries like China, whose citizens made up more than half of the passengers on the ill-fated plane, Vietnam, Singapore, Thailand, Indonesia, Philippines, Australia, and the United States, all joined forces in the unprecedented search [21]. The multinational team also demonstrated extraordinary cooperation among the mostly ASEAN countries, illustrating the transboundary nature of the crisis. The "search and rescue effort," was described as the most comprehensive and expensive in aviation history [22]. As the search continued, rumors, innuendos, and conspiracy theories filled social media. Questions arose about possible terrorism in connection with two passengers who were alleged to be travelling with stolen passports belonging to an Austrian and an Italian. They were subsequently identified as Iranians who had nothing to do with the missing aircraft [23]. Other rumors ranged from terrorism, intentional acts by the pilots, plane diverted to a remote island, international espionage, to United States Central Intelligence Agency (CIA) and military involvement and much more. None of these has been proven.

After much conjecture and false leads as to the location of the plane, the Malaysian government concluded that the plane could not be found. The Malaysian Prime Minister Najib Razak, announced in a press conference that, based on a "fresh analysis of satellite data tracking the flight," the missing flight MH370 may have plunged into the southern Indian Ocean [24]. Since the disappearance in 2014, parts of the plane have washed up in faraway places as Reunion Island, but neither the intact plane nor the black box has been found. While speculations abound, experts believe that MH370's disappearance would remain a mystery. This chapter focuses on one small, but important, aspect of the tragedy—crisis communication.

Crisis Stakeholder Audience

Given the uniqueness of the crisis situation, the whole world was baffled and it would not be far-fetched to say that the whole world was interested in what was unfolding and the mystery of the missing flight. Nevertheless, for our purposes, we outline the following as the key stakeholders for this crisis:

- The families and loved ones of the passengers and crew of MH370
- The governments and people of the passengers' home countries, a majority of who were from China
- All Malaysian people (including overseas Malaysians) and government
- Malaysian, regional, and international media as this was an unprecedented occurrence
- The families of the exclusively Malaysian crew that were on board
- The International Civil Aviation Organization (ICAO) which receives reports about airline accidents

Dealing with an Unprecedented Event: How the Government and MAS Responded

One can infer from media reports that the overarching goal was to find the missing aircraft and communicate that information, with compassion, to the family members of the plane's passengers and crew, the home governments of the passengers, the media and the world, and minimize speculation by providing accurate information. However, the strategies to achieving those aims were fraught with missteps that were complicated by the enormity of the crisis, culture, and technology.

Chief among those missteps were

- Contradictory and confusing information
- Mistakenly referring to Iranian passenger traveling on fake passport as Mario Balotelli
- Providing false hope to loved ones of the plane's passengers that their loved ones may have survived
- Not reporting the last ping heard from the aircraft
- Contradicting the last words allegedly spoken by the plane's captain

While it is easy to criticize MAS's response to the crisis, it is important to recognize that no country has dealt with the disappearance of an entire aircraft in recent times. Malaysia is no exception. This crisis in a social media era created unprecedented challenges for MAS and the Malaysian government. Prime Minister Najib Razak described the disappearance of Flight MH370 as an unprecedented situation. He noted that "In the first few days after the plane disappeared, we were so focused on trying to find the aircraft that we did not prioritize our communications" [1]. This was corroborated by Fuad Sharuji, MAS crisis director, who acknowledged in a published report that mistakes were made. He noted that his team identified "loopholes" in its response to the missing airline, but moved quickly to correct them [18].

MAS Strategies and Tactics

MAS used its social media to communicate messages to all target audience members, and correct inaccuracies, rumors, and innuendoes. It also used social media to show empathy for all the victims of the missing aircraft and their loved ones. On the morning of the disappearance of MH370, Malaysia Airline's first acknowledgement of the aircraft's disappearance occurred at 7:24 a.m., Saturday, March 8, in the form of a media statement posted on its website, Facebook, Twitter account, and Weibo (a popular Chinese microblogging website, similar to a hybrid of Twitter and Facebook). Although the time of the statement was 7:24 a.m., the actual post time was much later at 8:12 a.m. That was about 6 hours after the last communication with the plane. This was a basic incident report published in English and Mandarin, given that a majority of the doomed plane's passengers were Chinese (Figure 11.1).

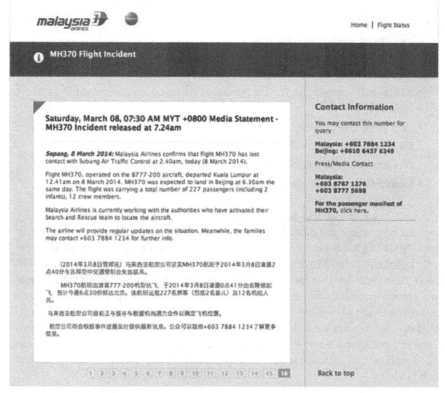

FIGURE 11.1. First media statement, published on the MAS website confirming the loss of flight MH370 [25]. At 7:24 a.m., on Saturday, March 8, about 6 hours after the last communication with the plane, Malaysia Airline's made its first public acknowledgement of the aircraft's disappearance. This was in the form of a media statement posted on its website, Facebook, Twitter account, and Weibo. Although the time of the statement was 7:24 a.m., the actual post time was much later at 8:12 a.m. This was a basic incident report published in English and Mandarin. Screenshot by Melissa Agnes, Crisis Management Strategist, in her 2014 analysis of Malaysia Airline's crisis response to MH370 which can be found at: http://melissaagnes.com/malaysia-airlines-crisis-communications-flight-mh370/ [27]. Used with permission.

The statement in English, read thus

> **Sepang, 8 March 2014:** Malaysia Airlines confirms that flight MH370 has lost contact with Subang Air Traffic Control at 2.40am, today (8 March 2014).
>
> Flight MH370, operated on the B777-200 aircraft, departed Kuala Lumpur at 12.41am on 8 March 2014. MH370 was expected to land in Beijing at 6.30am the same day. The flight was carrying a total number of 227 passengers (including 2 infants), 12 crew members.
>
> Malaysia Airlines is currently working with the authorities who have activated their Search and Rescue team to locate the aircraft.
>
> The airline will provide regular updates on the situation. Meanwhile, the families may contact +603 7884 1234 for further info. [25]

A second media statement was released at 9:05 a.m. acknowledging loss of the aircraft. This second release was posted at 9:36 a.m. A third statement at 10:30 a.m. listed the nationalities of the plane's passengers without their names, in accordance with the Malaysian Personal Data Protection Act 2010 [26].

Second Media Statement. Saturday, March 08, 9:05 AM GMT +0800 Malaysia Airlines MH370 Flight Incident

> We deeply regret that we have lost all contacts with flight MH370, which departed Kuala Lumpur at 12.41am earlier this morning bound for Beijing. The aircraft was scheduled to land at Beijing International Airport at 6.30am local Beijing time. Subang Air Traffic Control reported that it lost contact at 2.40am (local Malaysia time) today.
>
> Flight MH370 was operated on a Boeing B777-200 aircraft. The flight was carrying a total number of 239 passengers and crew – comprising 227 passengers (including 2 infants), 12 crew members. The passengers were of 13 different nationalities. Malaysia Airlines is currently working with the authorities who have activated their Search and Rescue team to locate the aircraft. Our team is currently calling the next-of-kin of passengers and crew.
>
> Focus of the airline is to work with the emergency responders and authorities and mobilize its full support. Our thoughts and prayers are with all affected passengers and crew and their family members. The airline will provide regular updates on the situation.
>
> The public may contact +603 7884 1234. For media queries, kindly contact +603 8777 5698/ +603 8787 1276.
>
> For the next-of-kin, please inform them **to Anjung Tinjau, Level 5, KLIA. Our staff will be there to assist. Transport will be provided to go to the South Support Zone Facility building for the next-of-kin.**
>
> **Or next-of-kin may head straight to the Support Facility Building at KLIA's South Support Zone.** [26]

Once MH370 was confirmed missing, the airline activated its "dark site," (a pre-made, but dormant site that is activated in the event of a crisis) and removed all appearances of business as usual, in order to convey the severity of the crisis. This seriousness was also reflected in all the company's social media accounts. Facebook and Twitter (hashtag #MASalert) notifications provided updates and responded to media stories and corrected innuendoes and rumors (see Figure 11.2).

FIGURE 11.2. MH370 Facebook page (left) and Twitter+Hashtag (right). Once MH370 was confirmed lost, the airline activated its "dark site," and removed all appearances of business as usual, in order to convey the severity of the crisis. All the company's social media, Twitter (hashtag #MASalert) and Facebook, that provided updates and responded to media stories and corrected innuendoes and rumors, reflected the seriousness of the situation. Screenshot by Melissa Agnes, Crisis Management Strategist, in her 2014 analysis of Malaysia Airline's crisis response to MH370 which can be found at: http://melissaagnes.com/malaysia-airlines-crisis-communications-flight-mh370/ [27]. Used with permission.

To show compassion, MAS sent out a "Go Team" (a team of investigators sent out to investigate accidents or attacks or any major crisis, volunteer caregivers, and MAS staff) to Beijing and kept one in Kuala Lumpur to provide support for families of passengers. Families were gathered in hotels where they were briefed about the situation. As news reports indicate, irate family members accused MAS and the Malaysian government of suppressing information. The Chinese government, having the largest number of its citizens on the plane, dispatched its officials to Kuala Lumpur demanding action.

Given that this was the first time in Malaysian Airline history that a crisis of this magnitude had occurred, especially in a social media era, the assumption was that the airline authorities would take advantage of the crucial first or golden hour of the crisis to focus on the most important audience, the families of the missing. It did not.

While the media statements posted on social media were acceptable, there was no consistency or brand new information with some of the earlier postings. Additionally, there were no links from the website that would allow for interactivity. At that early stage of the crisis, there was no "fact sheet" to provide basic facts about the unfolding crisis [28].

The Malaysia Airline's CEO, Ahmad Jauhari Yahya's, media briefing to provide updates about the crisis did not happen during that "golden hour." In fact, Malaysia Airline leadership, and by extension the government, was pilloried in the media for clumsy and contradictory responses, tardiness in releasing information, cover-up and nonsensitivity toward family members of the missing passengers. China's Xinhua News Agency, the official press agency of the Chinese government, led the charge. It said, "It is known to all that inaccurate, or at least incomplete information, led to the initial search in the South China sea" [29].

Fuad Sharuji, MAS crisis director, acknowledged in a published report that mistakes were made. He further said that the airline did the best it could under the extraordinary circumstance to respond to the crisis. He cited the activation of the company's "comprehensive and detailed" emergency response plans. He also noted that MAS's responsibility was to communicate its findings to the Rescue Command Centre, part of the Malaysian Department of Civil Aviation, which was ultimately "responsible for any search, rescue and repatriation efforts" [30].

Some Early Communication Mistakes

It is obvious MAS made some mistakes in its initial communication. For instance, official communication responses were slow, confusing, contradictory, and conveyed by too many spokespersons [31]. The airline's social media accounts were first updated 6 hours after a confirmation of the disappearance [18], opening up opportunities for conspiracy theorists and others to define the crisis for MAS. In an age where social media is literally the go-to place for information, especially breaking news, and seems to dominate the sharing of information, it (social media) should be the first channel of communication instead of the last. Additionally, the first statement should not have just stated the fact of the missing plane, but also convey empathy and seek to rebuild confidence during and after the crisis.

As noted earlier, official communications responses were slow, confusing, and had too many spokespeople involved. Some of the spokespeople were not properly trained for addressing the throng of international media and for a crisis of such magnitude. As the Prime Minister of Malaysia, Najib Razak, rightly noted in his editorial published in Wall Street Journal, effective communication was not prioritized in the first few days of the plane's disappearance [1].

The initial posts on MAS social media platforms were just facts with no attempt to convey empathy. Empathy should come across from the tone of the media statement; it should have a "human voice" [32]. While later posts conveyed empathy, overall, the government and airline's social media posts were inadequate. Important content such as maps, videos, and audio recordings that were used during the daily press conferences were missing from the posts.

Overall, the government and airline's social media posts were inadequate. Important content such as maps, videos, and audio recordings that were used during the daily press conferences were missing from the posts.

The airline missed the "golden hour," allowing for uncontrolled speculation, rumors, and innuendos to permeate social media. No press conference was scheduled within hours of the plane's disappearance, which meant family members, the media, and the public had to rely on the posted statements on MAS social media sites.

The statements posted did not have a "share" button making it impossible for people to expand the reach of the news or give them the option to ask questions or clarify information. The initial media statement was not posted at the time it was released.

Some contradictory messages from MAS and the government confused the public, who expressed their frustration on social media. Also, keeping the families in the hotel for a long period of time created a "media feeder," whereby the families came out each day after MAS briefings to speak to the media about their perceived lack of information or misinformation from MAS and the Malaysian government.

Sixteen days after the aircraft disappeared, MAS sent official condolences to the family members of the 239 passengers through text message stating: *"Malaysia Airlines deeply regrets that we have to assume beyond any reasonable doubt that MH370 has been lost and that none of those on board survived"* [33] (see Figure 11.3).

Notifying families through text message that everyone on the aircraft had died was insensitive. MAS officials had argued that it was another layer of communication tool. While it is, the use of such a tool in this context is inappropriate, lacks compassion, and could have a profound negative effect on the company's reputation. In summing up the social media response to the crisis, crisis expert, Pownall notes

Overall, both MAS and the Malaysian government appeared to be trying to manage the MH370 narrative primarily through traditional media, while using social media to push news in large part as they had existing official accounts and had to use them. But, in reality, MAS and the government had lost control of the story, something that became clearer the longer the plane was missing. [32]

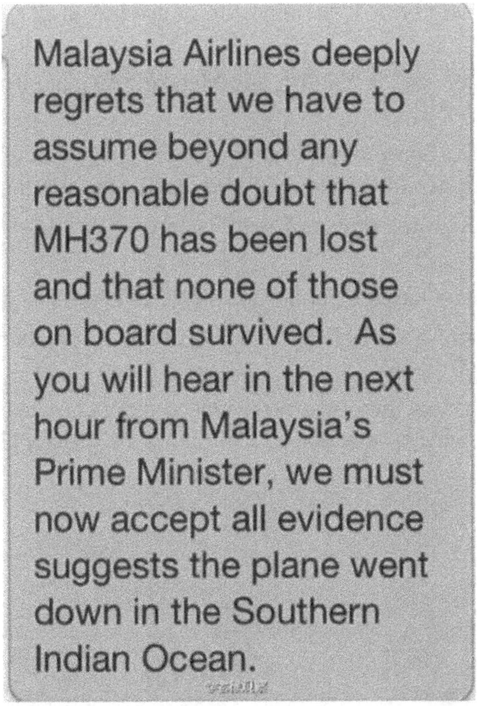

> Malaysia Airlines deeply regrets that we have to assume beyond any reasonable doubt that MH370 has been lost and that none of those on board survived. As you will hear in the next hour from Malaysia's Prime Minister, we must now accept all evidence suggests the plane went down in the Southern Indian Ocean.

FIGURE 11.3. **Image of text message from Malaysia Airlines to families of flight passengers and crew from the** *Daily Mirror* **of London [33].** Sixteen days after Flight MH370 disappeared, MAS sent official communication to the family members of the 238 passengers through text message, notifying them that their loved ones were presumed dead. This mode of communication was heavily criticized as being insensitive. Screenshot from CNN Breaking News on Twitter (@CNNbrk) on March 24, 2014.

What MAS Did Right (After the Initial Missteps)

In the midst of what seemed to be total confusion regarding how to handle such an unprecedented crisis event, MAS actually got some things right that are worth pointing out. Below are some noteworthy actions.

- Hired Ketchum's Singapore chief, John Bailey, an aviation PR expert, to handle the crisis as it was too big and unprecedented
- Removed all promotional images and text from all its communication channels

- Kept the public informed via statements of updates on all communication platforms
- Published statements in English and Mandarin (a majority of the passengers were Chinese)
- Deployed a "Go-Team" of MAS staff and volunteers to Beijing and in Malaysia to serve the needs of families and loved ones of the missing
- Asked the public for prayers for the safety of the passengers and crew of MH370
- Showed empathy through public statements and on social media
- Retired the flight codes MH370 as a sign of respect for the missing
- Created a *Wall of Hope* at the airport (see Figure 11.4) with the hashtag #MH370; however, there was no evidence that connected the Wall communication to online conversation streams about the tragedy [32]

FIGURE 11.4. Image of Malaysian women writing messages on the MH370 *Wall of Hope* at the Airport in Kuala Lumpur. One of the things that MAS did in the early days after the disappearance of MH370, was to create a *Wall of Hope* at the airport with the hashtag #MH370. While there was no evidence that connected the Wall communication to online conversation streams about the tragedy, the Wall was seen as one of the positive steps that MAS took in the aftermath of the initial announcement. Picture purchased from Alamy.com. Used with permission.

The Role of Culture in the Response

Given the magnitude of the crisis and its transboundary nature, there were bound to be cultural considerations and influences on the response provided by MAS and the Malaysian government. These considerations, in some cases, worked in their favor whiles working against them in other instances, resulting in a backlash. Below are a few that are worth pointing out.

a. The keeping of families in hotels was an act of compassion borne out of the cultural trait of consideration of others and generally seeking societal harmony on the basis of the principles of reciprocity [5,9]. Similar actions such as the call for the public to pray for the safety of the passengers and crew of MH370, showing empathy through public statements and on social media, retiring the flight codes MH370 as a sign of respect for the missing, and creating a Wall of Hope at the airport with the hashtag #MH370 can all be seen in this light. They were all actions that can be seen as emanating from a deeply religious and cultural concern for encouraging harmony.

b. The lack of open communication, which was the basis of complaints from family members of passengers, seems to have dogged the investigations to date. As of late August 17, 2016, it was reported that "Of greater concern to Australians is that Malaysia's apparent reluctance to be more open is tarnishing the reputation of (Australia's) crash investigators" [34]. Being a culture with high power distance [8] and also one that values harmony, and saving face [5,9], it is possible to surmise that these cultural traits did influence that behavior of officials and continues to do so.

c. The actual timing of the release of information about the missing flight can also be seen as culturally influenced. As noted earlier, the first announcement about the missing flight was issued nearly 6 hours after the confirmation of loss of contact from the Vietnamese authorities. As a culture that believes in the expansive nature of time—rubber time [5]—it is very likely that the delay in announcement would not have been considered a crucial matter, whereas many, particularly in the western (often low context) world, saw it as such because of their strict adherence to time. The timing could also be linked to the cultural trait where negative information is avoided as much as possible in the name of harmony and saving face is important [5,9].

d. Culture certainly influenced MAS officials in their response to the criticism of insensitivity, leveled against them. They found it difficult to accept that they should be criticized for using text message as an added layer of communication to notify family members of passengers, that their loved ones had died. The cultural attributes at play here are power distance, which expects subordinates to not question authority and saving face, which leads to the need for people in authority not to appear to be at fault in public.

Doing a Few Things Differently Could Have Helped

Given the varied reactions to the handling of the crisis and the accusations of poor organization, secrecy, and insensitivity, what could have been done differently to please particularly the grieving public? Pownall [32] suggests that Malaysian officials could have learned the lessons of Fukushima and approached the crowd as people they could work with rather than work against. His suggestions are very appropriate and worth citing.

- Openly encouraging members of the public to send in photographs and other documentary evidence.
- Making official data and analysis about the plane's flight public.
- Encouraging and even supporting plausible third-party crowdsourcing efforts.
- By being truly open, Malaysian authorities could have had a better chance of reducing misinformation and, perhaps perversely, regaining control of the narrative. [32]

Such a move would certainly have helped re-build trust with the families of the bereaved [32].

Interestingly, in the time since Pownall wrote, MAS has done all of the above and taken other corrective steps since the MH370 tragedy, including the following:

- Rebranded itself to the new name, MAB-Malaysia Airline Berhad. However, the rebranding process has not been what stakeholders expected. Christoph Mueller, a German "turnaround" specialist and the first non-Malay to head the airline stepped down in April 2016, before the end of his three-year contract. He slashed thousands of jobs and salaries and "focused the flight network on Asia"—moving away from a strategy of linking European cities to Australia [35]. Speculations surrounding his resignation point to interference by Khazanah, the majority shareholder and sovereign trust wholly owned by the government, the sole owner of MAB. The good news is that MAB posted a profit in February 2016, the first positive monthly result in years [35].
- Deployed a consistent social media strategy—evident in the response to the MH17 disappearance with "share" options in posts.
- Use of third party endorsers to reinforce perception of MAS (now MAB) as a safe airline. This was done after the MH17 crash.
- Instituted security measures that ensure that pilots are never alone in the cockpit at any given time. Other crew members must always be present to guard the door at all times, including bathroom breaks and meals.

Valuable Lessons for the Future

A crisis of this nature would invariably throw up many lessons that can be learned by those interested in crisis communication for the future. Below is a comprehensive, but not exhaustive, list of key lessons that can be gleaned from the crisis and the way MAS responded.

- A major crisis such as the disappearance of MH370 requires quick and coordinated action by an organization's crisis team and its allies.
- Minimize speculation and innuendos by providing timely and accurate information on the crisis. Updates should have new or additional information.
- Focus on the audience and customize messages for each group. Deliver bad news in a sensitive manner.
- Have a fact sheet and a Frequently Asked Questions (FAQ) about the incident available on the company's website and dark site.
- Have streamlined messages that are disseminated across multiple platforms.
- Recognize that most crises are transboundary, so audience should include "netizens" who may not share the same geographic, political, or philosophical space.
- Engage all social media and make them interactive with appropriate "share" buttons. Use social media not just to provide information, but to counter and correct inaccuracies and speculations.
- It is important to communicate to stakeholders using the appropriate tools. Sensitive messages such as loss of dear ones must be conveyed with compassion; texting lacks that. As Malaysia Airlines has learned, communications disseminated during a crisis has an immense impact on long-term company reputation.
- Social media is an incredibly helpful tool during a crisis. It can be used to convey empathy when written in a compassionate tone, generate support and participation by the audience.
- Use trained spokesperson(s) and ensure that the key messages are conveyed using the right tone.
- Do not prolong the agony of the families by keeping them for long periods with no additional or new information about their loved ones.
- Consistency, appropriate content, and visibility are crucial when posting information on social media accounts, so are facts. It is better to admit that one does not have an answer than to give wrong information.
- Leadership, especially in times of crisis, is crucial. The MH370 disappearance was a transboundary crisis that affected many countries whose citizens were passengers and a demonstration of effective leadership could have helped

assuage the ire of many stakeholders, especially the families of those onboard the flight. After the aircraft's wing was discovered on Reunion Island on July 29, 2015, distraught families continued to blame the airline for improper handling of the crisis.

• Leadership, especially in the decision-making process, is important, given the participation in the search and rescue effort by military personnel from many countries, some with vastly divergent political systems of government.

• The MH370 crisis reiterates the importance of a strong and tested crisis management plan. A strong crisis management plan can simulate most possible scenarios that an organization may face.

• There are tangible consequences of a crisis, in this case a steep decline in bookings. MAS lost 305.7 million Ringgit, or $97.2 million dollars, between April and June 2014. According to Business Insider, "The impact of the MH370 incident and intensified competition resulted in a 6.7 percent drop in bookings" [36]. Since then, MAS has rebounded and posted a small profit in February 2016 [37].

Practical Suggestions for Interested Parties

On the basis of the discussion in this chapter, people interested in issues and crisis communication in the specific context of Malaysia should consider the following as suggestions that might be useful:

Malaysia is a high context culture in which harmonious relationships, history, and traditions are valued. This means that in some situations, what might seem to be the optimal solution from an outsider's perspective, may not be culturally acceptable. Consequently, in such situations, both communication and action must take cognizance of such and must seek to create a harmonious win–win situation rather than take an approach that might result in winner-takes-it-all, and create disharmony.

Malaysia is a high power distance culture and as such irrespective of the occasion people in power expect such cultural protocols to be observed and within that context, there may be consequences for those who do not follow the norm.

Saving face is an important part of Malaysian culture, so one needs to be tactful in dealing with communication that points accusing fingers at people in authority. The lack of any critical analysis of the MH370 crisis and response from within Malaysia is ample evidence of the value placed on this cultural attribute.

Conclusion

On July 22, 2016, a meeting of Transport ministers from Malaysia, Australia, and the People's Republic of China was held in Putrajaya, Malaysia, to discuss arrangements in the event Malaysia Airlines flight MH370 is not located. At that meeting it was decided that should the aircraft not be located in the current search area, and in the absence of credible new evidence leading to the identification of a specific location of the aircraft, the search would be suspended upon completion of the 120,000 square kilometer search area [38]. Approximately 6 months later, on January 17, 2017, the tripartite Ministers of Australia, Malaysia and China announced that the search for MH370 has been suspended. They noted in a joint statement that, "the decision to abandon the search was not taken lightly, or without sadness". The statement further explained:

> Despite every effort using the best science available, cutting-edge technology, as well as modelling and advice from highly skilled professionals who are the best in their field, unfortunately, the search has not been able to locate the aircraft [39].

The outcome means that, this will go down in history as "one of the world's greatest aviation mysteries" [1]. The response to the crisis reveals some crucial points and lessons that can be learned in the areas of crisis communication; social media use in crisis communication, communication in a transboundary crisis context and even the airline industry. As Prime Minister Najib Razak rightly noted

> Malaysia is not the only party that must learn from MH370. There are also important lessons for the global aviation industry. One of the most astonishing things about this tragedy is the revelation that an airliner the size of a Boeing 777 can vanish, almost without a trace. In an age of smartphones and mobile Internet, real-time tracking of commercial airplanes is long overdue. [1]

Sadly, Shrivastava's [40] observation concerning the tragedy in the failure of organizations and organizational scholars to learn from prior crisis still holds true in this case. Even though investigators in the Air France 447 crash into the Atlantic Ocean recommended that the airline industry introduce improvements aimed at helping search teams quickly locate a crash site and reach any survivors, no action was taken [1]. While acting on those recommendations might not have prevented the loss of Flight MH370, it would very likely "make it harder for an aircraft to simply disappear, and easier to find any aircraft that did and certainly reassure the traveling public and reduce the chances of such a drawn-out disaster reoccurring" [1].

In the face of the uncertainty and the unfolding crisis, Malaysia managed to overcome diplomatic and military sensitivities and bring 26 different countries together to conduct one of the world's largest peacetime search operations.

On a positive note, one of the most powerful and most enduring lessons which can be learned is in the area of transboundary cooperation in times of crisis. In the face of the uncertainty and the unfolding crisis, Malaysia managed to overcome diplomatic and military sensitivities and bring 26 different countries together to conduct one of the world's largest peacetime search operations [1]. This, in the words of the Malaysian Prime Minister, "is no small feat" [1], and the world can and must learn from this example, as a way of forging ahead in our bid to live peaceably with one another at all times.

Also, from both a crisis communication and social media point of view, another point worth reiterating is that, this case has shown that in an age of unprecedented use of social media, having a social media strategy that reinforces the message disseminated in traditional media [41] is an absolute necessity. Ultimately, the overall value of this chapter lies in its demonstration of the need for responsiveness to "multiple cultures, value sets, and communicative practices of different nations" [42].

Discussion Questions

11.1 Given what you know of this crisis response, what do you think should be some of the factors that should have possibly overridden the cultural characteristics in crisis communication responses provided?

11.2 The case shows that Malaysia's cultural inclination for harmony and compassion influenced the decision to keep relatives of the passengers who were on board Flight MH370 in hotels; a decision which seemed to have backfired and provided an avenue for unwanted media feeds. Bearing this in mind, what would you recommend in a future situation like this, and why?

11.3 With the understanding that "saving face" is important in Malaysian culture and the suspicion/complaints that the Malaysian government has not been open enough, how would you suggest the diverse stakeholders (especially foreign governments like China, Australia, and an organization like The International Civil Aviation Organization) work together in trying to unravel the mystery of the lost plane?

11.4 Knowing how the Malaysian government and MAS responded in the first few hours when Flight MH370 disappeared and the reaction to their response, outline from a communications point of view, what would you have done in the first 12 hours after the realization hit that the plane had been lost. Identify and describe six main tasks that you think should be the most urgent.

11.5 Imagine a scenario where Flight MH370 is found, outline a series of activities that you would recommend to MAS officials and the Malaysian government to undertake in the 24 hours after it is confirmed that the plane has been found.

References

1. N. Razak. (2014, May 13). "Malaysia's lessons from the vanished airplane: My government didn't get everything right. Yet other parties, too, must learn from MH370—and make changes" [Online]. Available: http://www.wsj.com/news/articles/ SB10001424052702303627504579559170123401220, September 5, 2016 (last date accessed).

2. *Malaysia – The World Factbook—Central Intelligence Agency* https://www.cia.gov/ library/publications/the-world-factbook/geos/my.html, May 31, 2017 (last date accessed).

3. Malaysian Government. (n.d). "Malaysia" [Online]. Available: http://www.tourism. gov.my/, August 15, 2016 (last date accessed).

4. Department of Statistics Malaysia. (2016). "Current population estimates, Malaysia, 2014–2016" [Online]. Available: https://www.statistics.gov.my/index.php?r=column/ cthemeByCat&cat=155&bul_id=OWlxdEVoYlJCS0hUZzJyRUcvZEYxZz09& menu_id=L0pheU43NWJwRWVSZklWdzQ4TlhUUT09, August 15, 2016 (last date accessed).

5. R. Tajaddini and B. G. Mujtaba, "Stress perceptions and leadership orientation of Malaysians: Exploring their similarities and differences with Americans," *Chinese Business Review*, vol. 8, no. 8, pp. 26–42, 2009.

6. A. Davison. (2015, July 28). "Current issues in Malaysia and how it affects the economy" [Online]. Available: http://www.expatgo.com/my/2015/07/28/current-issues-in-malaysia-and-how-it-affects-the-economy/, September 5, 2016 (last date accessed).

7. D. C. Thomas and K. Au, "The effect of cultural differences on behavioral response to low job satisfaction," *Journal of International Business Studies*, vol. 33, no.2, pp. 309–326, 2002.

8. G. Hofstede, *Culture and Organizations: Software of the Mind*. New York: McGraw-Hill, 1997.

9. R. Fisher, W. Ury, and B. Patton, *Getting to Yes: Negotiating Agreement Without Giving in*, 2nd ed. Boston/New York: Penguin, 1992.

10. H. M. Dahlan, "Local values in intercultural management," *Malaysian Management Review*, vol. 1, pp. 45–50, 1991.

11. K. Kwansah-Aidoo, "Embarrassing Ghana to pay Brazil: The Ghana Black Stars player revolt at the 2014 FIFA World Cup," in *Culture and Crisis Communication: Transboundary Cases from Nonwestern Perspectives*, 1st ed., A. M. George and K. Kwansah-Aidoo, Eds. Hoboken, NJ: John Wiley-IEEE Press (IEEE PCS Professional Engineering Communication Series).

12. L. Huff and L. Kelley, "Is collectivism a liability? The impact of culture on organizational trust and customer orientation: A seven-nation study," *Journal of Business Research*, vol. 58, pp. 96–102, 2005.

13. M. L. Storz, "Malay and Chinese values underlying the Malaysian business culture," *International Journal of Intercultural Relations*, vol. 23, no.1, pp.117–131, 1999.

14. D. Kirkham and K. Muthaly, *Flying Through Crisis MH370: Lessons in Crisis Communication*. Kuala Lumpur: Calistro Consultants Ltd., 2015.

15. Malaysia Airlines. (n.d.). "Our story. Malaysian Airline systems" [Online]. Available: http://www.malaysiaairlines.com/us/en/corporate-info/our_story/about-us.html, September 5, 2016 (last date accessed).

16. J. Livesey. (2014, July 17). "Curse of Malaysia Airlines? 5 tragic moments in airline's history before MH17 and MH370" [Online]. Available: http://www.mirror.co.uk/news/world-news/curse-malaysia-airlines-5-tragic-3875868, September 5, 2016 (last date accessed).

17. A. Harjani. (2014, March 24). "Timeline of Flight MH370" [Online]. Available: http://www.cnbc.com/2014/03/11/timeline-of-flight-mh370.html, September 5, 2016 (last date accessed).

18. Malaysian ICAO Annex 13 Safety Investigation Team for MH370. (2015, March 08). "Factual information safety investigation for MH370 *(PDF) (Report). Malaysia*" [Online]. Available: http://mh370.mot.gov.my/download/FactualInformation.pdf, September 5, 2016 (last date accessed).

19. Malaysia Airlines. (2014, March 17). "Malaysia Airlines MH370 flight incident - MH370 press briefing by Hishammuddin Hussein, Minister of Defence and Acting Minister of Transport," [Online]. Available: https://web.archive.org/web/20141218104844/http://www.malaysiaairlines.com/ksd-maintenance/DarkSites.html, September 5, 2016 (last date accessed).

20. C. Ashton, A. S. Bruce, G. Colledge, et.al., "The search for MH370," *The Journal of Navigation*, vol. 68, pp. 1–22, 2015.

21. P. Armstrong. (2014, March 25). "Search for Malaysia Airlines flight 370: The technology," [Online]. Available: http://www.cnn.com/2014/03/24/world/asia/indian-ocean-search-for-mh370-hardware/, September 5, 2016 (last date accessed).

22. G. Botelho, M. Pearson, and J. Mullen. (2014, March 12). "Mystery Malaysia flight may have lost signal, gone hundreds of miles off course" [Online]. Available: http://www.cnn.com/2014/03/11/world/asia/malaysia-airlines-plane/index.html, September 5, 2016 (last date accessed).

23. S. K. Dehghan. (2014, March 12). "Iranians travelling on flight MH370 on forged passports 'not linked to terror,'" [Online]. Available: https://www.theguardian.com/world/2014/mar/11/passengers-malaysian-plane-mh370-iranian-forged-passports, September 5, 2016 (last date accessed).

24. "Flight MH370 'crashed in south Indian Ocean' - Malaysia PM," *BBC*, March 12, 2014. [Online]. Available: http://www.bbc.com/news/world-asia-26716572, September 5, 2016 (last date accessed).

25. Malaysia Airlines. (2014, March 08). "Media statement and information on Flight MH370 Incident released at 7:24 am MYT," [Online]. Available: http://www.malaysiaairlines.com/mh370, July 20, 2016 (last date accessed).

26. Malaysia Airlines. (2014, March 08). "Malaysia Airlines MH370 flight incident - 2nd media statement released at 9:05 am MYT," [Online]. Available: http://www.malaysiaairlines.com/mh370, July 20, 2016 (last date accessed).

27. M. Agnes. (2016, March 13). "A look at Malaysia Airlines' crisis communications during the crisis of flight MH370" [Online]. Available: http://melissaagnes.com/malaysia-airlines-crisis-communications-flight-mh370/, September 20, 2016 (last date accessed).

28. Media Training and Consulting. (n.d.). [Online]. Available: http://www.trinetizen.com/, September 5, 2016 (last date accessed).

29. J. Tilley. (2014, March 21). "Analysis: Malaysia Airlines' mishandled response to the MH370 crisis" [Online]. Available: http://www.prweek.com/article/1286333/analysis-malaysia-airlines-mishandled-response-mh370-crisis, September 5, 2016 (last date accessed).

30. A. Culbertson. (2014, March 18). "Malaysia Airlines admits it 'made mistakes' over handling of missing MH370" [Online]. Available: http://www.express.co.uk/news/world/653727/Malaysia-Airlines-made-mistakes-handling-MH370, September 05, 2016 (last date accessed).

31. S. Broderick. (2014, May 1). "First MH370 report details confusion in hours after flight was lost Aviation Week Network" [Online]. Available: http://aviationweek.com/commercial-aviation/first-mh370-report-details-confusion-hours-after-flight-was-lost, September 5, 2016 (last date accessed).

32. C. Pownall. (2014, May 26). "Malaysia Airlines, MH370 and social media crisis communications" [Online]. Available: http://www.business2community.com/crisis-management/malaysia-airlines-mh370-social-media-crisis-communications-0887855}AaaDsUjrAvSrOQ6X.97, September 5, 2016 (last date accessed).

33. D. Raven. (2014, May 26). "Malaysia Airlines flight MH370: Relatives screamed after being told of tragic news by TEXT" [Online]. Available: http://www.mirror.co.uk/news/world-news/malaysia-airlines-flight-mh370-heartbroken-3278066, September 5, 2016 (last date accessed).

34. "MH370: No mystery to flight's disappearance, says expert," *The Week*, August 31, 2016. [Online]. Available: http://www.theweek.co.uk/mh370/57641/mh370-plummeted-out-of-sky-at-up-to-20000ft-a-minute, September 5, 2016 (last date accessed).

35. J. Vasagar. (2016, April 19). "Malaysia Airlines chief Mueller quits early" [Online]. Available: http://www.ft.com/cms/s/0/21af7248-0631-11e6-9b51-0fb5e65703ce.html#axzz4JLPOlxak, September 5, 2016 (last date accessed).

36. "Malaysia Airlines' financial losses have nearly doubled since flight MH370 disappeared," *Business Insider*, August 31, 2016 [Online]. Available: http://www.businessinsider.com/afp-malaysia-airlines-loss-nearly-doubles-on-mh370-impact-2014-8, September 5, 2016 (last date accessed).

37. E. Ng, "Malaysia Airlines just turned its first monthly profit since before the MH370 crash," *Business Insider*, April 6, 2016. [Online]. Available: http://www.businessinsider.com/ap-ceo-says-malaysia-airlines-has-first-monthly-profit-in-years-2016-4, September 5, 2016 (last date accessed).

38. Australian Aviation. (2016, July 25). "Hunt for MH370 to be "suspended" once 120,000 sq. km search area completed" [Online]. Available: http://australianaviation.com.au/2016/07/hunt-for-mh370-to-be-suspended-once-120000-sqkm-search-area-completed/, September 5, 2016 (last date accessed).

39. H. Belot. (2017, January 17). "MH370: Search for missing Malaysia Airlines plane suspended," ABC News, [Online]. Available: http://www.abc.net.au/news/2017-01-17/search-for-mh370-suspended/8189066, May 31, 2017 (last date accessed).

40. P. Shrivastava, "Industrial crisis management: Learning from organizational failures," *Journal of Management Studies*, vol. 25, no.4, pp. 283–284, 1988.

41. David E. Johnson. (2015, December 29). "Malaysia Airlines: A lesson in crisis manage-
    ment" [Online]. Available: http://www.commpro.biz/corporate-communications/crisis-
    communications-corporate-communications/malaysia-airlines-crisis/, September 5, 2016
    (last date accessed).

42. M. Stohl, C. Stohl, and N. Townsley, "A new generation of global corporate social respon-
    sibility,". in *The Debate Over Corporate Social Responsibility*, S. May, G. Cheney, and J.
    Roper, Eds. New York: Oxford University Press, 2007, pp. 30–44.

Singapore 12

Cultural Impediment or Reflection of Global Phenomenon: State of Social Media Crisis Preparedness in Singapore

Augustine Pang and Christabel Reena David

Chapter Preview

Singapore has achieved fame as a hub of commerce, knowledge, and research and development in a fiercely competitive global environment. The national culture is characterized by diligence, continuous learning, improvement, growth, and always needing to be ahead of the curve. If there is an Achilles heel in Singapore's progress in this new economy, it would be its lack of crisis preparedness, particularly social media crisis (SMC) preparedness given the heavy social media use among organizations. Yet, even as local practitioners claim they understand the importance of crisis preparedness, few have actually put in place practical and rigorous mechanisms to help manage potential and actual crises. Is the practice of using social media to reach out to stakeholders in times of crises a function of Singapore's culture, or is it a global phenomenon?

Culture and Crisis Communication: Transboundary Cases from Nonwestern Perspectives, First Edition.
Edited by Amiso M. George and Kwamena Kwansah-Aidoo.
© 2017 by The Institute of Electrical and Electronics Engineers, Inc. Published 2017 by John Wiley & Sons, Inc.

After reading this chapter, you will be able to

- *Understand how organizations in Singapore prepare for social media crises*
- *Assess the level of preparedness for social media crises*
- *Know how different corporate culture types influence the style of communication they adopt, particularly on social media platforms*
- *Examine how practitioners operating in any country, in addition to understanding effective modes of communication, would also need to study the working cultures to understand when and how to push a social media preparedness agenda*

Brief Overview: Singapore and Its Working Culture

Singapore, a former British colony and a multicultural and multilingual Southeast Asian country [1], is a pluralistic society with a high income and competitive economy that provides a favorable entrepreneurial environment. Its population of 5.5 million consists of 74.35% Chinese, 13.35% Malays, 9.1% Indians, and 3.25% of other races [2], which constitutes diverse cultural and religious beliefs and practices. Today, Singapore is a prospering financial center and an economic "tiger" of Asia that is renowned for its conservatism, stringent laws, stability, and security [3]. According to Kaplan [4], founding father Lee Kuan Yew set about creating this modern republic society with a combination of Confucian principles and state-sponsored capitalism that has propelled Singapore into a first world country [5].

Singapore's culture is based on "Our Shared Values," which emphasizes "nation before community and society before self, family as the basic unit of society, community support and respect for the individual, consensus over conflict, and racial and religious harmony" [1]. The Shared Values bear close resemblance to Confucian values which are endorsed by the Government with the belief of providing a good foundation for inculcating Asian values in younger Singaporeans [1]. Among the many Confucian values, pragmatism, diligence, and lifelong learning/education for progress are observed to be most strongly reflected in Singapore and its people.

Due to its lack of natural resources, and driven by the need to survive and progress in a fiercely competitive global environment, pragmatism has influenced the way Singapore operates, characterized by utilization of limited human resources to increase efficiency and profitability [6]. As Singapore is a meritocratic society, the importance of diligence has been socialized in Singaporeans from a young age as they ascribe to the fear of stagnation [7]; thus, they advocate continuous learning, improvement, and growth [8]. The constant striving to better oneself and to be ahead of the curve is mirrored in the way plans—be they educational or infrastructural—are conceived in Singapore [9]. The aspiration is for the country to be a hub of commerce, knowledge, and research and development [9].

However, if there is an area that appears to be lacking, it would be the lack of crisis preparedness [10]. This chapter argues that for all its much-lauded competences, SMC preparedness among organizations in Singapore remains inadequate.

With social media having the ability to escalate any crisis [11], crisis preparedness must encompass SMC preparedness, particularly in the light of the heavy social media use in Singapore. Out of a resident population of 5.4 million, Singapore has 70% of social media penetration [12]. Most, if not all, organizations have turned to the online platform to engage their stakeholders in publicity and marketing efforts. LinkedIn® and Facebook® are the preferred B2B (Business to Business) social marketing platform in Singapore [12].

However, the practice of using social media to reach out to stakeholders in times of crises still remains relatively foreign to many organizations, even in the United States [13]. Only 13% of professionals surveyed said a social media strategy was incorporated in their organizations' crisis communications plans [13]. Arguably, the situation is similar in Singapore.

Of the practitioners who claim they understand the importance of crisis preparedness, few have actually put in place practical and rigorous mechanisms to help manage potential and actual crises.

Even for the practitioners who claim they understand the importance of crisis preparedness, few have actually put in place practical and rigorous mechanisms to help manage potential and actual crises. Wu and Dai [10] found that few organizations had a crisis management plan (CMP) in place. A PricewaterhouseCoopers (PwC) study in 2013 found that many organizations were not leveraging on social media as a crisis management resource [14]. Another study by the international law firm Freshfields Bruckhaus Deringer found that organizations do not cope well with online crises [15]. Like the findings worldwide, the lack of crisis preparedness among organizations in Singapore remains a gap to be addressed. The question remains: What cultural factors influence this phenomenon of the lack of preparedness?

Background of Crisis Communication Research

Research on crisis communication in Singapore has been episodic, symptomatic, and segmented [16]. Thus far, the segmented studies have examined only specific industries like hotels, tourist attractions, and property firms [17–19]; the episodic have examined selected major crises, like the SQ006 air crash [20] and the management of the National Kidney Foundation (NFK) crisis [21]; and the symptomatic examined how crises were managed and resolved, like the series of studies on Severe Acute Respiratory Syndrome (SARS) of 2003 [22].

Three research themes were identified [16]. First, research had focused on crises that the organizations had no control over, but the resultant impact was one the organization had to address. A key example was the research on the 2003 SARS virus that had spiralled into a worldwide crisis. On March 18, 2003, Singapore joined Canada, China, Hong Kong, and Taiwan in the World Health Organization's (WHO) list of SARS-hit countries. The following months marked the frenetic pace at which the Singapore Government worked to contain and communicate the SARS crisis with its different publics, eventually leading WHO to declare Singapore SARS-free on May 31. WHO praised the government's handling of the crisis as "exemplary" [22].

Second, research had focused on crises which could possibly (but not necessarily) be in the organization's locus of control, and may or may not have a negative impact on the organization's target audience, but nonetheless was a crisis to the organization. A key example is the impact of the Asian financial crisis that started in mid-1997, on tourism [17].

The third theme focused on crises which were attributed to the organization, be it through intentional or unintentional actions. A key example was how the Singapore Government's role as a regulator came under scrutiny in 2004 when allegations of mismanagement of funds and misrepresentation by top executives of the NKF, Singapore's largest charity organization then, caused widespread public outrage [21].

Thus, Pang [16] argues that much of the research on crisis communication appears to have been focused on the institutional and organizational perspectives. They invariably fall into either one of these categories

- They had national interests and/or international impacts
- They attracted extensive media coverage
- Studies focused more on crisis management and response than crisis planning or pre-crisis preparation

The only large-scale study on crisis preparedness was conducted by Wu and Dai [10]. Their survey of 200 organizations in Singapore found that many (76%) claimed they had planned for crises, but a little more than half admitted their organizations did not have either a written crisis plan or a crisis management team, even though more than a third (35%) of organizations reported they had been hit by crisis in the past 5 years. These statistics found traction in other studies [17–19, 23]. What all of this means is that crisis preparedness among organizations in Singapore is akin to what Wu and Dai [10] described as "overall slackening."

Role of Culture on Crisis Communication Practice

The role culture plays in Singapore's corporate practices is more ideological, that is, a way of doing things, characterized by pragmatism, rather than the pervading influence of any of the ethnic cultures. Low [24] conceptualized nine types of Singaporean corporate cultures. Three are evidently practiced. They are *Profit*, *Stability*, and *Bureaucratic* types.

- Organizations with *Profit* culture are concerned with profit-making and survival in an intensively competitive business environment; espousing the "can-do spirit" that resonates with the Singaporean value of achievement [6]. The Profit culture promotes perseverance and hard work; evidence of Singapore's Confucianism [6] and its high long-term orientation [25].

- The *Stability* corporate culture is the one that emphasizes playing "it safe" [24] as Singaporeans value political, social, and economic stability, as well as the government's role and assistance [24].

- The *Bureaucratic* culture is the one characterized as being "power-oriented, cautious, established, solid, regulated, structured, procedural, overly rule-bound, hyper-precautious, lack of risk-taking, terse and over-reacting" [24] as well as being less open in communication, preferring one-way communication, and slow to accept changes [24]. This coincides with Singapore's fixation on establishing an "elite economic bureaucracy" to steer economic development [24], as well as being consistent with the reflective, meticulous, reserved, stern, methodical, and conservative personalities of Singaporean managers [26].

The six remaining corporate culture types that are less evident are *Cooperative*, *Modernizing*, *Sole Proprietor*, *Role Model*, *Going Global*, and *Metamorphosis*.

- First, organizations such as cooperatives, charities, and governmental social agencies subscribe to the *Cooperative* corporate culture. They tend to prioritize and meet their members' and beneficiaries' interests and needs during difficult times, which characteristically demonstrate the Confucian practice of benevolence, compassion, and understanding [24].

- Next, corporations with *Modernizing* culture believe in improving their technologies and business techniques to meet competition in a modernizing environment. This is in line with Singapore's culture of advanced planning for holistic excellence [24], as well as demonstrating the national value of practicality and "continuous effort and being resilient" [24]. Examples of entities with such culture are modern companies and family businesses.

- Third, *Sole Proprietor* organizational culture is common in small companies, whereby business owners are highly involved and aware of the business situation and environs [27]. This close-knit culture stresses hierarchy of seniority, values relationships, and emphasizes personal reliability and trustworthiness, as well as embodying Singapore's high power distance and collectivism [25].

- Next, the *Role Model* culture, which embodies Singapore's weak masculinity [25], is apparent in education institutions and government-model firms, whereby they focus on operational efficiency and revere the teacher/role model as the main source of direction [24]. Large Singaporean corporations with international commerce and network, as well as those with potential and intention to globalize subscribe to the *Going Global* culture as they strongly welcome technology, networking opportunities, and strategically utilize local and foreign skills and knowledge to gain profits [24].

- Finally, *Metamorphosis* culture is present in hi-tech start-ups and environmental firms, whereby pragmatism, rationality, progress, and utilization of science and technology to achieve excellence and quick results are strongly valued [24].

For all its emphasis on efficiency and advancement, and given the pervasiveness of social media use, the irony is that many organizations in Singapore are not prepared for social media crises. Despite the findings of a 2012 Singapore social media study by the social media consulting firm, Rock Publicity, that the country currently "leads Asia in terms of social media usage and general tech-savviness," [28] the lack of effort in engaging audiences on social media could be due to Profit culture's pragmatism, Safety's prudence, and Bureaucratic culture's preference for one-way communication. Choo [29] concurred by attributing responsibility to corporate bureaucracy. The reticent approach to social media by local organizations could be a reflection of their conservative business approaches and cultures [28]. The practice among many organizations appeared to be for them to treat their social media platforms, like Facebook, as a promotion-centric advertising bulletin [30]. Most organizations perceive their forays into social media as "pilots" and remain cautious of it impacting their core businesses and core assets [28].

Case Study: The 2011 Subway Crisis

A crisis that epitomizes the lackadaisical approach organizations had toward social media use and the attendant lack of SMC preparedness occurred to Singapore's Mass Rapid Transit (SMRT) operator, in December 2011 in what was then known as the most serious and unprecedented train breakdown in SMRT's 24-year history [31]. The first crisis on December 15, 2011, lasted 5 hours, while the second, on December 17, 2011, lasted 7 hours.

With more than 220,000 commuters affected [32], confusion reigned. Trains were stalled in underground tunnels and some commuters had to be guided onto the tracks and walked in the dark along the tunnels to enter the stations [33]. When the doors of some trains did not open, and ventilation wore thin, train windows were smashed to let air in [34]. There was no respite for those who managed to leave the stalled trains to get into the stations. They were faced with customer service officers who had no formal training to deal with disruption and staffing was short and late in deploying [35]. Those who did get out of the station were faced with another set of disappointments. Bus bridging services to ferry them onward on their journeys came hours later [36].

Commuters were seething with anger. They vented and ranted and spared no emotion in lambasting SMRT publicly, online on blogs, chat forums, social-networking sites, e-mail distributions, and offline. Some SMRT staff reportedly received "some nasty remarks and scolding" from commuters [33]. One commuter perhaps summed up the general sentiment: "I don't think their (SMRT's) best is good enough yet" [37]. The Singapore Government acted swiftly. Within days, the Prime Minister Lee Hsien Loong announced the commission of a Committee of Inquiry (COI) to get to the root of the problem.

Weeks after the crises, Transport Minister Lui Tuck Yew declared during a parliamentary sitting that the crises "exposed gaps in emergency preparedness and crisis response, and we need to do better" [31]. The lack of crisis preparedness, it was to emerge later during the COI, came in several forms. Many pertained to operational deficiencies and lack of investment in maintenance [32].

Most disappointing—and some said amusing with a tinge of resignation—was the lack of social media preparedness. Even though SMRT apologized after the first crisis, its communication left much to be desired. When the first hint of train breakdown occurred on December 15, a message was sent out to taxi drivers, presumably to take advantage of the breakdown. The message, which was flashed on SMRT taxi drivers' screens, read: "Income opportunity. Dear partners, there is a breakdown in our MRT train services from Bishan MRT to Marina Bay MRT stretch of stations." A taxi passenger took a photo of the screen and posted it online. It went viral instantly and the message drew heavy criticisms for its insensitivity. SMRT apologized and explained that a wrong message template was used [38]. Communication updates from corporate communication could also have been more prompt using social media. SMRT's official Twitter® handle @SMRT_Singapore used to have this as description, "This is the official Twitter channel of SMRT. We're here, 9am-6pm, Mon-Fri (excl public holidays)." Lim [39] argued that SMRT had since realized that social media does not have "official hours" and has changed its Twitter description.

With this case as a springboard, to understand organizations' views on social media and SMC preparedness, the authors interviewed 15 practitioners who came from diverse industries including government, finance, education, consumer, retail, entertainment, and creative industries to understand SMC preparedness. The interviewees were chosen as they were able to provide insights into both the operational protocol and the policy decisions behind the practices. They held positions ranging from executive to senior managing directors in organizations representing Profit, Stability, and Bureaucratic types. The interviews were conducted from mid-September to mid-November 2013. Two Research Questions were examined

Research Question 1: How do organizations prepare for SMCs?
Research Question 2: What is the level of preparedness among Singapore organizations?

Situational Analysis

Research Question 1: How do organizations prepare for social media crises (SMCs)?

When asked about how their organizations would fare in a SMC, a variety of responses were received, with most claiming to be fairly well prepared. However, a clear observation was that respondents from the government sector were generally less confident, explaining that the hierarchical nature of the government proved too slow in social media response times. What was more interesting was that though none of the respondents claimed to have been through an SMC, a clear majority (13 out of 15) of interviewees felt that an SMC was a "very real concern."

Research Question 2: What is the level of preparedness among Singapore organizations?

Results showed that only 3 out of 12 respondents had monitoring teams and systems. Though almost all interviewees felt it was a relevant concern, not all actually took the further step of having/forming one. This trend was discovered to be more prevalent in the government sector. One of the respondents from a government entity explained that most corporate communications teams did not have a CMP and operated within the guidelines of Standard Operating Procedures (SOPs) passed down from the top management. Should a crisis happen, the prescribed line of action would be to "[follow] the SOP and [wait] for more information from top management."

Another respondent expressed little need for a CMP, much less a social media one, stating that "a crisis communication plan is only necessary for complicated structures" and that its flat organizational structure did not warrant the need for a plan. The interviewee further posited that occasional social media monitoring and tip-offs from stakeholders were sufficient for the communications manager to plan next steps.

Response of the Organizations

The interviews distilled several key learnings. First, findings showed that organizations in Singapore recognized the importance of social media and have begun incorporating it in their day-to-day work; they are increasingly savvy in choosing their social media platforms. Several organizations have expressed difficulties in creating content that could actively engage their target audience. Second, it was also observed that organizations in Singapore have begun to take notice of crises that start on or escalate on social media and the general insight is that many are aware of the ferocity and intensity of SMCs. Social media has now made the public an even more important stakeholder group and messages to the public will have to be sent at a faster speed before misinformation, rumors, spoofs, and spin-offs quickly spiral out of control and become accepted as public truth.

Social media has now made the public an even more important stakeholder group. Messages to the public will have to be sent at a faster speed before misinformation, rumors, spoofs, and spin-offs quickly spiral out of control and become accepted as public truth.

Though more practitioners were aware of the severity and negativity of an SMC, their lack of deeper understanding of the different definitions suggests that more attention and appreciation can still be given to the art of crisis preparation. While overall there have been significant developments in the preparation toward crisis management, there is still room for improvement in terms of the communications role.

Culture's Influence on Response

At present, Profit, Stability, and Bureaucratic corporate culture types are more apparent in many of Singapore's top organizations as they are characteristically cautious and prudent, which are reflected in their daily operations. As such, these corporate culture types share the commonality of maintaining status quo and preference for utilizing "safe" traditional media to exert control over communications [40], failure of which may result in debilitating financial and reputational losses for the company [41]. Organizations' preference for traditional communication channels over social media is an additional indicator of status quo heuristic [42] in organizational decision-making process, while Stability and Bureaucratic corporate cultures exert their respective influence of prudence and being reserved in communication [24].

This is manifested in several ways in the workplace. First, it is observed that forward-looking organizations like Singapore Airlines and the Singapore Government are proactive in preparing for social media crises by conducting simulation exercises. Many others do not appear to be sold on the idea of crisis preparedness. Pang and Yeo [43] argued this could be due to the fact that many organizations do not yet fully appreciate the value of communication.

Second, instead of taking a crisis preventive approach, some organizations would rather counter the negative publicity created by the crisis with more marketing and events in the hope that such endeavor would drown out the crisis. The mistaken perception remained that crisis management was media management [44].

Third, most organizations were more concerned with profitability and operational issues [45]. They did not have the financial resources to invest in consulting for a possible crisis.

Lessons Learned and Practical Suggestions

What can practitioners of corporate communications learn from the findings? First, any practitioner operating in any country, in addition to understanding effective modes of communication, would also need to study the working cultures to avoid making blunders. In the circuit of culture model posited by du Gay and colleagues, practitioners would be better placed to understand practice if they understood how social meanings are produced and reproduced [46]. They can develop such understanding if they study how management works and find ways to win the management over by gradually but surely impressing upon them the importance of SMC preparedness instead of rashly pushing the preparedness agenda. The subtleties and nuances embedded in the country's culture and organizations need time to absorb, articulate, and acclimatize.

In addition, work with and through organizations to create change, particularly for those who relocate to Singapore on assignments. Efforts have to be made to minimize issues like ethnocentrism, especially when one is on short-term assignments in another culture where time is not on one's side to fully understand the culture [47]. Given the general lack of crisis preparedness by organizations globally over the years [48–52], it appears that the lack of crisis preparedness is more than just an impediment of working culture. It could be a reflection of global phenomenon. If so, more patience is needed to effect change.

Beyond the influence of culture, Pang [53] offered two suggestions for crisis planning to be formalized. First, the anticipatory perspective, that is, how crisis planning can be further institutionalized as a critical function in organizations. Organizations often acknowledge the need for crisis planning without fully understanding its significance. Possessing a crisis plan is often used as an indicator of crisis preparedness [49]. More than that, beyond the conceptualization of the plans, how they should encourage organizations to move to next steps like conducting drills and simulation exercises to test out the rigors of the plans [54]. Low, Chung, and Pang [55] argue that strong leadership and a healthy communication culture can enhance the institutionalization of crisis plans. This stream of work is what Olaniran and Williams [56] described as anticipatory perspective, regarding how organizations anticipate and pre-plan for crises before they occur.

Second, we look at the management perspective, that is, how management can be more proactive in leading in crisis planning. One issue that was flagged in the SMRT crisis of 2011 was that even though SMRT did have a rail incident management plan, it was "too complicated," declared an expert witness. The witness observed that senior management lacked formal operational training and its "competency regime...deals only with theoretical training qualifications" [32].

The question remains: What does it take for organizational leaders to step up and take the lead? One perspective offered by Tichy and Bennis [57] argued that it boils down to making the judgment call. "Good leaders make a habit of sensing, framing, and aligning so that they are prepared for the call, which can arise any moment" [57]. One way is for communication practitioners to position themselves as trusted counsel to leaders. In that role, communication practitioners can "work in" the unique intra-organizational factors they are likely to encounter, such as a conservative corporate culture or less supportive top management, even as the social media preparedness plans are drawn.

Practitioners can subtly persuade and plod management, showing how the organization would be better served with an astute plan. Planning must include the organization's unique circumstances right from the early stages so that modifications could be made at the start rather than late in the process. For instance, if practitioners know that top management is less likely to agree to conduct more drills to test the plans, they can possibly advocate for *more* test drills in the plan to allow for top management to rationalize them to a figure that the practitioners originally had in mind. So if the practitioners think that three test drills would suffice, they could propose to conduct five drills to top management, who may eventually rationalize to three, instead of proposing three drills only for top management to rationalize to one [54].

Conclusion

We cite wholly from a 2012 study done by the social media consulting firm Rock Publicity [58], which concluded that Singapore was caught in what they (Rock Publicity) called a *paradoxical social media situation*. On the one hand, an overwhelming number of Singaporeans (almost 85% of the population) was wired in to the Internet. In fact, at the time of the study, it was also discovered that more than 70% of Singaporeans owned a smartphone, a number which is expected to have risen significantly by now. This smartphone penetration of population is said to be the highest anywhere in the world. On the whole, Singapore leads Asia "in terms of social media usage and general tech-savviness across the board" [58].

However, despite this apparent attraction to social media by users, social media marketing and communication as a whole by companies in Singapore is lagging behind the western world and is in the bottom 50% when compared to the rest of its Asian counterparts who use similar sites [58].

In all, Singaporean organizations were very slow to take up using social media as a tool for customer relations and brand building. A great number of the corporate businesses and brands in the country had no real social media presence at all. Of the ones that did, very few were doing anything that could be called proper implementation. As discovered in the study, it was taking the average company somewhere between 15 and 17 hours to respond to a question via social media, specifically on Facebook® and Twitter. However, even worse was that around 50% of companies were completely unresponsive [58].

One reason accorded for this was the lack of proper training, but the bigger reason assumed was that many companies still simply cannot see the full value of social media as any kind of platform, therefore leading to complacency.

In closing, Rock Publicity summarized a few words of advice for Singapore organizations: Organizations needed to understand the value of social media as more than a mere platform where customers can follow brands for more information. While being an excellent tool for updating people about general promotional news, its use extends to so much more than that. Social media provides a powerful medium that allows an organization's reputation to be shaped through "every single conversation or comment someone is making on the Internet about [it] ... all at the very moment they happen." It needs to be seen as the only tool that can offer organizations the ability to connect with people who are searching for what the brand can offer the moment they search for it, something with which organizations can resolve any customer issue the moment they make it public, as well as being able to influence more people at one time to think differently about your company.

Discussion Questions

12.1 How can organizations leverage the use of social media to communicate during crises?

12.2 How can top management globally be more proactive in crisis planning?

12.3 How can organizational leaders assume leadership in social media crisis preparedness?

12.4 How can communication professionals and other line managers in organizations be empowered to embark on crisis preparedness?

Acknowledgments

The authors would like to thank Malvin Chua, Sophial Foo, and Fiona Tan who provided research help for the interviews.

References

1. C. Tan, "Our shared values in Singapore: A Confucian perspective," *Educational Theory*, vol. 62, no. 4, pp. 449–463, 2012.
2. Department of Statistics Singapore. (2015, September). "Population trends 2015" [Online]. Available: http://www.singstat.gov.sg/docs/default-source/default-document-library/publications/publications_and_papers/population_and_population_structure/population2015.pdf, May 20, 2016 (last date accessed).
3. British Broadcasting Corporation. (2015, October 1). "Singapore country profile" [Online]. Available: http://www.bbc.com/news/world-asia-15961759, May 31, 2017 (last date accessed).

4. R. D. Kaplan, "Asia's rise is rooted in Confucian values," *Wall Street Journal*, February 6, 2015. Available: http://www.wsj.com/articles/asias-rise-is-rooted-in-confucian-values-1423254759, May 20, 2016 (last date accessed).

5. H. Beech and Z. Abdoolcarim. (2015, July 23). "Exclusive: Singapore Prime Minister Lee Hsien Loong speaks candidly with TIME" [Online]. Available: http://www.mfa.gov.sg/content/mfa/overseasmission/geneva/press_statements_speeches/2015/201507/press_20150723.html, May 20, 2016 (last date accessed).

6. K. C. P. Low, *Corporate Culture and Values: Perception of Corporate Leaders of Co-Operatives in Singapore*. Germany: VDM-Verlag, 2009.

7. K. C. P. Low, "Confucian ethics and social responsibility - The golden rule and responsibility to the stakeholders," *Ethics and Critical Thinking Journal*, vol. 4, pp. 46–54, 2008.

8. T. L. F. Leong, J. L. Huang, and S. Mak, "Protestant work ethic, Confucian values, and work-related attitudes in Singapore," *Journal of Career Assessment*, vol. 22, no. 2, pp. 304–316, August 2014.

9. K. C. P. Low and S. L. Ang, "Confucian leadership and corporate social responsibility (CSR), the way forward," *Asian Journal of Business Research*, vol. 2, no. 1, pp. 92–116, July 2012.

10. W. Wu and S. Dai, "A comparative study of crisis management planning in Singapore and Hong Kong," Research paper series, Faculty of Business Administration, RPS #2001-007, Singapore, 2001.

11. J. Siah, M. Bansal, and A. Pang, "New media and crises: New media – A new medium in escalating crises?," *Corporate Communications: An International Journal*, vol. 15, no. 2, pp. 143–155, 2010.

12. "Social media landscape in Singapore" (n.d). Hashmeta [Online]. Available: http://www.hashmeta.com/social-media-singapore-infographic/

13. S. R. Veil, T. Buehner, and M. J. Palenchar, "A work-in-process literature review: Incorporating social media in risk and crisis communication," *Journal of Contingencies and Crisis Management*, vol. 19, no. 2, pp. 110–122, June 2011.

14. PricewaterhouseCoopers. (2013). "Many companies still not leveraging social media as a crisis management resource" [Online]. Available: www.pwc.com/us/em/press-releases/2013/many-companies-still-not-leveraging-social-media, May 20, 2016 (last date accessed).

15. M. Quah, "Companies not coping well with crises in digital age: Freshfields," *The Business Times*, p. 3, November 5, 2013.

16. A. Pang, "Crisis communication research in Singapore," in *The Handbook of International Crisis Communication Research*, M. Loffelholz, A. Schwarz, and M. Seeger, Eds. Malden, MA: Wiley-Blackwell, June 2016.

17. J. Henderson, "Managing the Asian financial crisis: Tourist attractions in Singapore," *Journal of Travel Research*, vol. 38, pp. 177–181, 1999.

18. J. Henderson and A. Ng, "Responding to crisis: Severe Acute Respiratory Syndrome (SARS) and hotels in Singapore," *International Journal of Tourism Research*, vol. 6, no. 6, pp. 411–419, November 2004.

19. S. P. Low, D. K. H. Ho, and S. A. Yeap, "Crisis management: A survey of property management firms," *Property Management*, vol. 17, no. 3, pp. 231–244, 1999.

20. J. Henderson, "Communicating in a crisis: Flight SQ 006," *Tourism Management*, vol. 24, pp. 279–287, 2003.

21. J. M. H. Lee, J. L. Z. Lee, and A. Pang, "Credibility governance: Singapore government's management of charity scandal arising from the National Kidney Foundation (NKF) crisis," presented at the Asian Media Information and Communication Conference, New Delhi, 2009.

22. S. Khalik and S. M. Wong, "SARS-free, not to fine-tune crisis handling," *The Straits Times*, p. 1, June 1, 2003.

23. S. Lim, J. Goh, and K. Sriramesh, "Applicability of the generic principles of excellent public relations in a different cultural context: The case study of Singapore," *Journal of Public Relations Research*, vol. 17, no. 4, pp. 315–340, October 2005.

24. K. C. P. Low, "Types of Singapore corporate culture," *Business Journal for Entrepreneurs*, vol. 2, pp. 11–49, 2011.

25. "What about Singapore?" (n.d.). Hofstede Centre [Online]. Available: http://geert-hofstede.com/singapore.html, May 20, 2016 (last date accessed).

26. V. Tan and N. T. Tan, "Personality type and the Singapore manager: Research findings based on the MBTI," *Singapore Management Review*, vol. 21, no. 1, pp. 15–31, January 1991.

27. S. W. Sheh, "Chinese cultural values and their implications to Chinese management," *Singapore Management Review*, vol. 23, no. 2, pp. 75–83, 2001.

28. EASTWEST Public Relations. (2011, October 28). "Use of social media by Asia's leading companies" [Online]. Available: http://www.eastwestpr.com/2011/10/use-of-social-media-by-asias-leading-companies/, May 20, 2016 (last date accessed).

29. B. Choo. (2013, October 7). "This is the biggest social media mistake of Singapore companies" [Online]. Available: http://sbr.com.sg/media-marketing/commentary/biggest-social-media-mistake-singapore-companies, May 20, 2016 (last date accessed).

30. Mynewsdesk. (2015, March 11). "95 Percent of small businesses failed on social media" [Online]. Available: http://www.mynewsdesk.com/sg/jackchaz/pressreleases/95-percent-of-small-businesses-failed-on-social-media-1128644, May 20, 2016 (last date accessed).

31. L. Lim, "MRT breakdowns 'exposed gaps' in crisis response," *The Straits Times*, p. A10, January 10, 2012.

32. C. Tan, "Getting rail transport back on track," *The Straits Times*, p. D2, July 7, 2012.

33. M. Almenoar and R. Sim, "Train tunnels are now lit at all hours," *The Straits Times*, p. A6, April 24, 2012.

34. X. Li, "Confusion over the hybrid creature called the MRT," *The Straits Times*, p. A8, January 10, 2012.

35. M. Almenoar and R. Sim, "Back-up MRT staff turned up 1 hours late," *The Straits Times*, p. C6, April 27, 2012.

36. M. Almenoar and R. Sim, "Commuters waited 2 hours for shuttle buses," *The Straits Times*, p. B10, April 28, 2012.

37. J. Hong, "Passengers at Circle Line stations left scrambling," *The Straits Times*, p. A8, April 19, 2012.

38. J. Tan. (2011, December 16). "SMRT says sorry for 'income opportunity' alert" [Online]. Available: https://sg.news.yahoo.com/percentE2percent80percent98they-donpercentE2

percent80percent99t-seem-to-care-about-passengers-at-allpercentE2percent80percent99.
html, May 20, 2016 (last date accessed).

39. W. Lim. (2011). "SMRT train breakdowns on social media" [Online]. Available: http://
www.net-profit-marketing.com/smrt-train-breakdowns-on-social-media.html, May 20,
2016 (last date accessed).

40. C. Li. (2014, December 16). "PwC: Significant 'media gap' exists in Singapore"
[Online]. Available: http://www.mynewsdesk.com/sg/pwc-singapore/pressreleases/pwc-
significant-media-gap-exists-in-singapore-1099250 Nov 6, May 20, 2016 (last date
accessed).

41. Y. H. L. Hong, S. Y. J. Quek, and B. P. Ng, "A research on the cultural values of Singapore
and the impact on work related behaviours," unpublished.

42. E. H. James and L. P. Wooten, "Decision for the crisis leader," in *Leading Under Pressure:
From Surviving to Thriving Before, During, and After a Crisis*, E. H. James and L. P.
Wooten, Eds. New York, NY: Routledge, 2010, pp. 69–101.

43. A. Pang and S. L. Yeo, "Examining the expertise, experience and expedience of crisis consultants in Singapore," *Public Relations Review*, vol. 38, pp. 853–864, December
2012.

44. A. Pang, B. Nasrath, and A. Chong, "Negotiating crisis in the social media environment:
Evolution of crises online, gaining credibility offline," *Corporate Communication: An
International Journal*, vol. 19, no. 1, pp. 96–118, 2014.

45. M. H. Lee, A. Mak, and A. Pang, "Bridging the gap: An exploratory study of corporate
social responsibility among SMEs in Singapore," *Journal of Public Relations Research*,
vol. 24, pp. 299–317, August 2012.

46. T. K. Gaither and P. A. Curtin, "International public relations," in *Public Relations: From
Theory to Practice*, T. Hansen-Horn and B. D. Neff, Eds. Boston, MA: Pearson Allyn &
Bacon, 2008, pp. 281–299.

47. Y. Low, J. Varughese, and A. Pang, "Communicating crisis: How culture influences image
repair in Western and Asian Governments," *Corporate Communication: An International
Journal*, vol. 16, no. 3, pp. 218–242, September 2011.

48. J. J. Burnett, "A strategic approach to managing crisis," *Public Relations Review*, vol. 24,
no. 4, pp. 475–485, 1998.

49. R. Cloudman and K. Hallahan, "Crisis communications preparedness among US organizations: Activities and assessments by public relations practitioners," *Public Relations
Review*, vol. 32, pp. 367–376, September 2006.

50. S. Fink, *Crisis Management: Planning for the Inevitable*. New York: AMACOM, 1986.

51. M. K. Pinsdorf, "Flying different skies: How cultures respond to airline disasters," *Public
Relations Review*, vol. 17, no. 1, pp. 37–56, January 1997.

52. M. J. Tiller, "Is your disaster plan effective," *Management Review*, vol. 83, p. 57, April
1994.

53. A. Pang, "Derailed: The SMRT crisis of 2011," *Media Asia*, vol. 40, no. 2, pp. 124–127,
June 2013.

54. A. Pang, G. T. Cameron, and F. Cropp, "Corporate crisis planning: Tensions, issues, and
contradictions," *Journal of Communication Management*, vol. 10, no. 4, pp. 371–389,
December 2006.

55. L. Low, V. Chung, and A. Pang, "Efficacy of crisis management plans: Toward a revised synthesis model in managing crises," in *Pre Crisis Management: Preparing for the Inevitable*, B. Olaniran, D. Williams, and W. T. Coombs, Eds. New York: Peter Lang, 2012, pp. 171–197.

56. B. Olaniran and D. Williams, "The need for an anticipatory perspective in crisis communication," in *Pre Crisis Management: Preparing for the Inevitable*, B. Olaniran, D. Williams, and W. T. Coombs, Eds. New York: Peter Lang, 2012, pp. 3–16.

57. N. M. Tichy and W. G. Bennis, "Making judgment calls," *Harvard Business Review*, vol. 85, no. 10, pp. 94–102, October 2007.

58. Rock Publicity. (2012). "The 2012 Rock Publicity Singapore social media study" [Online]. Available http://www.slideshare.net/rockpublicity, May 20, 2016 (last date accessed).

South Korea 13

Going Nuts Over Nuts: The Korean Air Ramp Return Crisis

Jangyul Robert Kim and Kyung-Hyan Yoo

Chapter Preview

How did Korean Air manage its "ramp return" crisis? This "nut rage" crisis case differs from traditional western crisis cases in several aspects. Korean Air boasted a strong public relations department with seasoned crisis communication experts, but its crisis management system did not effectively operate in this unique owner-originated crisis. The Korean Chaebol culture combined with Confucianism negatively impacted Korean Air's crisis management. Social and mobile media also played a key role in exacerbating the crisis, touching on adverse sentiments of ordinary Korean citizens.

After reading this chapter, you will be able to

- *Understand the role of culture in risk and crisis communication practices*
- *Discuss the importance of developing crisis communication strategy that appropriately appeals to the general public*

Culture and Crisis Communication: Transboundary Cases from Nonwestern Perspectives, First Edition.
Edited by Amiso M. George and Kwamena Kwansah-Aidoo.
© 2017 by The Institute of Electrical and Electronics Engineers, Inc. Published 2017 by John Wiley & Sons, Inc.

- *Differentiate between conventional crisis management and owner-originated crisis management*
- *Identify the limits of the role of public relations experts when they fail to persuade the firm's top management*
- *Understand the difficulties in controlling today's communication channels, particularly social and mobile media*
- *Discuss the importance of timely response and honest communication in crisis management, prioritizing the interest of victims and publics over the interest of the owner of the company*

Overview of Korea and Its Culture

Korea is a peninsular nation located in East Asia, between China and Japan. It has a long dynastic history including Silla, Goryeo, and Chosun. The country has an affluent Buddhist culture and advanced technology with its own language and ingenious characters. Korea was forcibly occupied by Japan for 36 years (1909–1945), then was divided into North and South Korea after its independence from Japan, then experienced the Korean War from 1950 to 1953, which left the country completely devastated. Today, it is the only country divided into two different nations in the world by political systems. North Korea still maintains a communist regime while South Korea adopted democracy and capitalism.

Confucianism influenced Korea over its Chosun dynasty period and still remains part of its culture, represented by emphasis on collectivism and respect for elders. Scholars categorized Korea, China, and Japan as sharing many cultural similarities [1], mainly attributed to their high context culture [2]. South Korea was less known to westerners as compared to its neighboring countries, until the country hosted the Summer Olympics in 1988 and the World Cup in 2002. Today, South Korea is well known throughout the world, partly as a result of its flourishing economy, developed hi-tech industry, and so-called "Korean Wave" represented as healthy cuisines, K-pop music, and dramas.

South Korean Chaebol and Its Culture

One of the key factors that has contributed to the development of the South Korean economy to date is the role of the Chaebols, or large business conglomerates (typically family owned), unique to its culture. The Park Chung-Hee military regime (1963–1979) fully supported a few select South Korean firms to create jobs, vitalize its economy, and drive exports. These firms contributed immensely to the development of the South Korean economy while accumulating their own wealth in return.

They include global South Korean giant corporations such as Samsung®, Hyundai®, LG®, and Korean Air®.

South Korean Chaebols differ from conglomerates in western countries. While these are corporations or a group of corporations, a few founders (owners) and their families keep control of the corporations despite owning fewer stocks, and their second, third, and fourth generations assume reigns of the companies. Those descendants receive special and tailored education, study abroad (mostly in the United States) at renowned private universities, return to South Korea, and are ultimately trained to manage the firms. These descendants are promoted comparatively rapidly than their peers. One research showed that these young descendants of the owners' families of the top 30 South Korean conglomerates rose to executive levels just in 3.5 years while it takes 4 years for common college graduates to be promoted from one position to an assistant or deputy manager level [3]. Another data reports that fewer than 5 out of 1000 employees with a college degree are promoted to be an executive among South Korean conglomerates, taking over 22 years [4].

Due to this special treatment in favor of Chaebols and their families, some of the young generation of these families tend to perceive themselves as born differently than the average employee, and they take such privileges within their corporations for granted. Sometimes, they are known to have more power than CEOs and nonfamily executives, because they wield strong influence over the employees' promotion and their position assignments. Therefore, it is hardly imaginable to see employees of these corporations disagree with the decisions or requests of the owner families. One of the worst crisis cases originating from a Chaebol family was that of a second-generation Chaebol who beat a worker with a baseball bat for openly complaining about an employment issue due to the merger of his company, and then gave him 20 million Korean Won (approximately US$20,000) as "blood money" [5].

Role of Culture in Crisis Communication Practice

According to Hall's [2] study, East Asian countries are categorized as the representative high context culture whereas the United States and Germany are regarded as low context culture. In a high context culture, people distinguish between ingroup and outgroup members based on personal relationships rather than official business relationships [6]. The ingroup members share similar experiences and regard the ingroup members as their friends and allies, while they maintain minimal and official relationship with outgroup members. This high context and ingroup culture has influenced the crisis communication practice in South Korea.

Even though social media is an important communication channel, traditional media such as newspapers, magazines, and television remain the most relevant intervening public that needs to be reached, and, if possible, managed when a crisis breaks out. In general, to manage a crisis effectively and successfully, it is critical to control the information, and if the public relations practitioners have good personal relationships with journalists (i.e., if the journalists perceive the public relations practitioners as their ingroup members), it is more likely that the journalists will try to understand the corporation's position and therefore, be more cooperative. In particular, if the crisis or issue was related to the owners and their family members, an intimate personal relationship with journalists is more vital. In South Korea, crisis management is centered on this aspect more than western countries. This culture is reflected in the media relations of South Korean public relations practitioners. They spend more time and effort in building and maintaining personal relationships with journalists by playing golf, dining, and drinking together than typical western public relations practitioners [7].

In addition, one of the characteristics of South Korean culture that affects crisis communication practice is "saving face" which can be understood as part of justification strategy [8]. Because South Koreans place importance on keeping human relationships, it is assumed that if journalists and public relations practitioners have good personal relationships, the journalists would refrain from writing negatively to save the face of a company and its owner, and even when they have to blame the company, they may try to use less harsh expressions or tone down their descriptions.

The Crisis: Korean Air "Nut Rage" Case

On December 5, 2014, the Korean Air® Flight 86 departing from John F. Kennedy International Airport in New York for Incheon International Airport, South Korea, returned to the gate and ejected a senior flight attendant from the plane. The reason for this uncommon and abrupt ramp return was not a terrorist attack, hijacking, critical mechanical issue, or health-related emergency for one of the passengers. The reason was macadamia nuts. The incident began with the way a snack was served to the first-class passengers, that is, the macadamia nuts from Hawaii were served in a bag instead of being served on a plate. Why did it matter? Cho Hyun-ah, a Korean Air Executive Vice President on board was not happy with the way the snack was served and she ordered the captain to move back to ramp and eject Mr. Park Chang-jin, a senior flight attendant. This uncommon incident took place because she was not just one of the several EVPs, but the daughter of the chairman of the family-run conglomerate that operates the airline [9].

According to the initial announcement from Korean Air, Ms. Cho ordered Mr. Park to leave the plane because he was not well informed about food and beverage service regulations. It was reported that she yelled at him, insulted him by forcing him to kneel down, and beat his shoulder with a plastic file [10].

As soon as South Korean media reported this incident on December 8, 2014, it aroused rage and criticism among the South Korean community as it was regarded as an example of misuse of "excessive power and sometimes inappropriate behavior of the families who control the country's leading chaebol companies" [11]. This affair was extensively covered by most major international print media such as *New York Times*®, *Wall Street Journal*®, *Guardian News*®, *The Times*®, *The Financial Times*® as well as broadcast media including CNN®, ABC®, CBS®, BBC®, Bloomberg®, and almost all online news sites including Yahoo® and AOL®. The case was reported by many media under the headlines of "nut rage" and "nut queen," and also became the subject of mockery such as "going nuts over nuts" by some bloggers [9].

This crisis case demonstrates how culture influences the crisis response strategies in various aspects. The incident was widely covered in international media and blogs due to its uniqueness, and the subsequent responses from Korean Air differed from what western public relations practitioners would expect.

Objectives of the Crisis Communication

While no specific objectives were communicated by Korean Air, the following can be inferred from the way the company handled the crisis and communicated.

Objectives

1. To protect EVP Cho's reputation from being tarnished through criticism of her excessive behavior in the airplane until the crisis situation is resolved
2. To prevent the crisis from expanding into a larger crisis among internet users
3. To support EVP Cho during the prosecutor's investigation process to help mitigate the sentence or minimize the penalty
4. To restore Korean Air's image as a responsible corporate citizen among the target audience during and after the crisis

Stakeholders

We have collected in Table 13.1 the various stakeholders (publics or target audiences) that Korean Air needed to consider in its attempt to deal with the crisis.

Response from Korean Air: From Bad to Worse

As the case provoked enormously negative uproar, the public relations department of Korean Air attempted to settle the public rage by releasing an official position statement on December 8, 2014. However, the content was far from a relevant crisis response message. It tried to support the behavior of Ms. Cho and pointed an accusing finger at Mr. Park, the senior flight attendant.

This position statement failed to calm down the flaming anger of South Korean citizens because it tried to justify the behavior of Ms. Cho rather than to apologize

TABLE 13.1. Stakeholder Breakdown

Stakeholders	Descriptions
Immediate victims	Mr. Park Chang-jin, the senior flight attendant, and another flight attendant in the first-class cabin were the most urgent and important target audience that Korean Air needed to address with priority and sincerity.
Media	Both South Korean and international media were key intervening target audience that needed to be managed with transparency and authenticity based on facts.
Bloggers	Bloggers in South Korea and other countries were key intervening target audiences because of their influence on their readers.
Internet users	Both South Korea and other countries have internet users who read/watch the news and diffuse the news to other internet users—in particular, social media and smartphone users.
Korean Air employees	Employees are the internal ambassadors. They should be taken care of the same as the victims as they are the assets of Korean Air.
Korean Air stockholders	Those who own stocks (who invested in the company and who might suffer from lost opportunities) should be informed in a timely and honest manner.
Korean Air customers	Customers should be taken care of. They include current customers who frequently travel and who are loyal to Korean Air such as its privilege club (**SKYPASS**) members, other customers who travel with Korean Air, and potential Korean Air customers.
Prosecutors and judges	Even though these stakeholders are in the legal department, it is important to keep an eye on their decisions in order to respond accordingly.
Government officials	Government officials in the Ministry of Land, Infrastructure, and Transport should be informed of the situation immediately and correctly.

for her misdeeds. Despite stating "we apologize to our passengers for their inconvenience" in the first sentence, the statements that followed blamed the flight attendants, asserting that they ignored service regulations and processes, failed to use the service manual, and lied to Cho. The statement further put the blame on the captain, not EVP Cho, who ordered Mr. Park to leave the aircraft. As well, the statement emphasized that the company would strengthen the training of flight attendants to provide its passengers with better services and further guarantee safety. Many South Koreans, media, and bloggers were skeptical of the statement and suggested that it was not the flight attendants, but rather Ms. Cho, who needed training.

Within a few days, this statement proved to be false. Mr. Park disclosed what really happened inside the aircraft at an interview with SBS-TV on December 13, 2014. He admitted that he was physically and verbally assaulted by Ms. Cho and finally was ejected from the plane [12]. Moreover, a first-class passenger confirmed Mr. Park's revelation to be true. During the time the incident was happening, that passenger even sent several text messages describing the situation to her friend via KakaoTalk, the most popular mobile messenger service in South Korea [13].

On December 12, as public opinion on the matter worsened, Cho Yang-ho, Chairman of Korean Air, apologized on behalf of his daughter and announced that she would resign from all positions while maintaining her EVP title. However, the decision to allow Ms. Cho to keep her EVP title despite her resignation from all official positions backfired. The South Korean media and internet bloggers harshly criticized Chairman Cho's decision condemning it as a fake apology. Media began to portray the negative aspects of the Chaebol system of Korea. Activist groups and civic organizations began to protest against Korean Air calling for Ms. Cho's resignation from all official positions and titles.

Further, the negative public opinion led to the prosecution summoning Ms. Cho for investigation. In front of the prosecutor's office, she officially apologized for the first time (see Figure 13.1). The excessive treatment and strict control of a photo line to block journalists from approaching her by the Korean Air employees was badly

FIGURE 13.1. A bow of apology. Bowing EVP Cho. Former Korean Air Vice President Cho Hyun-ah bows in apology after she appeared for questioning at the West Seoul branch of the Supreme Prosecutors' Office on December 17, 2014. *Source*: Kim 2014 [14]. Reproduced with permission of The Hankyoreh.

criticized as it was seen as evidence of excessive loyalty to their owner. Moreover, Ms. Cho visited Mr. Park's home to offer an apology without an appointment. When she failed to meet him, however, she left a note on a piece of paper that she apologized for the case. The public condemned this act as well, seeing it as a lack of genuine interest in apologizing to the victim.

On December 16, 2014, Korean Air placed apology advertisements in most South Korean daily newspapers. It backfired on the company's image yet again. The advertisement was condemned for lacking details of action to further prevent the recurrence of such a mishap and for not apologizing to the victims but only to general public vaguely [15]. The fact that it was placed in the name of Korean Air (company), not by EVP Cho (individual), was also criticized. It was ironic that Korean Air (and its employees who were victims of this owner-originated crisis) placed large-scale ads at the company's own expense while Ms. Cho who caused the problem kept silent and hid from the public. The sincerity of the apology advertisement was doubted by most South Koreans [16]. Figure 13.2 is the apology advertisement in Korean language [17] and its verbatim translation in English by the author.

On top of these grudging and inept responses, it was discovered that an executive of Korean Air had attempted to cover up Ms. Cho's misdeed, destroyed evidence, and coerced Mr. Park and the other flight attendants into making false statements [18]. He even contacted a first-class passenger and asked her to verify the fact that Korean Air has apologized to her if she received any question from media, offering her a free model aircraft and calendar [19].

Prosecutors finally issued a warrant for Ms. Cho's arrest for ordering fabricated testimony [20]. Moreover, it was revealed that Korean Air executives attempted to leverage their personal connections with government officials in the Ministry of Land, Infrastructure, and Transport to acquire confidential details of the official inquiry

	Korean	English
(Title)	그 어떤 사죄의 말씀도 부족하다는 것을 절감하고 있습니다	No word of apology does justice
(Body)	최근 대한항공의 일들로 국민 여러분께 말로 형용할 수 없는 실망감을 안겨 드렸습니다. 지금까지 커다란 사랑을 주신 여러분께 큰 상처를 드렸습니다. 그 어떤 사죄의 말로도 부족하다는 것을 잘 알고 있습니다. 그래서 더욱, 국민 여러분의 질책과 나무람을 가슴 깊이 새기겠습니다. 다시금 사랑 받고 신뢰받는 대항항공이 되도록 환골탈태의 노력을 다하겠습니다. 새로운 대한항공이 되겠습니다.	We have disappointed you beyond explanation with our recent incidents. We have repaid your love with harm. No word of apology is enough. We take your critiques deeply to our heart. We will continue our best efforts to regain your love and trust. We will be a reborn Korean Air.
(Signature)	대항항공	Korean Air

FIGURE 13.2. Korean Air apology. Here is the direct wording, in Korean, for the apology advertisement placed in most Korean newspapers by Korean Air [17] and its English translation. Translation provided by the authors.

[21]. For instance, an ex-Korean Air government official in the transport ministry illegally conveyed the content of internal discussions and decisions in the ministry to the Korean Air executive during the investigation process via phone call and text messages so that Korean Air executives would know the information and respond accordingly. In addition, it was found that Korean Air provided these officials with benefits such as free upgrade to business/first class when they travelled with Korean Air, which is regarded as a form of bribery [22].

Consequences: Losing It All

The consequences of Ms. Cho's excessive order to return the aircraft to the gate and the series of inappropriate responses were detrimental. Ms. Cho resigned from all positions and titles. She was convicted of violating the aviation safety law by illegally forcing the flight back to the gate, and sentenced to a year in prison [23]. Not only was the reputation of Korea Air damaged but employee morale also suffered greatly. Korean Air became an object of mockery among global media, bloggers, and internet users. The company's employees became the subject of national and global sympathy. To date, a simple search using "nut rage" in Google.com yields more than 1.3 million results, with most of them being negative. If social media posts and shares are taken into consideration, the number of people exposed to the news increases exponentially.

The company's business was negatively affected as well. The incident occurred when international oil prices had plunged, providing a great opportunity for airlines to increase their revenue, coupled with rising stock prices. Thanks to the plummeting oil prices, Korean Air's stock price increased by 9% even a week after the incident was reported. In comparison, the stock price of Asiana Airlines, its South Korean competitor, significantly increased by 31.7%. In other words, even though Korean Air's stock price did not drop, the company lost an opportunity to leverage the favorable factor [24].

Ironically, the "nut rage" scandal made sales of macadamia nuts soar as South Koreans wanted to taste the nuts served only to Korean Air's first-class passengers. South Korean eBay reported a 12-fold increase in sales in the 5 days after the case was reported, and sales on another website jumped 20 times in a week as well [25].

Effect of Culture on Korean Air's Crisis Communication Practice

South Korea has a strong "saving face" culture [8] that influences communication practice and relationship between public relations practitioners and journalists. Further, the country has kept strong Confucianism heritage, including respect for elders and obeying the organizational hierarchy [1]. The influence of these nonwestern cultures can be seen in the response of Korean Air in managing the crisis. Simultaneously, the prevalent anti-Chaebol sentiment among the Korean citizen contributed to the exacerbation of the crisis.

This Korean Air "nut rage" case differs from traditional western crisis cases in several aspects.

This Korean Air "nut rage" case differs from traditional western crisis cases in several aspects. It extends beyond a simple incident, but rather an explosion of widely dispersed negative perception of the Chaebols within the South Korean society and against the excessive behaviors of the owner family.

In a typical western crisis, a corporation may respond based on a crisis management response scenario presumed by crisis communication scholars and consulting firms, and follow the guidelines. In a case of an airplane crash or a terrorist attack, for instance, safety and/or livelihood of the passengers and their loved ones become top priority. A corporation may apologize to the victims and community depending on the level of its responsibility and severity, do its best to save the victims, take care of their families, compensate the victims or the community, and follow up on the crisis until it is resolved [26].

However, such a crisis management scheme does not accommodate this case of owner-originated mishap, particularly because the owner's desire or will becomes a crisis management system itself, and eventually the standard of crisis communication manual. Moreover, the cause of the crisis was the owner's dissatisfaction with the way macadamia nuts was served in a bag, not on a plate. In South Korea's Chaebol system where the owner can exercise absolute power, any recommendation from the internal public relations department becomes futile unless the owner agrees.

Up until the incident, the public relations department of Korean Air had earned a high reputation thanks to its strong network with media and its own accumulated expertise. The company has experienced and survived various types of issues and crises both domestically and internationally, and has many experienced crisis communication professionals as employees or counselors. It is unfortunate that such a strong communication system and qualified communication professionals could not contribute to solving this owner-originated crisis.

In South Korea's Chaebol system where the owner can exercise absolute power, any recommendation from the internal public relations department becomes futile unless the owner agrees.

Lessons Learned

Ms. Cho and Korean Air should have acknowledged her responsibility and given a full and genuine apology from the beginning. Korean Air misjudged the public's response to their refusal to accept liability, underestimated the severity of the issue, responded hesitantly and dishonestly, missed timely responses, released a wrong statement and placed an erroneous advertisement, and escalated the crisis.

If Ms. Cho had fully and directly apologized immediately, she may not have had to resign from all positions. As she hid behind a curtain, let the company issue a position statement which pointed fingers at the employees who were also victims, the public's wrath grew. According to Coombs' situational crisis communication theory [27] and related research [28], Ms. Cho should have adopted a *full apology strategy* in this situation as she was fully responsible for the crisis and no one else deserved the blame. However, Ms. Cho missed this simple but crucial point.

The apology advertisements placed in daily newspapers should have addressed the victims and included a corrective action plan to prevent recurrence of such a nonsensical event. The advertisement should have been in the name of Ms. Cho and she should have borne the cost or together with Chairman Cho, her father, not in the name of Korean Air with the company shouldering the expenses. The equivocal content of the advertisement under the company name worsened the situation as more South Koreans doubted the sincerity of the advertisement.

Korean Air should have communicated openly and honestly. Evidence disclosed during the prosecutor's investigation process showed the company's attempts to cover up the case—such as an executive's clandestine connection with government officers and the illegal effort to acquire confidential information, coercion of its employees to make false statements to protect the company's owner, and concealment of evidence. The responses of Korean Air did not follow the basic "one voice" rule [26] in crisis communication which addresses the importance of sharing the same information and using the same talking points to maintain accuracy and credibility. In addition, some employees' explicitly excessive behavior to treat Ms. Cho as a VIP in public places (even though she was summoned to the prosecutor's office) harmed the company's reputation, and contributed to the public's trust as well. The crisis communication messages should have focused on demonstrating their intention to give an unqualified apology and propose corrective actions, and on protecting victims, their families, and the publics, not on protecting the owner and covering her culpability.

Practical Suggestions

For those seeking to communicate risk and crisis information or conduct business in South Korea, below are a few suggestions that may be of help.

1. Understand the country's culture. South Korea is one of the East Asian countries that adhere to the tradition of Confucianism that still affect the

practice of public relations and crisis communication. It is important to understand that Koreans regard "face-saving" as an important interpersonal skill.

2. South Korea is one of the high context culture countries. Like Chinese "Quanxi" which considers personal relations more important than laws and written agreement, it is important in South Korea to belong to "ingroup" with the stakeholders for efficient relationship with them [6].

3. South Korea is well equipped with high speed internet and highly developed telecommunication infrastructure. It is important to reach South Koreans not only via mass media, but also via online networks, social media, and mobile messages as crisis communication has no deadlines nor is it controllable due to the new communication ecology. All communication efforts should be candid and transparent.

Expert Commentary: Transparency is Key

The most significant insight gained from the crisis communication of Korean Air "nut rage" case is that of *transparency*. Corporate culture thus far has remained a private matter within each specific corporation. However, this incident shed a spotlight on the longstanding authoritative internal corporate culture, exposing it to public scrutiny.

Shortly following the controversy, Korean Air's mistakes continued in not understanding the value of transparency. This conglomerate failed to monitor and analyze the public's sentiments that evolved rapidly, and thus failed to respond in a timely and transparent manner. Further, transparency seemed to have been thrown off by the many internal decision-making and response processes driven by top-level executives (EVP Cho Hyun-ah and her family).

The crisis expanded as the company's illegal lobbying attempts were exposed to the public. Its "share one voice" initiatives through internal staff were portrayed as a gag by the media. Through this incident, transparency challenged the way South Korean corporations handled crisis that has been rampant with secrecy, protection, and silence. Transparency is an important ecological threat for South Korean conglomerates who used to be nontransparent.

Korean Air's "nut rage" crisis management case demonstrates the influence of new communication ecology and social stakeholders that emerged as a new social influencer. It is apparent that crisis management strategy should be based on transparency.

Reproduced with permission of James Chung.

Discussion Questions

13.1 If you were the communication director of Korean Air, what would you have done during the first 24 hours after the incident? Identify and describe five tasks that you think are the most urgent and important.

13.2 EVP Cho had to resign from all positions due to the deteriorating public opinion and finally sentenced to jail. Do you think an admission of full responsibility for the incident, and an unqualified apology from her at the outset could have prevented these happenings? What are the reasons for your answer?

13.3 The "nut rage" scandal not only harmed the reputation of Korean Air, but the perception of South Korea's transport ministry. If you are the communication director of the Ministry, what kinds of image recovery strategies would you develop to recover the Ministry's damaged image? Suggest one short-term and one long-term image restoration program.

13.4 Find any airline involved in crisis in your country. Compare the crisis with this case. What are the differences and similarities?

13.5 Discuss this crisis case with other students and write three lessons you have learned. Suggest alternate ways in which the airline could have responded.

References

1. G. Hofstede, *Culture's Consequences: International Differences in Work-Related Values*, 2nd ed. Beverly Hills, CA: Sage Publications, 1984.
2. E. T. Hall, *Beyond Culture*. New York: Doubleday, 1976.
3. H. Kim, "'Superfast promotion' of descendants of Chaebol owners, 3.5 years to become executives ... what about ordinary employees?" *Dong-A Ilbo*, January 8, 2015. [Online]. Available: http://news.donga.com/3/01/20150108/68982518/1, September 24, 2016 (last date accessed).
4. Y. Noh, "Only 4.7 became executive out of 1,000 employees with college degree," *Kookmin Ilbo*, November 3, 2014. [Online]. Available: http://news.kmib.co.kr/article/view.asp?arcid=0922833145&code=11151100&sid1=eco, September 24, 2016 (last date accessed).
5. J. Son, "SK Group family member accused of brutal assault on employee," *The Hankyoreh*, November 30, 2010. [Online]. Available: http://english.hani.co.kr/arti/english_edition/e_national/451375.html, September 24, 2016 (last date accessed).
6. J. O. Yum, "The impact of Confucianism on interpersonal relationship and communication patterns in East Asia," *Communication Monographs*, vol. 55, pp. 374–388, December 1988.
7. S. Jo and Y. Kim, "Media or personal relations? Exploring media relations dimensions in South Korea," *Journalism and Mass Communication Quarterly*, vol. 81, no. 2, pp. 292–306, 2012.
8. Y. Kim and J. Yang, "The Korean apology map: An analysis of apologies by types during the past 10 years," *Korean Journal of Communication and Information*, vol. 59, pp.180–210, Fall 2012.
9. S. Choi, "Korean Air executive resigns post after halting flight over snack service," *The New York Times*, December 9, 2014. [Online]. Available: http://www.nytimes.com/2014/12/10/world/asia/korean-air-executive-resigns-post-after-halting-flight-over-snack-service.html?_r=0, September 24, 2016 (last date accessed).

10. "'Nut rage' incident could result in sanctions against Korean Air," *The Guardian*, December 30, 2014. [Online]. Available: http://www.theguardian.com/world/2014/dec/16/nut-rage-incident-sanctions-korean-air, September 24, 2016 (last date accessed).

11. S. Mundy, "Korean Air "nut rage" executive charged," *Financial Times*, January 7, 2015. [Online]. Available: http://www.ft.com/intl/cms/s/0/89ea6f1e-9640-11e4-a40b-00144feabdc0.html}axzz3SVlU9mJ1, September 24, 2016 (last date accessed).

12. Uhm, M., "[Interview] Korean Air senior flight attendant "assaulted and verbally abused.... threw a file to him," SBS News, December 13, 2014. [Online]. Available http://news.sbs.co.kr/news/endPage.do?news_id=N1002733703, September 24, 2016 (last date accessed).

13. "KakaoTalk messages of a first-class passenger sent to her friend was revealed during Cho Hyun-ah 'Nut return,'" *The Kyunghyang Shinmun*, January 21, 2015. [Online]. Available: http://m.khan.co.kr/view.html?artid=201501211532331&code=940202, September 24, 2016 (last date accessed).

14. S. Kim, "Cho Hyun-ah accused of trying to cover up her abusive 'nut rage,'" *The Hankyoreh*, December 17, 2014. [Online]. Available: http://english.hani.co.kr/arti/english_edition/e_national/669694.html, September 24, 2016 (last date accessed).

15. Y. Kim, "Korean Air still isn't aware of what went wrong," *Yonhap News Agency*, December 16, 2014. [Online]. Available: http://www.yonhapnews.co.kr/bulletin/2014/12/16/0200000000AKR20141216174500003.HTML, September 24, 2016 (last date accessed).

16. D. Min, "The apology of the victims of nut rage?" *Media Today*, December 22, 2014. [Online]. Available: http://m.sisainlive.com/news/articleView.html?idxno=22088, September 24, 2016 (last date accessed).

17. "Apology advertisement," *Huffington Post*, December 17, 2014. [Online]. Available: http://i.huffpost.com/gen/2401000/original.jpg, September 24, 2016 (last date accessed).

18. S. Hong, "Park, Chang-jin, My company covered up systematically... no sincerity in its apology," *KBS-TV*, December 17, 2014. [Online]. Available: http://news.kbs.co.kr/news/NewsView.do?SEARCH_NEWS_CODE=2986073, September 24, 2016 (last date accessed).

19. K. Kim, "Korean Air attempts to appease the first-class passenger beside Cho Hyun-ah 'offering airplane model and calendar...'" *The Hankyoreh*, December 15, 2014. [Online]. Available: http://www.hani.co.kr/arti/society/society_general/669089.html, September 24, 2016 (last date accessed).

20. S. Oh, "Cho Hyun-ah accused of trying to cover up her abusive 'nut rage,'" *The Hankyoreh*, December 18, 2014, [Online]. Available: http://english.hani.co.kr/arti/english_edition/e_national/669694.html, September 24, 2016 (last date accessed).

21. S. Choi, "Former executive of Korean Air is indicted in "Nut Rage" episode," *The New York Times*, January 7, 2015. [Online]. Available: http://www.nytimes.com/2015/01/08/world/former-korean-air-executive-indicted-over-nut-rage-incident.html, September 24, 2016 (last date accessed).

22. D. Lee, "Prosecution expands investigation for suspicion of corruption between transport ministry and Korean Air," *Yonhap News Agency*, December 24, 2014. [Online]. Available:http://www.yonhapnews.co.kr/society/2014/12/28/0701000000AKR20141228044500004.HTML, September 24, 2016 (last date accessed).

23. S. Choi, "An instant of nut-fueled rage draws a year in South Korean jail," *The New York Times*, February 12, 2015. [Online]. Available: http://www.nytimes.com/2015/02/13/world/asia/former-korean-air-executive-Cho-Hyun-ah-convicted-in-nut-rage-episode.html?_r=0, September 24, 2016 (last date accessed).

24. P. Chun, "'Nut return'... loss of Korean Air stocker holders?" *Asia Business Daily*, December 19, 2014. [Online]. Available: http://www.asiae.co.kr/news/view.htm?idxno=2014121814432317208, September 24, 2016 (last date accessed).

25. S. Tomlinson, "How South Korea's 'nut rage' scandal has made macadamias all the rage: Sales soar after daughter of Korean Air Lines chief demand they be served on plate not in bag," Daily Mail, December 15, 2014. [Online]. Available: http://www.dailymail.co.uk/news/article-2874207/Sales-macadamias-soar-daughter-Korean-Air-Lines-chief-demand-served-plate-not-bag.html, September 24, 2016 (last date accessed).

26. W. T. Coombs, *Ongoing Crisis Communication: Planning, Managing, and Responding*, 2nd ed. Los Angeles, CA: Sage, 2012.

27. W. T. Coombs, "Protecting organization reputations during a crisis: The development and application of situational crisis communication theory," *Corporate Reputation Review*, vol. 10, no. 3, pp. 163–176, 2007.

28. H. Cha, J. Suh, and J. Kim, "Effect of issue obtrusiveness, issue congruence and response strategies on the acceptance of crisis communication messages," *Asian Journal of Communication*, vol. 25, no. 3, pp. 307–326, 2015.

IV

Middle East

Syria

14

A Battle for Hearts and Minds: Dealing with Syria's Intractable Humanitarian Catastrophe

Kwamena Kwansah-Aidoo and Ibrahim Saleh

Chapter Preview

The ongoing civil war in Syria which began in 2011 and still rages on in 2017, without any end in sight, has spawned a subsequent refugee crisis that has been described as the worst humanitarian disaster since World War II. The civil war has claimed over 200,000 lives and about 12 million Syrians have been forced to flee their homes into other parts of Syria as well as to some major European and Middle Eastern countries. While the war seems to be about getting rid of the current Syrian government of Bashar al-Assad, the different factions do not necessarily agree on exactly what they would want in place of the current al-Assad regime. In the meantime, the refugee situation continues to grow dire by the day. So what is the rest of the world doing in response to the humanitarian disaster unfolding right before their eyes? What are key Western and Middle Eastern countries doing to help resolve the refugee situation? How are the media covering the crisis and how does this coverage affect refugees in their efforts to settle in the new places that they find

Culture and Crisis Communication: Transboundary Cases from Nonwestern Perspectives, First Edition.
Edited by Amiso M. George and Kwamena Kwansah-Aidoo.
© 2017 by The Institute of Electrical and Electronics Engineers, Inc. Published 2017 by John Wiley & Sons, Inc.

themselves? Finding answers to such important questions helps bring to the fore the complex and problematic nature of the civil war in Syria and the refugee crisis that it has inevitably created.

After reading this chapter, you will be able to

- *Understand the beginnings of the Syrian civil war and why it continues to rage on 6 years down the track*
- *Discern the scale of the humanitarian crisis that has resulted from the Syrian civil war*
- *Interpret the role played by culture and religion in fueling the civil war*
- *Explain the nature of the al-Assad government's response to the crisis and the role played by culture in that response*
- *Discuss the response of key Western and Middle Eastern countries to the refugee crisis*
- *Appreciate the role played by media in framing the way refugees are seen and received in host countries*
- *Outline some of the key lessons to be learned from the ongoing Syrian humanitarian disaster and some communication strategies that may help in dealing with refugees*

Introduction: Overview of Syria and Its Culture

Syria is a Middle Eastern nation with a small strip of Mediterranean coastline that includes territory in the Golan Heights that has been occupied by Israel since 1967 [1]. It became an independent nation in 1946 and has been formally known as the Arab Republic of Syria since 1991 [1, 2]. The name Syria is probably derived from the Babylonian word "suri," but Arabs traditionally referred to it as "Al-Sham," which translates as the northern region, which historically included Jordan, Israel, and Lebanon between 2700 and 2200 BCE [3]. It was home to the "Ebla kingdom." Its strategic location on the coastal line gave way to prominence as a Phoenician trading post, but it was conquered by the Persians around 500 BCE, by the Greeks in 333 BCE, and by the Romans in 64 BCE. Muslim Arabs conquered Damascus in 635 CE, and in 1095, Syria was a target of the Crusades, but the Arabs ultimately defeated the Christian invaders [3].

Before the war started in 2011, Syria's population was estimated at 23 million [2, 4]. The country consists of 90.3% Arabs, and Kurds are estimated to constitute between 3% and 9% of the population. The demographics also include Turks, Armenians, and small numbers of Circassians, Assyrians, and Jews. The majority of Muslims "Alawis" live in the rural landscape of "Jabal an Nusayriyah," which reflects around 80% of rural dwellers. The Bedouins were initially Arabs from a distinct group, whom were originally nomadic, but many have been forced to settle in towns and villages [5].

Syrian culture is a melting pot of many subcultures and traditions but at its core, it prioritizes family, religion, and betterment of the self. Arabic is the official language with 90% of the population speaking it. The Syrian dialect (of the Arabic language) is very similar to Jordanian and Egyptian versions, and varies little from Modern Standard Arabic. Some ancient languages such as Maalua, and Aramaic, English, and French are still spoken [6].

Syrian culture is highly hierarchical, with a strong affinity for unequal distribution of power. Consequently, seniors in age and positions are benevolent autocrats, who tell younger people and subordinates what to do. It is a collectivist culture that expresses a very high degree of interdependence. This makes loyalty to family, then clan, and then the tribe paramount, in that order of importance [7]. According to *Countries and Cultures*, "Religion is perhaps the single most important marker of communal identity" in the Middle East region, which includes Syria and "Islam, the religion of the overwhelming majority of the population" [8].

Syrian culture is highly hierarchical, with a strong affinity for unequal distribution of power. Consequently, seniors in age and positions are benevolent autocrats, who tell younger people and subordinates what to do.

Though it gained independence in 1946, Syria's political culture remained highly unstable due to intense friction between different social, religious, and political groups. In 1970, Syria came under the authoritarian rule of President Hafiz al-Assad who focused on attaining national security, domestic stability, and recovering the Syrian territory that was lost to Israel in 1967. Assad drove Syria into an enormous arms buildup, which strained the national budget and left only marginal space for allocations to development in the budget.

After Hafiz al-Assad's death in 2000, his son Bashar al-Assad became President, and in the early stages of his rule, he started to show signs of leaning toward political reform. However, he quickly made an about-turn and followed closely his father's approach of authoritarian style of government, by using Syria's powerful military and security services to suppress political dissent [1], a situation that ultimately gave rise to the current civil war.

Researching and Communicating the Syrian Crisis

Since the outbreak of the Syrian war, the refugee crisis has become an attractive research topic [9–11]. Yet, most of the discourse around such research has focused on sensationalism, projecting a "mean world" [12] that exudes hostility and chaos without any consideration for human pain and suffering [13]. Most scholarly publications lack first-hand insights, local perspectives, and domestication of events and ideas, following a social distance approach and with very low indigenous theoretical features [14]. Such lack of depth and contextualization only add to the existing "managerial bias" [15], and disregard the multifaceted and multilayered aspects of crisis in the region [16].

Thus, the main corpus of research on crisis communication in Syria and the rest of the region is normative and only describes the host countries' policy responses and generally provide a non-Arab perception of the crisis [17–23]. Other research focus on the cost of hosting Syrian refugees [24–28], which means that research on communication and the assessment of burden/responsibility sharing is almost nonexistent [29,30]. Some other research investigate sectorial analysis of the rights of Syrian refugees such as the right to education [31–33], health care [34,35], and the right to work [36,37]. This shows a clear inadequacy of research that focus on all the different problems associated with hosting refugees in the Middle East and North Africa (MENA) region [38,39].

The Syrian Crisis: Child of the Arab Spring?

On December 17, 2010, a 26-year-old Tunisian man, Mohamed Bouazizi, set himself on fire in front of a local municipal office in protest after the Tunisian police had confiscated his fruit cart earlier and beaten him because he did not have a permit, and the municipal office workers had ignored his attempts to file a complaint [40]. The young man's actions in Tunisia set in motion an uprising in that country in December 2010, which eventually spread across parts of the Middle East— Egypt, Libya, Syria, Yemen, Bahrain, Saudi Arabia, and Jordan. These democratic uprisings which started independent of each other and spread across the Arab world in 2011, became known as the Arab Spring [40, 41]. In essence, it was a series of anti-government protests, uprisings, and armed rebellions that spread across the Middle East and were all aimed at bringing down regimes in the affected countries that were perceived to be autocratic and dictatorial. To date, "their purpose, relative success and outcome remain hotly disputed in Arab countries, among foreign observers, and between world powers looking to cash in on the changing map of the Middle East" [42].

In the specific case of Syria, pro-democracy protests erupted in March 2011 in the southern city of Deraa after the purported arrest and torture of 15 school children who supposedly painted revolutionary slogans/graffiti on a school wall. Security forces responded to these protests by opening fire on demonstrators, killing four of them in the process, and then killing another person during the burial of the four. After these events, more took to the streets, setting in motion a nationwide protest demanding the resignation of President Bashar al-Assad [2, 43, 44]. The government's use of force to crush the dissent merely hardened the protesters' resolve. By July 2011, several hundreds of people were protesting on a regular basis across the country and these groups that opposed the al-Assad regime, eventually started taking up arms, first to defend themselves and later to expel security forces from their local areas [44].

While the arrest and torture of the school children was seen as the immediate cause of the beginning of the protests, it is believed that many Syrians did not like Bashar al-Assad despite his regime allowing religious and other freedoms. For many, there was anger over the regime's failure to deliver on long-promised economic and political reforms, and emboldened by the Arab Spring uprisings, they began anti-government protests [2]. Many of those who took up arms were ordinary Syrians; some were also disenchanted former members of Assad's military. In due course, the skirmishes escalated into a full scale civil war and the group was joined by "a ragtag bunch of jihadists and others, who crossed borders to join the action on the side of the anti-government rebels" [2].

The Syrian Civil War has turned into a conflict so complicated, even the experts admit it almost defies description, and all factions in the civil war have different aims.

Six years down the track (2017), the war still rages on, and as Sharwood notes, "the Syrian Civil War has turned into a conflict so complicated, even the experts admit it almost defies description" [2] and all factions in the civil war have different aims.

What is certain though, is that, all the opposition, whether Islamists or Free Syrian Army, are united in one thing: "Assad must leave" [2]. In the meantime, the body count continues to grow. As of March 2016, it was estimated that approximately 240,000 people have died as a direct or indirect result of the conflict [2, 4, 43]. This situation of death, chaos, and uncertainty naturally leads to displacement of people and people fleeing to seek safety and comfort elsewhere, thereby creating a refugee situation which has been described variously as: "a humanitarian catastrophe" [45]; "the largest forced migration of peoples since World War II" [46]; and "the world's worst refugee crisis in a generation" [47].

People on the Move: A Forced Migration of Epic Proportions

Any war or conflict situation creates an exodus of people fleeing from the conflict and the extremely difficult situation that it throws up. The Syrian civil war is no different, and while it is difficult to ascertain the exact number of people who have been displaced by this civil war, it has been suggested that by most measures, as many as 11 million Syrians have been displaced. Out of this number, 4.5 million are believed to have fled the country and been registered as refugees with the United Nations High Commissioner for Refugees (UNHCR); most of them women and children [2, 43, 44].

While it is difficult to ascertain the exact number of people who have been displaced by this civil war, it has been suggested that by most measures, as many as 11 million Syrians have been displaced.

Close neighbors Lebanon, Jordan, and Turkey have struggled to cope with what is turning out to be one of the largest refugee exoduses in recent history. It is estimated that by the end of 2015, there were more than 2.2 million Syrian refugees in Turkey, 1.2 million in Lebanon, and more than 600,000 in Jordan [48,49]. About 10% of these refugees have fled to Europe, seeking the safety that they believe they can find in those environs, and sparking some intense political arguments over how to share the burden. A further 6.5 million people are believed to be internally displaced within Syria, with 1.2 million said to have been driven from their homes in 2015 alone [43,44].

For the year 2016, the UNHCR indicated that it would require $3.2 billion to help the 13.5 million people, including 6 million children, who would require some form of humanitarian assistance inside Syria in 2016 [43, 44]. Within Syria itself, about 70% of the population is said to be without access to adequate drinking water, and a third of the population is said to be unable to meet their basic food needs. Also, it is estimated that more than 2 million children are out of school, and approximately 80% of people are believed to be living in poverty [44]. All of this makes for what has been described as "the largest forced migration of peoples since World War II" [46].

Situational Analysis

Given the scale of the crisis and the humanitarian nature, there are bound to be many stakeholders. However, we will concentrate here on those that are immediately affected and those that are bound, either by duty or conscience to respond in some immediate way.

Key Stakeholders

Immediate Victims: Individuals and families who have been forced to flee the violence or displaced as a result of the incessant fighting. These people are either on their way to some set destination or at specific destinations—refugee camps, within or outside of Syria or in countries either in the Middle East or elsewhere in Europe or the rest of the world.

World Governments: If this is the worst humanitarian crisis of our times, then the government of every country is a stakeholder because of our shared humanity. But especially, governments of developed nations—those considered to be wealthy enough to be able to provide substantial help to the refugees. Particularly, Western European nations and the United States who have a strategic interest in the Middle East and are supposed to be guardians of world peace.

United Nations High Commissioner for Refugees (UNHCR): As the world's peak body for dealing with refugees and refugee situations everywhere in the world, the UNHCR is a key stakeholder in this refugee crisis, working together with governments to try and bring a semblance of normalcy to the lives of Syrian refugees both in Syria and elsewhere.

Global NGOs and Humanitarian Aid Organizations: Aside from the UNHCR, many international NGOs such as the International Red Cross, World Vision International, MercyCorps, Amnesty International, and many more, collaborate or partner with the UNHCR to bring relief to refugees all over the world as part of their mission.

The International Media: Given the high stakes and the fact that governments all over the world are key stakeholders, the international media represent an important key stakeholder. Their coverage and the framing of the whole war and ensuing refugee crisis would play a significant role in how the rest of the world views the unfolding events in both Syria and the countries that host refugees.

The Arab or Middle Eastern Media: There is a sense in which the Middle Eastern media can and should be distinguished from other international media as a distinct and key stakeholder. Covering the region and broadcasting mainly in Arabic, the media of these countries would approach the situation from the perspective of 'insiders," with a better knowledge of the region than other media outside of the region. Many of them would also be more influential among people in that region, than media outside of that region.

Response to the Refugee Situation

Given the nature of the refugee situation, it is important to look at the response from both within Syria and outside of the country.

Internal Response

By all accounts, the Syrian government led by al-Assad is a contributor to the refugee crisis and has made no direct effort to actually deal with its displaced citizens. In a desperate bid to retain power, the regime has arbitrarily arrested and detained many Syrians, and tens of thousands are believed to have disappeared [50]. With the help of Russian government forces, Syrian government forces have engaged in intense bombardment of sections of the Syrian community, including places such as Aleppo, where attacks targeted hospitals and other medical facilities. These same forces make it impossible for humanitarian aid deliveries to reach their intended refugee camp targets [45, 47, 50]. These bombings (by Syrian and Russian forces) and internal atrocities have resulted in a death toll of innocent civilians believed be more than 60,000 [51]. On that basis, it has to be argued that the singular objective of the al-Assad led government is to keep itself in power by crushing all forces that have arisen against it.

The Role of Culture It is possible to observe cultural influences in the response or nonresponse from the al-Assad led Syrian government. The al-Assad family has ruled Syria for a long time and one can argue that culturally they feel that they have a right to rule. As Sharwood explains

> Though it has pretences of being democratic, Syria has been led by the al-Assad family for 45 years. Hafez al-Assad ruled from 1970 to 2000. His first son died in a car crash and his second, Bashar al-Assad, has been president since 2000. [2]

On that note, it is possible to surmise that perhaps many Syrians, especially those under the age of 50 years, have only known an al-Assad as their country's ruler and accept that they would be ruled by that family. Another interesting observation regarding the influence of culture is the relationship between single family/monarchical type of rulership and the success of the uprisings in the Arab Spring. Any keen observation reveals that the countries where the uprising succeeded in overthrowing the ruling government—Tunisia, Libya, and Egypt, did not have a history of one family or a monarchy ruling the country for a long time. Bahrain, Saudi Arabia, and Jordan which are all ruled by monarchies, managed to quell the uprisings. In Yemen, where there is no monarchy or one family rule, rebels managed to chase President Hadi into exile and he returned only after Saudi backed forces had managed to force the rebels out of Aden [52]. There is an argument therefore to be made for the culture of one family/monarchy rule influencing the response to these uprisings, and also to a large extent, the success of the uprisings. In the specific case of Syria, despite the raging civil war, the country is still functioning.

> [T]he country itself is far from entirely dysfunctional. "Syria is going a lot better than Iraq thanks be to God," … "There is a fully functioning bureaucracy. Unlike Lebanon, where garbage has not been collected for months, the garbage is collected in Syria." As the country somehow stays functional in most areas, its people maintain their spirits. [2]

And Sharwood points out, "It would be ironic if this war, which started as an anti-Assad crusade, ends up making people feel that Assad is the safe option. But there is evidence that the chaos caused by all the various factions in this war may produce exactly that result among the Syrians left behind" [2]. Herein lies vindication for the staying power of countries ruled by single families/monarchies.

At the center of this intractable conflict is religion; it drives most of the combatants to do what they do, and they all believe they are right according to their own religious point of view. The non-Islamist group is also influenced by religion because they do not want the kind of Islamic rule that the other groups want.

Again, the strong-armed response by the al-Assad led government can be seen as influenced by culture. As indicated earlier, Syrian culture is very hierarchical and unequal distribution of power is a common feature which allows seniors in age and positions to be autocratic. The government's initial response to the school children's graffiti on the walls, with arrests and torture, and then the shooting of people who protested the arrest of these school children [43], was all influenced by this hierarchical culture in which people who occupy positions of power are autocratic and believe that they should not be challenged. In that sense, the government feels it is its right to be in power, hold on to power, and to tell the rest of the society what to do and not the reverse. Hence culturally, it would not make sense to acquiesce to the demands of the rebels.

Finally, the civil war continues to rage on in the way it does because of one factor: culture or better still, religious culture. Sharwood captures this sentiment succinctly thus

The non Islamist [rebel] groups don't like Assad, IS want to expand the caliphate, groups like Jabhat al-Nusra want Islamic rule in Syria under their leadership, other Islamist groups want Islamic government although what that looks like and how it might be achieved is never articulated. But they all want Islamic rule in one way, shape, or form. [2]

In other words, at the center of this intractable conflict is religion; it drives most of the combatants to do what they do, and they all believe they are right according to their own religious point of view. The non-Islamist group is also influenced by religion because they do not want the kind of Islamic rule that the other groups want.

What the World Outside Syria is Doing

Given the messy and ongoing nature of the crisis, we examine the world's response in terms of the refugee situation arising from the conflict, rather than political and military aspects which seem to defy any meaningful solution at this point in time [2].

The Middle East: Helping Arabs in Need? By reason of proximity to Syria, it is necessary to look at the way some of the Middle Eastern countries have responded to this Syrian refugee crisis.

- **Lebanon:** As of September 2015, Lebanon claimed to have taken in 1.1 million registered refugees and many more who are not registered. Government officials put the overall number at 1.5 million [48].
- **Jordan:** Claimed it had taken in 1.4 million Syrians, although according to the UNCRH there were 629,266 registered refugees by the end of 2015 [48].
- **Turkey:** When the war began in 2011, Turkey opened its borders to Syrians fleeing the conflict, but on March 9, 2015, Turkey decided to close its last open borders after taking in an estimated 2 million Syrians. According to the UNHCR, the Turkish government has spent more than $6 billion to help Syrian refugees [53]. Turkish military forces at the border have taken to shooting at Syrians trying to cross the border illegally and Amnesty International reports that dozens of Syrians have been shot dead since December 2013. It is believed that a greater number of Syrians reside in Turkey without official "guest" status, meaning that in reality the number of Syrians in Turkey is much higher than the estimated 2 million. Turkey has taken in the most refugees than any other country [48].

The Persian Gulf Arab Countries—Saudi Arabia, the United Arab Emirates, Qatar, Oman, Bahrain, and Kuwait As a collective, these countries have been criticized by human rights organizations for not offering enough help [48]. These countries are among the world's largest donors to Syrian refugees, via United Nations agencies and private charities, but they are also known for not pledging any resettlement places to Syrian refugees [54]. Amnesty International argues that because they are closer geographically to Syria, and have historical links with that country, and also because they share a common language and religion, there is a very good integration potential and so Gulf countries should make a significant contribution to the resettlement of Syrian refugees [54]. The stance of the Gulf nations is not seen as a specific case of being hostile to Syrian refugees; they are not signatories to the international conventions on refugee rights and statelessness [54]. So while they are happy to grant Syrian residents long-term residency permits, which means that they would not be asked to leave if their legal status expires, they will not participate in refugee resettlement [54].

It is worth pointing out that Open Source Investigations (OSI) disputes these claims. The group argues that it is a myth that was perpetuated by the Western media, particularly CNN, BBC, and Washington Post [49]. According to OSI, there is a logical explanation for this.

> Western media miscount the Syrian refugees because the primary data source, The United Nations High Commissioner for Refugees (UNHCR), does not count the refugees within the Gulf States. These states are not signatories to the Refugee Convention, their refugee relocations are not handled by the UNHCR". There are 2 million to 3 million Syrians in the Gulf countries, many of whom arrived since the war began, but they are not considered refugees and they are not part of the UNHCR statistics. They are classified as "Arab brothers and sisters in distress" instead of refugees covered by UN treaties. [49]

According to this source, Saudi officials say they do not deal with Syrians as refugees or put them in refugee camps so as to preserve their dignity and safety, and also give them complete freedom of movement [49]. They also claim that "the UAE has made it one of its foreign policy priorities to address this issue in a sustainable and humane fashion together with its regional and international partners" [49].

Israel The only country sharing a border with Syria that has not taken in any Syrian refugees is Israel. Israel has rejected all calls to take in refugees from Syria and elsewhere, saying that although Israel was "not indifferent to the human tragedy of the refugees," it was not in a position to take them in. Israel however claims to have provided medical care for more than 1000 injured Syrians, as well as aid to African nations to help deal with the flow of migrants [48].

Disagreeing on What to Do: Western Europe Struggles to Respond
Confronted with what the UN High Commissioner for Refugees, António Guterres, calls "the most dramatic humanitarian crisis the world has faced in a very long time" [47], the Western countries seem be struggling to provide a coherent response. There has been "huge and often sterile debate on how to address the crisis" [49] and it is claimed in some quarters that the debate is more often based on myths than facts [49]. As would be expected, many of the misconceptions about the refugee and migrant crisis have become part of mainstream political debates [49]. Some critics even questioned whether generous asylum policies would not act as enticement for more migrants to make the dangerous trek for Western Europe [48]. Below are individual responses from some key Western European countries, and their chief ally, the United States.

- **Germany:** Germany announced that it would receive 800,000 migrants in 2015, more than any other UN nation. A top German official actually mentioned that his country would be able to accept half a million refugees a year for years ahead. "I believe we could surely deal with something in the order of half a million for several years," Vice-Chancellor Sigmar Gabriel said. Germany also announced a €6 billion (US$9.6 billion) aid package to help ease the crisis [48]. There was however some opposition to the welcome and some far-right anti-immigration groups staged protests. There were also repeated incidents of arson of refugee shelters in some towns [48, 55].

- **Finland:** Though not used to mass immigration, and struggling to handle the situation amid deep spending cuts and rising unemployment in their recession-hit country, the Finnish government doubled its estimate for asylum seekers intake in 2015 to about 30,000 in order to accommodate more Syrian refugees [48]. The number is remarkable considering that Finland accepted only 3600 refugees the previous year. As a show of complete welcome to the refugees, the Finnish Prime Minister Juha Sipila decided to offer his spare house to host a refugee family in 2016 [48, 56].

- **Sweden:** The Nordic country announced that it was anticipating taking in 74,000 asylum seekers in 2015 of whom many would be Syrian refugees [48].

- **Austria:** The Austrian government initially decided not to carry out strict border checks, which allowed migrants arriving from Hungary without valid papers to pass through its territory to get to Germany. This was in spite of the fact that European Union (EU) rules dictated that refugees had to seek asylum in the country that they first arrived in, which would be Hungary, in this case. The decision was later rescinded "to move step-by-step away from emergency measures toward normality, in conformity with the law and dignity" [48], after 12,000 people were let through in just one weekend. Austria accepted 12,000 migrants in 2015, while making stringent efforts to reduce the influx.

- **Hungary:** More than 140,000 migrants entered Hungary in 2015. Initially, Hungary tried to prevent the migrants from moving on to other countries, insisting that they register in their country of arrival. However, it soon gave up and started providing buses to take thousands of marchers determined to reach Germany on foot. The Hungarian Prime Minister Viktor Orban seemed to be opposed to the idea of allowing Muslim migrants into his country. He claimed the crisis was a threat to Europe's prosperity, identity, and "Christian values" [48]. Hungry has built a 3.5 m high wall on its border with Serbia to prevent immigrants from getting in and closed its southern border [48, 55].

- **France:** Despite a series of Islamist terrorist acts in France over recent years, the French government continued to allow refugees from Africa and the Middle East to set up camps within its borders with migrant shelters spread throughout the country. France pledged to "take in 24,000 people from frontline European

Union nations" over 2 years [57]. The French far-right in France was however not happy with the decision, wanting rather to stop migrant intake into Europe. Their leader, Marine Le Pen, accused Germany of harboring ulterior motives by opening its doors to thousands of migrants and refugees: "Germany probably thinks its population is moribund, and it is probably seeking to lower wages and continue to recruit slaves through mass immigration," Ms. Le Pen told supporters [48]. France also agreed to set up a command and control center with Britain in Calais to stop people from risking their lives by stowing away on trains and trucks [48, 57].

- **Britain:** Even though Britain had accepted 25,000 refugees in 2014, the country pledged to take in 20,000 Syrian migrants over 5 years from camps near the Syrian border, not from the boat and train loads that would arrive unceremoniously. "What matters is that when they come they get a proper welcome and we look after them, and that is exactly what we'll do," David Cameron, the then British Prime Minister said [48, 57].

- **Italy and Greece:** To date, Italy and Greece remain the main Western European countries that have borne the brunt of the wave of migrants fleeing by boat from Libya and Syria. Their ports and systems have been seriously overburdened and both countries have sought help from the European Union to help them cope [48]. About 250,000 migrants are believed to have entered Europe through Greece's borders. Italy has received nearly 120,000 migrants arriving on its shores from North Africa, many of them Syrians [48].

- **European Union:** In August 2015, the European Commission approved €2.4 billion (US$3.6 billion) of aid over 6 years for countries including Greece and Italy. Italy was to receive the most aid—nearly €560 million, while Greece would also receive €473 million [48, 58]. The EU also came up with a blueprint for a further 120,000 who would be distributed among EU nations, "with binding quotas for each country and coordinated systems including new legal migration channels into Europe" [48, 59].

- **United States of America:** In the United States, President Barack Obama instructed his administration to take in a minimum 10,000 displaced Syrians by the end of 2016 [48, 60]. Later the Secretary of State John Kerry said at a closed-door meeting on Capitol Hill that overall refugee intake could rise over the next year—2016, leaving room for an additional number of Syrians to be resettled in the United States. Religious groups in the United States had been impressing upon the Obama administration to step up its response to the Syrian refugee crisis, including the global humanitarian organization, Church World Service, that represents 37 Christian denominations, which urged the US government to take in 100,000 Syrians by the end of 2016 [48, 61]. Until these measures were announced in September 2016, the United States had taken in only 1500 Syrian refugees since the war broke out in 2011, and most of them had been accepted in 2015 [48, 61].

Media and the Refugee Crisis

While the media, particularly the Western/international media, have provided broad coverage of the civil war and the ensuing refugee crisis, there is a view that despite the widespread coverage, "the refugees' own struggle and personal upheaval is sometimes left out, as well as the efforts of many around the world to help those in need" [62]. The media had simply provided human suffering stories that did not offer any real engagement with victims, making the narratives "highly charged" [63]. Some argue that deep analysis that focuses on the suffering of refugees and the impact of the war on displaced individuals was largely missing, particularly in the period prior to August 2015 [62].

This shortcoming apparently led to a decline in public sympathy and increasing resentment in many European/Western countries, where many started to see the refugees as so-called poverty-refugees who wanted to exploit the welfare system of their countries [64]. The situation inside the Middle East and North Africa (MENA) region was not any different, with 79% of Jordanians being opposed to receiving further Syrian refugees, 65% of Turks holding a strong position against the Syrian refugees and 30% urging authorities to send them back. And in Lebanon, over 90% perceived refugees as a threat to their economic livelihood and value system, while two-thirds perceived them as existential threats [65].

In the book *Humanitarianism and Suffering* [66], Wilson and Brown describe "the sentimental narrative" around coverage of the refugee crisis as sneaky tactics to appeal to the impoverished and their plight [67]. In many cases, communicating the crisis has lacked substance, context, deep understanding of the human rights laws, and basic awareness about the psychological impact of the cultural crisis [68].

The visual of the 3-year-old Syrian toddler, Aylan Kurdi, who had drowned with most of his family while trying to reach Turkey dominated global news and focused immediate attention by giving a human face to the Syrian refugees' pain and suffering.

The turning point in the media coverage occurred during the tragedy in Lampedusa in 2013, where several hundreds of refugees drowned in the Mediterranean Sea; that made the refugees an important beat in different mass media [51]. Later, the visual of the 3-year-old Syrian toddler, Aylan Kurdi, who had drowned with most of his family while trying to reach Turkey [69, 70], dominated global news and focused immediate attention by giving a human face to the Syrian refugees' pain and suffering [71].

Van Gorp [72] and Gale [73] have both pointed out that there are entrenched ambivalences in media reporting of any crisis, which project bipolar frames of the actors and voices involved, while deploying narrative macrostructures and linguistics microstructures to serve the intended screen power [74], and this is very true of the Syrian crisis. Thus, Arab nations have been condemned for their indifference, while the west have been criticized for their double standards and politicization of the crisis through a process of misrepresentation and polarization [75] and also a display of anti-Muslim sentiments [9].

Some reports, for example, depicted Syrian refugees as criminals, illegitimate refugees and potential threat to national identity and to the economy [76]. Others adopted a master narrative frame of the crisis that used dehumanizing references to "swarms" of refugees, and an emphasis on numbers rather than people. Geostrategic interests have also played a role in covering the crisis. For example, an Egyptian popular broadcaster faced widespread criticism on social media after airing a program on her show on *Al Nahar TV*, in which she used images of Syrian refugees in a Lebanese camp and called them "disrespectful, lost, and ruined" [77]. Ahmed Esmat, Editor of *Alex Agenda*, was also quoted as saying there is no news interest in covering stories that might reflect Syrian refugees' successful stories of how they are socially and culturally adapting within host cultures [77].

In some other cases, the international media have negatively represented refugees and projected an acute state of disharmony with hosts in Europe. For example, news reports framed refugees chanting Islamic slogans and shouting obscenities during clashes with Hungarian police as a clash of cultures, and by extension, a cultural crisis. *Russia Today* (RT) reported the arrests of suspects identified as extremists and linked to Islamic State (IS) who had sneaked across the borders [78]. There were also unverified reports from Italy, France, and Germany of locals clashing with refugees, and refugees clashing with police officers on a daily basis as a result of frustrations for having to live in squalid conditions [78]. In all, one can say that some of the media reporting of the refugee crisis has been quite unfriendly, leading the UN High Commissioner for Refugees to comment that "The human rights agenda is losing ground to the national sovereignty agenda, and that is making humanitarian work more and more difficult in several parts of the world" [79].

Some Emerging Matters of Concern

The whole Syrian situation—the civil war and the resulting refugee crisis—throws up a number of issues that are worth noting in the general context of crisis communication around war and humanitarian situations.

First, is that of proof or being a properly certified refugee. Syrian refugees, like all others, are required to prove that they are "Convention refugees" before they can be considered "legitimate," by showing that they have fled individual persecution in their home country and that they fear persecution should they return [53, 80]. Given the rather volatile situation from which people flee during war situations, it is a difficult expectation for them to fulfill.

Second, the forms of protection granted to refugees under the UN Refugee charter are neither inclusive nor mandatory to family reunification. This prolongs family separation and in many cases, prevents families from restarting their lives [81]. Given that Syrians are from a collectivist culture, it makes the process of resettlement in their host countries very difficult.

Third, given the increased activities, particularly bombings by terror groups that have Islamic affiliations, citizens of host countries are concerned about receiving refugees from poor nations with Islamic backgrounds with the justification that they could be physically endangering the host countries [82]. This in fact muddies the waters of the humanitarian agenda, makes the process of refugee resettlement an uneasy proposition, particularly in Western non-Islamic contexts.

Fourth, is the problem of the state of mind of refugees wherever they are. For example, an empirical study by the German Chamber of Psychotherapy released in September 2015 revealed that at least half of the Syrian refugees who had been accepted into Germany had mental health problems because of trauma suffered in war or during their dangerous escapes [83].

> Most common were post-traumatic stress disorder and depression, sometimes so severe that patients are suicidal. Forty per cent of refugee children had witnessed violence, and "26 percent had to watch family members being attacked" ... More than 40 percent of adult refugees have nightmares, and 50 percent have flashbacks where they relive a traumatic event "as if it were really happening again" ... Many refugees suffer from heightened noise sensitivity, jumpiness and insomnia, as well as an inability to cope with confined or crowded spaces, said the chamber. [83]

Finally, and perhaps most important of all, is the issue of resettlement and adjustment to host cultures, particularly in the Western countries. News reports have highlighted the growing problem of refugee resettlement—loss of status, identity confusion, language difficulties, poverty, and concern for separated or lost family members, guilt, isolation, host hostility, and countless other factors that add to the pressures on refugees in a strange land [84]. All of these factors influence the ability of refugees to cope with and/or adjust to the situation they find themselves in. The end result is that sometimes their response is less than ideal. For example, as reported by the head of a UNHCR camp: "In Bulgaria, they complained that there were no jobs. In Sweden, they took off their clothes to protest that it was too cold. In Italy, Muslim African 'refugees' rejected pasta and demanded food from their own countries. Refugees in Italy were throwing rocks at police while demanding free Wi-Fi" [85].

Charting a way Forward Through This Maze of a Crisis

The ongoing Syrian conflict and the subsequent refugee crisis is a challenging situation whichever way one looks at it. The following practical suggestions may however be helpful in terms of what needs to be done and communicated, in an attempt to deal with a situation that seems to have no end in sight.

For starters, anyone who is interested in dealing with Syrian refugees wherever they may be found, but particularly in the western world, must take cognizance of two things:

A. The culture of the refugees which, as noted in Chapter 1, influences how people respond to and communicate in crisis situations [86]. Outside the Middle East, most of the cultures that the Syrian refugees will find themselves in, in their host countries, will be noncollectivist and in opposition to their own collectivist Syrian culture. This is absolutely essential to consider in the immediate scheme of things.

B. The trauma that most of the refugees have gone through before getting to their host countries. As indicated earlier, empirical evidence shows that many of the refugees have mental health problems.

An acknowledgement of these two basic but important points from the outset will help host countries prepare better for their dealings with not just Syrian refugees but refugees from anywhere. Crisis communication from stakeholders in the host countries should be aimed at reducing the sense of alienation felt by refugees, and encourage them to embrace certain aspects of their host culture without necessarily giving up on their own.

For those seeking to communicate risk and crisis information or conduct field work in Syria, Arab region, or the Middle East, they need to understand that Syria and the Arab region as a whole is much more complicated than might be initially presumed. There are three regional dynamics that must be considered when dealing with any risk communication research: (a) there is what is largely a cultural conflict of reconciling a highly romanticized religious past [8] and a present that is filled with the harsh realities of conflict, poverty, and political suppression, which is compounded by group-thinking and polarized culture in a space which is a melting pot of many cultures; (b) the region is one large interconnected space that, as much as possible, utilizes force and patronization to suppress any dissent; and (c) politics and religion go hand in hand as part of the culture of the region and these are heavily ideological. There are some that dream of one region, a united Arab world, achieved through any, and every means possible—exclusion, oppression, and violence included. These cultural factors influence communication and perception of events in ways that sometimes cannot be fathomed.

In terms of media and communication, all concerned must communicate with a view to achieving the following:

• Protection of Syrian refugees from being stereotyped as illegal and criminal by others living in host countries

- Prevention of refugee resettlement problems from expanding into violence and agitations, while ensuring that agitations do not result in further anti-Muslim narratives
- Supporting Syrian refugees to adapt to host countries by explaining to all concerned the difficulties and differences to help improve dialogue and minimize hostility
- Treatment of Syrian refugees with dignity and restoration of their image as rightful victims of atrocities caused by others
- Orienting Syrian refugees to their new cultural settings while educating host communities about the cultural background of the refugees

Finally, with regards to specific actions and communication from Western nations, the following are suggested as a way of helping to bring some resolution to the humanitarian disaster and perhaps the wider conflict. Communication in this regard should aim to

- Unify and show that Western countries are prepared to provide leadership in refugee resettlement
- Demonstrate that refugee resettlement is not considered a danger to national security
- Send a powerful message to counter jihadi extremists' such as Islamic State's portrayal of the Western world as the enemy of Islam
- Create an alliance against resurgent anti-immigrant and anti-Western world populism orchestrated by some right wing factions within the West
- Support and stabilize Middle Eastern front line states—Turkey, Jordan, and Lebanon—in their own efforts to contain Syrian refugees on their doorsteps [46].

As has been rightly observed

The most important dimension of refugee policy is strategic communication .... The leaders of the Islamic State (IS) are masters of strategic disinformation. They want to convince Western publics that refugees fleeing barrel bombs and IS terror pose a security threat to states that give them refuge. [46]

A key weapon in dealing with any crisis is communication, and it is no different in this situation. It is especially vital in this context that communication is directly targeted at rebutting IS strategies of disinformation.

Conclusion: Battling for Hearts and Minds in a Crisis Beyond Borders

The Syrian refugee crisis is unlike any other crisis; it has several dimensions to it. Born of the intractable conflict that is the Syrian civil war, it represents a truly transboundary case; a crisis beyond borders which continues to be a challenge to world leaders, particularly the leaders of the Western world who must necessarily address it as a challenge to western values of care and compassion, and to humanity. Communication, particularly media coverage of the conflict and the refugee crisis that it has spawned, has been challenging in many respects. The criticism is, that, the prevailing media narratives have not adequately addressed the impact of the conflict on the refugees; neither has it dealt with the ambivalent attitudes and resentments among locals inside and outside the region, against the Syrians [62, 64].

The Syrian refugee crisis is unlike any other crisis; it has several dimensions to it. Born of the intractable conflict that is the Syrian civil war, it represents a truly transboundary case; a crisis beyond borders, which continues to be a challenge to world leaders, particularly leaders of the Western world who must necessarily address it as a challenge to Western values of care and compassion, and to humanity.

There is a perceived absence of in-depth analysis of the conflict and migration nexus, humanitarian protection, refugee burden sharing [29, 30], addressing mass influxes and public opinion formation in host countries, refugee health care, and refugee integration support with different aspects [87]. Another criticism has been that when it comes to the geopolitics of this particular crisis, the mainstream Western media outlets are "more wedded to the idea of pushing agendas and suppressing facts" [88]. Yet others have claimed that "rather than framing personal trauma in a salacious fashion" some of the reporting has done "a much better job of informing the world about what's really happening to the Syrian refugees" [69].

As the world, and in particular, the West grapples with how to deal with the most serious and most challenging humanitarian crisis since World War II, it is important to bear in mind the words of Curtis:

A great loss is taking place outside of the Syrian revolution, a loss that could be prevented, a loss of a highly skilled and educated generation of youth, of young women unable to ever experience self-determination, and of professionals blocked from work by bureaucracy and politics. Behind every conflict are the victims of violence. [53]

There are many important lessons to be learned from this crisis, but the most important one is this: only a concerted effort from the international community, led by Europe and the United States, and working together with Middle Eastern allies, to provide shelter and hope for families fleeing the conflict in Syria, can resolve the situation. Such an approach will also help to refute the jihadi messages of hate and division coming from some factions in that conflict [46].

A generous and humane refugee policy with effective strategic communication as the cornerstone is both a humanitarian and a strategic imperative from the leading nations of the world [46]. The Syrian refugee crisis clearly represents a battle for hearts and minds [46], and giving the refugees hope through good refugee policies backed by effective communication can help win that battle. As the discussion in this chapter has shown, ultimately, the Syrian refugee crisis is not just a Gulf Arab issue, it is one for the Gulf as well as Western countries to work on together [54].

Discussion Questions

14.1 Given that this refugee crisis has been tagged a battle for hearts and minds, imagine that you are the communication director at the European Union (EU) Secretariat, what are some of the key messages you would come up with in the immediate aftermath of media reports of thousands of refugees fleeing the conflict and trying to get into Europe? Who would be your key target audiences and why?

14.2 Many have criticized the Gulf Arab States for their unwillingness to take in refugees, and that is in part because they are not signatories to any international refugee treaties. This Syrian refugee crisis represents an opportunity to revisit the issue of signing the international refugee treaties and also taking in some Syrian refugees. Imagine that you work for the UNHCR and you have been given the opportunity to communicate with the rulers of these Gulf States on the matter. Develop a communication strategy with key messages that you would use to address these monarchs in order to convince them to achieve both aims. Apart from a one-off face-to-face meeting, which other communication channels and/or methods would you use to get your messages across?

14.3 Let us say you work in the Office of the German Chancellor as Director of Communication, what would you have done in the first 24 hours after news broke about resistance to Germany's offer of taking in that many Syrian refugees. Identify and describe five tasks that you think are the most urgent and important.

14.4 Who do you think are the most important publics given the different stakeholders in the situation, both within and outside of Syria? Imagine that you work as a communication specialist for the UNHCR which has the mandate for dealing with refugee matters worldwide, list six primary publics and prioritize them. Explain why you believe they are the most important in your chosen order and develop key messages for each of these publics.

14.5 Taking note of the fact that there are serious issues of culture clash and resettlement difficulties with refugees in host communities, what communication strategies would you suggest should be used in dealing with them and host community workers who deal with refugees, and what message(s) would you seek to pass on to them to try and prevent some of the refugee acts of resistance or disdain from reoccurring?

References

1. K. S. Salibi. (2015). Encyclopedia Britannica. [Online]. Available: http://www.britannica.com/place/Syria, May 16, 2016 (last date accessed).
2. A. Sharwood. (2015, September 9). "Syria explained in 10 simple points. A western perspective on the crisis" [Online]. Available: http://www.news.com.au/world/middle-east/syria-explained-in-10-simple-points-a-western-perspective-on-the-crisis/news-story/4463e6f61181946100517266bd648009, May 4, 2016 (last date accessed).
3. J. Galvin, *Divided Loyalties: Nationalism and Mass Politics in Syria at the Close of Empire*. Berkeley, CA: University of California Press, 1998.
4. MercyCorps. (2016, February 5). "Quick facts: What you need to know about the Syrian crisis" [Online]. Available: https://www.mercycorps.org/articles/iraq-jordan-lebanon-syria-turkey/quick-facts-what-you-need-know-about-syria-crisis, May 4, 2016 (last date accessed).
5. L. Wedeen, *Ambiguities of Domination: Politics, Rhetoric, and Symbols in Contemporary Syria*. Chicago, IL: University of Chicago Press, 1999.
6. O. Winkler, *Demographic Developments and Population Policies in Ba'athist Syria*. Sussex: Sussex Academic Press, 1998.
7. S. Standish, Syria-Culture Smart! The Essential Guide to Customs and Culture, London: Kuperard Publishers, 2012.
8. World Culture Encyclopedia. (2016), Countries and their cultures: Introduction to the Middle East – Religion (2016) [Online]. Available: http://www.everyculture.com/Africa-Middle-East/Introduction-to-the-Middle-East-Religion.html#ixzz48szIsLay, May 17, 2016 (last date accessed).
9. C. M. R. Sulaiman-Hill, S. C. Thompson, R. Afsar, et al., "Changing images of refugees: A comparative analysis of Australian and New Zealand print media 1998–2008," *Journal of Immigrant and Refugee Studies*, vol. 9, no. 1, pp. 345–366, 2011.
10. C. Coole, "A warm welcome? Scottish and UK media reporting of an asylum seeker murder," *Media, Culture and Society*, vol. 24, no. 1, pp. 839–852, 2002.
11. T. Wright, "Collateral coverage: Media images of Afghan refugees," *Visual Studies*, vol. 19, no. 1, pp. 97–112, 2004.

12. A. Eli, "Crisis communication, image restoration, and battling stereotypes of terror and wars: Media strategies for attracting tourism to Middle Eastern countries," *American Behavioral Scientist*, vol. 57, no. 9, pp.1350–1367, September 2013.

13. M. Eid, "Editorial: Risk and crisis communication," *Global Media Journal, Canadian Edition*, vol. 7, no. 1, pp.1–3, 2014.

14. M. Ayish, "Communication research in the Arab world: A new perspective," *The Public*, vol. 5, no. 1, pp. 33–57, 1998.

15. D. Waymer and R. L. Heath, "Emergent agents: The forgotten publics in crisis communication and issues management research," *Journal of Applied Communication Research*, vol. 35, no. 1, pp. 88–108, 2007.

16. H. Musallam, "Communication strategies of crisis and conflict management in the public and private sectors in the state of Kuwait," Ph.D. dissertation, Department of Mass Communication, University of Southern Mississippi 2004, Paper 2342. [Online]. Available: http://aquila.usm.edu/theses_dissertations/2342/, May 16, 2016 (last date accessed).

17. H. Naufal. (2012). "Syrian refugees in Lebanon: The humanitarian approach under political divisions" [Online]. Available: http://cadmus.eui.eu/handle/1814/24835, May 16, 2016 (last date accessed).

18. A. İçduygu. (2015, April). "Syrian refugees in Turkey: The long road ahead" [Online]. Available: http://www.migrationpolicy.org/research/syrian-refugees-turkey-long-road-ahead, May 16, 2016 (last date accessed).

19. O. B. Dinçer, V. Federici, E. Ferris, et al., Suriyeli Mülteciler Krizi ve Sonu Gelmeyen Misafirlik. Brooking Enstitüte and USAK, 2013.

20. M. M. Refaat and K. Mohanna, "Syrian refugees in Lebanon: Facts and solutions," *The Lancet*, vol. 382, pp. 763–764, 2013.

21. P. A. Döner, R. Özkara, and R. Kahveci, "Syrian refugees in Turkey: Numbers and emotions," *The Lancet*, vol. 382, no. 9894, p. 764, 2013.

22. C. Thorleifsson, "Coping strategies among self-settled Syrians in Lebanon," *Forced Migration Review, Special Issue: The Syrian Crisis, Displacement and Protection*, vol. 47, no. 1, pp. 23–25, 2014.

23. L. Achilli. (2015). "Syrian refugees in Jordan: A reality check" [Online]. Available: http://cadmus.eui.eu/handle/1814/34904, May 16, 2016 (last date accessed).

24. S. Al-Kilani, "A duty and a burden on Jordan," *Forced Migration Review, Special Issue: The Syrian Crisis, Displacement and Protection*, vol. 47, no. 1, pp. 30–31, 2014.

25. H. Öztuürkler and T. Göksel, "The economic effects of Syrian refugees on Turkey," Orsam, Center for Middle Eastern Strategic Studies, January 2015, Report Number 196. [Online]. Available: data.unhcr.org/syrianrefugees/download.php?id=13434, May, 31, 2017 (last date accessed).

26. B. Berti, "The Syrian refugee crisis: Regional and human security implications," *Strategic Assessment*, vol. 17, no. 4, pp. 41–53, 2015.

27. S. Ajluni and M. Kawar. (2014). "Impact of Syrian refugees on the Jordanian labour market: A preliminary analysis" [Online]. Available: http://www.ilo.org/wcmsp5/groups/public/—arabstates/—ro-beirut/documents/publication/wcms_242021.pdf, May 16, 2016 (last date accessed).

28. Y. E. Akgündüz, M. van den Berg, and W. Hassink, "The impact of refugee crises on host labor markets: The case of the Syrian refugee crisis in Turkey," IZA Discussion Papers, No. 8841, February 2015. [Online]. Available: http://ftp.iza.org/dp8841.pdf, May 16, 2016 (last date accessed).

29. K. Kirişci. (2014, May 12). "Syrian refugees and Turkey's challenges" [Online]. Available: http://www.brookings.edu/~/media/research/files/reports/2014/05/12-turkey-syrian-refugees-kirisci/syrian-refugees-and-turkeys-challenges-may-14-2014.pdf, May 16, 2016 (last date accessed).

30. S. A. Bidinger, D. Lang, Y. Hites, et al. (2015). "Protecting Syrian refugees: Laws, policies and global responsibility-sharing" [Online]. Available: https://www.bu.edu/law/central/ jd/programs/clinics/international-human-rights/documents/FINAL Full Report.pdf, July 23, 2015 (last date accessed).

31. M. Christophersen. (2015, May). "Securing education for Syrian refugees in Jordan" [Online]. Available: https://www.ipinst.org/wp-content/uploads/2015/05/IPI-E-pub-Securing-Education-for-Syrian-Refugees.pdf, May 16, 2016 (last date accessed).

32. H. M. Ahmadzadeh, J. A. Çorabatır, L. Husseini, et al. (2014, September). "Ensuring quality education for young refugees from Syria (12-25 years): A mapping exercise" [Online]. http://www.rsc.ox.ac.uk/files/publications/other/rr-syria-youth-education-2014.pdf, May 16, 2016 (last date accessed).

33. Reliefweb. (2016, March 13). "Jordan - Syrian refugee children enrolled in public schools – by directorates (2015-2016), as of 21 February 2016" [Online]. Available: http://reliefweb.int/map/jordan/jordan-syrian-refugee-children-enrolled-public-schools-directorates-2015-2016-21-february, May 16, 2016 (last date accessed).

34. M. M. Murshidi, M. Q. B. Hijjawi, S. Jeriesat, et al., "Syrian refugees and Jordan's health sector," *The Lancet*, vol. 382, no. 9888, pp. 206–207, 2013.

35. Z. El-Khatib, D. Scales, J. Vearey, et al., "Syrian refugees, between rocky crisis in Syria and hard inaccessibility to healthcare services in Lebanon and Jordan," *Conflict and Health*, vol. 7, no. 18, pp. 1–3, 2013.

36. International Labour Organization. (2015). "Access to work for Syrian refugees in Jordan: A discussion paper on labour and refugee laws and policies" [Online]. Available: http://www.ilo.org/wcmsp5/groups/public/—arabstates/—ro-beirut/documents/publication/wcms_357950.pdf, May 16, 2016 (last date accessed).

37. S. Bidinger. (2015, January 14). "Syrian refugees and the right to work: Developing temporary protection in Turkey" [Online]. Available: http://www.bu.edu/ilj/files/2015/01/Bidinger-Syrian-Refugees-and-the-Right-to-Work.pdf, May 16, 2016 (last date accessed).

38. C. Orchard and A. Miller. (2014, September). "Protection in Europe for refugees from Syria" [Online]. Available: http://www.rsc.ox.ac.uk/files/publications/policy-briefing-series/pb10-protection-europe-refugees-syria-2014.pdf, May 16, 2016 (last date accessed).

39. P. Fargues and C. Fandrich. (2012, September). "Migration after the Arab Spring" [Online]. Available: http://www.migrationpolicycentre.eu/docs/MPC percent202012 per cent20EN percent2009.pdf, May 16, 2016 (last date accessed).

40. SourceWatch. (2016, March 11). "Arab Spring" [Online]. Available: http://www.sourcewatch.org/index.php/Arab_Spring, May 4, 2016 (last date accessed).

41. R. Rifal. (2011, January 23). "Timeline Tunisia" [Online]. Available: http://www.aljazeera.com/indepth/spotlight/tunisia/2011/01/201114142223827361.html, May 4, 2016 (last date accessed).

42. P. Manfreda. (2014, November 25). "Definition of the Arab Spring" [Online]. Available: http://middleeast.about.com/od/humanrightsdemocracy/a/Definition-Of-The-Arab-Spring.htm, May 4, 2016 (last date accessed).

43. "What's happening in Syria?," *BBC*, March 15, 2016. [Online]. Available: http://www.bbc.co.uk/newsround/16979186, May 4, 2016 (last date accessed).

44. "Syria: The story of the conflict," *BBC*, March 11, 2016. [Online] Available: http://www.bbc.com/news/world-middle-east-26116868, May 4, 2016 (last date accessed).

45. Amnesty International. (2015, June). "The global refugee crisis: A conspiracy of neglect" [Online]. Available: http://www.amnesty.org.au/resources/activist/POL4017962015ENGLISH.PDF, May 11, 2016 (last date accessed).

46. M. Ignatieff, R. Abdelhamid, J. Keeley, et al. (2016, January 27). "The United States and the Syrian refugee crisis: A plan of action" [Online]. Available: http://shorensteincenter.org/united-states-syrian-refugee-crisis-plan-action/, May 10, 2016 (last date accessed).

47. Amnesty International. (2014). "Left out in the cold: Syrian refugees abandoned by the international community" [Online]. Available: http://www.amnestyusa.org/sites/default/files/left_out_in_the_cold_syria_refugees_resettlement_briefing_-_formatted_final_version_-_december_2014__cover-2.pdf, May 11, 2016 (last date accessed).

48. L. Timson. (2015, September 9). "Refugee crisis: How the world is reacting" [Online]. Available: http://www.smh.com.au/world/migrant-crisis/refugee-crisis-how-the-world-is-reacting-20150907-gjgxcw.html, May 10, 2016 (last date accessed).

49. Open Source Investigations. (2015, September 9). "Gulf States response to Syrian refugee crisis – A myth debunked" [Online]. Available: http://www.opensourceinvestigations.com/syria/gulf-states-response-to-syrian-refugee-crisis-a-myth-debunked/, May 10, 2016 (last date accessed).

50. Amnesty International. (2016, February 1). "About our safety for Syrians campaign" [Online]. Available: http://www.amnesty.org.au/crisis/comments/41176/?gclid=CPmcgeue0cwCFdcRvQodJ8YPGA, May 11, 2016 (last date accessed).

51. "The Syrian refugee crisis," *New York Times*, January 21, 2013, pp. 20.

52. "Yemen crisis: President Hadi returns to Aden from exile," *BBC*, September 22, 2015. [Online]. Available: http://www.bbc.com/news/world-middle-east-34323078, May 12, 2016 (last date accessed).

53. M. Curtis. (2015, October 7). "A reactionary world response to the Syrian refugee crisis" [Online]. Available: http://www.truth-out.org/news/item/33125-a-reactionary-world-response-to-the-syrian-refugee-crisis, May 10, 2016 (last date accessed)

54. R. Pollard. (2015, September 11). "Refugee crisis: Why aren't the rich Gulf Arab states doing more?" [Online]. Available: http://www.smh.com.au/world/migrant-crisis-why-arent-the-rich-gulf-arab-states-doing-more-20150909-gjj1hn.html, May 12, 2016 (last date accessed).

55. A. Smale. (2015, August 25). "Trudging toward Hungary as the border fence rises" [Online]. Available: http://www.smh.com.au/world/trudging-toward-hungary-as-the-border-fence-rises-20150824-gj6uaz, May 11, 2016 (last date accessed).

56. "Migrant crisis: Finland's PM Juha Sipila offers his home to Syrian refugees," *Sydney Morning Herald*, September 7, 2015. [Online]. Available: http://www.smh.com.au/world/migrant-crisis-finlands-pm-juha-sipila-offers-his-home-to-syrian-refugees-20150906-gjgicu.html, May 14, 2016 (last date accessed).

57. N. Birnbaum. (2015, September 8). "Europe's migrant crisis: Britain, France to accept some refugees as flow accelerates" [Online]. Available: http://www.smh.com.au/world/europes-migrant-crisis-britain-france-to-accept-some-refugees-as-flow-accelerates-20150907-gjh8vw, May 12, 2016 (last date accessed).

58. A. Saeedy. (2015, August 12). "European Union to provide \$3.6b funding for migrant crisis" [Online]. Available: http://www.smh.com.au/world/european-union-to-provide-36b-funding-for-migrant-crisis-20150811-giwevn.html, May 13, 2016 (last date accessed).

59. N. Miller. (2015, September 10). "Refugee crisis: EU president wants to distribute another 120,000 across Europe" [Online]. Available: http://www.smh.com.au/world/refugee-crisis-eu-president-wants-to-distribute-another-120000-across-europe-20150909-gjj190.html, May 13, 2016 (last date accessed).

60. D. Sanger. (2015, September 15). "US President Barack Obama directs administration to accept 10,000 Syrian refugees" [Online]. Available: http://www.smh.com.au/world/migrant-crisis/us-president-barack-obama-directs-administration-to-accept-10000-syrian-refugees-20150911-gjk6di.html, May 13, 2016 (last date accessed).

61. P. Zangerle. (2015, September 11). "Refugee crisis: US plans to increase refugee intake by 5000 next year" [Online]. Available: http://www.smh.com.au/world/refugee-crisis-us-plans-to-increase-refugee-intake-by-5000-next-year-20150909-gjj343.html, May 13, 2016 (last date accessed).

62. J. Erbentraut. (2015, October 15). "How the media are reporting on Europe's refugee crisis" [Online]. Available: http://www.huffingtonpost.com.au/entry/refugee-crisis-media-coverage_us_5615952ce4b0cf9984d850ec?section=australia, May 13, 2016 (last date accessed).

63. P. Marfleet, *Refugees in a Global Era.* New York: Palgrave Macmillan, 2006.

64. B. Jaya. (n.d.). "How does the media portrayal of the Syrian refugee crisis affect our moral attitude to it?" [Online]. Available: https://www.quora.com/How-does-the-media-portrayal-of-the-Syrian-refugee-crisis-affect-our-moral-attitude-to-it, May 31, 2017 (last date accessed).

65. EDAM. (2014, January). "Reaction mounting against Syrian refugees in Turkey" [Online]. Available: http://www.edam.org.tr/en/File?id=1152, May 16, 2016 (last date accessed).

66. R. A. Wilson and R. D. Brown, *Humanitarianism and Suffering: The Mobilization of Empathy.* Cambridge: Cambridge University Press, 2011.

67. J. Moore. (2012, August 2). "The white correspondent's burden: We need to tell the Africa story differently" [Online]. Available: https://www.bostonreview.net/world-us/white-correspondent percentE2 percent80 percent99s-burden-jina-moore, May 16, 2016 (last date accessed).

68. C. Johnson. (2015, June 21). "The problem with the media's coverage of sexual assault" [Online]. Available: http://national.deseretnews.com/article/4923/the-problem-with-the-medias-coverage-of-sexual-assault.html, May 16, 2016 (last date accessed).

69. L. Palmer. (2015, September 7). "Sensationalism or a call to action: Covering the Syrian refugee crisis" [Online]. Available: https://ethics.journalism.wisc.edu/2015/09/07/

sensationalism-or-a-call-to-action-covering-the-syrian-refugee-crisis/, May 13, 2016 (last date accessed).

70. B. Giggs. (2015, September 3). "Photographer describes 'scream' of migrant boy's 'silent body'" [Online]. Available: http://edition.cnn.com/2015/09/03/world/dead-migrant-boy-beach-photographer-nilufer-demir/, May 13, 2016 (last date accessed).

71. A. Wright. (2015, September 8). "The Arab Twitterati reacts to Syrian refugee crisis" [Online]. Available: http://www.alaraby.co.uk/english/blog/2015/9/8/the-arab-twitterati-reacts-to-syrian-refugee-crisis, May 16, 2016 (last date accessed).

72. B. Van Gorp, "Where is the frame? Victims and intruders in the Belgian press coverage of the asylum issue," *European Journal of Communication*, vol. 20, no. 4, pp. 484–507, 2005.

73. P. Gale, "The refugee crisis and fear: Populist politics and media discourse," *Journal of Sociology*, vol. 40, no. 4, pp. 321–340, 2004.

74. M. Khosravinik, "The representation of refugees, asylum seekers and immigrants in British newspapers during the Balkan conflict (1999) and the British general election," *Discourse Society*, vol. 20, no. 4, pp. 477–498, 2009.

75. Question More. (2015, September 16). "Western double standards hit Russia's Syrian efforts" [Online]. Available: https://www.rt.com/op-edge/315571-syria-russia-us-isis/, May 16, 2016 (last date accessed).

76. A. Hanyes, E. Devereux, and M. Breen. (2004). "A cosy consensus on deviant discourse: How the refugee and asylum seeker meta-narrative has endorsed an interpretive crisis in relation to the transnational politics of the world's displaced persons" [Online]. Available: http://www.ulsites.ul.ie/sociology/sites/default/files/A percent20Cosy percent20Consensus percent20on percent20Deviant percent20Discourse.pdf, May 16, 2016 (last date accessed).

77. Media Diversity Institute. (2015, October 9). "Arab media coverage of the refugee Crisis" [Online]. Available: http://www.media-diversity.org/en/index.php?option=com_content&view=article&id=2996:arab-media-coverage-of-the-refugee-crisis-&catid=35:media-news-a-content&Itemid=34, May 16, 2016 (last date accessed).

78. J. Hall. (2015, September 9). "Syrian refugees have turned Lesbos into a war zone" [Online]. Available: http://www.dailymail.co.uk/news/article-3227436/Syrian-refugees-turned-Lesbos-war-zone-residents-claim-migrants-chant-f-Hungarian-police-amid-fears-ISIS-using-crisis-enter-Europe.html, May 16, 2016 (last date accessed).

79. N. Noman. (2015, September 2). "The tragic reality of the Syrian refugee crisis, in one gut-wrenching photo" [Online]. Available: http://mic.com/articles/124788/the-tragic-reality-of-the-syrian-refugee-crisis-in-one-gut-wrenching-photo#.BTQJ3gr1U, May 16, 2016 (last date accessed).

80. A. Jeffers, *Refugees, Theatre and Crisis Performing Global Identities.* London: Palgrave Macmillan, 2012.

81. M. Phillips and K. Starup, "Protection challenges of mobility," *Forced Migration Review*, vol. 47, pp. 27–30, September 2014.

82. S. Gormley. (2015, September 21). "Yes, let's be rational about the Syrian refugee crisis" [Online]. Available: http://ottawacitizen.com/news/politics/gormley-yes-lets-be-rational-about-the-syrian-refugee-crisis, May 16, 2016 (last date accessed).

83. Medical Xpress. (2015, September 16). "Half of refugees traumatised: German psychotherapists" [Online]. Available: http://medicalxpress.com/news/2015-09-refugees-traumatised-german-psychotherapists.html, May 12, 2016 (last date accessed).

84. European Resettlement Network. (2014). "Cultural orientation for Syrian refugees under the Norwegian Cultural Orientation (NORCO) programme" [Online]. Available: http://www.resettlement.eu/news/cultural-orientation-syrian-refugees-under-norwegian-cultural-orientation-norco-programme, May 12, 2016 (last date accessed).

85. D. Greenfield. (2015, September 4). "The Syrian refugee crisis is not our problem: We didn't cause it. We don't have to solve it" [Online]. Available: http://www.frontpagemag.com/fpm/260020/syrian-refugee-crisis-not-our-problem-daniel-greenfield, May 12, 2016 (last date accessed).

86. K. Kwansah-Aidoo and A. George, "Communication, culture and crisis in a transboundary context," in *Culture and Crisis Communication: Transboundary Cases from Nonwestern Perspectives*, 1st ed., A. M. George and K. Kwansah-Aidoo, Eds. Hoboken, NJ: John Wiley-IEEE Press.

87. C. Gregoire. (2015, September 18). "Psychological toll of the Syrian refugee crisis" [Online]. Available: http://www.huffingtonpost.com/entry/refugee-crisis-mental-health_55f9b694e4b00310edf55c73, May 17, 2016 (last date accessed).

88. Activist Post. (2016, May 3). "Mainstream journalist slams MSM coverage of Syrian crisis: 'Incomparably worse' than coverage of Iraq war" [Online]. Available: http://www.activistpost.com/2016/05/mainstream-journalist-slams-msm-coverage-of-syrian-crisis-incomparably-worse-than-coverage-of-iraq-war.html, May 13, 2016 (last date accessed).

Turkey 15

"Nothing Will Ever Be the Same": The Borusan Case and the Socio-Cultural Dynamics of Crisis in Turkey

Ebru Uzunoğlu and Selin Türkel

Chapter Preview

The 2011 Borusan crisis in Turkey revealed the complex relations between business, culture, politics, and religious sensitivities. The company withdrew sponsorship for a woman race car driver giving the official reason as budget cuts. However, it was alleged by others that the real reason was because the woman wore a headscarf in a television interview which did not sit well with the company's policy of political and religious neutrality. In this case, the controversy regarding the true meaning of a headscarf, in terms of what it represents—religious devotion or political Islam—became an issue that exemplified how sociopolitical, cultural, and religious differences and inclinations interacted to turn what looked like a simple business decision, into a full-blown crisis, aided by social media. The Borusan crisis is regarded as the first major crisis occurring along the sociocultural fault line, that Turkish corporations witnessed and one that the business world was not prepared for and was unable to deal with in a satisfactory manner. But it also reveals that

Culture and Crisis Communication: Transboundary Cases from Nonwestern Perspectives, First Edition.
Edited by Amiso M. George and Kwamena Kwansah-Aidoo.
© 2017 by The Institute of Electrical and Electronics Engineers, Inc. Published 2017 by John Wiley & Sons, Inc.

reputational credit, stemming from corporate social performance can help a
company in times of crisis. The various philanthropic activities of Borusan acted as
a reservoir of goodwill which helped the conglomerate overcome the crisis with
minimal damage. Ultimately, the case shows that sociocultural factors have major
influences on business success, while highlighting recently amplified sensitivities of
the Turkish society.

After reading this chapter, you will be able to

- *Understand the competing cultural identities in Turkey*
- *Verify the place of Islam (religion) in the politics and culture of Turkey*
- *Appreciate the complex relations between business, culture, politics, and religious sensitivities in Turkey*
- *Unpack how sociopolitical, cultural, and religious differences and inclinations can interact to cause a full-blown crisis, aided by social media*
- *Evaluate the important role that sociocultural factors can play in business success*
- *Analyze the value of corporate philanthropy/social responsibility in times of crisis.*

Overview of Turkish Cultural Identities

It is important to pay attention to shared beliefs, values, and cultural variations since they are all aspects that need to be considered in developing crisis communication strategies. Addressing the significance of cultural orientation in processes of communication, Hall emphasizes the link between these two notions as "Culture is communication and communication is culture" [1]. Since communication is expected to satisfy the diverse needs of stakeholders and the broader community, the major role of culture cannot be denied.

To better grasp the cultural mindset of different societies, it is possible to harness the notion of cultural types as described by Hall [2] and Hofstede et al. [3]. Regarding cultural types, Hofstede et al.'s [3] individualism and collectivism dimensions serve as an explicative framework on Turkish cultural contexts and traits. According to Hofstede et al. [3], Turkish culture is portrayed as high on collectivism. Consequently, in Turkey, group loyalty is valued to ensure harmony and avoid conflicts within family, relatives, and friends [4]. Turkey also reveals characteristics of high context culture where a subtle way of communication is utilized [5]. Apart from a theoretical perspective, a brief overview of Turkey's recent history will be useful to understand the underlying assumptions of Turkish culture.

Kemal Atatürk, the first president of Republic of Turkey between 1923 and 1938, was not only a military leader, but also an impressive statesman who initiated various reforms that have impacted Turkey, both economically and socially. At the core of the reforms was Kemalism "a set of ideological prescriptions regarding

272 "NOTHING WILL EVER BE THE SAME"

nationalism, republicanism, secularism, populism, reformism, and statism that were embedded in the ruling People's Party program" marking a distinct departure from Ottoman past [6, p. 2], that maintains its influence today.

The assumption of the modernist approach is that traditional societies should abandon religious dogmas and adopt rational and positivist values [7]. Turkish modernization as a civilization project has come into conflict with local Islam as being inconsistent with science and reason [8]. In Turkey, "secularism can be thought of as a product of modernization" [9]. The term *secularism* denotes a lifestyle based on reason and scientific thinking [7]. Accordingly, it can be considered that the ruling People's Party's (Cumhuriyet Halk Partisi) aim was to replace traditional Islamic lifestyle with a secular one, favoring science over religion.

In the 1990s, the media began to use two binary labels, "white" and "black"' Turks [10]. The former leads a secular lifestyle, "which include drinking alcohol and not covering one's head" [11]. In contrast to this politically left of center, mainly urban population, Black Turks are generally from rural areas, and hold Islamic values [12]. Black Turks are believed to be the majority in Turkey.

The relations between the Turkish secular republic and Islam have been historically complicated and strained, as highlighted by the headscarf issue. Using headwear for women is a tradition, and the reason for its widespread use is summarized as follows: "it's used in traditional rural village society, within the emerging Islamic urban middle class, as a statement of Islamic belief, as an object of mass-fashion, and as a statement of the right to express one's beliefs" [13]. However, under Turkish Republican secularism, it was considered that headscarves should be excluded from the public sphere, being restricted to the private sphere [14].

In addition, secularists make a distinction between *headscarf* (başörtüsü) and the *türban,* accepting the former as traditional headcover but rejecting the latter as a blatant political symbol. However, Islamic women deny its political symbolism, calling it a sign of faith [15]. The conservative Justice and Development Party (AKP), first came to power on November 2002, and has governed Turkey ever since. Under the AKP governments, the active role of the Muslim urban middle class in both political and business life emerged into public view [16]. According to Göle [17], these people, benefitting from educational opportunities in cities and possessing both economic and political power are no longer Black Turks, but grey; meaning "partially whitened." However, as the two polar groups now live in close proximity in urban areas, they are experiencing increased contact and conflict.

Crisis Communication in Turkey: Reflections from Academia and Practice

A content analysis of Turkish academic articles published between 2006 and 2014 demonstrates the existence of over 1000 studies with "crisis management" in the title. However, only 70 studies were found on the topic of "crisis communication."

As stated by Çığ and Çığ [18], both crisis literature and practices were closely related to neoliberalism and grew at a rate that closely matched the rate of neoliberal transformation. The timing of the crisis management literature clearly coincides with the influential neoliberal policies of Turgut Özal, the Turkish prime minister, during the 1980s.

Even though crisis communication emerged as a separate field in the late 1980s, the original studies in this area on Turkey were mostly published after 2000. Before the 2000s, the subject was mostly dealt with in relation to management studies. Since crisis communication is a function of public relations, the lack of public relations undergraduate degrees before 1992 may possibly account for the absence of studies. The main subjects of crisis communications (2006–2014) include tourism, food, political and financial related issues, both natural and human-made disasters, and terrorism. They focus more on practical aspects, such as strategy development, process planning, and suggestions on communications. Moreover, to the authors' best knowledge, few academic studies are devoted to the role of culture in crisis communication [19, 20].

Turkish crisis communication practices were examined by the authors via the media coverage of crisis events between 2006 and 2014. Accordingly, economic crisis was the most prevalent topic among crisis news. The 2008–2009 global economic crisis is considered to be the underlying reason for this. The second most frequent news was about the Soma mining disaster in May 2014. Due to the lack of preparedness of the victims, the final death toll reached 301. Political and international crises, which dealt with different countries and political parties including the governing party, were also common topics. Most often, the governmental agencies were criticized for not ensuring safe work environments.

In the context of international crises, strained relations between Turkey and neighboring countries are covered. The food industry seemed to be the most vulnerable sector. The negligence of food safety and hygiene issues can be the possible reason for this frequent coverage. The evidence revealed that celebrity crises were also salient and attention worthy. These were mostly personal scandals involving entertainment and sports stars who disregarded the moral rules of the society. The media also covered terrorism, which had its beginnings in the 1960s and, emerged as a serious threat after the 1980s. Finally, safety crises in the construction and transportation industries were observed. In at-risk sectors, such as airline and automotive sectors, the importance of communication in terms of crisis management is clearly seen in this analysis.

The Role of Turkish Culture in Crisis Communication Practice

The context, which ensures the message reception in the way sender aims to deliver, has a vital role in communication. Therefore, Turkish communication style, with its high context cultural feature, demonstrates indirect, implicit form with an emphasis on nonverbal, emotional cues and high tolerance for ambiguity [5]. Kartarı [21] points out that, in Turkish culture what is said is nowhere near as important as how it is said. The finding of Lvina et al.'s study [22], which indicated that an individual's facial gestures are critical factors in decoding messages delivered by others, support Katari's claim. Furthermore, the source of verbal communication is significant in addition to paralinguistic cues such as intonation, loudness, gestures, body postures, facial expressions [21].

Apart from national values, it is vital to pay regard to cultural backgrounds that necessitate different communication approaches. Consisting of diverse cultural groups based on political, religious, ethnic, and regional backgrounds, Turkish culture makes it imperative for organizations to plan their crisis communication strategies in a more sensitive manner. Hence, organizations acknowledging these requirements should implement training, preferably at CEOs level, to enhance cultural competence. The case of Borusan Group, discussed below, exemplifies the role of culture in Turkish crisis communication.

It is vital to pay regard to cultural backgrounds that necessitate different communication approaches.

The Borusan Crisis: Nothing Will Ever Be the Same Again

To have a better grasp of the intricacies of the case, two in-depth interviews were conducted with Ali Cem İlhan, owner of Tribeca, Borusan's communication consultancy and Şule Yücebıyık, Head of Corporate Communication at Borusan Holding. Concurrently, we conducted content analysis of the media coverage over 212 news stories between January 28, 2011 and February 7, 2012, which also provided extended information about the issue.

Overview and Background of the Borusan Group

Borusan Group, established in 1944, is one of the Turkey's top industrial family conglomerates with operations in steel, distributorship, and energy industries. The distributorship encompasses worldwide known brands, particularly in the automotive and construction equipment industries: BMW®, Mini®, Land Rover®, and Caterpillar®. Having an emphasis on added value for Turkey's economy, the Group also enhances the cultural and social life of Turkey through Borusan Culture and Arts (BKS). Asım Kocabıyık, the founder, was considered a prominent industrialist of the early Turkish Republican period [23]. His business approach symbolizes the values of the early Republic. One of the striking examples of this approach is revealed in the company's annual report which states that: "Borusan deems the development of classical music to be a significant contribution for the country and the society's modernization process" [24].

More Than a Simple Slip of the Tongue

On December 28, 2011, the Yeni Şafak daily published the headline "Başörtülü binince BMW bozuluyor (When a headscarved driver gets in a BMW, it is damaged)" [25] on the front page, sparking an escalating crisis for the Borusan Group.

The story began on August 17, 2011, when a settlement in principle for sponsorship was reached between Borusan Group and the women's rally champion, Burcu Çetinkaya. Three months later, she started to host a TV show called Otomobil Sevdası (The Love of Automobile) for a national channel, Kanal24. Çetinkaya test drove a Mini Cooper with a guest on the show, Merve Sena Kılıç, a reporter for the daily paper Yeni Şafak. A photo of the two in front of the car appeared in Kelebek, a supplement of Hürriyet daily, in which Kılıç was wearing a headscarf. Following this interview, Çetinkaya was cautioned by Borusan Group Mini Brand Manager, Hakan Bayülgen, saying that "we saw your photos with the Mini and a veiled woman in the press. And this created an image problem for us. Those abroad [implying headquarters of Mini owner BMW] do not want this" [26]. Within a short period, Borusan withdrew the sponsorship agreement. Although Borusan officials attributed this to budget cutting, the issue was reflected in the media as a concern with company image.

One of the main factors in spreading the crisis message was a *tweet* sent by Cüneyt Özdemir, the Turkish journalist with the highest number of followers on Twitter®. Özdemir, stated very directly and tactlessly that

> Borusan overturned the sponsorship deal, saying that headscarved presenter disrupts their image. Take your brand … [three dots used to imply inappropriate language]. We have a Mini. I am selling it immediately. I spit in your valuable image, which you say must not to be damaged. [27]

Similarly, another journalist mentioned the issue on his Twitter account, saying

> The first headscarved woman to burn her BMW in front of Borusan Headquarter will become a heroine! [27]

Through these messages, the crisis emerging in the press shifted to social media and spread like wildfire. Apart from media reactions, the cancelation of sponsorship triggered negative responses from various stakeholders, such as the Turkish Motorcycle Federation, The Center for Consumer Rights, Spor Toto Organization, and Religious Affairs Foundation's Officers' Union of Turkey.

Apologetic Response from Borusan

Following the viral spread of unexpected messages, Borusan's reputation and strong relationships with stakeholders were at stake. Hence, the priority was minimizing reputational risk. Accordingly, a reputation management goal was established at the onset of the crisis. Ali Cem İlhan, one of the interviewees, has clearly noted that the crisis was considered a matter of reputation, and added that senior management deemed reputation a priority. Acceptance objectives [28] can be considered to apply to the Borusan crisis case. They were vital, in line with reputational effect of the crisis's impact, to result in positive attitudes of stakeholders.

Ideally, it is suggested to try to resolve the crisis immediately in the place where it occurred [29]. Relying on this suggestion, Borusan aimed to address the ongoing negative conversation, particularly on Twitter. Hakan Bayülgen, the brand manager, published an apology on Twitter.

Original
Çıkan bir haberde saygı duyduğum bazı değerleri istemeden incittiğimi gördüm. Haberin özü bu olmasa bile kamuoyundan, kurumum ve markamdan, yarattığım hassasiyet için özür dilerim. [30]

Translated into English
In the news, I saw that I had unintentionally hurt some values I respect. While this is not the essence of the news, I apologize for the [lack of] sensitivity I have caused the public, the Group and my brand.

As involvement of the CEO is vital in crisis communication, potential consequences of the situation were recognized by the upper administration, resulting in a declaration by the CEO, Agah Uğur again on Twitter.

Original
Bugün yayınlanan haberden ötürü … büyük üzüntü duydum… Borusan Otomotiv'in ekonomik gerekçelerle durdurduğu bir sponsorluk görüşmesi maalesef ülkemiz için çok hassas bir konu ile özdeşleştirilmiştir. Borusan Otomotiv'in din, dil, inanç, ırk gibi konularda ayrımcılık yapması söz konusu bile olamaz. [31]

Translated into English
Because of the news published today, …I felt great sorrow… Sponsorship, which has been withdrawn due to economic reasons by Borusan Automotive, has unfortunately been associated with a very sensitive issue for our country. Discrimination on the basis of religion, language, belief and race is not even a matter of discussion for Borusan Automotive.

The importance of the crisis for the Board of directors was stated by Ali Cem İlhan. He reported that 28 managers were involved in the crisis, after the failure of personal messages. Thus, crisis communications shifted toward a more structured and impersonal approach.

On January 1, 2012, 3 days after the appearance of the news in Yeni Şafak, the crisis management team issued a full-page advertisement in 13 mainstream newspapers with a message expressing regret for the misunderstanding. The message translated below by the authors, read thus

Original
Kamuoyuna saygıyla:
Herkesin dil, din, ırk, inanç, giyim ve yaşam tarzına saygımız sonsuzdur; ayrımcılık yapmamız asla söz konusu olamaz. Son günlerde Borusan Otomotiv ve Borusan Grubu hakkında, bir sponsorluk görüşmesi ile ilişkilendirilerek ortaya atılan "ayrımcılık" iddialarıyla ilgili ifadeleri kabul etmemiz mümkün değildir. Yanlış algılanmaktan ötürü son derece üzgünüz. İstemeyerek bir parçası olduğumuz bu durumdan etkilenen herkesin hassasiyetini içtenlikle paylaşıyoruz. [32]

Translated into English
With respect to the public:
We unconditionally respect everyone's language, religion, race, belief system, dress, and lifestyle. Discrimination is not even a matter of discussion. In recent days, it is not possible to accept statements regarding discriminatory allegations that are associated with Borusan Automotive and Borusan Group's sponsorship negotiations.

We are extremely sorry for this misunderstanding. We sincerely share the sensitivity of everyone affected by this situation in which we have unintentionally become involved.

The next day, the crisis management team organized a press conference with the participation of Borusan Group CEO, Agah Uğur, and Chief Executive of Borusan Automotive, Eşref Biryıldız. In contrast to the previous message, which expressed regret for a misunderstanding, this time Agah Uğur offered a clear apology to the general public.

Original
Hangi dil, din, ırk, inanç, giyim ve yaşam tarzında olursa olsun tüm vatandaşlardan içtenlikle özür dileriz...Bir yol kazası olduğunu düşünüyorum. Yeni bir yol kazası olmaması için ne yapmak gerekiyorsa onu yapacağız. [33]

Translated into English
Regardless of language, religion, race, belief system, dress, and lifestyle, we
sincerely apologize to all our citizens…I think it was a road accident… We
will do our best to avoid any other similar incidents.

During the press conference, Agah Uğur also announced the resignation of Hakan
Bayülgen, the Mini Brand Manager. Agah Uğur admitted that the sponsorship process was poorly handled, citing professional mismanagement by Hakan Bayülgen. In
terms of commercial consequences, Agah Uğur mentioned that three orders had been
cancelled. In response to a question raised by a journalist, Agah Uğur stated that
the company was considering providing training on corporate stance regarding the
wearing of the headscarf and belief systems for all employees, including distributors.
After the press conference, the news of the announcement received extensive coverage in both mainstream and local media. Particularly, Agah Uğur's direct headscarf
apology was the most highlighted message among the headlines. Over the following
3 days, the news focused on the messages given in the press conference. However,
the issue remained on the public agenda for almost a month, although the emphasis
changed. The crisis management process of Borusan was subject to criticism by both
journalists and communication experts.

Strategic Approach

Aiming to minimize the reputational risk, Borusan authorities highlighted three priority stakeholders as the employees, the media, and the general public.

Effective internal communication is key to crisis communication. Ali Cem İlhan
emphasized both the importance of keeping employees well informed during the crisis, and how they kept employees informed via memos and meetings. Since the manager resigned shortly after the incident, the employees' concerns could not be ignored,
according to Ali Cem İlhan. He added that these concerns were addressed through
transparent dialogue. The absence of negative reactions, he believed, was an indi-
cation of the correct approach. He also emphasized the significance of leader presence, highlighting the visibility of Borusan Holding Chairman of the Board, Ahmet
Kocabıyık, and his personal contact with staff on Employees' Day.

Another influential stakeholder group was the media, since negative publicity
can result from a crisis. Other than providing timely and truthful information, it was
ensured that the misleading information was quickly corrected on time. One example concerns the Turkish Motorcycle Federation. Chief Executive of Borusan pointed
out that the company had no agreement with the Turkish Motorcycle Federation and
so claims of a suspension of the agreement as a protest by this organization could
not have been true. Finally, to identify the short-term results, a perceptual survey of
attitudes toward Borusan Automotive was conducted on behalf of Marketing Türkiye

Magazine in January of 2012. The survey found that 52% of respondents held neutral attitudes, while negative and positive attitudes were expressed by 28% and 20%, respectively [34]. Twenty-eight percent negative attitudes is considered low given that the incident was so recent and was sensitive in Turkey.

Coomb's Situational Crisis Communication Theory framework [28] is an appropriate tool for analyzing the response strategy of Borusan. The Group employed *Apology*, a rebuild crisis response strategy. In this strategy, the organization accepts full responsibility for what it has done and asks stakeholders to forgive the misstep [35]. It is a good fit for crises that have "strong attributions of crisis responsibility (preventable crises), regardless of crisis history or prior relationship reputation" [36]. Borusan, with its positive relationship reputation, and with no crisis history, is a good example of this, and accordingly, it was able to prevent the crisis with an early intervention.

It was also a threat for Borusan, a distributor of an international brand, that is, Mini-BMW, to have international consequences. However, as the content analysis of media coverage revealed, there were no negative concerns directed at headquarters of BMW except two minor mentions.

The Influence of Culture on Borusan's Response

When the Borusan case is examined from a cultural perspective, the apologetic response seems appropriate. As a cultural concept, apologies should be performed cautiously in Turkey, since they pose a serious threat to those using them. That is to say, "the speaker admits that s/he has done something wrong, thus, s/he exposes his/her face" [37]. It should be noted that saving face has major importance in Turkish culture. The idiom "don't bring down our face" (*yüzümüzü yere eğdirme*) is evidence of the significance of saving one's face at all costs. However, accepting one's mistakes and apologizing are also appreciated in Turkish culture [38]. According to Özyıldırım's research [39], explicit expression of apology is acceptable when the offense is deemed serious.

As expected in a high context culture, crisis communication necessitates a sincere approach where nonverbal communication addresses emotional concerns. Accordingly, Borusan executives arranged a press conference to express their responsibility, rather than sending only a press statement. During the meeting, Borusan's CEO conveyed an apologetic message which appeared in both print and broadcast media. However, we, the authors, found the message delivery insincere. To verify this assertion, the video [40], was shown to a naturally formed group of 12 students. The group of participants was a nonrandom convenience sample of six female and six male Public Relations and Advertising students enrolled in Marketing Communication Research during the fall 2015 semester in a focus group setting. Participants perceived the speech as a monologue read without any eye contact, interaction, and vocal variety.

It lacked emotional content. Despite these observations, the *apology* itself was strong enough to meet the expectations of the general public since it expressed *loss of face*.

Assessment of Outcome in Borusan Crisis

As stated earlier, the crisis caused very little financial harm. According to Ali Cem İlhan, Borusan managed to control the crisis in a relatively short time, 4 days. In particular, apologizing to publics appeared to be a success factor. The generally sympathetic tone of the media coverage is evidence of the effectiveness of the crisis communication approach. Also, positive results were found in the perception survey conducted by the Borusan Group in March, which revealed that the crisis had lost its importance for the general public. Accordingly, no additional precautions or actions were considered necessary.

Borusan Automotive, being the Turkish distributor of BMW automobiles, has a joint venture relationship with GIWA Holding, operating in Germany. The crisis, which had potential to impact the BMW brand, inflicted no long-term damage. According to Ali Cem İlhan, this result is an achievement of crisis management. The content analysis also affirmed this view. Especially, after the press conference, almost all news mentioned Borusan rather than BMW, showing a shift in the focus of the crisis.

Consequently, it should be noted that the reputational credit, which stemmed from corporate social performance of Borusan was able to safeguard the company against the crisis. The social investments of the company were mentioned in dailies such as Sabah [41] and also Yeni Şafak, where the crisis started [42]. The various philanthropic activities of Borusan, most notably, Borusan Istanbul Philharmonic Orchestra, are believed to have acted as a reservoir of goodwill which helped the conglomerate to overcome the crisis with minimal damage.

Lessons Learned

The main lesson of the Borusan crisis is the importance of learning from sociocultural mistakes. If not all, many crises are predictable and avoidable. It is possible to argue that the Borusan case is one that could have been foreseen.

Specific to Turkey, cultural sensitivity is an increasingly vital area needing effective proactive management. Unless the crisis is avoidable, different cultural identities need to be considered in post-crisis stages. It is important that the acceptance of diverse cultural identities permeates the culture of organizations. In terms of aspects of culture such as the language of organization, extreme caution is needed. In particular, as Ali Cem İlhan noted, it is important to use appropriate words, such as, using "headscarf" instead of "turban," which has different connotations. Apart from words, communication style is at the heart of crisis communication particularly, in a high context culture. Thus, this case provides culture-specific insights for executives who are willing to communicate properly.

It is important that the acceptance of diverse cultural identities permeates the culture of organizations.

The other lesson is about the crisis response strategy utilized in the case study. The importance of the strategy was also put forward by Ali Cem İlhan in the following terms: "Borusan has marked a new epoch by apologizing to a religious public" [43]. The apologetic response seems to be direct and proper corporate conduct in collectivist Turkish culture where polarization is a constant issue and conflicts need to be avoided.

Remarks on the Borusan Crisis Communication Process

The Borusan crisis indicates that sociocultural factors have major influences on business survival. However, an organization cannot be isolated from its organizational culture and value system that mainly originates from its founder. Accordingly, the Western, secular, and modern values of the founder of Borusan are clearly still embodied in its corporate culture [44]. The initial unfortunate statement, which the Group claimed was the view of one individual, the brand manager of Mini, was associated with corporate identity by the religious-conservative media. Furthermore, the issue, which first appeared on the agenda with the Borusan case, received intense media attention, and became a subject of discussion. The controversial issue regarding the true meaning of headscarf, in terms of whether it represents religious devotion or political Islam, became prevalent again. The people favoring Islamic lifestyle, more powerful and visible than before the AKP came to power in 2002, have encountered secularists more often in the cities, leading to tensions. A popular columnist drew attention to this dramatic change stating: "If it were in the past, Borusan would not mind the issue, or other than being a runner up, a headscarved woman would not attend a fashion TV show" [45]. The Borusan crisis exemplified the sensitivities of the society. Kılıç, an educated urban headscarved grey Turk, was in a news story concerning a corporation that identifies with a modernist stance. This was evidence of the conflict involving the confrontation of a grey Turk with a supposedly secular corporation.

The crisis has significance for the Turkish business community. According to Ali Cem İlhan, it is acknowledged that crisis management was generally limited to product and service related issues among business in Turkey. During a personal interview with the authors, Ali Cem İlhan said "...this is the first major crisis that the Turkish corporations have witnessed occurring along the socio-cultural fault line, a situation which they are not accustomed to coping with." Thus, the examined crisis can be considered a sign of transformation in the crisis communication field, particularly in Turkey. In other words, *nothing will ever be the same*.

During this period, one well-known brand communication expert, Güven Borça, indicated that the Borusan crisis was a strong warning for the business community to shift its mindset [27]. Similarly, one academic, Hale Bolak who criticized Borusan's handling of the crisis, claimed that it might be interpreted as a sign of increasing sensitivity toward different cultural identities [46].

Though it came as a surprise, as Ali Cem İlhan mentioned, the company was able to deal with this crisis and initiated a crisis communication plan in a relatively short time. Initially, using a controlled communication tool, that is, the crisis advertisement, Borusan offered a partial apology "as an expression of concern and regret" [47]. Immediately after, the message was transformed into a full apology by the company's spokesperson at the press conference. It seems inconsistent at first glance that within a day the apology type changed. Additionally, brand expert, Yelda İpekli, criticized the advertisement itself on the grounds that it was an inappropriate means of communication on such an occasion [48]. Instead, leveraging endorsement of their own headscarved employees might have been a better strategy, as this would have enhanced credibility of the company. However, it should be noted that advertisement could have been considered a legitimate tool for the organization to ensure the presence in print media. It was not possible to guarantee the attendance of large numbers of journalists at the press conference since it coincided with New Year celebrations. Yücebıyık, the Corporate Communications Director of Borusan Group, confirmed in one news report, that both the advertisement and press meeting were preplanned to stay ahead of the rapidly changing news agenda [49]. The content analysis of the print media coverage showed that the company's efforts were effective to a certain degree. Following the crisis communication implementations of Borusan, the majority of published news stories were neutral, with even a few positive accounts from the nonreligious press.

Practical Suggestions

Some practical suggestions and ideas to assist organizations and others interested in doing business in Turkey to effectively manage crisis situations and build mutually beneficial relationships with stakeholders are given below.

- Turkey is a high context culture, and so in times of crisis, all communication should be delivered in a culturally appropriate manner, taking cognizance that how the message is delivered is more important than the actual content of the message being delivered.
- In Turkey's collectivist culture, despite the fact that maintaining face is a matter of concern, explicit statements of apology are regarded as acceptable for the

purpose of crisis communication depending on the perceived seriousness of the issue. Apology is, therefore, an acceptable crisis management strategy in certain circumstances.

- In the Turkish context, a good corporate philanthropy program can be useful in times of crisis and so organizations need to have such programs so as to be able to take advantage of goodwill when crisis strikes.

- There are sensitivities in the Turkish society around sociopolitical, cultural, and religious differences that can interact to turn a simple business dealing into a full-blown crisis, aided by social media. Therefore, an organization must have the ability to adapt quickly in a changing crisis environment and have in place the right strategies to communicate with diverse groups.

Discussion Questions

15.1   What additional strategic approach would you advise Borusan to take that fits the high context culture of Turkey?

15.2   Borusan's executives' initial response to the crisis was given through Twitter. Discuss whether it was an appropriate act or not.

15.3   What implications can be drawn for crisis communication experts in a society of numerous subcultures in light of the Borusan case?

15.4   What are the primary crisis communication lessons that can be taken away from the Borusan case?

Acknowledgments

The authors would like to thank Ali Cem İlhan, owner of Tribeca Communication Consultancy and Şule Yücebıyık, Head of Corporate Communication at Borusan Holding, for their support and on behalf of Media Monitoring Center, Berk Ertürk for his valuable contribution in providing the material used in media content analysis.

References

1. E. T. Hall, *The Silent Language*. New York: Doubleday, 1959.
2. E. T. Hall, *Beyond Culture*. New York: Doubleday, 1976.
3. G. Hofstede, G. J. Hofstede, and M. Minkov, *Cultures and Organizations: Software of the Mind*, 3rd ed. New York: McGraw-Hill, 2010.

4. A. Bakay, "Does interpersonal trust influence organizational behavior?" *Eurasian Journal of Business and Economics*, vol. 8, no. 15, pp. 219–238, May 2015.

5. A. S. Sargut, *Kültürler Arası Farklılaşma ve Yönetim*. Ankara: İmge Kitabevi, 2001.

6. J. M. VanderLippe, *The Politics of Turkish Democracy*. Albany, NY: State University of New York Press, 2005.

7. E. Özbudun, "Secularism in Islamic countries: Turkey as a model," in *Constitutionalism in Islamic Countries: Between Upheaval and Continuity*, R. Grote and T. J. Röder, Eds. New York: Oxford University Press, 2012, pp. 135–145.

8. N. Göle, *The Forbidden Modern: Civilization and Veiling*. Ann Arbor, MI: University of Michigan Press, 2003.

9. T. Keskin, "Market oriented post-Islamism in Turkey," in *Secular State and Religious Society: Two Forces in Play in Turkey*, B. Turam, Ed. New York: Palgrave Macmillan, 2012, pp. 121–142.

10. D. Demiröz and A. Öncü, "Türkiye'de piyasa toplumunun oluşumunda hegemonyanın rolü: Bir gerçeklik projesi olarak beyaz Türklük," in *Şerif Mardin'e Armağan*, A. Öncü and O. Tekelioğlu, Eds. İstanbul: İletişim Yayınları, 2005, pp. 171–199.

11. J. White, *Muslim Nationalism and the New Turks*. Princeton, NJ: Princeton University Press, 2013.

12. J. B. White, "The end of Islamism? Turkey's Muslimhood model," in *Remaking Muslim Politics: Pluralism, Contestation, Democratization*, R. W. Hefner, Ed. Princeton, NJ: Princeton University Press, 2005, pp. 87–11.

13. M. R. Breu and R. T. Marchese, "The power of cloth: Popular culture that intersects sociopolitical boundaries," in *The Fabric of Life: Cultural Transformations in Turkish Society*, R. T. Marchese, Ed. New York: Global Academic Publishing, 2005, pp. 85–98.

14. A. A. An-Na'im Na, *Islam and the Secular State: Negotiating the Future of Sharia*. Cambridge: Harvard University Press, 2008.

15. I. Ozgur, *Islamic Schools in Modern Turkey: Faith, Politics, and Education*. New York: Cambridge University Press, 2012.

16. K. Hart, *And Then We Work for God: Rural Sunni Islam in Western Turkey*. California: Stanford University Press, 2013.

17. N. Göle. (2005, December). "Europe: A Common Dream?" [Online]. Available: www.signandsight.com/features. 514.html, March 22, 2015 (last date accessed).

18. E. Ç. Çığ and Ü. Çığ, "Neoliberal akılsallığın bir semptomu olarak kriz iletişimi ve yönetimi," *Atılım Sosyal Bilimler Dergisi*, vol. 3, no. 1–2, pp. 79–97, December, 2013.

19. İ. Erdoğan, *Teori ve Pratikte Halkla İlişkiler*. Ankara: Erk, 2014.

20. F. B. Peltekoğlu, *Halkla İlişkiler Nedir?* İstanbul: Beta Yayınları, 2012.

21. A. Kartarı, *Kültür, Farklılık ve İletişim*. İstanbul: İletişim Yayınları, 2014.

22. E. Lvina, G. Johns, D. C. Treadway, et al., "Measure invariance of the Political Skill Inventory (PSI) across five cultures," *International Journal of Cross Cultural Management*, vol. 12, no. 2, pp. 171–191, August, 2012.

23. Hürriyet. (2012, December.). "Borusan'ın Kurucusu Asım Kocabıyık Hayatını Kaybetti" [Online]. Available: http://www.hurriyet.com.tr/ekonomi/22250812.asp, March 24, 2015 (last date accessed).

24. Borusan Holding. (2007). "2007 Annual Report of the Borusan Holding" [Online]. Available: http://www.borusanyatirim.com/BorusanFaaliyet/2007/sitemap.html, March 24, 2015 (last date accessed).

25. "Başörtülü Binince BMW Bozuluyor," *Yeni Şafak*, December 28, 2011, p. 1.

26. "Başörtüsü BMW'nin Kimyasını Bozdu," *Yeni Şafak*, December 28, 2011, p. 14.

27. "Başörtülüden Bozuk BMW!" *Yeni Şafak*, December 29, 2011, p. 14.

28. R. D. Smith, *Strategic Planning for Public Relations*. New York: Routledge, 2013.

29. A. Jacques. (2009, August). "Domino's delivers during crisis: The company's step-by-step response after a vulgar video goes viral" [Online]. Available: www.prsa.org/Intelligence/ TheStrategist/Articles/view/8226/102/Domino_s_delivers_during_crisis_The_company_ s_step?utm_source=prsa_website&utm_medium=facebook_like&utm_campaign=face book_like, March 26, 2015 (last date accessed).

30. On5yirmi5. (2011, December). "Borusan'dan Başörtüsüyle İlgili Açıklama!" [Online]. Available: http://www.on5yirmi5.com/haber/guncel/medya/72805/borusandan -basortusuyle-ilgili-aciklama.html, May 31, 2017 (last date accessed).

31. "BMW'ye Pistte Ambargo," *Milliyet*, December, 29, 2011 p. 11.

32. Borusan, "Kamuoyuna Saygıyla," *Türkiye Gazetesi*, January 1, 2012, p. 3.

33. "Borusan 'Yol Kazası' Dedi Olanlar İçin Özür Diledi," *Milliyet*, January 3, 2012, p. 8.

34. P. A. Yıldız, "Borusan Mini' Krizini Yönetebildi mi?" *Marketing Türkiye*, no. 236, pp. 66–70, January 15, 2012.

35. W. T. Coombs. (2007, October). "Crisis management and communications" [Online]. Available: http://www.instituteforpr.org/crisis-management-and-communications/, May 31, 2017 (last date accessed).

36. W. T. Coombs, "Protecting organization reputations during a crisis: The development and application of situational crisis communication theory," *Corporate Reputation Review*, vol. 10, no. 3, pp. 163–176, Fall 2007.

37. Ç. Hatipoğlu, "Level of imposition and explicit electronic apologies," in *Essays on Turkish Linguistics*, S. Ay, Ö. Aydın, I. Ergenç, et al., Eds. Wiesbaden: Harrasowitz Verlag, 2008, pp. 277–286.

38. U. R. Çetinavcı, "Apologizing in Turkish language: An intracultural and intercultural exploratory study," *Contemporary Online Language Education Journal*, vol. 1, no. 1, pp. 72–104, 2012.

39. I. Özyıldırım, "The level of directness in Turkish apology forms in relation to the level of education," *Edebiyat Fakültesi Dergisi*, vol. 27, no.1, pp. 179–201, June 2010.

40. Borusan, "Borusan Holding CEO'su Agah Uğur'un Basın Toplantısı Konuşması," Vimeo, 2016. [Online]. Available: https://vimeo.com/34457284, May 31, 2017 (last date accessed).

41. H. Uluç, "Sanal medyada linç merakı," *Sabah*, January 5, 2012, p.17.

42. Y. Z. Cömert, "Bitsin artık şu yobazlıklar," *Yeni Şafak*, December 29, 2011, p.14.

43. A. C. İlhan, "Bir Krizin Ardından Sınıfta Kalanlar," in *Aklıma Düşenler*, 2012. [Online]. Available: http://kuzguncuk.blogspot.com.tr/2012/01/bir-krizin-ardindan-sinifta-kalanlar.html, April 4, 2016 (last date accessed).

44. E. Diler, "BMW ve başörtüsü," *Takvim*, December 29, 2011, p. 16.
45. C. Semercioğlu, "Vali Mutlu: Havai fişeği kontrol altına alacağız," *Hürriyet Kelebek*, January 4, 2012, p.3.
46. E. Tatlıpınar, "Fetiş mi, siyasi taktik mi, iyi niyet işareti mi?" *Akşam Pazar*, January 8, 2012, p.9.
47. W. T. Coombs, *Ongoing Crisis Communication: Planning, Managing, and Responding.* Thousand Oaks, CA: Sage, 2012.
48. N. Akman, "Ders kriz yönetimi, konu Borusan örneği," *Zaman Pazar*, January 8, 2012, p.1.
49. "Kurumlar da Özür Dileyebilir," *Marketing Türkiye*, January 15, 2012, p. 72.

V

Latin America

Brazil 16

Gone with the Mud: Learning from the Niterói Disaster in Brazil

Regina Coeli da Silveira e Silva and Amiso M. George

Chapter Preview

Natural disasters due to heavy rains, landslides, and flooding are recurrent in South and Central American countries. Government response to rich and poor residents who live in high-risk areas in these countries contrasts sharply. The poor are disproportionately affected and are usually the last to recover, if at all. We use Hofstede's Power Distance concept to understand the underlying cultural reasons for such unequal government response toward these natural disasters.

This chapter examines a landslide disaster which occurred in Niterói, Rio de Janeiro, Brazil. It presents a situation where two factors came together and turned a natural disaster into an avoidable tragedy. The disaster was compounded by a sequence of careless activities strongly affected by cultural attitudes, existing state and municipal government (in)action, and lack of preparation for effective crisis management.

Culture and Crisis Communication: Transboundary Cases from Nonwestern Perspectives, First Edition.
Edited by Amiso M. George and Kwamena Kwansah-Aidoo.
© 2017 by The Institute of Electrical and Electronics Engineers, Inc. Published 2017 by John Wiley & Sons, Inc.

As of this writing, a dark cloud hangs over Brazil as a result of political corruption scandals that have swept up former and current presidents and financial corruption at Petrobras, the country's national oil company, which has now ensnared some of the nation's top business leaders and legislators. These criticisms coupled with the handling of the Niteroi disaster of 2010, highlight how culture and politics negatively influence Brazil's response to crisis. They also provide lessons on the importance of effective risk analysis and crisis communication and the value of life versus electoral votes.

After reading this chapter, you will be able to

- *Understand the symbiotic relationship between Brazil's history and its political system*
- *Discuss some Brazilian cultural dimensions and their impact on politics*
- *Describe the role of "Jeitinho Brasileiro" in understanding crisis management in Brazil*
- *Analyze the response of the Niterói Municipal Government and Mayor to the Bumba Hill disaster*
- *Understand why effective crisis management for poorer communities appears elusive in Brazil*
- *Comprehend the lessons from Brazil's crisis response for neighboring countries with similar political systems*

Brazilian History and Political System

The largest and most populous country in South and Latin America with a population of 200.4 million, Brazil occupies 47.3% of the South American continent. It is also the world's fifth largest country with the largest Portuguese-speaking population. The country boasts an Atlantic Ocean coastline of 4655 miles and borders every South American country except Ecuador and Chile. Brazil is rich in biodiversity and natural resources and is the world's seventh largest economy. It is also home to one of the world's most diverse populations; however, the disparity between rich and poor is staggering [1, 2].

The Brazilian political system has its origin in the Imperial period (1822–1889), which had a strong impact on Brazilian cultural behavior. The country gained its independence in 1822 after more than three centuries as a Portuguese colony. Ruled by a monarchy, the country was declared a republic by the military in 1889.

With the new government came a new flag and subsequently, a new constitution was introduced. However, wealthy landowners and coffee magnates in Rio de Janeiro and São Paulo controlled political power during the Republican era. These businessmen-politicians passed laws that gave them exceptional rights, income, and power. They also defined election results, especially in the poor states in the northern parts of the country. The poor were simply forced to vote in ways that kept the political elite in power. Despite mandatory voting, the right to vote was denied to women, indigenous people, illiterate people, the military, and priests [3].

In 1930, new president, Getúlio Vargas, wrested power and turned Brazil into a dictatorship. The new centralized government gave women the right to vote in 1932 and promoted unprecedented development of the country [4]. Today, every Brazilian has the right to vote. Vargas went from a dictator to a democratically elected president who fought against communism and for workers' rights. He is hailed in Brazil today as protector of the poor.

In 1964, during the Cold War, the military seized power in order to avoid a communist revolution in the country. During this period (1964–1985), direct elections were suspended. Only Congress had the right to vote. Only two political parties: ARENA—Aliança Renovadora Nacional (National Renewal Alliance)—a center right party, also known as the situation party, and MDB—Movimento Democrático Brasileiro (Brazilian Democratic Movement)—a centrist party, which was also the opposition party were approved. The ARENA party always presented a four-star army general for president, while MDB, the opposition party, did not care who it presented as its candidates since everyone already knew MDB would lose the elections.

In 1985, the Armed Forces returned the government to civilian rule. Since then, Brazilians have had elections for every political office or issue. Today, Brazil is a republic run by three independent powers: the Executive, the Legislature, and the Judiciary. Voting is mandatory for Brazilians between 18 and 70; however, the country amended its constitution in 1988 to allow 16- and 17-year olds to vote voluntarily [5]. Thus, every eligible Brazilian votes to elect the president who holds executive power. The governor of each state is elected by the citizens of that state, and the mayor of each city elected by the citizens of the city. The president, state governors, as well as city mayors, all have 4-year terms, and they can be reelected once. The legislature is composed of the House of Representatives (Congress) and the Senate. Citizens of each state elect their senators for an 8-year term; while members are elected for a 4-year term [1]. The Judiciary is in charge of evaluating and applying the law. There are judges at several levels, with the highest level, the "Tribunal Superior da Justiça," being equivalent to the US Supreme Court. Appointed by the president and subject to the Congress, this higher court is the only court that can judge elected officials [5].

In 2002, Luiz Inácio Lula da Silva, known as "Lula," a member of the Workers' Party, became President of Brazil and was reelected in 2006. In 2010, Dilma Rousseff, also a member of the Workers' Party under Lula, became the first woman to be elected president. Rousseff was reelected in 2014 for a new 4-year term that ends in 2018. However, in May 2016, Rousseff was suspended from office when the Brazilian Senate voted 55 to 22 to try her on charges of manipulating the budget. Despite the fact that she was not charged with corruption, Rousseff was impeached and removed from office in August 2016, in what she referred to as a "parliamentary coup" [6].

Brazilian Cultural Dimensions

The word *culture* is derived from a general sense of how different people live. It refers to how people think, feel, and act. Culture is defined as "the collective programming of the mind distinguishing the members of one group or category of people from another" [7]. The category includes nations, regions within or across nations, ethnicities, religions, occupations, organizations, or the genders. Culture is "the unwritten rules of the social game."

Hofstede notes that national cultures seldom change; rather, what changes "in response to changing circumstances are practices: symbols, heroes, and rituals, leaving the underlying values untouched" [7]. Hence, this concept helps in understanding the Brazilian Government's response to this case study.

Hofstede's Cultural Dimension of National Culture #1-*Power Distance* concept refers to the extent to which power is distributed unequally. Power distance is the extent to which the less powerful members of organizations and institutions (like the family) accept and expect that power is distributed unequally [8]. Because of this power difference and expectations, those at the top of society are not much concerned about the ones at the bottom; meanwhile, the ones at the bottom do not expect much from the ones on top. Hofstede, in his 1970s study of 40 countries, found Brazil to rank as a high power distance country [9]. Brazil exemplifies Hofstede's Power Distance concept because it is an elitist society where the rich dominate and the poor know and accept their place.

Brazilian political culture, much like its business culture, is considered paternalistic—a superior/subordinate relationship, in which the superior guides and protects and the subordinate is loyal and respectful [10, 11]. This paternalism has been the norm in Brazil even before independence; therefore, in order to analyze Brazil's response to crisis, one must understand the nexus between Brazilian culture and politics.

Culture and Politics: Being a Politician Has Its Privileges

Most people become politicians to improve the lives of their citizens. It is no different in Brazil. However, there are also some in Brazil who enter politics due to the benefits accorded to Brazilian politicians. For such persons, seeking political office is a quick and easy way to riches. Among the multitude of advantages of an elected office holder are political power, high income, and every imaginable privilege. Politicians usually have a fully maintained government car, telephones, air tickets, even for private trips, full health insurance, housing, and full payment of salary for life, even if he or she is dismissed for misconduct. Other benefits like assistants, consultants, private drivers, free transportation all around the country, priority in airplanes, are also provided. For many years, elected officials could even hire relatives and friends for government jobs; however, that privilege is now illegal.

In 1979, just before the end of military rule, politicians who had been exiled by the military government were granted amnesty by the Brazilian Government [12]. This amnesty resulted in a tidal wave of returnee former politicians who, playing on the desire of the population to be free from military dictatorship, formed several political parties that quickly became popular. Given the paternalistic nature of the culture, politicians pledged to provide more freedom and better economic conditions for all in exchange for loyalty and votes from the citizens. They campaigned and easily won elections.

In reality, a majority of these politicians just wanted the benefits of public office for themselves and their families. It is no surprise that Brazilians do not trust politicians. In fact, Brazilians consider politicians unreliable. Every year, IBOPE (Instituto Brasileiro de Opinião Pública e Estatística—in Portuguese) or the Brazilian Institute of Public Opinion and Statistics conducts a nationwide opinion research ranking Brazilians' confidence in major Brazilian institutions. Results of the 2015 study showed that Brazilians consider firefighters, the church, and the military most reliable, in that order; whereas, they find the Federal Government, the National Congress, and political parties the least reliable, also in that order [13].

Since early 2015, national political crises and government corruption have involved ministers of the Federal Government, Congress, and the Senate, and many private companies working for national oil company, Petrobras. The federal police has investigated and prosecuted many CEOs and high level officers of these private companies; however, politicians involved in the corruption scandals have not been investigated. Brazilian law grants not only privileges to politicians, but also protection from prosecution. One of the laws states that high level politicians may only be prosecuted by the Tribunal Superior de Justiça—the Higher Court of Justice. This two-tier system of justice does not engender confidence in the Brazilian political system.

While mandatory voting for political leaders (with some exception) is part of the Brazilian culture, it is also part of the culture that, after taking office, almost nothing can be done to politicians irrespective of how they conduct themselves. In 2015, approximately 273 out of 513 members of Congress and 45 out of 81 senators had civil cases pending in forums all over the country, but they may not be judged, except by the Higher Supreme Court [14]. This provision in the law makes it easy for politicians, especially at the municipal government and mayoral levels, to reward their families, friends, and supporters with official positions after each election. Their objective is to build relationships and networks with people who can help them maintain their positions in power, so that they can keep on making money.

This practice of political benevolence extends to approval for the construction of commercial and residential buildings. Project approvals are expedited if the contractor bribes the civil servant or political appointee as exemplified by the wave of high level corruption scandals that are now public [15, 16]. Such euphemisms as "give away something" are often used to describe the transactions between contractors and city officials. Sometimes, the officials can make specific demands (purportedly prescribed by technical personnel) in order to bring one's project to priority position. In Brazilian culture, most people understand and accept "Jeitinho"—a way to achieve a goal by skirting rules or social conventions, in this case, speeding up the process of attaining a favorable contract [17]. The concept of "Jeitinho Brasileiro" or the "Brazilian way of doing things" is derived from the expression "dar um jeito," which means "find a way." The International Football Federation, FIFA, even adopted the slogan as an anthem for the 2014 World Cup hosted by Brazil [18].

In Brazilian culture, most people understand and accept "Jeitinho"—a way to achieve a goal by skirting rules or social conventions, in this case, speeding up the process of attaining a favorable contract [17]. The concept of "Jeitinho Brasileiro" or the "Brazilian way of doing things" is derived from the expression "dar um jeito," which means "find a way."

The concept of Jeitinho is very attractive to political candidates because they know that these "helpers" in such positions will have many "followers" just because of the vast dispensation of political favors. Therefore, these "helpers" become useful for future election campaigns. Ostensibly, public officials from mayors to governors officially claim ignorance of Jeitinho; thus, they would not dismiss errant officials just for a few infractions. For instance, a mayor knows that as a politician, he or she will probably need these same people as campaign supporters in future elections. Additionally, such behaviors are not perceived as terrible crimes because political parties routinely benefit from these procedures.

Home Ownership and Politics

Brazilians are always eager to vote, mainly in presidential elections. Before the Republican political system of 1889, one needed to own property in order to vote. It literally meant that one would not be considered a citizen without land or home ownership [19].

Until 1950, majority of Brazilians did not own property; most families lived in rentals. Therefore, owning a home became everyone's highest dream. This quest led to the evolution of slums in Brazil. Poor homeless people built small shanty houses around the cities or downtown or in the hills, but close to their work places. These tiny homes usually lacked electricity and sanitary facilities. Although the authorities were supposed to inspect every construction to ensure adherence to building codes; in reality, they inspected very few. Of those inspected, much attention was given to expensive buildings, while the cheap houses received minimal or no inspection. Slum constructions fared even worse—they were seldom inspected. Poor people who could not afford to provide valuable favors saw their dream of home ownership fade away. They ended up building without proper inspection or advice. The wealthy, who wanted their homes finished on time, paid to expedite the process.

This practice of "Jeitinho"—a way to achieve a goal by skirting rules or social conventions, was and remains a part of the Brazilian culture [20]. It is understood and accepted by a majority of Brazilians as a way of doing business.

However, the political climate in Brazil is changing. Massive demonstrations have been buoyed by media reports on several corrupt politicians such as Federal Government ministers, the president of the Congress, the president of the Senate, and even former President Lula da Silva, who are under investigation by the Brazilian justice system [21].

Culture and Crisis Communication

Unlike large countries with extensive research in crisis communication, Brazil has negligible research in crisis communication. In fact, few formal research pieces on crisis communication in Brazil exist. A disaster guideline published by Oliveira [22] highlights the need for attention to crisis and risk communication in Brazil. Citing the Niteroi case, he notes that the frequency and "intensity of natural disasters in Brazil" merits serious consideration from the government, politicians, and scientists. A few studies at Brazilian universities and academic papers have also been published [23–25]. Despite the limited number of studies on crisis communication, the government at the three levels—federal, state, and municipal—is concerned with facing and managing natural disasters or accidental crises caused by technical or human errors. Some actions have been taken to improve communities' and companies' awareness of natural disasters and how to respond and protect victims during a crisis [26]. Several government guidelines have also been published on the subject [27]. However, none of these books, papers, or even doctoral theses discusses the importance of crisis communication.

The Case: Bumba Hill, Niterói—Gone with the Mud

With a population of nearly half a million, Niterói is a city in the state of Rio de Janeiro. It is directly across the Guanabara Bay from Rio de Janeiro City. Considered a financial powerhouse with a high quality of life, Niterói is described as comfortable and peaceful, with nice and beautiful beaches, good schools, restaurants, and universities. People commute everyday across the Guanabara Bay to work, study, or do business in either of these two cities. The commute could be a 12-minute trip on a ferryboat, which carries 100,000 people daily [28] or by a 10-mile long bridge that averages 140,000 vehicles daily [29].

The Night of the Disaster

Three days before the disaster in April 2010, the cities surrounding Guanabara Bay were deluged with torrential rains. On Wednesday, April 7, at 8:00 p.m. explosions were heard at a neighborhood called Bumba Hill (Morro do Bumba), a shantytown built on an old landfill in Niterói City. Landslides followed the explosions. As the heavy mud came crashing down the hill, it brought down everything in its path, including bushes, trees, and houses. Electric power outages and continuing heavy rain made emergency help almost impossible in the first hours. This very difficult scenario prevented immediate survivors from running to safety.

The landslide took place in three different sequences with explosions that destroyed houses and caused people to disappear into the mud. Those who had not been buried under the mud and garbage which came up from the soil all at once were found either burned or cut in pieces. Those who had miraculously survived had lost their relatives and neighbors. News reports indicate that about 200 people were buried in the mudslide. The disaster also left 4000 families homeless with thousands more at risk [30]. Some of the dead and missing have not fully been accounted for as of this writing (see Figure 16.1).

The Bomb Underneath the Houses

Landslides were not the worst danger. There was also a potentially deadly cocktail of garbage underneath the houses of which the residents were unaware. Unfortunately,

FIGURE 16.1. Cleanup efforts after the slide. The devastating mud slide buried neighborhoods, houses, and families without remorse. The efforts to clean up the debris from the slide can be seen here. Reproduced with permission of Evaldo Fernandes.

for most poor people who wanted jobs in Rio, this was the neighborhood in which they could afford to live. Although they knew their homes were built atop a landfill, they believed it was safe given that the landfill had not been used for decades; but in reality, the soil was like a bomb ready to be triggered by strong continuous heavy rain [31, 32].

Those houses were unknowingly built over solid residue surface which had been crushed and mixed with rain, water, and a variety of materials such as arsenic, carbon tetrachloride, lead, and organic and inorganic products. The combination of all types of waste and chemicals turned into biogas composed of methane, carbon dioxide, and sulfuric gas [33]. If methane, the main component of this biogas, came into contact with oxygen in the air, it often resulted in an explosion. Thus, it was no surprise that those houses, which had literally been sitting over flammable gas for some time, exploded during the landslide. For the residents of Bumba Hill, the danger of the explosion and eventual fire that destroyed their homes and their lives were attributed to the negligence of government and civil defense.

Stakeholders

Given the kind of crisis in this case study, the whole city of Niterói was strongly affected by this natural disaster. Nonetheless, the main stakeholders were Bumba Hill residents, who were victims or lost loved ones and homes; residents of neighboring streets, whose homes were also built over a disused garbage dump; and Niterói residents who feared that they might be at risk. Niterói sits between the coast and the mountains surrounded by many beautiful beaches. Many unapproved homes dot the mountains.

Other stakeholders included the media, which provided comprehensive live coverage of the unfolding disaster for national and international audience. They were prompt in finding survivors and telling their stories. They also focused on the culpability of the municipal and state governments in allowing people to build their homes on land that was once a garbage dump. The Niterói mayor and the municipal government whose crisis responses were criticized completed the list of stakeholders.

Bumba Hill: Decades-Old Problems

The causes for this disaster date back decades. In 1970, Niterói mayor expropriated an old farm called Fazenda do Saraiva due to nonpayments of municipal taxes [34]. The city turned that land into a garbage deposit. Land and property in the neighborhood lost economic value. The environment also suffered, as trees were cut. The land soon was infested with insects and rodents and the whole area gave off an unpleasant odor, causing people to move away. However, in 1982, the garbage dump was deactivated after having daily received several tons of garbage for 12 years [35]. As trees and bushes grew back, the area became free land to fulfill poor residents' dream of building their own homes. The municipal government cautioned citizens against building houses in that area, despite the return of vegetation. However, the caution fell on deaf ears.

In the early 1990s, as Brazil celebrated the end of military rule, many leftist leaders were elected as state governors and city mayors, including Rio de Janeiro state, PDT Party Governor Leonel Brizola and PDT Party Niterói Mayor Roberto Silveira [36]. Brizola and Silveira were concerned with providing low-income citizens with more freedom and better life conditions. Thus, they approved construction and development of urbanized slum ("favela") areas. Bumba Hill in Niterói was one of those poor neighborhoods. State and municipal governments helped to build public schools and nurseries, and provided the area with sanitation. Three other special state government projects were developed to urbanize the Bumba Hill area. The government provided electricity ("A Light in the Darkness"—Uma Luz na Escuridão); drinkable water ("Clean and Drinkable Water in the Slums"—Água Limpa e Potável nas Favelas); and the promise of legal papers for their properties ("Each Family, a Plot"—Cada Familia, Um Lote). The government made sure to invite the media so the news about such improvements would be made public. The governor himself intended to run for president, while Niterói Mayor Silveira intended to run for state governor, in subsequent elections [37].

Eager to improve social conditions in that neighborhood and state, municipal leaders had invested in urbanizing the place without checking what lay underneath the poor housing which had been gradually built by homeless people. Government authorities just wanted to finish up any new project, program, or construction improvement so they could inaugurate it.

Government efforts toward urbanizing Bumba Hill led residents to believe they lived in a safe area. People were certain that had there been any danger whatsoever, government would not have provided the area with all those urban amenities. Anyway, warnings about the danger of building in such an area would have gone unheeded, because residents believed the government would not allow them to live there if it were unsafe.

Crisis: Government Response

A crisis is a sudden and unexpected event that threatens to disrupt an organization's operations and poses both a financial and a reputational threat [38]. Crisis response must be quick and effective. Niterói mayor's response to the crisis was neither fast nor effective. Had he and his assistants acted quickly to contain the disaster, the outcome of the crisis on April 7, 2010 might have been better for most of the stakeholders, for the municipal government, and for himself.

Summer rain is an annual occurrence, so municipal governments should have been prepared for floods and landslides during that period, but they were not. The

Niterói disaster might have been preventable given that it was a combination of heavy rains and houses constructed in unsafe terrain. Residents needed information as to what action to take, but they were told to stay and wait for help. Additionally, the mayor's first priority should have been the residents' safety; instead, he tried to minimize his responsibility by noting that he was not aware Bumba Hill had been a garbage dump in the past.

It is obvious from news reports and government response to the crisis that lack of a strategic plan and the Brazilian paternalistic culture were at work.

The mayor only arrived at the scene 16 hours after the disaster and stayed only briefly. Although his first reaction was to express sympathy, he denied responsibility. He was quoted as saying: "No one held the Asian governors responsible for the [2004] tsunami or the Chileans for the earthquake" [35].

His reaction may be explained by Hofstede's Cultural Dimension of National Culture #1-Power Distance concept, which refers to the extent to which power is unequally distributed [8]. Had the disaster occurred in a rich and well-connected neighborhood, would the mayor have waited 16 hours before showing up? Would the mayor attempt to deny or shift responsibility of the landslide to the terrain and the victims who built their homes on a former landfill? Because of this power difference and expectation, those at the top of society are not too much concerned about the ones at the bottom; meanwhile, the ones at the bottom do not expect much from the ones at the top. Brazil is an elitist society; thus, the mayor's lack of urgency in response to the crisis is not unusual. It simply reinforces the noncommitment to poor people's lives or safety [35].

Additionally, the mayor's slow response to the crisis and denial of responsibility aptly illustrate the culture of Brazilian politicians who look out for their own self-interest and seek ways to perpetuate their stay in power. This behavior is also perhaps influenced by the fact that the Brazilian Constitution protects political authorities from being investigated, convicted, or jailed [39, 40].

While we do not have access to government documents regarding its response to the crises, one can deduce the goals and objectives from the actions and rhetoric by government officials reported in the media [31, 41, 42].

Goal: The overall goal of the crisis response was to contain the crisis and return the situation to normal as soon as possible.

The following objectives, strategies, and tactics are deduced from the media coverage and government actions.

Objective 1: To rescue trapped residents of Niterói, specifically Bumba Hill and neighboring communities

Strategy: The government urged people to stay in their homes.
Tactic: Emergency rescue teams found and identified 16 bodies, although news reports estimated 150–200 bodies were thought to be buried under the mud.

Objective 2: To safeguard citizens of Niterói, especially Bumba Hill and neighboring communities

Strategy: The government made plans to relocate the displaced to safer places.

Tactic: The government moved Bumba Hill residents to different locations far from their work, schools, and churches.

Objective 3: To show concern and compassion for the victims

Strategy: City government dispatched officials to the scene to survey damage.

Tactic: The mayor showed up at the disaster scene 16 hours after the landslide.

Objective 4: To improve living conditions for residents of Bumba Hill

Strategy: Relocate displaced Bumba Hill residents to safer ground.

Tactic: The mayor ordered the bulldozing of 300 homes after the landslide and hired contractors to build new homes elsewhere. The process took 5 years. Residents were unhappy due to the length of time and location of new homes.

Outcome of the Crisis

Since 1999, presidents, governors, and mayors had been given the option of running for a second consecutive term. Mayor Roberto Silveira of Niterói and his staff had controlled the Niterói Municipal Government since 1992, and he sought to be reelected in 2012. Early in the campaign, all the stakeholders (victims, citizens, and especially the media) started a campaign against the mayor and his staff. The media kept pressing him with questions about the Bumba Hill disaster in just about every interview. He ended up having to admit that he had not been efficient in handling the crisis.

> I was not efficient in managing that special crisis in the city. I was disturbed by information that my government knew about the danger caused by the garbage deposit in the Bumba Hill community, and that was not true. So, I became extremely worried since I had never lied to Niterói. I never lied to my citizens. I became too concerned about this condition. At that time, people demanded that the mayor acted as their father, protecting the city when facing the crisis. But I am also a part of the citizens, and I myself was also in crisis, and as everybody else, I felt like a victim too. But now that crisis has passed. It is gone. We need to look ahead. I believe Niterói is getting through that crisis. [43]

The pressure was such that in October of that same year, 2010, Silveira gave up his quest for a second term as mayor. Not only that, his party also lost the election.

It is obvious that the mayor's response exemplifies both Hofstede's Power Distance and the Brazilian paternalistic view of the poor.

The newly elected municipal government became concerned with both planning and being able to take effective action toward diminishing the risk as well as the magnitude of a natural disaster, should it strike the city again.

The houses in Bumba Hill that disappeared under mud and garbage were homes to about 300 families. Five years later, in 2015, only 147 families live in a nearby community under a municipal program called social rent. About 100 other families live in a nearby condominium under the Federal Government "Minha Casa, Minha Vida" (My Home, My Life) program, a public–private partnership whose goal is to reduce the housing crisis among the poor [44]. The program does this by easing credit and financing constraints for the poor and lower middle class. While the program has been praised, it has also been criticized for shoddy housing, faulty electrical wiring, and inability to deliver the minimum number of housing units promised [45].

Subsequent municipal administration established a natural disaster prevention program: the installation of a weather detection system (a meteorological station), an Alarm Aware System (Sistema de Alerta e Alarme), 26 automatic pluviometers for monitoring weather conditions, and the development of an Emergency Exit Plan for neighborhood and areas under risk. The municipal administration also established a natural disaster action training course for the community. Trained community disaster teams are responsible for identifying and reporting dangerous conditions to the Civil Defense Agency as early as possible so that lives could be saved should a disaster occur [46, 47].

The municipal government also founded an extensive program of rainwater control in more than 10 neighborhoods aiming at preventing landslides. The neighborhood reconstruction cost US$20 million. The government also provided an emergency toll free number "199" for phone alert that makes it easy and fast to report disaster conditions [48].

What Should Have Been Done and Potential Outcomes

1. The mayor and his team should have gone to the scene as soon as media started providing information about the disaster. His presence and urgent decisions would have shown his concern about the victims' well-being, lives, and homes.

2. The mayor should have requested additional help for urgent transportation, removal, and care of injured people.

3. The authorities should have immediately gathered all possible information regarding the cause and history of the area in order to show awareness of the

victims' situation as well as to alleviate the victims' immediate and long-term suffering.

4. The authorities should have ensured that most of the information about the disaster came from or was channeled through the municipal government in order to show that there was strong crisis leadership from the mayor.

5. The government should have established a crisis team consisting of members of the municipal government, in collaboration with the Brazilian Red Cross, the fire fighters, the disaster and risk management team, police, and other civil organizations to contain the crisis, provide stakeholders with basic needs (shelter and food), and to support the area.

6. That municipal government's crisis team, which should have been formed, would also have been charged with collaborating with local hospitals and welfare organizations to respond to recovery plans for the victims affected by the natural disaster.

7. The mayor should have continuously answered all questions related to the stakeholders, and presented all the actions and results of the municipal government to improve victims' conditions.

Lessons Learned

This case study highlights certain issues about crisis communication, culture, and politics in Brazil.

1. Political leaders lost what they valued the most—their patronage-based political positions—in their attempt to ignore a crisis that affected a poor community.

2. The politicians' response illustrates the culture of Brazil—one in which an elite cadre at the top plays the role of the benevolent superior, who in turn expects loyalty and service from the subordinate or those in the lowest rung of society. This lack of attention to and care for poor citizens was obviously unacceptable by the stakeholders involved in this crisis. This lack of attention is evident in the unwillingness or inability to enforce building codes that would have saved families; prevented people from building in unsafe areas, and acted quickly to minimize the impact of the crisis on the most vulnerable stakeholders.

3. This is a good example for Brazilian leaders as well as those of other countries with similar relationship between political leaders and the poorest citizens.

4. This crisis case study shows that negligence as well as the culture of negligence by politicians caused the loss of political power for the mayor and his staff.

5. The media are powerful and when they turn against any public official, the consequences could be politically devastating. Mayor Roberto Silveira of Niterói and his staff learned that lesson the hard way.

6. The need for immediate action and the best possible and effective communication are crucial in a crisis situation.

The analysis indicates that the Bumba Hill, Niterói, landslide was partly a result of a terrible series of management misconduct which ignored building of homes in a dangerous terrain; absence of an effective civil defense, risk and crisis management system; and poor political leadership. It damaged a community and the lives of those who lost loved ones and neighbors. Additionally, the Niterói case shares similar characteristics with South and Central American countries where there is a high risk of natural disasters affecting poor people, an elite ruling class with a paternalistic relationship with the poor, and the nonexistence of effective crisis management [49].

It is obvious that an effective crisis plan: (1) prevention—preparing before a crisis occurs; (2) managing—containing and communication during the crisis, and (3) recovery—communicating post-crisis [50], would have made a difference in the outcome of the Niterói case. Most important is the willingness to manage the crisis that affects poor communities. This lack of competence, insensitivity to key stakeholders' concerns, a perpetuation of the Brazilian paternalistic leadership style led to the collapse of a continuous political power base of over 20 years in the Niterói community. The Niterói disaster illustrates the importance of understanding how Brazilian culture affects crisis response.

Discussion Questions

16.1   List and describe three of the most important lessons you have learned about the relationship between Brazilian culture and politics that will guide you if you were to work or do business in Brazil. What steps would you take to avoid cultural pitfalls?

16.2   Describe how the concept of "Jeitinho Brasileiro" is detrimental to effective crisis management. If you were to conduct business in Brazil, how would you handle this? What alternative suggestions would you provide?

16.3   The response of the Niterói Municipal Government and Mayor to the Bumba Hill disaster was ineffective. If you were the public information officer for the city of Niteroi, prepare a detailed outline of a crisis communication plan for use in response to the Bumba Hill disaster.

16.4   What are the lessons of the Niterói disaster and what kind of risk assessment would you propose should be done to mitigate a future occurrence?

References

1. CIA. (2015). "The world factbook-Brazil" [Online]. Available: https://www.cia.gov/library/publications/the-world-factbook/geos/br.html, December 20, 2015 (last day accessed).

2. IBGE. (2015). [Online]. Available: http://www.7a12.ibge.gov.br/voce-sabia/curiosidades/municipios-novos, December 20, 2015 (last day accessed).

3. F. Koifman, *Presidentes do Brasil*. Universidade Estacio de Sá-São Paulo: Cultura editores, 2002.

4. J. E. Hahner, "The beginnings of the women's suffrage movement in Brazil," *Signs*, vol. 5, no. 1, pp. 200–204, 1979.

5. R. A. Hudson, ed. (1997). *Brazil: A Country Study*. Washington: GPO for the Library of Congress. [Online]. Available: http://www.countrystudies-us/brazil/100.htm, December 20, 2016 (last date accessed).

6. J. Watts and D. Bowater (Sept. 1, 2016) "Brazil's Dilma Rousseff impeached by Senate in crushing defeat," *The Guardian*, [Online]. Available: https://www.theguardian.com/world/2016/aug/31/dilma-rousseff-impeached-president-brazilian-senate-michel-temer, May 31, 2017 (last day accessed).

7. G. Hofstede. (2015). "Culture" [Online]. Available: http://www.geerthofstede.nl/culture, December 20, 2015 (last date accessed).

8. G. Hofstede. (2015). "Dimensions of national culture" [Online]. Available: http://www.geerthofstede.nl/dimensions-of-national-cultures, December 20, 2015 (last date accessed).

9. G. Hofstede. (2015). "Brazil" [Online]. Available: https://geert-hofstede.com/brazil.html, February 20, 2016 (last day accessed).

10. A. Ardichvili, D. Jondle, J. Wiley, et al. "Building ethical business cultures: BRIC by BRIC," *The European Business Review*, March 10, 2013. [Online]. Available: http://www.europeanbusinessreview.com/?p=1930, December 20, 2015 (last date accessed).

11. R. C. Silva and A. C. Chen. "Diana: A multi-nation study of news values and practices," in *International Communication Bulletin*, EUA, vol. 36, nos. 3–4, pp. 2–15, 2002.

12. L. Paim, "Anistia traz de volta os exilados e torna real o sonho da redemocratização," *Sul 21*, April 4, 2014. [Online]. Available: http://www.sul21.com.br/jornal/anistia-traz-de-volta-os-exilados-e-torna-real-o-sonho-da-redemocratizacao, December 20, 2015 (last date accessed).

13. R. Azevedo, "Em quem os brasileiros mais confiam," *Exame*, July 31, 2015. [Online]. Available: http://www.exame.abril.com.br/brasil/noticias/em-quos-brasileiros-mais-confiam, December 20, 2015 (last date accessed).

14. I. Franco, "Panorama político: Na linha de tiro," *Jornal O Globo*, August 23, 2015, p. 2.

15. S. Eisenhammer, "Brazil corruption probe threatens Rio Olympics preparations," *Reuters*, July 31, 2015. [Online]. Available: http://www.reuters.com/article/us-olympics-construction-petrobras-idUSKCN0Q51LL20150731, January 20, 2016 (last date accessed).

16. L. Magalhaes, "Brazil judge sentences OAS executives over Petrobras corruption scandal," *Wall Street Journal*, August 5, 2015. [Online]. Available: http://www.wsj.com/articles/brazil-judge-sentences-oas-executives-over-petrobras-corruption-scandal-1438817426, January 20, 2016 (last date accessed).

17. R. Levine, *Brazilian Legacies*. New York: M. E. Sharpe, 1997.

18. "FIFA World Cup chooses 'Dar um Jeito (We will find a way)' as official anthem," *Global News*, March 28, 2014. [Online]. Available: http://globalnews.ca/news/1237257/fifa-world-cup-chooses-dar-um-jeito-we-will-find-a-way-as-official-anthem/, January 16, 2016 (last date accessed).

19. T. E. Skidmore, *Uma História do Brasil*. São Paulo: Paz e Terra S.A., 1998, p. 107.

20. R. Levine, *Brazilian Legacies*. New York: M. E. Sharpe, 1997.

21. J. Watts. (2016, Mar 13). "More than a million Brazilians protest against 'horror' government" [Online]. Available: http://www.theguardian.com/world/2016/mar/13/brazil-anti-government-protests-dilma-rousseff-rio-de-janeiro, May 13, 2016 (last day accessed).

22. M. D. Oliveira, *Manual de gerenciamento de desastres*. SC, Brasil: CEPED-Universidade Federal de Santa Catarina, 2009.

23. J. H. Souza, "Sistemática para priorização de atendimentos emergenciais de engenharia," Tese de doutorado, Universidade Federal Fluminense, Niterói, RJ, 2015.

24. G. Santos, "Metodologia para avaliação de áreas susceptívies à escorregamento de solo," Tese de doutorado, Universidade Federal Fluminense, Niterói, RJ, 2015.

25. A. M. A. Pinto and S. Wainer, "Examining 2007 São Paulo City subway line 4 construction site accident," in *Proceedings of the 2011 IAJC-ASEE International Conference*, Nashville, TN, 2008.

26. S. B. Araújo, *Administração de desastres. Engenharia de segurança*. Rio de Janeiro, Brasil: Sygma Fire Protection Engineering, 2010.

27. M. D. Oliveira, *Curso de gestão integrada em defesa civil*. Ministério da Integração Nacional, Secretaria Nacional de Defesa Civil, 161 pages, Brasilia, DF, 2010.

28. CCR Barcas. (2015). [Online]. Available: http://www.grupoccr.com.br/barcas, January 16, 2016 (last date accessed).

29. P. Henrique and Z. Ventura, *Rio Ponte Niteroi*. Brazil: Editora Melhoramentos, Ltda, 2003.

30. "Fresh Brazil landslide leaves 200 feared buried," *BBC News*. [Online]. Available: http://news.bbc.co.uk/2/hi/americas/8608718.stm, January 20, 2016 (last date accessed).

31. Associated Press. (2010, April 8). "200 believed buried in deadly Brazil landslides," cited in *New York Daily News*. Available: http://www.nydailynews.com/news/world/200-believed-buried-deadly-brazil-landslides-article-1.165629, January 20, 2016 (last date accessed).

32. "200 Feared Buried in Brazil Mudslides," *CBS News.com*, April 8, 2010. [Online]. Available: http://www.cbsnews.com/news/200-feared-buried-in-brazil-mudslides/

33. U.S. Energy Information Administration. (n.d.). "Landfill gas and biogas" [Online]. Available: http://www.eia.gov/Energyexplained/?page=biomass_biogas, December 20, 2015 (last date accessed).

34. M. N. S. Azevedo, "Risco das Águas de Março: O Morro do Bumba em Niterói," Anais do I encontro Nacional da Associação Nacional de Pesquisa e Pós-Graduação em Arquitetura e Urbanismo, Rio de Janeiro, 2010.

35. M. Fox, "Rio de Janeiro's Katrina: Rains, tragedy and segregation," *Axis of Logic*, April 30, 2010. Available: http://axisoflogic.com/artman/publish/Article_59638.shtml, January 20, 2016 (last date accessed).

36. L. Paim, "Anistia traz de volta os exilados e torna real o sonho da Redemocratização," *Sul 21*, April 4, 2014. [Online]. Available: http://www.sul21.com.br/jornal/anistia-traz-de-volta-os-exilados-e-torna-real-o- sonho-da-redemocratizacao, December 20, 2015 (last date accessed).

37. O. Manaschy and A. Oseas, *Vida e Obra de Leonel de Moura Brizola*. Rio de Janeiro: PDT-RO, 2011.

38. T. Coombs, "Protecting organization reputations during a crisis: The development and application of situational crisis communication theory," *Corporate Reputation Review*, vol. 10, pp.163–176, 2007.

39. A. Secco, "Im(p)unidade," *Veja*, July 12, 2000. [Online]. Available: http://veja.abril.com .br, January 20, 2016 (last date accessed).

40. D. L. J. Rodrigues, "Imunidade parlamentar: A impunidade continua?" *Ordem dos Advogados do Brasil*, August 18, 2006. [Online]. Available: http://boletimjuridico.com/ doutrina/texto.asp?id=977, May 31, 2017 (last date accessed).

41. A. Barrionuevo, "Rescuers work to save scores buried in a Brazil landslide," *New York Times*, April 8, 2010. [Online]. Available: http://www.nytimes.com/2010/04/09/ world/americas/09brazil.html, January 20, 2016 (last date accessed).

42. A. Brasileiro, "Rio residents told to stay home as flooding kills 95," *Bloomberg News*, April 6, 2010. [Online]. Available: http://www.bloomberg.com/news/articles/2010-04-06/rio-mayor-urges-people-to-stay-home-as-rains-kill-25-flood-neighborhoods, January 20, 2016 (last date accessed).

43. L. Valle, "Niterói sob influência de Plutão, Urano e Netuno," *O Globo*, April 4, 2012. [Online]. Available: http://oglobo.globo.com/rio/niteroi-sob-influencia-de-plutao-urano-netuno-4649544, December 20, 2015 (last date accessed).

44. B. Camboriu, "If you build it: A scheme to promote working-class home owner-ship is off to a good start," *The Economist*, February 16, 2013. [Online]. Available: http://www.economist.com/news/americas/21571893-scheme-promote-working-class-home-ownership-good-start-if-you-build-it, December 20, 2015 (last date accessed).

45. G. Ribeiro, "Cinco anos depois da tragédia no Morro do Bumba, famílias vivem em casas condenadas pela Defesa Civil," *Jornal EXTRA*, April 5, 2015. [Online]. Available: http://extra.globo.com/noticias/rio/cinco-anos-depois-da-tragedia-no-morro-do-bumba-familias-vivem-em-casas-condenadas-pela-defesa-civil-15780575.html, December 20, 2015 (last date accessed).

46. A. Barrionuevo, "After deadly mudslides in Brazil, concern turns to preparedness," *New York Times*, January 16, 2011. [Online]. Available: http://www.nytimes.com/2011/01/17/ world/americas/17brazil.html?_r=0, December 20, 2015 (last date accessed).

47. L. Flueckiger, "Niterói receives weather warning system," *The Rio Times*, September 17, 2013. [Online]. Available: http://riotimesonline.com/brazil-news/rio-politics/niteroi-receives-weather-warning-system/, January 20, 2016 (last date accessed).

48. G. Ribeiro, "Cinco anos depois da tragédia no Morro do Bumba, famílias vivem em casas condenadas pela Defesa Civil," *Jornal EXTRA*, April 5, 2015. [Online]. Available: http://extra.globo.com/noticias/rio/cinco-anos-depois-da-tragedia-no-morro-do-bumba-familias-vivem-em-casas-condenadas-pela-defesa-civil-15780575.html, December 20, 2015 (last date accessed).

49. United Nations Office for Disaster Risk Reduction – Regional Office for the Americas (UNISDR AM). (2015, November 27). "Americas hit hard by El Niño" [Online]. Available: https://www.unisdr.org/archive/46864, January 16, 2016 (last date accessed).

50. A. M. George and C. B. Pratt, *Case Studies in Crisis Communication: International Perspectives on Hits and Misses*. New York: Routledge, 2012.

Colombia and Guatemala

17

When Conflict Shifts: An Analysis of Chiquita Brands' Transnational Crises in Colombia and Guatemala

Juan-Carlos Molleda and Gabriel C. Stephen

Chapter Preview

The Chiquita Brands' crisis focuses on two countries in Latin America—Colombia and Guatemala— and represents a very good example of a transboundary crisis. The case involves US-based transnational corporation (TNC) Chiquita Brands International®, which was involved in crises originating in Colombia and Guatemala, each of which rapidly spread to the United States with different consequences in each respective nation. As these crises shifted from the corporation's host countries (Colombia and Guatemala) to Chiquita's home country (the United States), and the organization adopted certain specific and controlled public relations and communication strategies and tactics to try and address these challenging situations. The case is important because it demonstrates (a) the need to understand crises in the context of global public relations in a globalizing world, (b) TNCs need to understand how cross-national conflict shifts happen. Corporations need to have the ability to develop a "glocal" strategy that

Culture and Crisis Communication: Transboundary Cases from Nonwestern Perspectives, First Edition.
Edited by Amiso M. George and Kwamena Kwansah-Aidoo.
© 2017 by The Institute of Electrical and Electronics Engineers, Inc. Published 2017 by John Wiley & Sons, Inc.

responds to the needs and concerns of different publics in the home and host
countries. They can use Cross-National Conflict Shifting Theory (CNCS) as a basis
for building a practical framework for addressing transnational crises.
After reading this chapter, you will be able to

- *Describe the CNCS and its application*
- *Identify the roles of culture in crisis communication practice*
- *Discuss effective crisis response strategies with reference to Image Restoration Theory*
- *Explain the importance of a "glocalized" response plan*
- *Summarize the role of communication in transnational crises*

Introduction

Since 2007, the US-based TNC Chiquita Brands International has been involved in crises originating in Colombia and Guatemala, each of which rapidly spread to the United States with different consequences in each respective nation. In Colombia, the crisis became public when Chiquita disclosed, in the United States, that it had paid $1.7 million to paramilitary groups in the South American nation. In Guatemala, a crisis arose when a Seattle-based nonprofit organization filed a lawsuit alleging that Chiquita was responsible for water contamination near schools and homes. This chapter describes these crises, the way they shifted from the corporation's host countries (Colombia and Guatemala) to Chiquita's home country (the United States), and the specific controlled public relations and communication strategies and tactics followed by Chiquita to face those challenging situations.

Understanding these crises in the context of global public relations is essential. In a globalizing world, TNCs need to understand how cross-national conflict shifts happen. These corporations need to have the ability to develop a "glocal" strategy that responds to the needs and concerns of different publics in the home and host countries. In this regard, Taylor [1] said

> Globalization means that what happens to an organization in one part of the world will affect the organization in other parts of the world. The implications for public relations are clear: successful organizations must understand the intercultural and international aspects of public relations.

To provide a practical framework for addressing these transnational crises, the CNCS is used for analysis from a global public relations perspective. Corporate responses to the crises in both countries will be compared to the 10 theoretical propositions of the CNCS theory.

Cross-National Conflict Shifting Theory (CNCS)

In the global public relations field, CNCS explains how a TNC may face crisis that originates at an international operation (host country) and then transfers to the country where the corporation has its headquarter (home country). CNCS posits that a crisis that starts in a host country has consequences in both host and home country environments; in some cases, a crisis may even have consequences in other countries or markets where the TNC operates or is well known. These types of transnational crises can impact more than just an organization's reputation; the legal and financial stability of a TNC in home and host locations is simultaneously threatened. Molleda [2] provided a definition of CNCS.

> Cross-national conflict shifting (CNCS) is the transfer of incidents or crises faced by a transnational corporation (TNC) from the country where the situation originates to another or multiple world countries where the TNC is headquartered or executes major operations. Reversed CNCS is when the conflicting situation occurs in the home country where the main office of the TNC functions and shifts to other host environments.

The CNCS theory was first introduced by Molleda and Connolly-Ahern [3] who analyzed different transnational crises—including those by Taylor [1] and Frietag [4]—concerning culturally-driven responses of European publics and the nature of international news coverage. The CNCS theory, which explains that crises are not isolated to the country where they originated, was then expanded by Molleda and Quinn [5] who used case studies to articulate the characteristics of a transnational crisis, the way a local conflict reaches home and transnational stakeholders, and the list of publics involved or impacted by the transnational conflict almost simultaneously. Molleda and Quinn said

> A national issue can become international in an instant, impacting host, home, and transnational publics. Public relations professionals practicing in more than one country are challenged by conflicts that impact their organizations' or clients' activities and reputation in more than one location at the same time. [5]

Molleda and Quinn [5] presented 10 propositions that constituted the basic principles of the CNCS theory in global public relations. After years of refining through empirically supported qualitative and quantitative testing through several studies [2, 6–11], the 10 theoretical propositions were revised and reorganized by Molleda [2] to state the following:

1. CNCSs are mainly related to corporate social performance issues, negative economic consequences of globalization, actions of home or host countries'

governments, and diplomatic or trade conflicts among countries of the world where transnational organizations (TNOs) operate.

2. National conflicts shift to the international arena when primarily global non-government organizations (NGOs) or media report the situation to audiences in different world locations, as well as when common citizens creatively use emergent communication technologies to denounce the conflict situation. However, there will be occasions during which the TNO itself alerts home authorities to improper actions in which it is involved in other countries. Similarly, home authorities could uncover, prosecute, and punish TNOs for their businesses overseas.

3. CNCSs with a great human interest focus are likely to be shifted to be of interest to the international community and will attract greater attention of home, host, and transnational stakeholders.

4. Direct involvement of a TNO in a CNCS will produce greater consequences and demand a more comprehensive set of responses and public relations techniques and efforts than an organization that is embedded in a multi-industry consortium or business partnership or is indirectly related to the crisis.

5. TNOs that produce or commercialize tangible, boycottable products or are led by high profile executives are more likely to receive attention by home, host, and transnational publics than those who produce and commercialize intangible services, and whose top executives do not have a high profile position outside the organization.

6. The magnitude of a CNCS will increase when it starts in an emergent or developing economy because of the greater pressure the TNO will face in both host and home countries and from the transnational activist community.

7. A greater number of involved parties will characterize a CNCS in which a developed nation's TNO is the principal participant of the crisis because they will be better known and have greater global impact than those organizations from emergent or developing economies progressively expanding to host locations.

8. The life of a conflict that occurs in developed nations, often where its headquarters are located, will be shorter and will produce low or no impact in host countries when the incident only involves home consumers and/or legal actions and the organization has been proactive in self-denouncing its wrongdoings or accepting blame. In contrast, the crisis will last longer when it involves corporate wrongdoing in host countries and is punished at home by regulatory authorities.

9. Therefore, a lower number of involved parties will characterize a CNCS in which a developing nation or emergent economy organization is the principal responsible for the crisis situation.

10. TNOs headquartered in developed nations that produce or are part of a conflict situation in host locations will attract significant attention from global NGOs, international regulatory bodies, national governments, organized citizen groups, and international newswire agencies and global media outlets.

Research on CNCS has also shed light on the type of media coverage that occurs when a transnational crisis develops, including the use of sources, the amount of news detail, the focus, and the type of quotes used in the news stories. The most interesting findings note that the use of sources, the amount of detail, the focus, and the type of quotes used in the news stories will significantly vary according to the country where the news story originates. In plain words: The media will cover the crisis differently according to the country where the media operates and the prominence of the TNC involved in the situation, which may indicate the need for focused and contextual corporate responses to the crisis.

Kim and Molleda [6] found that publics in host countries perceive and frame transnational crises differently than home country locations. And Molleda and Quinn concluded that "a greater understanding of cross-national conflict shifting would allow a TNO to avoid or diminish the negative effects of conflicts or crises that originate in one of its subsidiaries or offices in a host country" [5].

Globalization requires organizations to consider international cultures and the implications of culture on business operations in both home and host countries. Cross-cultural studies in marketing, public relations, and advertising are plentiful (see 12–14]) and, as a result, there are numerous approaches to defining the characteristics of culture. Cultural dimensions (i.e., categorized patterns of values and beliefs) are commonly used to compare the characteristics of culture [12]. Varying levels of culture—from organizational to national to continental—have provided numerous frameworks for evaluating dimensions of culture [12]. Hofstede's cultural dimensions have been the most salient tool used to compare cultures. Terlutter, Diehl, and Mueller outlined the dimensions.

> Power Distance, societal desire for hierarchy or egalitarianism; individualism, society's preference for a group or individual orientation; masculinity vs. femininity, a sex-role dimension; and uncertainty avoidance, a culture's tolerance for uncertainty. Later research resulted in the addition of a fifth dimension, long-term orientation [...], the cultural perspective on a longterm vs. a short-term basis. [14]

According to Hofstede's dimensions of culture, both Colombian and Guatemalan cultures are collectivistic with high power distance and high uncertainty avoidance [15]. An interpretation of the scores generally indicates that as collectivistic cultures, people are in-group oriented—emphasizing the importance of loyalty, family, and close friends [15,16]. High power distance scores indicate a relatively high level of comfort with inequality in society and government [15]. Lastly, high uncertainty avoidance scores indicate a low tolerance of ambiguity; this characteristic may be manifested in the desire for conservation and order, which may come in the form of religion or detailed rules to govern society [15].

The political and civil travails of Colombia and Guatemala have influenced the cultures of the Latin American countries [17–20]. Historically, both countries—as many other regions throughout Latin America—had been occupied and acculturated by the Spaniards for nearly three centuries [17, 18], respectively, each country has been significantly shaped by that European influence [19]. For example, ethnicity is used as a measure of social status or caste of families and individuals [19,20]. Generally, whites (unmixed European heritage) and mestizos (mix of European and indigenous heritage) comprise the upper class, occupy urban areas, work in white-collar professions, and have a disproportionate share of national wealth and political power [19,20]. Just as the Europeans were the controlling groups during colonization, white and fair skin is still associated with wealth and having a place of prominence in the community [20]. Meanwhile, Garífunas (African/Caribbean descent) and indigenous people (natives) are commonly considered to be lower class, live predominantly in the coastal or remote regions, work in agriculture or trade industries, and typically live in poverty [19].

Historically, Colombia and Guatemala were both plagued by government corruption, leading to radicalization and the formation of anti-government guerilla groups [20]. Even in the mid-twentieth century, Chiquita was involved in a transnational crisis in Guatemala. In 1954, Chiquita (then called the United Fruit Company) was at the center of Guatemalan government collapse [21]. Following the strategy set forth by Edward Bernays—the founding father of public relations—the TNC assisted in the instigation of a national revolution; by manipulating the CIA into taking covert action against the left-leaning government, Chiquita sought to protect business interests threatened by new leadership [21].

Government corruption, regardless of the cause, led to civil unrest between government and insurgent groups. In Guatemala, violence from anti-government guerilla groups went on for decades; in Colombia guerilla activity was so pervasive that violent crimes are commonly referred to as *sangre muertes* or blood deaths [17, 18, 20]. With funding from drug cartels and funding from locals (collected as taxes), guerilla movements have become terror organizations for people in rural areas (i.e., Garífunas and natives) [20]. Tracing the post-colonial history and cultural dimensions of these Latin American countries informs the analysis of Chiquita's crises in each respective territory.

Case Study—Chiquita Brands and Its Transnational Crisis Originated in Colombia

The transnational crisis for Chiquita in Colombia started in 2003 [22]. The peak of the crisis came when Chiquita alerted the US Department of Justice that it has been paying paramilitary groups for the last 7 years through its Colombian subsidiary, Banadex, to protect the safety of employees, most likely from guerilla groups. Chiquita sold Banadex in 2004. In March of 2007, US federal prosecutors charged Chiquita with "doing business with a terrorist organization," saying that the corporation agreed to pay about $1.7 million between 1997 and 2004 to an organization that, in 2001, was identified by the US government as a terrorist group [23]. Confronting these charges, Chiquita pleaded guilty in the US District Court in Washington, DC to one count of doing business with a terrorist organization. The company said that it was "forced to make payments to ensure workers' safety," but agreed to pay a $25 million fine [23].

Between June and November of 2007, human rights groups and relatives of victims allegedly killed or injured by paramilitary groups in Colombia that received payments from Chiquita's former subsidiary filed lawsuits against the company. Four civil lawsuits were filed in US federal courts in the District of Columbia, Florida, New Jersey, and New York. The lawsuits claimed that Chiquita should be held legally responsible for the deaths of hundreds, maybe thousands of people in Colombia because of the support received by the paramilitary groups through the payments given by the then Ohio-based TNC (currently headquartered in Charlotte, NC). One of the three civil suits sought a total of $7.86 billion in unspecified damages for nearly 400 plaintiffs [23]. Another one of the three suits asked for more than $13 billion for 600 plaintiffs [22].

In February 2008, all four lawsuits were transferred to the US District Court in Miami, FL. Chiquita lawyers have insisted that the money the company paid over a 7 year period to the right-wing United Self-Defense Forces of Colombia (AUC, Spanish acronym) has no direct connection to the criminal acts committed by AUC in the region [22]. Chiquita has also admitted to paying the left-wing Revolutionary Armed Forces of Colombia, or FARC. The United States lists both as terrorist groups who engage in murder, torture, kidnappings, and violence [22]. The lawsuits also claim that Chiquita allegedly provided AUC with cash, weapons (such as AK-47s), military supplies, and access to the banana ports for trafficking cocaine [22]. With this material support, according to the lawyers of the hundreds of Colombian plaintiffs, AUC injured or killed Colombian labor leaders, attacked FARC guerrillas, and became "rulers" of a region formed by about 200 Chiquita farms. The lawsuits were brought under the Alien Tort Act. It allows non-US citizens to make claims in US courts for acts that violate international law [22]. In July 2014, US federal appeals court dismissed the lawsuit against Chiquita, finding that the case was out of the court's jurisdiction [24].

Case Study—Chiquita Brands and Its Transnational Crisis Originated in Guatemala

The transnational crisis for Chiquita in Guatemala started in late 2013 [25]. The crisis became salient when a Seattle-based nonprofit organization—Water and

Sanitation Health (WASH)—sued Chiquita with allegations of misleading consumers with inaccurate marketing claims [25]. According to WASH, Chiquita made false claims about the environmental soundness and sustainability of its operations, a practice also known as *greenwashing* [25]. The lawsuit alleged that "Chiquita's millions of pounds of bananas are produced in ways that harm ecosystems and contaminate water supplies" [26]. WASH alleged that the organization would not have purchased thousands of bananas from Chiquita if not for the TNCs inaccurate portrayal of environmentally responsible and sustainable farming [25].

In October 2013 and May 2014, legal representatives of WASH surveyed a number of Chiquita's growing operations in Guatemala [25]. Water samples collected from farms in southern Guatemala were found to have had unsafe levels of pollutants—in some cases, 10 times above safe levels for consumption—including, pesticides, herbicides, and fungicides [25]. Chemical residue was found near community playgrounds and schools—where locals reported sicknesses from rashes to vomiting [25]. By December 2014, Chiquita had reached a settlement with WASH for an undisclosed sum—preventing further legal action from the nonprofit against the corporation—but the precedent of the settlement set the stage for more lawsuits from other complainants against Chiquita and its partners in Guatemala [25].

From the beginning of 2015, Seattle-based law firm Hagens Berman has filed numerous class action lawsuits against Chiquita Brands—in one case, seeking as much as $5 million in damages [27–29]. Hagens Berman attorneys have encouraged California residents, who purchased Chiquita bananas, to consult with the firm about taking legal action [29]. Attorneys claimed that Chiquita knowingly hide environmentally destructive business practices from the public at the expense of the Guatemalan people and ecosystem [29]. The firm estimated that as many as 7200 people have been affected by contamination caused by Chiquita partners and subsidiaries [27].

Chiquita's Responses to the Crises

Part of understanding a transnational crisis involves understanding the types of responses that a TNC provides during the conflict. In this case, Benoit and Brinson's [30] typology of corporate apologies—part of Image Restoration Theory—is used to categorize Chiquita's responses in Latin America and in the United States as either denial of the situation, blame shifting, evading responsibility arguing that there was provocation, evading responsibility arguing that there were good intentions involved, reducing the offensiveness of the event by minimizing the importance of the situation, offering corrective action, showing mortification (admitting the wrongful act and asking for forgiveness), or other crisis response [31].

Official responses came from the Chiquita headquarters in Ohio for the crisis in Colombia, and from the relocated headquarters in North Carolina for the crisis in Guatemala. The goal of Chiquita's response to the crisis in Colombia was to repair and/or maintain the TNCs positive reputation to the public. The corporation's objectives were to cooperate with the US courts during the prosecution with minimal pushback, and to be transparent in communicating Chiquita's role in the crisis. To accomplish the goals and objectives during this crisis, Chiquita's strategy was to garner sympathy for the corporation; Chiquita sought to endear the organization to the public by portraying the company as another victim of paramilitary extortion. According to Image Restoration Theory, Chiquita utilized two types of responses in Colombia: evading responsibility by arguing that there were good intentions involved and evading responsibility by arguing that there was provocation of the paramilitary groups.

Chiquita commonly argued that the company was not at fault for the crisis, because the TNC was forced by paramilitary groups to pay for the protection of employees [31]. In a high profile interview with CBS' 60 Minutes, Chiquita's CEO Fernando Aguirre explained that the payments were used to save the lives of their employees stating, "these lands were lands where there was no law. It was impossible for the government to protect employees. [...] The responsibility of any murders are the responsibility of the people that made the killings, of the people who pulled the trigger" [32].

Chiquita's corporate response was stronger in the United States than in Colombia. For news reports in the United States, corporate responses were more frequently reported and came directly from then CEO Fernando Aguirre (in two statements released in 2007 and 2008). Those tactics indicate a tightly managed, centralized corporate response—the implications of which meant that the Colombian media had only limited or indirect access to the corporate response.

The goal of Chiquita's responses to the crisis in Guatemala was to maintain the reputation of an environmentally responsible organization in the public eye. To meet the organization's goal, Chiquita's objective was to minimize the legitimacy of the conflict in the public eye by avoiding salient company actions in addressing the legal process. Chiquita's strategy was to largely ignore the issue to reduce the impact of the crisis in the United States. Image Restoration Theory informs Chiquita's two responses to the crisis in Guatemala: denial of the situation and other crisis response.

Chiquita restricted the company's responses to this crisis. When Chiquita did choose to respond to the crisis in US news reports, the primary message was denial of the situation by reaffirming the company's claims of environmentally sustainable practices [25, 26]. In rare instances, Chiquita threatened a countersuit against WASH for defamation [26]. In both cases, Chiquita's response to the crisis in Guatemala did not come from an executive; rather, responses came directly from a company spokesperson [25].

At first glance it may seem as though culture had little influence in Chiquita's response in the company's transnational crises, in actuality there were several inferential cultural influences involved in the TNC's responses. As mentioned earlier,

Colombia and Guatemala both have long histories of colonial rule; Guatemala, in particular, was subject to economic colonialization by Chiquita in the early 1950s [21]. Additionally, both Latin American countries are collectivistic and showed a high score on the power distance index of Hofstede's cultural dimensions. Therefore, an argument can be made that the cultures of both nations may be relatively uniform in their relative comfort with inequality. In each culture, Chiquita—as a large and influential TNC—epitomizes the sort of powerful entity that people may consider a part of their societal structure. Arguably, Chiquita is then not hurt by restricted and singular responses to crises in those Latin American countries because of the culture in each nation.

To a lesser degree, colorism in the cultures of Colombia and Guatemala may also influence the reception of Chiquita's crisis response strategies. Also attributable to the post-colonial cultures of each nation, persons of European heritage have a privileged place in society, while Garífuna and Indian people are commonly subjugated or secluded. In present day, violent guerilla groups in Colombia, and destroyed ecosystems in Guatemala disproportionately affect Garífunas and natives. Despite Chiquita's dispassionate responses to transnational crises in Latin America, the cultures present in Colombia and Guatemala indirectly benefit the TNC because the victims are historically undervalued members of society.

How the Chiquita Crisis Fits as a CNCS

We will now use the CNCS framework to provide perspective on the national and cultural challenges faced by Chiquita in Colombia and Guatemala.

- Proposition One: The Chiquita CNCS is related to a corporate social performance issue and negative consequences of globalization, where a US corporation paid almost $2 million to paramilitary groups in Colombia and is alleged to have destroyed ecosystems in Guatemala. For Colombia, in particular, the crisis involved violent crimes against Colombians and US citizens. Proposition one is supported.

- Proposition Two: In both cases, the CNCS took place in developing countries and increased as a result of external pressure. The crisis in Colombia was a case where the TNO itself alerted authorities of improper actions; as a result, authorities in the TNO's home country prosecuted and punished Chiquita for illegal actions taken overseas. Proposition two is supported.

- Proposition Three: Chiquita's actions in each crises triggered interest from the international community, as well as stakeholders in home and host countries. Transnational stakeholders may be interested in Chiquita's crisis in Colombia (issue of terrorism), while home country stakeholders will most likely be interested in the crisis in Guatemala (issue of greenwashing). The human interest issue and general newsworthiness of the crisis most likely contributed to this phenomenon. The third proposition is also supported.

- Proposition Four: The direct involvement of Chiquita in both CNCSs—from a global public relations perspective—created a substantial demand for the TNC to take reasonability for the results of each crisis. At the peak of the crisis in Colombia, Chiquita was facing lawsuits with monetary grievances numbering in the billions. Therefore, the fourth proposition is supported.
- Proposition Five: In Colombia and, especially, Guatemala, Chiquita is a well-known and highly visible company that produces tangible, boycottable products. Respectively, each crisis attracted attention of home, host, and transnational publics. Proposition five is supported too.
- Proposition Six: In Colombia, the CNCS for Chiquita started in the host country and continued to increase in magnitude until reaching its zenith, leading to prosecution in the United States. The company faced pressure from news media outlets in both nations, from international news agencies, and from TNOs. In the CNCS case in Guatemala, Chiquita was pressured in the United States by multiple lawsuits from nonprofit organizations and private parties. Proposition six is supported.
- Proposition Seven: Concurrently, the party considered as the principal participant in a crisis is often the defendant in legal action coming as a result of crisis. In Colombia, Chiquita was prosecuted by the US federal courts and sued by thousands of Colombians claiming that the TNC should be held accountable for the crisis. In Guatemala, multiple class actions suits against the TNC provide evidence to the TNCs identification as the principal participant in the crisis; and after successful legal action, partners of Chiquita in Guatemala are not being targeted for legal action. Thus, proposition seven is supported.
- Proposition Eight: The CNCS of Chiquita in Colombia was a lengthy process—lasted from 2007 to 2014 (although the conflict that led to the crisis started nearly a decade earlier). The conflict occurred in a host country, and the regulatory authorities of the home country applied the punishment. Therefore, the eighth proposition is supported.
- *Proposition Nine is not applicable to either of Chiquita's cases.*
- Proposition Ten: The Chiquita conflict in Colombia attracted significant attention from international newswire agencies, global media outlets, two national governments, and several global NGOs; the company was then headquartered in Cincinnati, OH (home country and developed nation), and was facing a crisis in a host location. The conflict in Guatemala attracted attention from organized citizen groups as well as two national governments. Proposition 10 is supported.

A Glocal Response to Chiquita's Crises

We offer these recommendations.

Strategic Plan Goals

For public relations professionals' representing organizations facing a transnational crisis, the goal of the strategic plan should be *glocal*. All the following elements of the crisis communication plan—the objectives, strategies, and tactics—must to be localized in accordance with the unique cultural characteristics and the stakeholders' expectations in the host country.

Objectives

The objectives in transnational crisis communication that multinational organizations can strive for in consideration of the Chiquita cases in Latin American are threefold: be accountable for a crisis in both the home and host countries, respond to a crisis with a strategic plan that is glocal and has relevance to the local culture, and engage host country stakeholders by cultivating relationships.

Strategies

Public relations professionals need to identify an organization's key stakeholders, and engage in a relationship building and cultivation process that includes both the local and organizational cultures. In a country such as Colombia, nurturing relationships with government officials at each level of government (executive, legislative, judicial) would be essential. In the United States, even more primary stakeholders must be engaged as a transnational crisis has the capacity to attract the attention of global media outlets, International Nongovernmental Organisations (INGOs), international regulatory bodies, news agencies, and activists. In that respect, public relations practitioners should expect a more complex crisis plan for the United States than in Latin America. As stakeholder groups and nationalist governments in the subcontinent increasingly become more active, this reality may soon see a progressive change. Through social media and other web communications, multitudes of voices from host countries are making transnational crises even more challenging to manage in Latin America.

Tactics

Not only were the frequencies and lengths of news stories different in each country, the headlines and leading remarks were not uniform. From the selection of journalists and media vehicles, to the quotes provided for the stories, even to details on the crisis itself—the transnational crisis communication plan lacked a unified glocal approach.

The corporate response from Chiquita in Colombia was consistent. Chiquita was forced to make illegal payments to the Colombian paramilitary groups, and the TNC acted with good intentions to protect its employees. The consistency of that message was not equally voiced in each country. The corporate voice of Chiquita was more prevalent in the United States because it was easier to disseminate; accordingly, Colombia did not receive equal treatment in access to the company's corporate responses. The decisions in a transnational crisis should not be made out of convenience. And account-ability during crises should not favor only a TNCs home country. The lack of access to a company's response—whether it is through a spokesperson or CEO—will not stop journalists' from reporting on the story. Having such little influence on reports of a transnational crisis has the potential to only further damage the reputation of an organization in the host country.

Practical Suggestions/Actions Plans

The authors of this case firmly believe, as many other scholars and professionals, that US-headquartered TNCs must behave overseas as they would behave at home. The US Foreign Corrupt Practices Act, to only name a legislation, "was enacted for the purpose of making it unlawful for certain classes of persons and entities to make payments to foreign government officials to assist in obtaining or retaining business" [33]. Other countries, such as the United Kingdom, have such overreaching law (i.e., Bribery Act). It is a moral obligation for TNCs of all nationalities to behave ethically and lawfully in an ever interconnected global marketplace. Public relations and com-munication management professionals are called to be part of the decision-making process and dominant coalition table and, therefore, to advise organizations that cross borders to be responsible with their decisions, actions, and communications.

Placing corporate policies and codes of conducts/ethics upfront would help cor-porate, agency and global public relations professionals to guide their strategic advis-ing function. Having said that, cross-national crises or conflicts are almost unavoid-able in an increasing complex international environment, in which a myriad of smart stakeholders and involved consumers are closely watching corporate behaviors and demanding corporate and government accountability. Here, the global issues identifi-cation, monitoring, and management function is also essential to avoid an escalation of a controversial situation. Public relations professionals should be trained and then should assume this function actively. They would gain greater access to top manage-ment, as a consequence.

If a transnational crisis or cross-national conflict happens, global crisis commu-nication must be activated. In the case of Chiquita, the company has been active in presenting and making available its versions of the situations. It has gone beyond responses to compliance and corrective actions. Public relations professionals servicing TNCs would benefit from having a well-oiled coordinated communication network inside and outside their organizations. They also must understand the transnational crisis cycle and the levels of expectations and demands of home, host, and transnational publics.

Moreover, global issues management and crisis communication plans should be developed and vetted with top management as part of an organizational crisis prevention program. All procedures should be rehearsed annually or on a regularly scheduled basis; so that when a crisis occurs, implementation will be on target to ensure the effectiveness of the plans. Finally, the responses must be under constant monitoring, identifying where adjustments are needed. The outcomes of the plans should be evaluated against the measurable objectives set at the beginning of the process. Home and host spokespeople are integral elements of a global crisis plan. Public relations professionals should media train them, and they also need to understand their personalities and communication style for the spokesperson to be perceived as authentic and efficient. Strategic message response to the organization's global identity and local constituencies is also a significant feature of any plan.

Out-behaving the Competition: The Role of Communication in Transnational Crises
Expert Commentary by Robert Grupp.

In this age of ubiquitous communications flow and hyper-transparency, the world is more connected than ever before. Because of this rapid and incessant transfer of information, companies are more visible and publicly accountable than ever. Everything we say and do is cast within a cross-national context of interdependence, where everything we know about one another is dependent on the flow of information, whoever generates it and whatever its sources.

We have become interconnected and interdependent, where our stakeholders and publics feel the right—even a sense of self-defined obligation—to critique our organizations, products, and people. As the authors point out, our ever-expanding communication and technology require *glocal* strategies that respond to the concerns of different publics in both home and host countries.

It used to be that an organization's ability to manage its reputation—especially during crises—was the key to its success. While still true to a degree, for organizations to succeed today, it is not just a question of perception but the deeper idea of who they really are and how they go about business that has become a key differentiator. The *corporate character,* the most authentic alignment between an organization's expressed values and behaviors that can be observed, is what makes a crucial difference to reputations. Character creates reputation and becomes a critical element of the capacity of Chiquita and others to manage cross-national conflict while maintaining productivity.

Today, organizations like Chiquita are striving not just for behavior that will allow them to be well perceived by their stakeholders, but *out-behaving* to create a reputational margin for error. If you out-behave consistently, you create social license and give yourself room (and permission) for mistakes to happen—and since mistakes are inevitable, it is important to have that reputational cushion for a potential misstep or full-blown transnational crisis.

It can be said that an organization's truest character emerges during a crisis, and this usually refers to how an organization reacts to the crisis, and not necessarily the crisis itself. How we judge an organization's actions and behavior post-crisis is our measuring stick by which future reputation is determined.

No matter how skilled a team may be at developing and sustaining corporate character, there will always be moments when individuals or a company like Chiquita make errors in judgment. When that occurs, our responses say more about our character than does the mistake. As former baseball player Wade Boggs [34] said, "Our lives are not determined by what happens to us but how we react to what happens."

For organizations embroiled in transnational crisis, the impact is clear. Since we no longer have the capacity or, some would even argue, control over our own narrative, it has become more important than ever that our performance and behavior be beyond reproach. Our well-thought-out values should be more than placeholders in our marketing tools but in fact, truly lived and exhibited through our behaviors, especially during crisis. The Chiquita Brands' transnational crises in Colombia and Guatemala provide the perfect case in point.

Robert W. Grupp is the president of Grupp Global Partners LLC, an independent management consultancy providing communication and public relations services to leading multinational corporations and to emerging entrepreneurial organizations worldwide. Grupp also is adjunct instructor and director of the Master's Degree Program specializing in global strategic communication at the University of Florida.

Discussion Questions

17.1 Chiquita Brands responded to the cross-national crisis in Colombia with a few official statements from the headquarters in the United States. How might audiences in Colombia perceive such a response?

17.2 Using CNCS's propositions, how could Chiquita provide a better corporate response to the cross-national crisis in Colombia?

17.3 Who are the key audiences that Chiquita needed to engage and inform during the cross-national crisis in Guatemala? What actions should be taken to address the concerns of those affected by contaminated natural resources?

17.4 What improprieties in Chiquita's business practices may have contributed to the company's repeated cross-national crises? How might Chiquita take measures to avoid similar crises in the future?

17.5 How might CNCS theory be improved? What are the limitations?

References

1. M. Taylor, "Cultural variance as a challenge to global public relations: A case study of the Coca-Cola scare in Europe," *Public Relations Review*, vol. 26, pp. 277–293, 2000.
2. J. C. Molleda, "Cross-national conflict shifting: A transnational crisis perspective in global public relations," in *Handbook of Public Relations*, 2nd ed., R. Heath, Ed. Thousand Oaks, CA: Sage Publications, 2010, pp. 679–690.
3. J. C. Molleda and C. Connolly-Ahern, "Cross-national conflict shifting: Conceptualization and expansion in an international public relations context," presented at the Convention of the Association for Education in Journalism and Communication, Miami, FL, 2002.
4. A. Frietag, "International media coverage of the Firestone tire recall," *Journal of Communication Management*, vol. 6, no. 3, pp. 239–256, 2002.
5. J. C. Molleda and C. Quinn, "Cross-national conflict shifting: A global public relations dynamic," *Public Relations Review*, vol. 30, pp. 1–9. 2004.
6. J. R. Kim and J.C. Molleda, "Cross-national conflict shifting and crisis management: Analysis of Halliburton's bribery probe case in Nigeria," *presented at the 8th International Public Relations Research Conference*, Miami, FL, March, 2005.
7. H. Lim and J. C. Molleda, "The influence of a cross-national conflict shift on a transnational corporation's host customers," presented at the International Communication Association 59th Annual Conference, Division of Public Relations, Chicago, May, 2009.
8. J. C. Molleda, "Advancing the theory of cross-national conflict shifting: A case discussion and quantitative content analysis of a transnational crisis' newswire coverage," *International Journal of Strategic Communication*, vol. 5, no. 1, pp. 49–70, 2011.
9. J. C. Molleda, C. Connolly-Ahern, and C. Quinn, "Cross-national conflict shifting: Expanding a theory of global public relations management through quantitative content analysis," *Journalism Studies*, vol. 6, no. 1, pp. 87–102, 2005.
10. T. M. Oliveira and J.C. Molleda. (2008). "Withdrawal of Vioxx in Brazil: Aligning the global mandate and local actions". in *The Evolution of Public Relations: Case Studies From Countries in Transition*, 3rd ed., J. V. Turk and L. Scalan, Eds. Institute for Public Relations, 2008, pp.181–194, [Online]. Available: http://www.instituteforpr.org/evolution-of-pr-third-edition/
11. Y. Wang, "Cross-national conflict shifting: A case study of the DuPont Teflon crisis," M.S. thesis, Department of Mass Communication, University of Florida, Gainesville, FL, 2005.
12. A. M. Soares, M. Farhangmehr, and A. Shoham, "Hofstede's dimensions of culture in international marketing studies," *Journal of Business Research*, vol. 60, no. 3, pp. 277–284, 2007.
13. K. Sriramesh and D. Verčič, *The Global Public Relations Handbook: Theory, Research, and Practice*. New York: Routledge, 2009.
14. R. Terlutter, S. Diehl, and B. Mueller, "The GLOBE study—Applicability of a new typology of cultural dimensions for cross-cultural marketing and advertising research," in International Advertising and Communication: Current Insights and Empirical Findings, R. Terlutter, S. Diehl and R. Terlutter, Eds. Wiesbaden, Germany: DUV, 2006, pp. 419–438.
15. G. Hofstede, G. J. Hofstede, and M. Minkov, "Cultures and organizations: Software of the mind." New York: McGraw-Hill, 2010.

16. P. G. Northouse, "Culture and leadership," in *Leadership: Theory and Practice*, 4th ed. Sage Publications, 2007, pp. 301–340.

17. Central Intelligence Agency. (2015a, June 24). "The world factbook" [Online]. Available: https://www.cia.gov/library/publications/the-world-factbook/geos/co.html

18. Central Intelligence Agency. (2015b, June 24). "The world factbook" [Online]. Available: https://www.cia.gov/library/publications/the-world-factbook/geos/gt.html

19. N. L. González. (n.d.). "Guatemala. Countries and their cultures" [Online]. Available: http://www.everyculture.com/Ge-It/Guatemala.html

20. S. Márquez and D. C. Broadfield. (n.d.). "Colombia. Countries and their cultures" [Online]. Available: http://www.everyculture.com/Bo-Co/Colombia.html, June 27, 2015 (last date accessed).

21. B. Fischer. (2010). "A banana republic once again? PR Watch" [Online]. Available: http://www.prwatch.org/news/2010/12/9834/banana-republic-once-again

22. C. Anderson, "Chiquita seeks dismissal in Colombian case", *The Associated Press*, [Online]. Available: http://www.sandiegouniontribune.com/sdut-chiquita-seeks-dismissal-in-colombian-case-2013sep21-story.html, May 31, 2017 (last date accessed).

23. E. Wulfhorst and E. Beech, "Chiquita sued in NY over killings in Colombia," *Reuters*, November 14, 2007. [Online]. Available: http://www.reuters.com/article/us-chiquita-colombia-usa-idUSN1421157820071114

24. E. Larson and C. Smythe, "Chiquita wins dismissal of U.S. suits on Colombia torture," *Bloomberg Business*, July 27, 2014. [Online]. Available: LexisNexis Academic database.

25. S. Shemkus. "Better bananas: Chiquita settles lawsuit over green marketing, but the legal battle isn't over," *The Guardian*, December 19, 2014 [Online]. Available: LexisNexis Academic database, June 22, 2015 (last date accessed).

26. J. L. Hardcastle, "Chiquita fights back against lawsuit," *Environmental Leader*, September 2, 2014 [Online]. Available: http://www.environmentalleader.com/2014/09/02/chiquita-fights-back-against-lawsuit/

27. "Chiquita faces another eco-lawsuit," *Fresh Fruit Portal*, February 11, 2015 [Online]. Available: LexisNexis Academic database.

28. "Class action says Chiquita's banana production in Guatemala harming environment," *Legal Newsline*, April 28, 2015 [Online]. Available: LexisNexis Academic database.

29. "Hagens Berman files lawsuit against Chiquita bananas alleging environmentally disastrous production methods," *The Pak Banker*, February 9, 2015, [Online]. Available: LexisNexis Academic database.

30. W. L. Benoit and S. L. Brinson, "AT&T: Apologies are not enough," *Communication Quarterly*, vol. 42, no. 1, pp. 75–88, 1994.

31. V. Bravo, J.-C. Molleda, A. F. G. Davilla, and L. H. Botero, "Testing cross-national conflict shifting theory: An analysis of Chiquita brand's transnational crisis in Colombia," *Public Relations Review*, vol. 39, pp. 57–59, 2013.

32. S. Kroft, "The price of bananas," *CBS' 60 Minutes*, May 11, 2008. [Online]. Available: http://www.cbsnews.com/news/the-price-of-bananas/

33. "An overview," *The United States Department of Justice*, 2015. [Online]. Available: http://www.justice.gov/criminal-fraud/foreign-corrupt-practices-act

34. W. Boggs. (n.d.). "BrainyQuote" [Online]. Available: http://www.brainyquote.com/quotes/authors/w/wade_boggs.html

VI

Conclusion

Looking Ahead

18

Planning for Crisis Communication Across Cultural and Transboundary Contexts

Amiso M. George and Kwamena Kwansah-Aidoo

Chapter Preview

As the chapters in this book, Culture and Crisis Communication: Transboundary Cases from Nonwestern Perspectives, have shown, and as history has consistently taught us, most organizations and institutions will experience a day of crisis in their lifetime. If that day of crisis is almost a certainty, then it makes sense to put in place plans for that day. In an era where a local crisis can quickly cross boundaries—physical, ideological, or virtual, and become an international crisis, and crisis seemingly happening far off from a nation's shores can quickly become a matter of concern for local authorities away from the maiden point of crisis, planning for that day of crisis has become even more imperative. The increasing domination of crisis events in the global news headlines shows that crisis is not limited to one context. There is usually a common theme running through most crises; that is, failure to plan in advance. While preceding chapters have examined how crises are communicated and perceived from a viewpoint that is often ignored

Culture and Crisis Communication: Transboundary Cases from Nonwestern Perspectives, First Edition.
Edited by Amiso M. George and Kwamena Kwansah-Aidoo.
© 2017 by The Institute of Electrical and Electronics Engineers, Inc. Published 2017 by John Wiley & Sons, Inc.

in most crisis literature—the nonwestern perspective, this last chapter attempts to tie it all together with tips on preparing for that day of inevitability. When a crisis hits, what is said in the early moments can go a long way to not just define how the crisis is perceived, but how the organization recovers from the crisis. In crisis situations, things can be more chaotic than the crisis handlers would like, and usually implementing any plan at all, is challenging. Nonetheless, planning is essential and this chapter seeks to provide some guidelines on how to plan for communication on that crisis day that is bound to come. Despite the focus on culture and transboundary concerns, certain commonalities can be found among crises across all settings that allow for the provision of broad guidelines in planning and preparation.

After reading this chapter, you will be able to

- *Recognize what crisis is, and the definition of crisis that we have adopted throughout this volume*
- *Understand the goal and objectives of a crisis communication plan (CCP)*
- *Appreciate the nature of strategy and actions as outlined in a CCP*
- *Comprehend that effective crisis communication encompasses three phases—before, during, and after the crisis*
- *Assess the importance of examining crisis communication from the three-phase perspective*
- *Understand the value of this concluding chapter in terms of how it ties the volume together by providing guidelines for future crisis planning*

Introduction: The Certainty of Crisis and the Need for Planning

The growth in frequency, magnitude, and complexity of crises and disasters over the past few decades, has resulted in calls for organizations and society in general, to pay more attention to crisis management and research [1]. Events between 2014 and 2016 alone, such as the disappearance of Flight MH370, the downing of flight MH17 over Ukraine, the intractable war in Syria, the outbreak of Ebola in parts of West Africa, and the threat of the Zika virus in South America bear testimony to that observation. Such occurrences present challenges to communicators [2], given that an organization's success in managing a crisis depends on what it says and does after the crisis hits [3]. It has been estimated that in a crisis or emergency situation, communication issues take up anywhere between 70% and 80% of the activities of the team that is managing the situation [4]. This communication is important not only during the crisis, but also in the immediate aftermath of the crisis [2].

Once a crisis hits, the media would be out there to get as much information as they can. Whether one likes it or not, they will get their story. An organization could either choose to give the media the information they seek, or they will find a way to get it. So, how should an organization respond to the media to avoid a potentially negative media spotlight, loss of public confidence, reputation, or credibility?

Whatever the crisis may be, the priority is to act to minimize the damage to victims and the possibility of reoccurrence. The second is to prepare for media onslaught by activating the crisis management team (CMT) and a CCP. This chapter provides a basic CCP that can be adapted to fit the needs of specific organizations in different contexts.

Whatever the crisis may be, the priority is to act to minimize the damage to victims and the possibility of reoccurrence. The second is to prepare for media onslaught by activating the CMT and a CCP.

Crisis Defined

Definitions of *crisis* abound; however, a common denominator is that a crisis is any situation that negatively affects the reputation of an organization. It is also described as "a major occurrence with a potentially negative outcome affecting the organization, company, or industry, as well as its publics, products, services, or good name" [5]. Crises may have elements of surprise (such as a major natural disaster), create uncertainty, pose a threat that must be dealt with immediately, and is highlighted by negative media attention that may be sustained over a long period of time [6].

Crisis expert, Otto Lerbinger [7], identified eight types of crises.

1. Natural disaster (such as earthquakes, tsunamis, tornadoes, and volcanic eruptions)
2. Technological crises (such as computer software failures, industrial accidents, and human caused security data breaches)
3. Confrontation (such as boycotts, sit-ins, blockade, and picketing an organization)
4. Malevolence (such as kidnapping, terrorism, espionage, product tampering, and rumors)
5. Organizational misdeeds (such as management misconduct or deceit)
6. Workplace violence (such as homicide)
7. Rumors (such as spreading misleading information about an organization or its products with the intent to damage the organization's image)
8. Terrorist attacks/human-caused disasters (such as 9/11)

Whether the crisis is caused by the organization or not, the focus is on the organization's response, the media coverage of the response, and the public perception of the response.

The Crisis Communication Plan

Goal

The CCP outlines the roles, responsibilities, and procedures that will guide the organization in quickly disseminating information to its audiences during and after a crisis or emergency. A component of the organization's emergency management plan, the CCP provides overall guidance that would help to minimize reputational damage and threats to the organization.

The CCP typically resides in and is managed by the communication or public relations department. For some organizations, it may reside in the human resources (HR) department.

One of the goals of the organization during a crisis is to provide the media and the public with accurate information about the crisis while also correcting innuendos and inaccuracies. The organization shares information as quickly as possible following the adage: "Tell it all, tell it fast, and tell the truth." While that approach may not be feasible in all cultures, it is important to remember that if accurate information is not disseminated quickly (at least an initial statement via a tweet), someone with a smart phone who knows or is witness to the crisis would get that information out with partial or unverifiable facts.

Given that most people get their information about a crisis from the media, release of accurate and timely information is imperative. The organization should always seek to be honest and courteous in its relations with the media.

Sample Plan

The goal of this CCP is to establish guidelines for dealing with a variety of crisis situations to minimize reputational damage and threats to the organization.

Situation Analysis

A situation analysis is an examination of the circumstances the organization faces, not just about the immediate crisis, but also its overall strengths, weaknesses, opportunities, and threats (SWOT). Such an analysis should be broad enough to be adapted when the actual crisis occurs. Details of the actual crisis would be added as needed. Thus, in the event of a crisis, the situation analysis provides a proper context for a description of the crisis situation and its significance.

TABLE 18.1. Audiences, Stakeholders, and Partners in a Crisis Situation

Target Audience	Stakeholders	Partners
• Employees • Local and regional residents • Local and county officials • Business and civic leaders	• City/local residents • Elected and appointed officials • Fire department • Police department • Hospitals and local clinics • Civic organizations (Red Cross/Red Crescent) • Business and civic leaders • Local schools • Local, regional, and national media	• Elected and appointed officials • City and county government • Local and regional hospitals and clinics • Fire department • Police department • Civic organizations (Red Cross/Red Crescent)

Compiled by Amiso M. George and Kwamena Kwansah-Aidoo.

Example Statement Wording

[*Insert name of organization*], just experienced [*name or brief description of crisis*]. As a result, we have activated our emergency response plan and are taking action to address the situation and protect all those affected. About [*insert numbers, if you have them; otherwise omit*] of our employees have been evacuated to safety, so have neighboring businesses. As usual, our priority is our employees [*insert other relevant public and reiterate organization's mission statement*].

Target Audience, Stakeholders, and Partners

Target audience, stakeholders, and *partners* are those who are directly affected by the crisis; they are invested in the crisis or assist in responding to the crisis.

Identification and definition of this audience prior to the crisis is imperative, as they should be informed of the crisis. Incorporating them into the CCP ensures that their concerns about safety are addressed. While they all play different roles, their roles complement each other and are helpful to the organization during a crisis.

Objectives

Objectives describe what should happen or be achieved in order to attain the organization's goals in a crisis. They should be specific, attainable, measurable, and time bound.

Examples

- Activate our CCP within an hour.
- Gather as much information as possible about the crisis.
- Notify our organization's leadership and employees within an hour.
- Notify the appropriate law enforcement authorities and media. This action depends on the type and severity of the crisis.
- Activate organization's "Dark Site"—a pre-made, invisible web site that is activated when a crisis or emergency occurs. The site stores general information about the crisis, but as specific details emerge, they are added just before the site is activated. The site is regularly updated as new information about the crisis is obtained.
- Communicate streamlined messages that reinforce the organization's brand and vision.
- Effectively and efficiently disseminate information to all stakeholders across multiple media platforms.
- Be honest and transparent with the media in all communication.
- Identify and communicate ways the organization is trying to resolve the crisis so as to engender public confidence and ensure business continuity.

Strategies

Strategies are general methods that explain how objectives would be accomplished and justification for the approaches chosen.

Examples

- In the event of a crisis, the CCT will coordinate all communication among all departments to ensure efficient and effective execution of the crisis plan. This team will also manage communication with external stakeholders, including the media.
- The CEO/president of the organization or a designee (Director of Communication or Public Relations) will serve as a spokesperson during the crisis. All media inquiries should be directed to the spokesperson(s).
- Good media relations are imperative; therefore, all inquiries from the media would be documented and responded to. If unable to respond to requests such as releasing personnel information, inform the media accordingly.
- Whenever possible, responses to the media should be proactive and reinforce the values of the organization.

Tactics/Action Steps

Tactics are the specific and visible activities or steps that are taken to implement objectives associated with each strategy.
Examples

- Hold a press conference.
- Stream live video of corrective action being taken by the company in response to the crisis.
- Post media statements on activated "Dark Site."
- Get third party endorsers to speak positively about the company or express support on social media.

Effective communication with all stakeholders in all three phases of a crisis (before, during, and after) is imperative, because it minimizes reputational damage to the organization and confusion as to what actions have been or would be taken.

Phase 1: Before the Crisis.

Step 1. Form a Crisis Management Team

This CMT which includes the CEO, head of the Office of Public Relations, security or safety officer, technology, legal, and other department heads where the crisis occurred, provides leadership and determines what action should be taken during a crisis and who speaks for the organization. The communication lead on this team is responsible for both internal and external communication during and after the crisis.

Given the nature of crises that can occur when team members are not necessarily in the same geographic location, ability to remain in close contact at any time is essential; hence, the need for a directory of team members.

This directory should include names, titles, home and cell phone numbers, e-mail, and social media contacts as illustrated below.

Example: Crisis Management Team Directory

Name/Title	Cell	Home	Office	Social Media Twitter Handle	E-mail
Marian Doe (CEO)	123-555-7890	234-555-8901	567-555-9012	@mariandoe	Marian.doe@org.com
Joe Baba CCT leader	098-555-5432	109-555-5432	567-555-6543	@joebaba	Joe.baba@org.com
Ty Gomez Safety	099-555-3245	108-555-3245	567-555-3456	@tygomez	Ty.gomez@org.com

Step 2. Identify and Train Spokespersons

    A. A primary spokesperson will speak on behalf of the organization. In a major crisis, that person would be the CEO/president. Surrogate spokespersons should be identified and be prepared to step in when the key spokesperson is unable or unavailable.

    B. Additionally, there should also be technical experts or content specialists to provide technical information related to specific aspects of the crisis.

    C. All spokespersons should be trained to speak succinctly and answer questions without rambling, avoid using the oft ill-advised phrase "No comment," or using too much technical jargon. They must be comfortable in front of the camera, appear sincere, confident, believable, calm, and knowledgeable about the crisis and the organization.

Step 3. Establish a Media Crisis Center

    A. This center should be away from the main offices of the organization, but close by. For some organizations, it could be a nearby hotel or a conference room within the vicinity of the organization.

    B. The center should have all the necessary equipment such as podium with company logo, desks, chairs, multiple outlets, and other technical essentials that would enable the staff and reporters to do their job.

    C. This center should be used for briefing the media.

Step 4. Establish an Emergency Operations Center

    A. A dedicated space such as a large conference room can be established as an emergency operations center (EOC).

    B. The EOC should be activated in the event of "a major crisis that causes significant property damage, potential or actual business disruption, or has the potential to cause a significant impact on the business" [8].

    C. The US Homeland Security outlines what a well-equipped EOC, would contain

        • Mobile and landline phones, including speakerphones, fax machines, and other communication systems used by the organization to ensure business continuity.

        • Computers and printers with Wi-Fi to allow access to e-mails, electronic copies of crisis response, business continuity and CCPs that can be printed on demand.

        • TV monitors, DVRs, projection units, or flipcharts with easel and markers to compile and display information, and white boards.

        • Hard copies of crisis tool box containing crisis response, business continuity and CCPs, contact/telephone lists, resource inventory, and diagrams of facilities and systems.

- Stationery, business and incident management forms, pens, pencils, markers, and supplies.
- Food, water, and dining supplies for EOC staff [8].

Step 5. Develop a Crisis Communication Plan (CCP)

A. Ensure that plan is signed and approved by CEO and top officials.

B. Prepare a list of crisis team member names, contact information and responsibilities.

C. Identify process of notification of crisis.

D. Identify process and agreement on how crisis information would be approved and disseminated.

E. Designate a spokesperson, additional spokespersons, and content and technical experts.

F. Develop messaging for different audiences and at different times during the crisis.

G. Use pictures and videos to communicate your story. Develop other collateral materials, such as brochures, fact sheets, frequently asked questions (FAQs), and load them on your website, but also make available upon request.

H. Activate and integrate your own social media into your crisis plan. Your "Dark Site" should be activated and be the repository of all information about the crisis.

I. Develop a contact list of regional, national, local media, and influential bloggers.

J. Develop a contact list of external partner organizations, such as police, fire department, hospitals, and social welfare organizations. Also contact other crisis experts to lend a hand, especially in an intense crisis that lasts for several days (see Appendices A and B).

Step 6. Review Your Crisis Communication Plan

A. Adapt the strategies and tactics in the plan to suit your organization's needs.

B. Make electronic and hard copies of plan accessible to all members of the crisis team.

C. Create an electronic and hard copy wallet-sized quick tips reference card.

Step 7. Plan Exercises to Simulate Your Crisis Communication Plan

A. Play out different crisis scenarios (see Appendix C). A necessary scenario should be that of data breach which has garnered tremendous media attention and has devastating consequences on organizations and government.

B. Train spokespersons on how to respond to media questions.

C. Make adjustments to crisis plan, if needed.

Phase 2: During the Crisis.

IMMEDIATE RESPONSE.

Step 1. Gather Information About the Crisis
- What happened?
- Where did it happen?
- When did it happen?
- Who is affected/involved?
- Why/How did it happen? (If known)

Often, employees at the scene of the crisis gather basic information. Immediately, prepare incident reporting forms or incident fact sheets, using the 5Ws and How (Who, What, When, Where, Why, and the How). Make it easy for anyone to report the information following the organization's protocol (see Appendix D.).

Step 2. Notify the Crisis Communication Team (CCT) Leader (Director of the Office of Communication) and the CEO
The CCT leader should be the first person to be called. That person, together with the CEO, should assess the situation and decide on the proper course of action.

Step 3. Activate Communication Notification Tree to Get Other CCT Members on Board
For full details and processes, see Appendix G.

Step 4: The CCT Leader and Team will Assess the Level or Intensity of the Crisis to Determine the Organization's Response
The crisis may range from mildly intense (barely attracting attention) to very intense (attracting intense multimedia live coverage featuring angry or frightened stakeholders). The intensity determines the response. A holding statement or an initial media statement is always useful (see Appendices E and F).

Step 5. Manage Communication Channels
Manage messaging (Activate the "Dark Site" on your company's website). Dark site is an already prepared web page with information devoted to the crisis.

A. Identify your target audiences.
B. Keep your internal audience up-to-date with crisis information via Intranet.
C. Keep your external audience up-to-date through your activated "Dark Site" and your social media channels. All communication channels should be integrated to allow audiences opportunities to comment and share information about the crisis.

D. Begin an inquiry/contact log for media and public (see Appendix H).

E. Assign spokespersons. The CEO is the spokesperson on high level or intense crisis. Following the CEO's initial media statement or conference, the CCT leader or other designee can perform that task.

- The spokesperson must be articulate and comfortable in front of cameras.

- Media training is highly recommended for such a person and understudy as part of pre-crisis preparation.

Step 6. Determine Logistics

A. Designate CCT staff at crisis site.

B. Designate a Media Center designed for press conferences or briefings about the crisis.

C. Designate an EOC away from the location of the crisis.

D. Ensure that the EOC has all the supplies for the CCT (if they have to stay there for a few days) and also Wi-Fi access and necessary technology for the media (see Appendix B).

E. Set up a virtual EOC. That means all CCT members must be able to reach each other via cell phone and/or other mobile technology wherever they may be, until they are able to get to the location of the crisis.

ONGOING RESPONSE.

Step 7. Develop Messages

The CCT leader (and assistants) should develop messages based on the information gathered and confirmed on the incident form.

A. Develop messages to communicate vital information about the crisis (see Appendices I and J).

B. Anticipate questions that could be asked by key audiences and provide those responses in the messages.

C. Consider the political implications of the messages (depending on the country in which your organization operates).

D. Determine the most efficient, effective, and appropriate way (media platforms) to disseminate important messages to all target audiences.

E. Develop new messages or modify old ones based on new or additional information. Communicate all messages via all media channels.

F. The CCT leader and team should continue to monitor the crisis and update all target audiences through the same multiple media platforms regularly used to communicate with them. The updates will be based on new information about the crisis and will continue until the organization returns to its pre-crisis state.

Step 8. Approve and Disseminate Crisis Messages

A. All messages must be vetted and approved by the CCT leader, legal counsel, operations manager, and the CEO or president of the company.

B. Once approved, the messages are ready to be disseminated to the target audiences.

C. In the event of fatalities, family members must be notified before the information is released to the public.

D. Messages to family members about loss of life should, as much as possible, be delivered in person, and by a senior member of the management team.

E. The streamlined message(s) will be disseminated through multimedia platforms to all the target audiences. For employees, it would be internal communication (Intranet).

F. Depending on the severity of the crisis, the messages, also communicated via multimedia platforms, could be released as if coming directly from the CEO.

Phase 3: After the Crisis. The CCT will monitor media messages and provide its stakeholders with information about recovery or corrective actions the organization has taken. Additionally, the team will review lessons learned in the organization's relationship with the media and its response to the crisis, and honor heroes or heroines of the crisis.

COMMUNITY/CONSUMER/STAKEHOLDER RELATIONS.

- The CCT should ascertain what specific stakeholder issues the media focused on during the crisis.
- The CCT should determine if the messages were effective with the various target audiences.
- The CCT should establish if the responses of target audiences to the organization's handling of the crisis were positive, negative, or neutral.
- The CCT should communicate to stakeholders, corrective actions or remedies that the organization has taken regarding the crisis.
- The CCT should declare, if applicable, the end of the crisis.

MEDIA RELATIONS.

- The CCT should continue to monitor media coverage of the crisis, key audience's reactions, and correct misinformation or innuendos as quickly as possible. This should be an ongoing action during and after the crisis.
- The CCT should determine if the media coverage was positive, negative, or neutral during and after the crisis.

- The CCT should ascertain which coverage got the most positive response, the most negative response.
- The CCT should pay special attention to local media coverage as that is important to the local audience.
- The CCT should monitor influential blogs or chat rooms to ascertain various stakeholders' perception of the organization's crisis response.
- It is important that company representative not respond to or comment on blogs as that could create a negative perception by the blogger or "netizens." The CCT should conduct Internet searches to ascertain if the crisis is still trending after it is officially declared over.

CRISIS COMMUNICATION.

- The CCT should evaluate the effectiveness of its CCP.
- The CCT should ascertain how well team members perform their assigned roles.
- The CCT should identify the key lessons that team members could incorporate into a revised CCP.

RECOGNIZING/HONORING THE HEROES AND HEROINES.

- The CCT should identify heroes/heroines, including team members, employees, volunteers, and community members who emerged during the crisis.
- The CCT should publicly recognize and honor members and others who went above and beyond the call of duty during the crisis.

Conclusion: The Value of Planning

The goal of this chapter has been to show the importance of being prepared, from a communication perspective, before disaster strikes. While human error that sometimes causes crisis cannot be eliminated in its entirety, and while some crisis events such as the missing MH370 (discussed in detail in Chapter 11) can be unprecedented, it is still an organization's responsibility to engage in preventive efforts that require anticipation of such errors and events [9], and to plan accordingly. Planning effectively represents the contours of best practice and "if the organization has prepared, its response is likely to be better structured (and more effective) than one that has not" [2].

It is still an organization's responsibility to engage in preventive efforts that require anticipation of such errors and events and to plan accordingly.

In the long run, as Benoit [3] rightly points out, an organization's success in dealing with a crisis is partly dependent on what it *says* (communication) after the crisis erupts [2,3]. This, makes the value of communication during a crisis and the need to have a communications plan ready, trialed, and tested before disaster strikes, very apparent [2]. The Swedish Emergency Management Agency (SEMA) handbook captures the value of communication planning before a crisis by noting that, "how well the communication works during a real crisis depends on how well an authority [sic] has prepared itself before the crisis" [4]. This means that an organization should be able to anticipate potential crisis situations and develop communication plans for such would-be crises.

In line with such thinking, we hope that this chapter has shown not only how to plan for a crisis, but also the value of planning in advance of the crisis event and the need to plan to obtain value in communication. We also hope that the entire book will contribute to understanding how crisis communication occurs in nonwestern cultures, and the basic principles involved in planning for crisis communication in all contexts, and thereby improve efforts at dealing more effectively with crisis events whenever and wherever they may occur.

Acknowledgements

Special thanks to Carolyn G. Bobo, MS, APR, Fellow PRSA, Fort Worth, TX, who compiled the disaster toolbox and provided advice on many aspects of the crisis plan, and to colleagues at the Greater Fort Worth Public Relations Society of America (PRSA), Fort Worth, TX (http://www.fortworthprsa.org), for their professional insights.

References

1. G. R. Webb, "Some issues to consider," presented at the Future Crises, Future Agendas: An Assessment of International Crisis Research International Workshop, Nice, France, 2004.
2. C. Galloway and K. Kwansah-Aidoo, "Getting to grips with issues management and crises communication," in *Public Relations Issues and Crisis Management*, C. Galloway and K. Kwansah-Aidoo, Eds. Melbourne: Thomson/Social Science Press, 2012, pp. 1–12.
3. W. L. Benoit, "Image repair discourse and crisis communication," *Public Relations Review*, Vol. 23, no. 2, pp. 177–186, 1997.
4. Swedish Emergency Management Agency, *Crisis Communication Handbook*. SEMA's Educational Series, Stockholm: SEMA, 2003.
5. K. Fearn-Banks, *Crisis Communications: A Casebook Approach* (Routledge Communication Series) 3rd Edition. NY: Routledge, 2009.
6. Seeger, M. W., Sellnow, T. L., and Ulmer, R. R. (1998). "Communication, organization, and crisis". *Communication Yearbook.*, vol. 21, pp. 231–275.

7. O. Lerbinger, *The Crisis Manager: Facing Disasters, Conflicts, and Failures*, 2nd ed. New York: Routledge, 2011.

8. U.S. Department of Homeland Security. (n.d.). "Crisis Communication Plan" [Online]. Available: https://www.ready.gov/business/implementation/incident, September 15, 2016 (last date accessed).

9. B. A. Olaniran and D. E. Williams, "Anticipatory model of crisis management: A vigilant response to technological crisis," in *Handbook of Public Relations*, R. L. Heath, Ed. Thousand Oaks, CA: Sage, 2001, pp. 487–500.

Sample Crisis Plan

Administrative or Executive Crisis Plan

Name of organization/Logo

Crisis Communication Plan

Written: Date, 20xx

Tested:_____

Updated: Date, 20xx

Culture and Crisis Communication: Transboundary Cases from Nonwestern Perspectives, First Edition.
Edited by Amiso M. George and Kwamena Kwansah-Aidoo.
© 2017 by The Institute of Electrical and Electronics Engineers, Inc. Published 2017 by John Wiley & Sons, Inc.

Crisis Plan Revision Table

Plan Revised Date	Revised by	Approved by	Comments

I. **Goal**

The goal of this plan is to provide guidance to senior management regarding public response to an issue that is of public interest and requires executive/administrative response. Such issues include, but are not limited to, the following:

- Board of Trustees and Board of Directors actions
- Personnel issues such as hirings, firings, and grievances
- Labor union activity or unrest
- Workplace violence
- Sexual harassment
- Employee drug use
- Financial improprieties such as embezzlement, fraud
- Product tampering
- Internet tampering/data breach
- Lawsuits
- Activism, such as consumer protests, neighborhood issues
- Executive death
- Executive arrest

This policy is separate from crisis and disaster plans related to response to computer operations, manufacturing or production issues, patient care or weather response.

II. **Administrative Crisis Response Team**
   The Administrative Crisis Response Team includes the following:
   - President and/or CEO
   - Public relations senior executive
   - Operations executive
   - Legal representative
     The president and CEO may also ask that senior management representatives of Human Resources, Security and Risk Management join the Administrative Crisis Response Team.
     - The team, will among others, develop communication templates, such as holding statements, media release, social media updates, etc.
     - Identify all communications channels, including social media, e-mail, phone, and traditional media.
     - Identify key external audiences, what they need to know, and how best to communicate with them.
     - Instruct employees of the company's policy, including social media, in relation to external audiences, especially during crisis.

III. **Activation**
   The Administrative Crisis Response Team will be activated when the chief executive officer, board chair or other senior executive determines that an issue exists which may
   - Affect reputation
   - Affect sales, referrals
   - Affect production, manufacturing, service
   - Affect financial support
   - Affect political support

IV. **Administrative Crisis Response Team Response**
   The Administrative Crisis Response Team will do the following:
   - Review the situation or event:
     - ✓ What happened?
     - ✓ When did it happen?
     - ✓ Where did it happen?
     - ✓ Why did it happen?
     - ✓ With what impact?
     - ✓ With what response?
     - ✓ With what results?
     - ✓ Who was involved?

✓ Who is involved now?

✓ Prior history of a similar event?

- Assess damages and/or potential for damage (physical, reputational, legal)
- Identify messages and methods of response for multiple audiences, such as, board of trustees/directors, customers, news media, social media, employees, competitors
- Identify the appropriate executive spokesperson
- Identify appropriate communication tactics
- Monitor and revise messages as needed

V. **Recovery**
   After an event and/or response to an event, the Administrative Crisis Team will authorize the following:

- Formal or informal research to measure public understanding
- Steps to correct misinformation or inaccuracy as appropriate
- Continued communication with key publics about actions taken to prevent future problems, results of investigations, regulatory agency findings and similar after-event information
- Recognize or honor "heroes" of the crisis

B

Public Relations Crisis Tool Kit

Putting Facts at Your Fingertips: Prepare a Public Relations Crisis Tool Kit

Strategic Preparation
- Tool kit is ready, especially when a speedy response is needed
- Crisis can happen here, so preparedness is key

Why Create a Tool Kit?
- Useful when there is no time to deliberate
- Supports organizational plan and mission
- Useful for reputation management
- Useful information overall
- Assists news media in their reporting

Culture and Crisis Communication: Transboundary Cases from Nonwestern Perspectives, First Edition.
Edited by Amiso M. George and Kwamena Kwansah-Aidoo.
© 2017 by The Institute of Electrical and Electronics Engineers, Inc. Published 2017 by John Wiley & Sons, Inc.

Where Should Tool Kit Be Located?
- PR Department
- Command center
- Senior management office
- Risk manager's office
- Security office
- Maintenance office

Disaster Plans
- Crisis assessment form
- Fire safety plans
- Hazardous materials plans
- Location-specific plan(s)
- Organization plan
- Public relations plan
- Terrorism response plans

Disaster Identification
- Company call center phone message
- Disaster code names, policies
- Evacuation protocol
- Flow charts
- Public relations staff duties
- Suspicious letter checklist
- Threatening phone calls checklist
- Web page response, social media posts

Media Questions Anticipated
- What happened?
- Who did it?
- When did it happen?
- Where did it happen?
- Why did you let it happen?
- Is the situation under control?
- Where else will it happen?
- Which victims can we interview?

- Who in your organization can talk about it?
- Who will be sued?
- When will the facility be able to provide/resume normal services?
- What will the organization do after the investigation?
- What are the interview guidelines?

Disaster Phone Logs

- Hold harmless release
- Media phone calls log
- Miscellaneous forms
- Obituary forms
- Phone scripts
- Social media pre-written posts
- Victim information forms

Control Center Phone Numbers (Alphabetically)

- Cell phones, pagers
- Crisis response center, hotlines, computer center, activated phones
- Headquarters departments, plants, security offices
- Satellite facilities
- Social media pages, websites
- Wireless addresses

Media Directory (Alphabetically)

- Home phones (for internal use only; not for public release)
- International media
- Local bureaus
- National media
- Radio stations
- Regional media
- Relationship media
- Social media sites
- Television
- Trade media
- Web sites
- Wire services
- Wireless addresses

Public Relations Support (Alphabetically)
- Department directory
- Disaster check list
- On-call information, digital contacts
- Specialized department members (computer programmers, firefighters, emergency management service)

Organization Leadership
- Management chart
- Administrative staff
- On-call managers/supervisors, special assignments
- Hotlines
- Home and personal contacts

External Assistance
- Police, fire, Red Cross/Red Crescent, state or national security agency, national emergency service, social services, maintenance
- Vendors, suppliers, customers
- PR contacts at competitors
- Financial representatives
- Trade associations
- Chamber(s) of Commerce
- Neighborhood groups, civic organizations
- PR and legal counsel, ad agencies
- Translators

Political Officials (Alphabetically)
- City, village, township councilmembers
- Congress/Parliament contacts
- County commissioners
- National officials (government departments and regulatory agencies)
- Other elected officials
- School trustees, utility district officers
- State agency contacts
- State government officials

Maps (Alphabetically)
- Bus, subway routes
- Company headquarters
- Crisis site
- Hazardous materials routes
- Major thoroughfares, interstates
- Nuclear plants
- Police, fire, ambulance stations
- Power stations, water tanks, sewer systems
- Railroads
- Satellite, remote facilities
- Schools, social service facilities
- Surrounding property owners

Security Assistance (Alphabetically)
- Bioterrorism agent information
- City, county response plans
- Evacuation procedures
- Military procedures
- National security advisory system
- Trade/industry association response systems, plans, protocols

Crisis Response Scenarios
- Bioterrorism
- CEO, executive death
- Computer virus, data breach
- Consumer activism, boycott
- Cultural insensitivity
- Customer injury, death
- Ethics issues
- Executive malfeasance
- Explosion, fire
- Financial fraud
- Hazardous materials
- Kidnapping, hostage situation

- Labor unrest
- Litigation
- Operational crisis
- Product recall
- Product tampering
- Protest, demonstration
- Sabotage
- Sexual harassment
- Stock price decline
- War
- Weather
- Workplace accident
- Workplace violence

Miscellaneous Information for Preparedness Team
- Bibliographies
- Crisis management literature
- Other relevant samples, guides
- PRSA Silver Anvil winners (USA)
- Sample plans, case studies
- Scenarios *(Johns Hopkins Center for Civilian Biodefense Strategies, University of Pittsburgh Center for Biosecurity, Centers for Disease Control)* (USA)

Crisis Tool Box
- Flashlights, batteries, recorders, tapes, phones, notepads, pens
- Hard hats, shoes, clothing, bumbershoots
- Safety vests, name badges
- Snacks, toiletries, medications

Evaluation
- Incorporate updates into post-event review
- Update officials, out-of-date information
- Update phone numbers, pager numbers, digital contacts

C

Administrative Crisis Response Scenario: Internal Facility Disaster

This scenario is a hypothetical example *of a situation that would be addressed by the Administrative Crisis Team and the Administrative Crisis Policy. This is based on* an actual incident.

Situation

During the heat of the summer, a city water line breaks, shutting off water to a local hospital. Without water, the hospital's chillers cannot supply air conditioning to the hospital; staff members, as well as patients and visitors, cannot wash their hands; bottled water must be provided for drinking purposes; toilets will not flush; dishwashers cannot be operated. The hospital calls a disaster code, which is overheard by media monitoring fire and police scanners.

An area fire department brings a pumper truck to fill chillers and operate air conditioning—a patient safety concern, not merely for comfort. Air conditioning to all nonpatient care buildings is turned off. Box fans are distributed.

Culture and Crisis Communication: Transboundary Cases from Nonwestern Perspectives, First Edition.
Edited by Amiso M. George and Kwamena Kwansah-Aidoo.
© 2017 by The Institute of Electrical and Electronics Engineers, Inc. Published 2017 by John Wiley & Sons, Inc.

Staff are instructed to sterilize hands using a waterless, antibiotic cleansing product. Bottled drinking water is brought for staff, patients, and families. Patients and families are directed to centrally located restrooms, not patient room toilets, and staff use bottled water to periodically flush in-room toilets. The restaurant uses disposable products for food service.

Media arrive *en masse*.

Example Plan

Responses are drafted for the following audiences:

1. **Employees and physicians of the hospital and on-campus clinics**
   - Nursing and administrative staff can provide information about patient care.
   - No employees/physicians are authorized to release information or make public statements on behalf of the hospital.

2. **Parents and relatives of patients at inpatient units, in the ER and in clinics**
   - Code Yellow (disaster) paged overhead.
   - The incident is not affecting care and safety of patients.
   - Please use centralized toilets instead of room toilets.
   - Clinical staff will provide drinking water.
   - Clinical staff and families should use waterless cleansing product for hand washing.
   - Additional information will be provided as quickly as possible.

3. **News media**
   - Facts as we know them: water main broken, city responded, fire department providing pumper truck for air conditioning.
   - Information about steps we are taking to wash, flush, and drink.
   - Reassurance that patient care is not compromised.
   - Appreciation for the fire department and other community assistance.

4. **Additional staff responses to media coverage**
   - Security monitors media arrivals.
   - A public information center is set up in the Board Room. Media are directed there.
   - PR Team identifies spokesperson for hospital, possible location for photos, TV footage.
   - Water department PR Person paged to scene.

Things to Emphasize

- Our goal in this crisis is to continue to provide appropriate medical care.
- We are monitoring each patient.
- We have ample supplies of bottled water; we are minimizing water use.
- This is a significant event; however, we prepare disaster plans and our staff members practice response to situations such as this.

Things to Remember

- Media outlets may be on campus throughout the incident, even if it lasts several hours.
- An incident of this significance could attract national media attention.
- Media may attempt to approach families of patients, but may be politely restricted to public property when not accompanied by a PR representative.
- Employees and physicians should not comment to the media on behalf of the hospital, unless requested to do so by the Public Relations Department.

Incident Report Form

An incident reporting form provides a brief written overview of a subject; generally limited to one page. It is prepared following the "5 Ws and H" format using headings, short phrases, key statistics, etc. It is not necessary to write in complete sentences. Write in the third person and in a clean concise manner.

General Information on Incident

What happened?_____
_____
_____

Who is affected or involved?_____
_____
_____

Where did it happen?_____
_____

Culture and Crisis Communication: Transboundary Cases from Nonwestern Perspectives, First Edition.
Edited by Amiso M. George and Kwamena Kwansah-Aidoo.
© 2017 by The Institute of Electrical and Electronics Engineers, Inc. Published 2017 by John Wiley & Sons, Inc.

When did it happen?_____

_____

How did it happen? (if known)_____

_____

_____

Extent of property damage/fatality _____

_____

_____

Why did it happen? (Often, this information is not readily available until investigation
is completed to ascertain the cause of the crisis.)_____

_____

_____

E

Holding Statement

A *holding statement* is a message developed for use immediately following a crisis. Holding statements are usually prepared in advance and can be used as a temporary response until the organization gets the facts about the crisis. A holding statement is ideally suited as an initial tweet about a crisis.

Example Wording

"We are aware of the (name of crisis) that occurred today and are responding to it. Our primary concern is the well-being and safety of all those affected. Our thoughts and prayers are with them. We will provide additional information on our website when it is available."

Culture and Crisis Communication: Transboundary Cases from Nonwestern Perspectives, First Edition. Edited by Amiso M. George and Kwamena Kwansah-Aidoo.
© 2017 by The Institute of Electrical and Electronics Engineers, Inc. Published 2017 by John Wiley & Sons, Inc.

F

Initial Media Statement

What happened?
At approximately_____(time) today_____(date), a
(nature of crisis)_____occurred on the _____site of the
_____(place or building).

Describe response:
Our organization (name of organization) is responding with assistance
from_____ (other local emergency or response team). Our response
team includes (list local medical, police, fire, etc.).

Show concern:
Our primary concern is for the safety and well-being of our staff, volunteers, nearby
community (whichever one applies) and the public—and to reduce the effect of the
(crisis).

Describe next action:
We are in the process of establishing what happened and will make efforts to minimize
the damage. We will provide more details as they become available.

Culture and Crisis Communication: Transboundary Cases from Nonwestern Perspectives, First Edition.
Edited by Amiso M. George and Kwamena Kwansah-Aidoo.
© 2017 by The Institute of Electrical and Electronics Engineers, Inc. Published 2017 by John Wiley & Sons, Inc.

G

Crisis Communications Roles and Responsibilities

Role and Responsibility	Name/Title
Crisis Communications Team (CCT) Leader • Manages all communication responses • Manages message development and approval of all distributed communication • Plans meetings and all activities with crisis team and management • Coordinates with teams at crisis site and main office • May serve as spokesperson Note: The CCT is usually the PR manager.	
CEO • Acts as chief spokesperson, especially in high intense crisis • Approves messages, approves budget and other responsibilities deemed appropriate	

Culture and Crisis Communication: Transboundary Cases from Nonwestern Perspectives, First Edition.
Edited by Amiso M. George and Kwamena Kwansah-Aidoo.
© 2017 by The Institute of Electrical and Electronics Engineers, Inc. Published 2017 by John Wiley & Sons, Inc.

Role and Responsibility	Name/Title
Legal Counsel • Provides legal advice on message strategies to all key audiences • Approves messages before they are disseminated	
Vice Presidents • Working closely with the CCT, vice presidents of the divisions affected by the crisis provide their team members with the appropriate language to use when responding to specific stakeholders • They may serve as content experts if needed	
Secondary Spokesperson(s) • **Other assigned technical and content experts may serves as spokespersons, depending on the nature of the crisis** • **Such spokespersons work in conjunction with the main spokesperson (the CEO or the CCT leader) at a media briefing**	
Information Technology Coordinator • Ensures that the technology needs of the CCT and the media are met	
Web Site/Social Media Coordinator • Updates the website and social media information • Keeps track of comments about the crisis by "netizens" and reports back to the CCT	
Operations Coordinator • Ensures that the EOC and media center have everything that the CCT team and the media would need • Works with CCT leader to ensure that phone lines are covered and other logistical needs of the team are met	

Sample Media Contact Log

Name of employee...............................Position....................................

Name	Phone/ E-mail	Date/ Time	Media Organization	Communication Type (TEV)	Question	Action	Comments

Culture and Crisis Communication: Transboundary Cases from Nonwestern Perspectives, First Edition.
Edited by Amiso M. George and Kwamena Kwansah-Aidoo.
© 2017 by The Institute of Electrical and Electronics Engineers, Inc. Published 2017 by John Wiley & Sons, Inc.

Media Statement

Example: Shooting Incident

The shooting that occurred at our facility in (location and time) has triggered a comprehensive emergency response. Our crisis team has prepared for incidents like this.

The shooting was limited to our warehouse in (name of location). While we will continue to investigate, our other warehouses continue to be fully operational.

At this time, we cannot confirm any fatality. However, law enforcement authorities at the scene say three people were injured. That is all the detail we can provide as State and Federal privacy laws prevent us from providing any additional information until family members are notified.

The following city emergency personnel and agencies responded to this incident: (insert emergency services).

Our thoughts and prayers go out to the injured. At (company name), our top priority is always the safety and well-being of our employees, customers, and other businesses near us.

Culture and Crisis Communication: Transboundary Cases from Nonwestern Perspectives, First Edition.
Edited by Amiso M. George and Kwamena Kwansah-Aidoo.
© 2017 by The Institute of Electrical and Electronics Engineers, Inc. Published 2017 by John Wiley & Sons, Inc.

J

Key Message

Key messages are the information that the audience should know about the organization, its response to the crisis, and its ability to resume normal operations. While an organization may develop up to ten key messages for each crisis, it is best to keep it to three for brevity's sake.

Develop your Key Messages

- Who needs to know about the crisis? (key stakeholders)
- What happened?
- When did it happen?
- Where did it happen?
- How did it happen?
- Who was affected or concerned?
- Why did it happen?
- What do the media want to know about the crisis?

Culture and Crisis Communication: Transboundary Cases from Nonwestern Perspectives, First Edition.
Edited by Amiso M. George and Kwamena Kwansah-Aidoo.
© 2017 by The Institute of Electrical and Electronics Engineers, Inc. Published 2017 by John Wiley & Sons, Inc.

- How should you show empathy? Do you apologize, express sadness or what?
- What is your organization doing to minimize the impact of the crisis/prevent it from happening again?
- When will you have additional or new information about the crisis?

The key message would be updated as soon as there is new information.

Key Message Form
Limit key messages to three. They will be communicated to the media, but adapted to specific publics.

1._____

_____

_____

2._____

_____

_____

3._____

_____

_____

Sample Key Messages
- The shooting that occurred at our facility in (location) has triggered our crisis response plan. We are fully prepared to deal with such emergency situations.
- The (name crisis) occurred in (location). As we commence our investigation of this crisis, our other factories (identify if business will continue normally or other).
- Our main concern is the safety and well-being our employees and customer and other businesses near the area.

Index

Note: Page numbers followed by "t" indicate tables.

Culture and Crisis Communication: Transboundary Cases from Nonwestern Perspectives, First Edition.
Edited by Amiso M. George and Kwamena Kwansah-Aidoo.
© 2017 by The Institute of Electrical and Electronics Engineers, Inc. Published 2017 by John Wiley & Sons, Inc.

Books in the
**IEEE PCS PROFESSIONAL ENGINEERING
COMMUNICATION SERIES**

Sponsored by IEEE Professional Communication Society

Series Editor: Traci Nathans-Kelly

This series from IEEE's Professional Communication Society addresses professional communication elements, techniques, concerns, and issues. Created for engineers, technicians, academic administration/faculty, students, and technical communicators in related industries, this series meets the need for a targeted set of materials that focus on very real, daily, on-site communication requirements. Using examples and expertise gleaned from engineers and their colleagues, this series aims to produce practical resources for today's professionals and pre-professionals.

*Information Overload: An International Challenge for Professional Engineers and
   Technical Communicators* · Judith B. Strother, Jan M. Ulijn, and Zohra Fazal

*Negotiating Cultural Encounters: Narrating Intercultural Engineering and
   Technical Communication* · Han Yu and Gerald Savage

*Slide Rules: Design, Build, and Archive Presentations in the Engineering and
   Technical Fields* · Traci Nathans-Kelly and Christine G. Nicometo

A Scientific Approach to Writing for Engineers and Scientists · Robert E. Berger

*Engineer Your Own Success: 7 Key Elements to Creating an Extraordinary
   Engineering Career* · Anthony Fasano

International Virtual Teams: Engineering Global Success · Pam Estes Brewer

*Communication Practices in Engineering, Manufacturing, and Research for Food
   and Water Safety* · David Wright

*Teaching and Training for Global Engineering: Perspectives on Culture and
   Professional Communication Practices* · Kirk St.Amant and Madelyn Flammia

*The Fully Integrated Engineer: Combining Technical Ability and Leadership
   Prowess* · Steven T. Cerri

*Culture and Crisis Communication: Transboundary Cases from Nonwestern
   Perspectives* · Amiso M. George and Kwamena Kwansah-Aidoo

Printed in the USA
K073162SCI121117   01S29053000000002602